Ius Gentium: Comparative Perspectives on Law and Justice

Volume 90

Ius Gentium is a book series which discusses the central questions of law and justice from a comparative perspective. The books in this series collect the contrasting and overlapping perspectives of lawyers, judges, philosophers and scholars of law from the world's many different jurisdictions for the purposes of comparison, harmonisation, and the progressive development of law and legal institutions. Each volume makes a new comparative study of an important area of law. This book series continues the work of the well-known journal of the same name and provides the basis for a better understanding of all areas of legal science.

The *Ius Gentium* series provides a valuable resource for lawyers, judges, legislators, scholars, and both graduate students and researchers in globalisation, comparative law, legal theory and legal practice. The series has a special focus on the development of international legal standards and transnational legal cooperation.

More information about this series at http://www.springer.com/series/7888

Laura Ervo · Pia Letto-Vanamo · Anna Nylund
Editors

Rethinking Nordic Courts

Springer

Editors
Laura Ervo
School of Law, Psychology
and Social Work
University of Örebro
Örebro, Sweden

Pia Letto-Vanamo
Faculty of Law
University of Helsinki
Helsinki, Finland

Anna Nylund
Faculty of Law
University of Tromsø–The Arctic
University of Norway
Tromsø, Norway

ISSN 1534-6781 ISSN 2214-9902 (electronic)
Ius Gentium: Comparative Perspectives on Law and Justice
ISBN 978-3-030-74850-0 ISBN 978-3-030-74851-7 (eBook)
https://doi.org/10.1007/978-3-030-74851-7

This Springer imprint is published by the registered company Springer Nature Switzerland AG
The registered company address is: Gewerbestrasse 11, 6330 Cham, Switzerland

Preface

This book is the result of a project founded by NOS-HS, the joint committee for Nordic research councils in the humanities and social sciences. The funding enabled us to gather Nordic legal scholars with an interest in courts and court proceedings as institutions embedded in the national, Nordic and European legal cultures, as well as courts as key institutions of democratic societies. Researchers from all five Nordic countries gathered to discuss the past, present and future of Nordic courts and court proceedings from a legal-cultural perspective at two workshops. The first was held in Örebro, Sweden, in September 2018, and the second in Helsinki, Finland, in February 2019. The contributions in this book are the outcome of the presentations and discussions that took place during these workshops. We are very pleased to have such enthusiastic and insightful colleagues; to be able to add to the body of knowledge on court culture as a specific form of legal culture in the Nordic context; and to contribute to the understanding of the value of multiple forms of Nordic cooperation.

We would like to thank all peer reviewers for their insightful and constructive comments and suggestions.

We are also happy to have been able to work with Springer to disseminate the results of our work.

Örebro, Sweden
Helsinki, Finland
Tromsø, Norway
February 2021

Laura Ervo
Pia Letto-Vanamo
Anna Nylund

Preface

Contents

Rethinking Nordic Courts: An Introduction

Anna Nylund

1 Introduction

Europeanisation, globalisation, privatisation, diversification and digitisation are trends that all exert an influence on courts and the justice system. Still, our understanding of the interrelationship between these currents in the legal landscape and national court culture is limited, which in turn impedes our comprehension of the on-going, potentially transformational processes related to courts. Nordic courts and court proceedings are, naturally, influenced by these trends both directly and indirectly, and their reactions to the developments are contingent on the underlying legal culture.

We argue that a distinctly Nordic procedural or court culture exists; that is, a set of ideas and values that in combination constitute the core of a regional legal culture can be identified in addition to the national legal cultures in the Nordic countries. Studying primarily Nordic rather than national court cultures is fruitful in that it shifts focus away from details to overarching, core ideas, while still allowing us to discuss variations among the Nordic countries. Deepening our understanding of the genesis and formation of Nordic courts and justice systems will give us a richer comprehension of contemporary Nordic legal culture, including the similarities and differences between the Nordic countries. For instance, we can explore how what could seem to be haphazard historical choices have engendered tangible, enduring differences in some respects. It will also enable us to develop tools for conceptualising procedural or court culture in general. A legal cultural approach can provide invaluable insight into how current processes of change shape courts both in the Nordic countries and elsewhere.

A. Nylund (✉)
UiT, The Arctic University of Norway, Hansine Hansens veg 18, 9037 Tromsø, Norway
e-mail: anna.nylund@uit.no

L. Ervo et al. (eds.), *Rethinking Nordic Courts*, Ius Gentium: Comparative Perspectives on Law and Justice 90, https://doi.org/10.1007/978-3-030-74851-7_1

The Nordic countries—Denmark, Finland, Iceland, Norway and Sweden—form a distinct group with close historic, cultural, societal and legal ties.[1] Studying them is interesting for several reasons. In addition to enabling us to treat courts as a legal-cultural phenomenon, findings on historical processes, for instance in the uptake of ideas from abroad and the variation in the sources of inspiration, can be contrasted with observations on current processes of change.[2] A legal-cultural approach helps to explain how Nordic legal cultures react to current changes, and by juxtaposing past and present processes of change we could gain unique insights into the factors and mechanisms propelling or restraining change.

Studying the Nordic countries is also valuable from a comparative perspective. At least some of the past and present processes shaping Nordic procedural law and courts are parallel to similar developments in other countries. Hence, although our study is limited to the Nordic countries, the insights could reflect trends in many other countries as well and, thus, could bring forward new knowledge that is applicable in a wider context. Even if the Nordic situations diverges from that of other countries, the findings will lend themselves to comparisons and to exploration of the mechanisms thrusting legal cultures in different directions. Moreover, as the gap in procedural differences among civil law and common law countries is shrinking, the Nordic countries are in an ideal position, as they have evaded the civil law/common law dichotomy, possessing some traits from both and some typical 'Nordic' traits.

The Nordic countries are an interesting object of study: the countries are similar in terms of cultural, economic, political, religious and societal factors, yet each has its own flavour. Their relationship to the EU, in particular the Area of Freedom, Justice and Security varies. Denmark, Finland and Sweden are EU members, but Denmark has opted out of cooperation in justice affairs and hence participates in only when it wishes to do so. Iceland and Norway are members of the European Free Trade Agreement (EFTA) and the European Economic Area (EEA) Agreement but still participate in some elements of judicial cooperation, in particular the Schengen Agreement and law related to it. Thus, the Nordic countries are a perfect laboratory for studying multi-speed integration and whether the same input can have different results even in similar countries. Furthermore, the research presented in this volume can be used to juxtapose findings from other countries to achieve comparative insights.

2 Changing Landscape of Courts and Court Proceedings

As mention above, Europeanisation, globalisation, privatisation, diversification and digitisation are key factors influencing the legal landscape in which courts operate and dispute resolution takes place. This part gives a short introduction of these trends.

---

[1] E.g., Letto-Vanamo et al. (2019), Nylund et al. (2019), Husa (2010), Husa et al. (2007), Bernitz (2007), Agell (2001) and Lando (2001).

[2] Hjort (2021), Letto-Vanamo (2021), Sunde (2021) and Tamm (2021).

Legal input comes increasingly from supranational organs: in Europe, the European Union (EU) has evolved into a powerful actor by being a continuous source of new hard law, case law and soft law.[3] Courts must enforce EU law effectively and equally and ensure that both the outcome and the proceedings adhere to the rights enshrined in the European Convention on Human Rights and the EU Fundamental Rights Charter. EU law also contains numerous rules with both direct and indirect procedural content.[4] Supranational European law has shifted the balance among the state powers by making courts key players through judicial review and by increasing the role of case law as a source of law.[5] In regard to commercial disputes, globalisation has contributed to an acceleration in the shift from litigation in national courts to arbitration[6] and, more recently, from litigation in regular courts to courts specialising in resolving international commercial disputes.[7] Nevertheless, the impact of globalisation is so far almost impalpable, particularly since it is interconnected with other trends, notably the privatisation of justice.

'Privatisation' of dispute resolution in the Nordic countries is pervading and has long historical roots. As discussed above, Nordic justice systems are based on out-of-court dispute resolution in *inter alia* consumer dispute resolution boards and family counselling services and have thus been 'privatised' for decades. Moreover, many of these dispute resolution boards are public entities, or at least publicly funded, and many are corporatist (i.e., corporate groups that consist of persons with the same type of interests, such as labour associations, traders' associations, tenants' associations, consumer associations, and agriculture associations are included in decision-making processes that concern areas related to their interests). Therefore, categorising these organs as private would be misleading. A more recent trend in 'partial' privatisation is making facilitation of settlement a task for the judiciary, through court-connected mediation, plea bargaining and judge-facilitated settlement during the course of court proceedings. Consequently, arbitration is largely the only form of pure privatisation of justice in the Nordic countries. The key factor propelling the use of arbitration is a desire for a private dispute resolution process as such and an efficient procedure, which the lack of a possibility to file an appeal augments.[8] Additionally, the increasing complexity and diversification of legal norms brings about a desire for experts to adjudicate cases; however, since Nordic judges are generalists, the courts are not able to appoint a panel of specialist judges to decide a case.[9]

---

[3]E.g., Krans and Nylund (2020a, b), Law and Nowak (2020) and Nylund and Strandberg (2019a, b).

[4]E.g., Krans and Nylund (2020b), Law and Nowak (2020) and Krans (2015).

[5]See Helenius (2021), Nylund (2021a), Sunnqvist (2021) and Thorsteinsdóttir (2021).

[6]E.g., Petersen (2021) and Cordero-Moss (2013).

[7]E.g., Kramer and Sorabji (2019a, b).

[8]Roschier Disputes Index 2021. Dispute Resolution Trends. https://www.roschier.com/publications/RDI2021/#p=1, p. 10 (Accessed 15 Feb 2021).

[9]Roschier Disputes Index 2021. Dispute Resolution Trends. https://www.roschier.com/publications/RDI2021/#p=1, p. 10 (Accessed 15 Feb 2021).

Arbitration also reflects the trend of privatisation of justice, since the proceedings are governed by international conventions, recommendations and rules issued by private bodies, and the outcome is often determined by soft law, some sort of *lex mercatoria* or other forms of private ordering. Many companies prefer to resolve their disputes in non-public, confidential proceedings and to appoint a private investigator to uncover disloyal employees and corporate crime rather than to rely on the government to investigate and persecute the possible crimes.[10] Another driving factor of privatisation is the government encouraging the parties to a dispute to resolve their case out of court in dispute resolution boards, mediation, negotiation processes or arbitration. Finally, and perhaps most interestingly, facilitation of settlement has become a task for the judiciary, through court-connected mediation, plea bargaining and judges facilitating settlement during the course of court proceedings.[11]

However, resorting to private processes can augment societal inequalities: large companies and well-funded organisations can afford a private investigation, whereas small and medium size companies and many non-governmental organisations cannot. Similarly, wealthy and knowledgeable consumers, tenants and employees can afford a legal counsel or have access to legal advice through insurance policies and membership in organisations, whereas less affluent citizens may be unable to do the same.[12] The use of private dispute resolution processes might also be problematic for enforcing mandatory law and using law to achieve policy-goals.[13]

Diversification of court proceedings (i.e., procedural rules tailored for a specific type of case) is interrelated with the other trends, although it is also concurrently discordant with them.[14] Enacting special procedural rules applicable only for a specific set of cases can contribute to increased party influence on the course of the proceedings and the court proceedings being tailored to fit each case. Small claims proceedings, for instance, could increase access to justice,[15] and flexible rules could serve as an incentive to select litigation over arbitration. However, the fragmentation and flexibilisation of procedural rules have some tangible drawbacks related to lack of coherence, either through lack of internal coherence of the special proceedings or by reducing the coherence of the rules of civil and criminal procedure in general.[16]

Digitisation is also important, despite the fact that it has so far meant transferring the activities of courts online, into a digital environment; thus far, however, it has had limited impact on how the courts are organised or the content and conduct of the proceedings.[17] Although the COVID-19 pandemic has signified a leap forward,

---

[10] Rui and Søreide (2019).

[11] See Ervo (2021a, b), Linnanmäki (2021) and Nylund (2021b).

[12] See, example, Fiss (1984), Resnik (2008), Cohen (2009) and Glover (2014).

[13] Petersen (2021).

[14] E.g., Krans and Nylund (2020b).

[15] E.g., Jensen (2021).

[16] E.g., Jensen (2021), Galič (2020), Hau (2020) and Krans and Nylund (2020b).

[17] E.g., Condlin (2016), Koulu (2016) and Ortolani (2016).

its long-term effect on courts is not known at the time of writing this chapter.[18] Uncontested pecuniary claims are among the proceedings that have been digitised to the greatest extent. Despite the fact that the Nordic countries are known for being among the most technologically advanced countries,[19] Nordic courts are still not at the forefront, perhaps with the exception of Danish courts. Nevertheless, small steps towards digitisation, either individually or in their combined effect, could eventually amount to a fundamental shift in the role of courts and court proceedings.

A final observation is that decreasing expenditure on courts appears to be a factor driving court reforms.[20] While efficiency has been a goal of court reforms for centuries and is certainly highly desirable, current reforms focus on saving government expenditure even if doing so generates costs for those who use courts, decreases access to justice and threatens the quality of the proceedings and the outcome.

3 Courts and Court Proceedings as a Legal-Cultural Phenomenon

Court proceedings are inherently a legal-cultural phenomenon deeply embedded in societal structures, values, concepts and ideas; in other words, they reflect the 'purpose to be served by the administration of justice: … the purpose of justice and … the choice of many procedural arrangements.'[21] As Oscar Chase wrote in his seminal book *Law, Culture,and Ritual*:

> Dispute processes are in large part a reflection of the culture in which they are embedded; they are not an autonomous system that is predominantly the product of insulated specialists and experts. More, they are institutions through which social and cultural life is maintained, challenged, and altered, or as the same idea has been expressed, 'constituted' or 'constructed.' These institutional practices importantly influence a society and its culture–its values, metaphysics, social hierarchies and symbols–even as those practices themselves reflect the society around them.[22]

Catherine Piché has discussed how legal culture—or, more precisely, litigation culture—is reflected in and shaped by class actions, as well as how each actor in court proceedings discloses, explicitly or implicitly, values, beliefs, ideas and norms. The judge decides which of these that will prevail.[23] Legal-cultural analysis of courts and court proceedings—that is, the analysis of litigation or court culture—is fruitful for understanding courts as key societal institutions that produce, interpret and enforce norms; that resolve disputes; and that are in constant interplay with

[18]See Krans and Nylund (2020c), and more specific observations on the Nordic countries in Ervo (2020), Nylund (2020) and Petersen (2020).

[19]Schwab (2019).

[20]E.g., Mekki (2016), Marcus (2013), Genn (2012) and Genn (2009).

[21]Damaška (1986), pp. 10–11.

[22]Chase (2005), p. 2.

[23]Piché (2009), pp. 114.

the surrounding society and culture. Litigation or court culture is reflected in, and shaped by, court proceedings: each actor in court proceedings discloses, explicitly or implicitly, values, beliefs, ideas and norms related to courts and dispute resolution.

In the endeavour to explore legal culture, doctrinal analysis and comparison of statutory and case law fall short of providing sufficient tools to account for variation in attitudes towards judicial discretion and the balance of formalism and pragmatism; they also fail to explain the extent and mechanisms of the influence these exert on other aspects of the justice system and court proceedings (i.e., the role of legal 'mentality').[24] Thus, we must explore the underlying ideas, values, concepts and practices and investigate courts as central societal institutions with various roles, including solving disputes and producing legal norms.

Judicial review serves as an example, in that providing courts with the power to perform judicial review does not necessarily induce courts to exercise those powers.[25] Whether and how courts use their power to review statutory law reflects the role of courts in society and thus also *inter alia* the interplay and relative power of different state organs, the role of supranational law, and the self-perception of judges. Understanding these differences necessitates an exploration of the foundational conceptions and ideas of procedural law.

A contextual, legal-cultural approach is also necessary to understand differences in the uptake of innovations. For instance, since the enactment of the 2008 EU Mediation Directive, many countries have implemented rules on court-connected mediation for both purely domestic and cross-border disputes. However, the extent to which court-connected mediation takes place varies significantly even among the Nordic countries.[26] Hence, understanding the underlying legal-cultural differences becomes important, as well as exploring whether and how mediation moulds litigation practices.

In this book, we will not attempt to define legal culture, or, more specifically, the legal culture of procedural law, in a conclusive manner. It suffices to say that we study courts as key institutions in society and that we are interested in treating procedural law primarily as a set of paradigms and practices, rather than a set of rules.[27] We focus specifically on legal culture that is connected to courts and court proceedings. In civil procedure, litigation culture and procedural culture are used as synonyms for court culture. However, for the purposes of this book, litigation culture is too narrow and even misleading. Litigation implies civil procedure, either in a broad or a narrow conception, whereas this book encompasses criminal procedure and to some extent administrative procedure as well. A narrow conception of litigation culture downplays the activities other than adjudication that occur outside courts and the role of dispute resolution mechanisms outside courts, such as arbitration, consumer dispute resolution and the use of administrative organs in the justice system.

---

[24] Husa et al. (2019), Kischel (2019) and Mankowski (2018).

[25] Sunnqvist (2021).

[26] Ervo (2021a), Linnanmäki (2021), Nylund (2021b), Adrian (2016), Ervo (2016) and Nylund (2016).

[27] Michaels (2005), Valcke (2004) and Van Hoecke and Warrington (1998).

Many of the contributions in this book do not address court culture or procedural culture explicitly, let alone attempt to define legal culture. Nevertheless, all authors discuss legal-cultural change, though implicitly, without clearly defining the particular elements as regulatory or cultural. One reason for this is that the two are intertwined, and the demarcation between them is therefore blurred.

4 Nordic Courts and Court Proceedings: A Brief Overview

4.1 Historical and Cultural Foundations

Understanding the past is paramount for understanding the present and predicting the future: Prominent comparatists refer to 'the presence of the past', or perhaps the 'pastness' of the present.[28] Hence, tracing the genealogy of current ideas and structures is indispensable for explicating current Nordic court culture, responding to current challenges and assessing future developments.

Nordic procedural law and court culture is not monolithic; on the contrary, it is fluid, is far from coherent and has been open to influences from abroad. Hence, rethinking the past of Nordic procedural and court culture calls for questioning the genesis and evolution—and even the existence—of 'Nordic' procedural law and culture. Did it emerge and unfold organically, or is it a product of deliberate moulding, or perhaps a combination of the two? If it is at least partially a product of an intentional process of carving out a Nordic form of dispute resolution, then the question arises of what processes, methods and sources of inspiration have been foremost in shaping contemporary law and legal culture.[29]

The basic tenets of the Nordic legal culture, and most other Western legal cultures, can be traced to the Weberian idea of modernity. Therefore, this volume takes the mid-1800s as a starting point for its analysis. Another reason for choosing Weberian modernity as the baseline is that current developments erode, or outright undermine, its precepts, and in doing so they reflect a paradigm shift. In the Weberian tradition, the nation state is understood as the sovereign and the sole legitimate source of legal norms, and consequently courts and state enforcement agencies are understood as the sole legitimate organs for enforcing legal norms. Norms are then inherently national and specific for each nation state. The state is the epitome of the law. Law is uniform; it is unified in coherent codes or acts of parliament and one jurisdiction enforcing it. The production and enforcement of law ultimately requires a single, supreme, sovereign authority, reflecting the slogan 'one King, one law, one measure, and one weight' from the French revolution.[30] The law is the same for everyone and is to be equally applied. All court cases follow the same path, unless the subject matter or the

---

[28]Legrand (1996), pp. 63 and 71 ff.

[29]Hjort (2021), Letto-Vanamo (2021), Sunde (2021) and Tamm (2021).

[30]Murphy and Murphy (1997), pp. 1–2.

value at stake (i.e., the disputed amount or the possible criminal sanction) requires otherwise.[31] Thus, the legal classification, not the parties involved, determines the forum. Courts, then, must be rational, bureaucratic organisations. The rule of law is at centre stage: law ensures equal and predictable outcomes and proceedings, and law is a central tool for implementing values, ideas and policies.

The second half of the nineteenth century was a time for building the nation state, both in the Nordic countries and in Europe at large. In parallel, Scandinavianism, or the pan-Scandinavian movement, spurred the idea of a Nordic culture distinct from other European cultures and legal cultures. Pan-Nordic efforts could also serve to propel innovation and modernisation of law in the Nordic countries through the creation of formal and informal modes of cooperation.[32] In the Nordic countries, the relation between national identity and a Nordic identity is hence characterised by mutual amplification rather than by one excluding or reducing the other.[33] Since influences from abroad engender legal reform, understanding the sources of inspiration and factors influencing the choice of sources is highly relevant, such as linguistic, structural and practical circumstances.

Today, the Nordic countries can be characterised as relatively small, affluent, homogenous and egalitarian. These characteristics have an impact on the Nordic legal culture and Nordic courts.[34] Late modernisation, urbanisation and professionalisation are still reflected in many legal institutions, *inter alia* in low specialisation among judges and the relatively high use of lay judges.[35] The state is considered 'good', and the boundary between civil society and the state is blurred compared to many other countries.[36] This is reflected *inter alia* in private organs, such as dispute resolution boards, having an important role in resolving disputes and in flexible rules giving the decision-maker discretion to find the most practicable solution.[37] As in any legal-cultural comparison, what matters for defining 'Nordic-ness' is not whether a single factor is unique for the Nordics but rather whether the combination of the factors constitutes 'Nordic-ness'.

The contributions in the first part of this book explore the legal-cultural and historical underpinnings and development of Nordic courts, court proceedings and dispute resolution practices.[38] Hence, legal-cultural and historical aspects will not be discussed in further detail in this chapter.

---

[31] See, example, Weber and Kalberg (2005), pp. 221–224 and 238–244.

[32] See Hjort (2021) and Letto-Vanamo (2021).

[33] Letto-Vanamo et al. (2019).

[34] Niemi et al. (2019) and Petersen et al. (2019).

[35] Nylund et al. (2019).

[36] Letto-Vanamo et al. (2019), pp. 8–9.

[37] Letto-Vanamo et al. (2019), pp. 9–12.

[38] Letto-Vanamo (2021), Sunde (2021) and Tamm (2021).

4.2 The Nordic Courts and Court Proceedings

The court system in the Nordic countries is simple: the West-Nordic countries (Denmark, Iceland and Norway) have only general courts, and the East-Nordic countries (Finland and Sweden) have general and (general) administrative courts.[39] In the absence of constitutional courts, supreme courts perform judicial review. However, Nordic courts have historically been reluctant to exercise those powers.[40]

There are almost no special courts. With few exceptions, all civil and criminal cases start in courts of first instance (*byret* in Denmark, *käräjäoikeus* in Finland, *héraðsdómstól* in Iceland, *tingrett* in Norway and *tingsrätt* in Sweden). Courts of appeal (*landsret* in Denmark, *hovioikeus* in Finland, *landsréttur* in Iceland, *lagmannsrett* in Norway and *hovrätt* in Sweden) are second-tier courts. The Supreme Court (*Højesteret* in Denmark, *Korkein oikeus* in Finland, *Hæstiréttur* in Iceland, *Høyesterett* in Norway and *Högsta Domstolen* in Sweden) is a third-tier court. In the absence of constitutional courts, supreme courts perform judicial review. However, Nordic courts have historically been reluctant to exercise those powers.[41] In Finland and Sweden, administrative courts form a parallel hierarchy of courts. In Finland administrative courts (*hallintotuomioistuin*) are courts of first instance and the Supreme Administrative Court (*Korkein hallinto-oikeus)* is the second and final instance. In Sweden, administrative courts (*förvaltningsrätt*) are courts of first instance, Administrative Appeals Courts (*kammarrätt*) are the second instance, and the Supreme Administrative Court (*Högsta förvaltningsdomstolen*) is the final court.

The role of Nordic supreme courts is also a characteristic of Nordic court culture. Today, the Nordic supreme courts, including the Finnish and Swedish supreme administrative courts, are de facto courts of precedent. They give leave to appeal to 100–150 cases annually based on whether the cases raise important legal issues in need of clarification or development. Although the rulings are not formally binding on lower courts, they have a de facto binding effect on lower courts. A lower court will not depart from the ruling unless there are exceptional reasons for challenging a case, such as a new ruling from the European Court of Human Rights or the Court of Justice of the European Union.

Generally speaking, all cases follow the same path and the same procedural rules and are heard by the same set of judges.[42] Furthermore, judges are mostly generalists who hear many different types of cases.

There are some exceptions, however. Labour courts (*arbeidsdomstol*, *arbetsdomstol*, *työoikeus*) and the Danish Maritime and Commercial High Court (*Sø- og handelsretten*) are the main exceptions in civil cases. Labour Courts hear only cases concerning the interpretation of collective labour agreements, whereas general courts hear cases arising from individual labour contracts. The Danish Maritime and Commercial High Court specialises in commercial matters, particularly cases

[39]For a more detailed discussion, see Nylund (2021b).

[40]E.g., Husa et al. (2019).

[41]E.g., Sunnqvist (2021) and Husa et al. (2019).

[42]For a more detailed discussion, see Nylund et al. (2019).

requiring specialist knowledge (e.g., intellectual property rights) and in which the amount in dispute is high. It has a dual function as both a court of first instance and a court of appeal, depending on the type of case. In the domain of public law, both Finland and Norway have an Insurance Court (*vakuutusoikeus*, *trygderetten*) for social security, unemployment and sickness benefits, and the Finnish Market Court (*markkinaoikeus*) hears *inter alia* patent and competition law cases. In the West-Nordic countries, administrative organs serve as quasi-courts in many types of administrative cases.[43]

The use of out-of-court dispute resolution is ubiquitous in the Nordic countries. The Nordics are known for their consumer dispute resolution system, where complaint boards constitute a key institution that provides affordable and simple dispute resolution mechanisms. Although the decisions of the boards are not binding in Finland and Sweden, the vast majority of traders comply voluntarily. Consumer organisations blacklist non-complying traders.[44] Consumer Ombudspersons also have an important role in enforcing consumer law and hence reduce the need for consumers to file individual claims. The prevalence of out-of-court dispute resolution is reflected in the low number of court cases.[45]

Criminal policy in which social problems are regarded as the key factor explaining deviant behaviour has resulted in low levels of repression, low incarceration levels, and the use of alternatives to punishment, such as victim-offender mediation and the use of community service combined with education and addiction treatment.[46] If the source of criminality is social problems, not the evil character of the perpetrator, then criminal proceedings need not be punitive and retributive in form and instead can encompass 'therapeutic' or 'problem-solving' elements.[47]

Moreover, many forms of deviant behaviour are sanctioned outside the criminal law system through administrative sanctions such as parking sanction fees and fees for other minor traffic violations. The police have the power to issue fines for minor crimes, including traffic violations, simple theft and disorderly conduct. The fines become final and enforceable unless the perpetrator appeals the fine to the district court. If the court upholds the fines, the perpetrator must pay them and compensate the state for legal costs. Since perpetrators wish to avoid the additional burden, most perpetrators refrain from appealing, unless they have a prospect of prevailing on appeal. As a result, most criminal cases are resolved outside courts by the means of fines issues by the police or the prosecutor or through (conditional) decisions on non-indictment. Studies have found that 92.9% of all criminal offences in Norway and 87.4% in Finland were resolved outside courts; however, these figures do not include non-indictment.

---

[43]See Nylund (2021b).

[44]For the Nordic EU Member States, see the national reports of Clement Salung Petersen (Denmark), Anna Nylund (Finland) and Eva Storskrubb (Sweden) in Law and Hess (2019), pp. 371–372, 379, 524, 534 and 538.

[45]Nylund (2019b) and Nylund et al. (2019).

[46]Helenius (2021), Lappi-Seppälä et al. (2019) and Nylund (2021a).

[47]Ervasti (2018), Diesen (2012) and Diesen (2007).

The Nordic labour courts embody corporatism in two ways. First, labour courts only hear disputes arising from collective labour agreements. Second, employers' associations and labour associations appoint a third of the judges each.[48] These judges are usually appointed on a part-time basis. The existence and role of labour courts illustrate the pivotal role of collective labour agreements: the labour courts do not have jurisdiction on individual labour agreements, only a right to interpret collective agreements regardless of whether the dispute pertains to a single case or a large number of similar cases. The labour courts are quorate in panels with an equal number of judges from each of the three groups: lawyers—usually judges or professors—with no ties to labour or trade organisations, representatives of labour organisations and representatives of trade organisations or the government as an employer. The Danish Tenancy Courts (*boligretten*) are another example, where the court is quorate either with a single professional judge or with a panel of one professional judge and two lay judges, one representing tenants' interests and the other landlords' interests.[49]

Many administrative appeals boards and CDR boards also adhere to the ideal of corporatism, with the chief and all chairpersons being 'neutral' and the rest of the members being appointed by corporate groups.[50] The chairpersons must usually possess the same qualifications as judges, but the requirements pertaining to the rest of the members are, with few exceptions, not defined. Furthermore, some persons are disqualified as members, so as to prevent persons from acting as judges in their own cases or cases they could be a party to.[51]

One could argue that labour court judges representing trade and labour organisations are not independent and impartial: after all, they have been appointed to promote the interest of one of the parties. However, the goal is not to forcefully argue for a specific party but rather to search for common ground and balanced, workable solutions. Having an equal number of representatives is expected to create a fertile ground for constructive debate in order to avoid strained relations.[52] Corporatist composition of the organs is believed to strengthen trust and confidence in the decision-making of the boards, especially among the members of the corporations that appoint the members of the boards.[53]

On a more intellectual or ideological level, Nordic court proceedings reflect a pragmatic approach with flexible rules that leave ample discretion to the judge. Many procedural rules state that the judge shall take a particular action unless he or she finds another option to be more appropriate, for instance due to the simplicity

[48]In Denmark lov om arbejdsretten og faglige voldgiftsretter 2017–08-24 nr. 1003, ss. 2 and 9; in Finland laki oikeudenkäynnistä työtuomioistuimessa 1974:676, ss. 3 and 8, in Norway lov om arbeidstvister 27 January 2012 no. 9, s2. 34–39; and in Sweden lag om rättegången i arbetstvister 1974:371, Chaps. 2 and 3.

[49]https://www.domstol.dk/alle-emner/boligret/ (Accessed 16 June 2020).

[50]Betænkning nr. 1401 (2001), pp. 128–129, HE 2006/115, and Difi-rapport 2014:2 p. 30.

[51]Difi-rapport 2014:2, pp. 28–31.

[52]Komiteanmietintö 2003:3, pp. 385–397.

[53]Difi-rapport 2014:2, p. 30.

or complexity of the case. The structure of court proceedings is based on the main hearing model.[54] Although the preparatory stage of the proceedings is central in both civil and criminal matters, the form and extent of preparation is highly discretionary. In criminal cases, preparatory hearings are used in complex cases and in cases raising complex procedural issues. In many simple criminal cases, the preparatory stage is limited and written. In civil cases, preparatory hearings are the norm; however, the length, number and content of the hearings can vary. Judges have ample discretion to form the preparatory stage.[55]

Trust in courts and the government is a prerequisite for entrusting judges to form the proceedings as they see fit. Nordic citizens and companies trust their courts,[56] which is hardly surprising considering that the Nordic countries are high-trust societies. A recent report from the Nordic Council of Ministers even called trust 'the Nordic gold'.[57] The use of lay judges has been identified as an important factor in building and maintaining trust in courts.[58]

A final characteristic of Nordic court culture is that the government actively uses courts to enforce policies and to create a level playing field. This is manifested in the duty of judges to give guidance to the parties to reduce the need for legal counsel and to actively manage the proceedings to ensure that expedient and economic proceedings are not dependent on whether a party can afford an expensive lawyer. Furthermore, there is a trend of openly acknowledging that enforcement of policies engenders differences in the role of judges depending on the subject matter of the case.[59]

5 Aim, Methods and Structure of This Book

This book seeks to analyse and assess the impact of selected aspects of the aforementioned trends on Nordic courts and court proceedings. To do so, we must first understand the history and present state of Nordic courts and court proceedings as part of Nordic society and legal culture. The identification of the 'Nordic' elements is intertwined with the historical analysis and with an examination of more recent developments that put Nordic courts and court proceedings into a broader societal context. This approach recognises that legal culture is both plastic and immutable and that change is gradual: an initially small step can unfold into a completely new direction. Although the analysis is limited to the Nordic countries, the findings shed light on shifts occurring in many other countries as well and deepen our understanding of court culture. However, pinpointing 'Nordic-ness' is difficult, since all cultures are fluid: they are not carved in stone, nor are they easily delimited from each other.

[54]Nylund (2018).

[55]Nylund et al. (2019), Nylund (2019a), Ervo (2016), Juul-Sandberg (2016) and Nylund (2016).

[56]European Commission (2019), pp. 44–46.

[57]Andreasson (2017).

[58]See Letto-Vanamo (2021) and Sunde (2021).

[59]Fredriksen and Strandberg (2019), p. 181 and Andersson (2019), pp. 161–162.

The fact that a trait is identified as Nordic does not preclude it from being present in other legal cultures as well, nor does the existence of a Nordic procedural culture exclude variation among the Nordic countries. Moreover, legal cultures result both from attempts to deliberately forge them and innate processes. Many of the authors will discuss how Nordic cooperation and the desire to maintain a certain degree of alignment among the Nordic countries is essential for maintaining Nordic unity and a distinctly Nordic court culture.

This volume aims also to understand the future of Nordic courts and procedural culture by investigating ongoing processes of change. Determining whether the current trends constitute an unruly tempest or a gentle breeze, as well as understanding the dynamics of the potential transformation, requires in-depth study of procedural law and practices and an understanding of the quintessential parameters of the current Nordic court culture. A legal-cultural approach is fruitful for understanding whether some aspects of the justice system and court proceedings are more likely to adopt innovations or to resist change, as well as for understanding why some trends might exert more tangible, or perhaps simply more perceptible, influence than others.

The authors in this book apply different methodological approaches. Some have a more pronounced legal-cultural approach, wherein societal aspects and underlying ideas, concepts and values are explicitly addressed, while others apply a more traditional legal doctrinal approach, albeit with clear comparative elements.

The book consists of three parts. The first part contains contributions that re-examine and question the genesis and evolution of Nordic procedural law and culture and its components. The chapters sketch an outline of Nordic courts and court culture by identifying and discussing quintessential parameters of Nordic court culture, thus laying the groundwork for rethinking current procedural rules and court culture. To some extent, they also explore the linkages to society at large.

The second part investigates the impact of Europeanisation on Nordic courts and procedural law, drawing on the insights from the first part. What is the role of European human rights law and EU law in shaping Nordic court proceedings? Has Europeanisation altered the role of courts in society and, if so, how? How does Europeanisation influence Nordic procedural law, and from which countries are new influences sought?

The third part of the book examines how the diversification, privatisation and flexibilisation of procedural rules mold Nordic procedural law and court practice. It also discusses shifts in the intended functions of the justice system and role of the structure and institutions of the civil justice system. The fourth, and final, part consists of concluding observations on the past and future of Nordic courts.

References

Adrian L (2016) The role of court-connected mediation and judicial settlement efforts in the preparatory stage. In: Ervo L, Nylund A (eds) Current trends in preparatory proceedings—a comparative study of Nordic and former communist countries. Springer, Cham, pp 209–231

Agell A (2001) Is there one system of family law in the Nordic Countries. Eur J Law Reform 3:313–330

Andersson T (2019) *Ex Officio* application of the unfair terms directive cases against consumers: a Swedish perspective. In: Nylund A, Strandberg M (eds) Civil procedure and harmonisation of law. Intersentia, Cambridge, pp 153–170

Andreasson U (2017) Trust—the Nordic gold. Nordic Council of Ministers, Copenhagen

Bernitz U (2007) What is Scandinavian law? Concept, characteristics, future. Scand Stud Law 50:13–29

Betænkning nr. 1401/2001 (2001) Retsplejerådets betænkning nr. 1401/2001 om reform af den civile retspleje I

Chase OG (2005) Law, culture, and ritual: disputing systems in cross-cultural context. New York University Press, New York

Cohen AJ (2009) Revisiting against settlement: Some reflections on dispute resolution and public values. Fordham Law Rev 78:1143–1170

Condlin RJ (2016) Online dispute resolution: stinky, repugnant, or drab. Cardozo J Confl Resolut 18:717–758

Cordero-Moss G (2013) International commercial arbitration: different forms and their features. Cambridge University Press, Cambridge

Damaška MR (1986) The faces of justice and state authority. Yale University Press, New Haven

Diesen C (2007) Therapeutic jurisprudence: an introduction from a Swedish perspective. Scand Stud Law 51:131–162

Diesen C (2012) Therapeutic jurisprudence and the victim of crime. In: Oei TI, Groenhuijen MS (eds) Progression in forensic psychiatry: About boundaries. Kluwer, Amsterdam, pp 579–585

Difi-rapport 2014: 2 (2014) Viltvoksende nemnder? Om organisering og regulering av statlige klagenemnder. Direktoratet for forvaltning og IKT, Oslo

Ervasti K (2018) Problem-solving justice in criminal and civil justice in Finland. Utrecht Law Review 14:19–30

Ervo L (2016) Swedish-Finnish preparatory proceedings: filtering and process techniques. In: Ervo L, Nylund A (eds) Current trends in preparatory proceedings: a comparative study of Nordic and former communist countries. Springer, Cham, pp 19–56

Ervo L (2020) Corona-jurisdiction in Finland. Krans B et al. Civil jusitce and covid-19. Septentio Reports 5:20–22

Ervo L (2021a) Culture and mentality in East-Nordic courts. In: Ervo L et al (eds) Rethinking Nordic courts. Springer, Cham

Ervo L (2021b) Plea bargaining changing Nordic criminal procedure: Sweden and Finland as examples. In: Ervo L et al (eds) Rethinking Nordic courts. Springer, Cham

European Commission (2019) The 2019 EU Justice Score Board. Communication from the Commission to the European Parliament, the Council, the European Central Bank, the European Economic and Social Committee and the Committee of the Regions COM(2019) 198/2

Fiss OM (1984) Against settlement. Yale Law J:1073–1090

Fredriksen HH, Strandberg M (2019) *Ex Officio* application of EU consumer protection law in Norwegian courts. In: Nylund A, Strandberg M (eds) Civil procedure and harmonisation of law. Intersentia, Cambridge, pp 171–191

Galič A (2020) Procedural autonomy between EU law and the Slovenian law of civil procedure. In: Krans B, Nylund A (eds) Procedural autonomy across Europe. Intersentia, Cambridge, pp 165–182

Genn H (2009) Judging civil justice. Cambridge University Press, Cambridge

Genn H (2012) What is civil justice for: reform, ADR, and access to justice. Yale J Law Human 1:397–417
Glover JM (2014) Disappearing claims and the erosion of substantive law. Yale Law J 124:3052–3092
Hau W (2020) Who is afraid of European civil procedure? A German perspective on the waning procedural autonomy of the member states. In: Krans B, Nylund A (eds) Procedural autonomy across Europe. Intersentia, Cambridge, pp 81–100
HE 115/2006 Hallituksen esitys Eduskunnalle laeiksi kuluttajariitalautakunnasta ja Kuluttajavirastosta annetun lain muuttamisesta
Helenius D (2021) Nordic and European judicial cooperation in criminal matters. In: Ervo L et al (eds) Rethinking Nordic courts. Springer, Cham
Hjort MA (2021) Sources of inspiration of Nordic procedural law: choices and objectives of the legal reforms. In: Ervo L et al (eds) Rethinking Nordic courts. Springer, Cham
Husa J (2019) Constitutional mentality. In: Letto-Vanamo P et al (eds) Nordic law in European context. Springer, Cham, pp 41–60
Husa J (2010) Nordic constitutionalism and European human rights-mixing oil and water? Scand Stud Law 55:101–124
Husa J et al (2007) Nordic law: between tradition and dynamism. Intersentia, Cambridge
Jensen C (2021) Small claims procedures in the Scandinavian countries. In: Ervo L et al (eds) Rethinking Nordic courts. Springer, Cham
Juul-Sandberg J (2016) Reform and development of preparatory proceedings in the Danish civil justice system: towards (even) more efficient courts. In: Ervo L, Nylund A (eds) Current trends in preparatory proceedings: a comparative study of Nordic and former communist countries. Springer, Cham, pp 81–107
Kischel U (2019) Comparative law. Oxford University Press, Oxford
Komiteanmietintö 2003:3 Tuomioistuinlaitoksen kehittämiskomitean mietintö. https://julkaisut.valtioneuvosto.fi/bitstream/handle/10024/75857/omkm_2003_3_tuomioistuinlaitoksen_kehittamiskomitean.pdf?sequence=1
Koulu R (2016) Blockchains and online dispute resolution: smart contracts as an alternative to enforcement. Scripted 13:40–69
Kramer X, Sorabji J (2019a) International business courts. Eleven, The Hague
Kramer X, Sorabji J (2019b) International business courts in Europe and beyond: a global competition for justice. Erasmus Law Rev 12:1–9
Krans B (2015) EU law and national civil procedure law: an invisible pillar. Eur Rev Private Law 4:567–587
Krans B, Nylund A (2020a) Aspects of procedural autonomy. In: Krans B, Nylund A (eds) Procedural autonomy across Europe. Intersentia, Cambridge, pp 1–12
Krans B, Nylund A (2020b) Comparative insights on procedural autonomy. In: Krans B, Nylund A (eds) Procedural autonomy across Europe. Intersentia, Cambridge, pp 227–243
Krans B, Nylund A (2020c) Concluding remarks on covid-19 and civil justice. Krans B et al., Civil justice and covid-19. Septentrio Rep 5:54–57
Lando O (2001) Nordic countries, a legal family? A diagnosis and a prognosis. Global Jurist 2
Lappi-Seppälä T, Nuotio K (2019) Crime and punishment. In: Letto-Vanamo P et al (eds) Nordic law in European context. Springer, Cham, pp 179–199
Law S, Hess B (2019) Implementing EU consumer rights by national procedural law. Beck, Hart, Nomos, München, Oxford, Baden-Baden
Law S, Nowak JT (2020) Procedural harmonisation by the European court of justice: procedural autonomy and the member states' perspective. In: Inchausti FG, Hess B (eds) The future of European law of civil procedure: coordination or harmonisation? Intersentia, Cambridge, pp 17–68
Legrand P (1996) European legal systems are not converging. Int Comp Law Q 1:52–81
Letto-Vanamo P (2021) Courts and proceedings: some Nordic characteristics. In: Ervo L et al (eds) Rethinking Nordic courts. Springer, Cham

Letto-Vanamo P, Tamm D (2019) Nordic legal mind. In: Letto-Vanamo P et al (eds) Nordic law in European context. Springer, Cham, pp 1–19
Linnanmäki K (2021) Mediation: a change in Finnish court culture? In: Ervo L et al (eds) Rethinking Nordic courts. Springer, Cham
Mankowski P (2018) Rechtskultur. Mohr Siebeck, Tübingen
Marcus R (2013) Procedure in a time of austerity. Int J Proc Law 3:133–160
Mekki SA (2016) L'economie procedurale. Int J Proc Law 6:7–31
Michaels R (2005) Two paradigms of jurisdiction. Michigan Journal of International Law 27:1003–1069
Murphy T, Murphy W (1997) The oldest social science?: configurations of law and modernity. Oxford University Press, Oxford
Niemi J (2019) Promoting gender equality. In: Letto-Vanamo P et al (eds) Nordic law in European context. Springer, Cham, pp 79–95
Nylund A (2016) Preparatory proceedings in Norway: efficiency by flexibility and case management. In: Ervo L, Nylund A (eds) Current trends in preparatory proceedings. Springer, Cham, pp 57–79
Nylund A (2018) The structure of civil proceedings: convergence through the main hearing model? Civ Proc Rev 2:13–39
Nylund A (2019a) Case management in a comparative perspective: regulation, principles and practice. RePro—Revista Do Processo 292:377–398
Nylund A (2019b) Comparing the efficiency and quality of civil justice in Scandinavia: the role of structural differences and definitions of quality. Civ Just Q 38(4):427–439
Nylund A (2020) Civil procedure in Norway and covid-19: some observations. Krans B et al., Civil justice and covid-19. Septentrio Rep 5:39–42
Nylund A (2021a) Europeanisation of Nordic civil procedure: does the map natch the terrain? In: Ervo L et al (eds) Rethinking Nordic courts. Springer, Cham
Nylund A (2021b) Institutional aspects of the Nordic justice systems: striving for consolidation and settlements. In: Ervo L et al (eds) Rethinking Nordic courts. Springer, Cham
Nylund A, Sunde JØ (2019) Courts and court proceedings. In: Letto-Vanamo P et al (eds) Nordic law in European context. Springer, Cham, pp 201–213
Nylund A, Strandberg M (2019a) Civil procedure and harmonisation of law: the dynamics of EU and international treaties. Intersentia, Cambridge
Nylund A, Strandberg M (2019b) Conclusions on civil procedure and harmonisation of law. In: Nylund A, Strandberg M (eds) Civil procedure and harmonisation of law: the dynamics of EU and international treaties. Intersentia, Cambridge, pp 231–242
Ortolani P (2016) Self-enforcing online dispute resolution: lessons from bitcoin. Oxf J Leg Stud 36(3):595–629
Petersen JH (2019) Nordic model of welfare states. In: Letto-Vanamo P et al (eds) Nordic law in European context. Springer, Cham, pp 21–39
Petersen CS (2020) Denmark. In: Krans B et al (eds) Civil Justice and Covid-19. Septentrio Rep 5:15
Petersen CS (2021) The public policy-implementing role of Nordic courts in civil dispute resolution. In: Ervo L et al (eds) Rethinking Nordic courts. Springer, Cham
Piché C (2009) The cultural analysis of class action law. J Civ Law Stud 101–145
Resnik J (2008) Courts: in and out of sight, site, and cite-the Norman Shachoy lecture. Villanova Law Rev 53:771–810
Rui JP, Søreide T (2019) Governments' enforcement of corporate bribery laws: a call for a two-track regulatory regime. Tidskrift for Rettsvitenskap 132(2):132–162
Schwab K (2019) The global competititiveness report 2019. World Econ Forum, Cologne
Sunde JØ (2021) The history of Nordic legal culture and court culture: the story of what should not have been, but still came to be. In: Ervo L et al (eds) Rethinking Nordic courts. Springer, Cham
Sunnqvist M (2021) The changing role of Nordic courts. In: Ervo L et al (eds) Rethinking Nordic courts. Springer, Cham

Tamm D (2021) Courts, law, language and culture. In: Ervo L et al (eds) Rethinking Nordic courts. Springer, Cham
Thorsteinsdóttir H (2021) Globalisation and court practice in Iceland: new case law of the Supreme Court in relation to the EEA Agreement and European Convention on Human Rights. In: Ervo L et al (eds) Rethinking Nordic courts. Springer, Cham
Valcke C (2004) Comparative law as comparative jurisprudence: the comparability of legal systems. Am J Comp Law 52(3):713–740
Van Hoecke M, Warrington M (1998) Legal cultures, legal paradigms and legal doctrine: towards a new model for comparative law. Int Comp Law Q 47(3):495–536
Weber M, Kalberg S (2005) Max Weber: readings and commentary on modernity. Wiley-Blackwell, Hoboken

The Historical and Legal Cultural Underpinnings of Nordic Courts

Courts and Proceedings: Some Nordic Characteristics

Pia Letto-Vanamo

Abstract This paper will discuss the characteristics of the court system and proceedings in the Nordic countries. The analysis is based on the idea of Nordic legal systems as a group bound both by historical similarities between them and by advanced legal cooperation between different legal actors. First, the main features of socio-legal developments, legal theory and legal practices characterising Nordic legal systems are discussed. Then, ideas, methods and results of cooperation in the field of law are described. 'Nordicness' within legal and judicial institutions is highlighted with three examples. The first example concerns popular participation, especially the importance of lay judges. The second example concerns the relationship between the legislator and the judiciary and the non-existence of constitutional courts. Finally, the third example discusses the many modes of conflict resolution typical in the Nordic countries.

1 Introduction

There is no such thing as Nordic law, yet it is easy to refer to a Nordic legal mind—a concept that characterises the peculiarities of and similarities between the legal systems of the Nordic Countries.[1] In fact, the Nordic countries comprise five countries with different histories and different laws. Generally speaking law is always national, even if national law itself needs not be of national origin: it can be a result of borrowing law or legal institutions from other countries or other legal systems. Also, the laws of

[1] Letto-Vanamo et al. (2019).

P. Letto-Vanamo (✉)
University of Helsinki, Yliopistonkatu 3, 00014 Helsinki, Finland
e-mail: pia.letto-vanamo@helsinki.fi

L. Ervo et al. (eds.), *Rethinking Nordic Courts*, Ius Gentium: Comparative Perspectives on Law and Justice 90, https://doi.org/10.1007/978-3-030-74851-7_2

the Nordic countries are firmly based on principles that have their origin in a common European past.[2]

In comparative analyses, however, Nordic legal systems are categorised as their own group. This is also my starting point, along with features of Nordic court systems and court proceedings.

The peculiarities of development seen in the Nordic systems are usually explained by reference to a certain historical delay in accepting such ideas and institutions as are considered to belong to the 'European mainstream'. For instance, the phenomena of a university-trained legal profession (with an exam) and legal science only appeared in the Nordic countries in the eighteenth or nineteenth centuries.[3] Hence, it was comparatively late that so called learned law and university educated legal professionals started to have an impact on law-making and dispute resolution.

At the same time, the idea of 'Nordicness' is quite recent. Only in the nineteenth century did the idea of a specifically 'Nordic law' become popularly supplanted the old division between Danish-Norwegian law on the one hand and Swedish law (including Finland) on the other, especially as a tool to promote cooperation in the field of law. Since then, Nordic legal unity has been formed by active cooperation, through which many former differences were bridged. This cooperation started in 1872 when several prominent lawyers were invited to the first meeting between lawyers from all the Nordic countries for the purpose of formulating answers to the common challenges the Nordic countries and their laws faced at the time of early industrialisation.[4]

One of the main arguments put forward in favour of Nordic cooperation by those invited to this first meeting of Nordic lawyers referred to a 'common way of legal thinking'.[5] Therefore, understanding the characteristics of Nordic legal thinking and legal practices requires considering both historical similarities between the Nordic legal systems and advanced legal cooperation.

Thus, the main features of socio-legal developments, legal thinking and legal practices characterising the Nordic Countries are discussed here first. Then, ideas, methods and results of cooperation in the field of law between the Countries are described. Nordicness within legal and judicial institutions, is highlighted with three

[2]The law of the Church, Canon law, was important in forming legal thinking in the Nordic countries. The Canon law scholars also played a significant role in the process of writing down local law, which mostly occurred in the twelfth and thirteenth centuries. However, the early wave of Roman law influence (that of the *ius commune*) did not have the same impacts as elsewhere in Europe. Roman law influence came later and indirect, mostly via (Roman-)German impacts in the Nordic legal scholarship in the nineteenth century.

[3]Tamm and Slottved (2009), Björne (2002).

[4]The inspiration for the meeting came from similar German and English institutions; H.Tamm (1972), Carsten (1973).

[5]Since the first meeting of Nordic lawyers in Copenhagen in 1872, these have been held every three years except for the periods between 1903–1918 and 1938–1947. The meeting in Helsinki in 2017 was attended by around 900 lawyers—judges, civil servants, practising lawyers and legal scholars—from all the Nordic countries. To enhance their importance for general debate on law, since the first meetings conference papers, talks and partly discussions among participants have been printed and published. See https://nordiskjurist.org/meetings/ (last visited 18th of January 2021).

examples. The first example concerns popular participation, especially the importance of lay judges. The second example concerns the relationship between the legislator and the judiciary and the non-existence of the constitutional courts. Finally, the third example discusses the many modes of conflict resolution typical in the Nordic Countries.

2 Active and 'Good' State

As noted, comparative lawyers typically group the Nordic countries together as one legal entity or at least as a subfamily of the so-called civil law family. In fact, many quite well-known similarities exist between the Nordic countries, some of which still play a role in the development of legal institutions, practices and theory. One can speak of rather small, quite homogenous, even egalitarian[6] societies. For a long time, cities in the Nordic countries were small, and a great majority of population was rural.

Social and legal, as well as procedural and judicial, cultures in the Nordic countries have therefore been characterised as determined by a peasant or rural culture. The impacts of the strong Monarchy introduced in the wake of the Lutheran Reformation in the sixteenth century cannot be neglected either. One can also speak of one-norm societies with an interplay between state and church that later could provide fruitful soil for modern, universal practices in Nordic welfare states.[7]

The Nordic countries and their law were modernised relatively recently, largely during the nineteenth century, with the first wave of industrialisation. In this process the state played an important role. In fact, the Nordic countries are often characterised as countries in which the borders between the state and civil society are blurred. Indeed, the concepts of state and society do seem to be interchangeable in many ways. In this, we can see at least some origins of the dominance of the Nordic idea of a 'good' state and the reasons for implementing the social state, inclinations which also characterise the Nordic legal system's approach to conflict resolution. The state is actively involved, e.g., in consumer protection, as well as many other alternatives to litigation.[8]

Also, more generally, a social dimension has been typical of Nordic legal theory, for example the focus on protecting the weaker party in contract law.[9] At the same time, many societal and legal institutions have in a way been corporatist by nature in order to ensure representation of various social interests—for instance, boards with conflict-solving or advising functions or committees for drafting new legislation.[10]

[6] Petersen et al. (2019) and Niemi et al. (2019).

[7] Stenius et al. (2013).

[8] Bärlund et al. (2019).

[9] Wilhelmsson (1987); see also Bärlund et al. (2019).

[10] Letto-Vanamo (2014).

Nordicness can also be found in the comparatively late professionalisation of the legal field. For a very long time, one could speak of non-expert or lay-dominated legal cultures. This again has defined court systems and legal procedures, but also explains at least partly why the Nordic legal mind even today is characterised by 'pragmatism'[11]—reflected, for instance, in attitudes among judges towards their roles both in litigation and its alternatives.[12] At the same time, popular involvement and a common-sense understanding of justice have, to varying degrees, been brought into court proceedings through participation by laymen, as will be discussed later in this chapter.

Even today, the public sector and public administration occupy a huge sphere and play an important role in all Nordic countries. However, their respective systems of conflict resolution between public authorities and citizens vary to a high degree. For instance, in Sweden and Finland, litigation between administration and citizen is dealt with by specific administrative courts organised in a hierarchy which differs from that of ordinary courts. The other Nordic countries, however, have no such administrative court system. For example, administrative cases in Denmark are dealt with by a plurality of different organs or boards, most of which are set up for specific administrative complaints such as taxes, social benefits, environmental protection or energy providers, while the ordinary courts (with some notable exceptions) normally have the last word in these matters.[13]

3 Harmonising Law and the Legal Mind

More detailed studies in legal institutions or in legal theory reveal not only similarities but also differences between the Nordic countries. As mentioned above, administrative courts exist in Sweden and Finland but not in other Nordic countries, while Scandinavian Realism, which played an important role in discussions on modernisation (democratisation) of court procedure and on judicial argumentation, was mostly a Swedish and Danish phenomenon.

Important principles of local law were written down in all the Nordic countries as early as in the Middle Ages. Even if many similarities can be found in their texts, significant differences arose due to local peculiarities. Hence, in order to understand how law and legal contacts developed and functioned between the Nordic countries, it is important to stress the ways in which the remains of earlier unions between the

[11]Uncomplicated and unformal style is partly linked to non-existence of modern civil law codification such as the French code civil (1804) or the German BGB (1900). Civil law issues, such as contract or tort law, have been regulated by more or less independent acts. Also generally, the Nordic countries have been resistant to these large-scale law projects, and have chosen to enact the necessary legislation separately in discrete statutes, many of which were drafted on the basis of Nordic initiatives and discussions.

[12]Esp. in so-called court annexed mediation, discussed in the Chap. 16.

[13]Mäenpää et al. (2019).

countries are still visible. To this effect, we can talk of the western Nordic countries consisting of Denmark, Norway and Iceland, and the eastern Nordic countries consisting of Sweden and Finland. Denmark and Norway were united under the same King beginning in 1380 and remained so until 1814. Finland formed part of Sweden until 1809. The law of the Danish-Norwegian Monarchy (which also included Iceland) developed differently from that of the Kingdom of Sweden. In the late seventeenth century, Danish and Norwegian laws were unified on the basis of two major law books or codes (in principle containing basic rules in all fields of law), the Danish Code of 1683[14] and the Norwegian Code of 1687. The Norwegian Code was based on the Danish Code and superseded much of old Norwegian law. Thus, Danish and Norwegian law for centuries were in large part virtually identical. To a certain extent, the idea of common Danish-Norwegian legal thought persisted after 1814, the year Norway entered into a union with Sweden (until 1905), which it did without adopting Swedish law.

Sweden and Finland have always had a common legal basis, most notably the Swedish Code of 1734. In fact, Swedish laws remained the laws of Finland, and Swedish the official language,[15] even after 1809 when Finland became an autonomous Grand Duchy (until 1917) within the Russian Empire. Still, this relationship with Russia has had a lasting impact on Finnish society as well as on social and legal thought, which may manifest in some of the differences between Finland and the other Nordic countries. For instance, attitudes towards law have been more legalistic[16] in Finland than in the other Nordic countries. Furthermore, Finland became involved in Nordic cooperation later than the other Nordic countries, only after becoming a sovereign state.

Nonetheless, strong similarities exist between Sweden and Finland, for example, in the preparation of new legislation. In Swedish legal tradition, including in judicial argumentation, preparatory works for new legislation (*travaux préparatoires*) play an important role, as they do in Denmark and Norway. Reference to Swedish material has often been used when drafting new Finnish legislation. Swedish models were actively followed also in reforming the Finnish court system and court procedures in the 1970s and 1980s.

It is possible that the Nordic countries might have continued two or more clearly distinct legal groups had such legal-political developments not been counterbalanced by active collaboration since the nineteenth century. This cooperation was based not only on common or similar histories and on the idea that the Nordic countries share a common idea of the law, but also on the conviction that the need for necessary legal reforms due to rapid developments in trade and commerce could best be met by common efforts. The cooperation started in the 1870s, and has perhaps been the

[14]See Tamm (1984).

[15]Today, Finland has two official languages, Finnish and Swedish; For instance, legislation is always published in both languages.

[16]In the so-called Russification period (during the decades before and after 1900) legalism was a concept that referred to retaining Swedish legislation that was (still) in force in Finland as a symbol of 'the rule of law'.

most successful result of the so-called Scandinavian movement of the early nineteenth century, which after centuries of warfare between the Nordic countries, pleaded for unity, collaboration and friendship among the nations of the North.

All the Nordic countries were, and remain, relatively small, and many then topical questions were unknown to their scholars. Working together and using the potential from several countries was the obvious solution, and success immediately followed. The purpose of this cooperation was to find a joint Nordic approach to questions posed by industrialisation and the rapid development of international commerce. Challenges were posed *inter alia* by new instruments of payment and other issues attached to international trade.[17]

In addition to the meetings between Nordic lawyers, the harmonisation of Nordic law had its beginnings in the 1870s. Since then, active legislative collaboration has been a decisive feature in classifying the Nordic countries as a legal family closer to civil-law countries (countries with statutory law) than to so-called common law countries (countries with case law), or even as a family all to its own. This cooperation takes the form of discussions among representatives of the different countries about common, novel legal solutions, but at the same time it is left to each country's lawmakers, and thus to a political decision, whether and to what degree any such new legislation will actually be drafted and adopted in their country.

In 1962, Nordic legal cooperation acquired a written foundation in a treaty concluded in Helsinki. From a legal perspective, the Helsinki Treaty could be seen as a codification of former cooperation.[18] According to the Helsinki Treaty, the Nordic countries would work for legal unity, for 'uniformity of regulation throughout the Nordic countries in as many respects as possible'. The aim is to attain the greatest possible uniformity in private law as was traditionally the scope of cooperation. However, the Treaty also mentions as a goal the promotion of unity as regards penal (criminal) law and penal sanctions.

Nor does cooperation mean that common courts or other organs have been established to create what could be called a 'Nordic common law'.[19] At the same time, national lawyers, judges and law professors are free to formulate their own interpretations of the law. Court decisions, legal rules and legal literature are national; those of other Nordic countries can be cited, and regularly are, but they only serve an advisory function, in the same way as any other foreign law, or as sources of inspiration when making decisions.

Nonetheless, this 'soft' method of harmonising the law, which does not aim at unification but respects local peculiarities and wishes, has led to an impressive series of important statutes within basic fields of law such as commercial law, especially

[17]When the first Nordic lawyers' meeting was convened, the invitation stressed that because of a common understanding of law and of the common origin of many legal institutions, it was only natural that development of those institutions would need common action. The topics mentioned for cooperation were the law of commerce and issues of court procedure in civil and penal matters Carsten (1993).

[18]It has also been seen as a result of Denmark's and Norway's interest in cooperating with the European Economic Community (EEC); see further Letto-Vanamo and Tamm (2016).

[19]Common law here in the meaning of Patrick Glenn; Glenn (2005).

common statutes on contracts and the law of buying and selling,[20] but also within fields often considered more national and culturally sensitive, such as family law.[21]

Nordic legal collaboration is a characteristic feature of what in a broader sense could be called 'Nordic legal culture'[22]—a sense of coming from and having studied the law of a Nordic country is part of a Nordic lawyer's identity. The Nordic lawyers' meetings, started in 1872, have since continued at different stages. Matters of common legal interest have remained on the agenda. At the same time, the meetings, which are in principle only conducted in Nordic languages,[23] contribute to the feeling among Nordic lawyers of having more in common amongst themselves than with lawyers from other countries.

Procedural law has never been harmonised by common-Nordic statutes, but questions concerning courts, the judiciary and procedure have regularly been on the agenda of the Nordic lawyer's meetings.[24] Since the first meetings, judges (especially from the supreme courts) have comprised the biggest group among the participants. National lawmakers have actively followed reforms and models from other Nordic countries, while informal and formal Nordic contacts (networks) form a natural part of courts' and judges' work.[25] The Nordic Association for Procedural Law (*Nordiska Föreningen för Processrätt*) was founded in 1981.[26]

4 Nordicness: Popular Participation

Legal modernisation has often been connected to the term democratisation: (legal) modernisation of the Nordic countries should happen with the help of legislation but also with the participation of the people, including the participation of laymen in dispute resolution in the courts. In Sweden, procedural law and court reforms were initiated during the nineteenth century in order to change the aristocratic model of the judiciary, and to implement modern procedural principles such as orality and so on. During the 1920s and '30s, 'democratisation of the judicial system' was one of the main goals of Swedish Social democratic legal policy.[27] Still, reform of the court system and legal procedure continued in the country as late as 1948. In Norway and

[20]See further Bärlund et al. (2019).

[21]See further Lund-Andersen et al. (2019).

[22]Early results of Nordic legal 'identity' included the Nordic legal encyclopaedia (Nordisk Retsencyklopedi 1878–1899) and the Nordic journal Tidskrift for Retsvidenskab (today Tidsskrift for Rettsvitenskap, 1888-); There are also Nordic associations and/or yearly meetings for scholars and other lawyers within different legal fields.

[23]For participants from Finland, however, this means only the Swedish language.

[24]Boucht (1999), pp. 764–766.

[25]Since 1950s reports of the Nordic supreme courts´ decisions have been published in *Nordisk Domssamling*.

[26]See in more details Bylander (2013); see also Bylander and Nylund (2015).

[27]Modéer (1999).

Denmark, this had happened some years earlier, but in Finland as late as during the 1990s, though the reform process had started two decades earlier.

In Finland, comments on and attitudes towards the court system and local, first instance dispute resolution have stressed the importance of maintaining informality and the 'Nordic peasant tradition'. Even in the 1970 and 1990s, proposed reforms for modernisation of court procedure (e.g., eliminating differences between courts and procedures in towns and in the countryside) were mainly based on Swedish examples. Later, however, Finnish reforms have been foremost justified by reference to European developments, especially obligations based on the ratification of the European Convention on Human Rights (ECHR).[28]

It can be said that for a very long time—and to a certain extent even today—the legitimacy of justice and judicial decisions arose from the conviction, or at least the assumption, that the courts obeyed the law (laws) and that the law was an expression of the will of the people. At the same time, the local, first-instance, courts were the main fora for conflict resolution, dealing with criminal and civil cases as well as with family law matters and various registration tasks.[29] Popular control and a common sense of justice were brought into the proceedings by the participation of the panel of laymen[30]—and (state) supervision of legality by the (Parliamentary) Ombudsman. Today, however, the legitimacy of decisions is with increasing frequency sought elsewhere, *inter alia,* from alternatives to traditional dispute resolution in court.

Of course, the ancient, 'communal' method of conflict resolution (in rural areas) was also in use elsewhere in Europe. In other European countries, however, the abiding rule was that a judiciary with an academic education gradually came to supersede earlier modes of dispute resolution. It was only in the nineteenth century that laymen were again accepted as court members—mostly as result of the French Revolution of 1789 and the democratisation of Western European societies, courts included.

The same process also took place in Norway and Denmark, but not in Finland or Sweden. In the latter countries, participation of laymen in the administration of justice continued uninterrupted. In part, this was a result of the comparatively late modernisation of those societies, but also of the overall slow rate of change in their court systems. Some reasons were ideological—it was important to safeguard the idea of a folksy and egalitarian character of the court procedure—but in Finland finances also played a part.[31]

In every case, justifications for lay participation changed from time to time. References to local knowledge became fewer, while popular control and democracy gained currency. In the debates in Sweden of the first half of the twentieth century, and in Finland of the 1960s and '70s, the prevailing arguments pertained precisely to the

---

[28]See further Letto-Vanamo (2010).

[29]Moreover, the procedure in the court of first instance was a blend of judicial interventionism and folksy informality.

[30]In Swedish '*nämnd*'.

[31]A system composed of a few circuit judges 'sitting ting' (and partly paying administrative costs by themselves) with lay panels placed little demand on the public purse.

democratisation of justice and to popular control over the judiciary. Interestingly, in 2003 the Finnish Commission for Development of the Court System advocated so-called procedural justice with a more active role taken by the parties, and regarding arrangements towards court-annexed mediation, proposed that the use of lay judges be severely curtailed on the basis that lay participation could only be justified at all by reference to its very long tradition. Today, lay judges are still used in Finland, but only in (some) criminal law cases at the first-instance courts. In Sweden, however, they also participate in administrative and appellate courts.[32]

5 Nordicness: Legislator Above Judiciary

In all the Nordic countries the most important source of law—and the key instrument for legal-societal changes—has been parliamentary legislation. Thus, the most important legal actor is the legislator. The countries do not have constitutional courts, and the judiciary has not been willing to question the authority of the legislator.[33] In fact, the Nordic countries are among the very few in Europe and the world that do not organise constitutional review through a special court. Nevertheless, a tradition of constitutional/judicial review exists.[34] Indeed, one can speak of several models of constitutional review in the Nordic Countries.[35] Differences between the models have historical bases, but the fundamental principle is the same: the parliament is the most important legal actor; it is the parliament, not the judiciary, that has the last word on the law.

Thus, Nordic judicial systems greatly respect their national parliaments as democratically chosen legislators. Furthermore, none of the Nordic supreme courts plays such a political role as do constitutional courts. At the same time, none of the supreme courts or other controlling organs possesses the competence to formally nullify parliamentary acts. Nevertheless, the non-existence of constitutional courts does not mean that Nordic legal systems do not share some features of the continental European legal tradition. For instance, key constitutional documents are written or codified even though they are supplemented by other formal acts, amendments, constitutional conventions or customary praxis.

Constitutionality is safeguarded first and foremost by mechanisms for review by the ordinary courts of the constitutionality of legislation. However, constitutional arrangements differ as to how such judicial review is organised. Denmark has no explicit constitutional provision concerning judicial review.[36] Nonetheless, it tentatively recognises judicial review. Finland and Sweden have written constitutional provisions concerning judicial review, although in practice these provisions

[32] See also Nylund and Sunde (2019), pp. 209–210.

[33] Wind and Føllesdal (2009).

[34] Sunnqvist (2014); see also Sunnqvist (2021).

[35] For a brief comparative overview see Husa et al. (2019); see also Husa (2002).

[36] For the Danish constitutional system see Krunke (2014).

are applied quite cautiously. Norway added judicial review to its constitution by a 2015 amendment.

Furthermore, a difference exists between each country's degree of 'judicial activism'. Sweden, Finland, Denmark and Iceland all are less active, whereas in Norway the Supreme Court has been playing an active role in judicial review.[37] Despite any such differences, all Nordic countries share a spirit of constitutionalism and rule of law with general respect for the rules of the constitution and for the hierarchy of legal rules. This spirit is reflective of a parliamentary system that respects the will of the legislator and that endeavours to avoid conflicts between the parliament and the supreme courts, in alignment with the ideology of separation of powers and consensual democracy.

The Norwegian Constitution Act,[38] adopted in 1814, is the second oldest written constitutional document in the world still in force, and the role of customary constitutional law is greater in Norway's system than in the other Nordic systems of law. Furthermore, the constitution enjoys a stronger political and cultural position in Norway[39] than in the other Nordic countries.[40] To Norwegians, their constitution symbolises freedom, independence and democracy. Norway's exceptional role in the Nordic constitutional landscape is linked its active exercise of *ex post* control of the constitutionality of legislation.

The central actor is the Supreme Court (in Norwegian '*Høyesterett*'), which reviews whether a statute is in conflict with the constitution. This judicial task was not included in the written Constitution Act before 2015. Nevertheless, a tradition of constitutional review by the judiciary emerged as early as in the nineteenth century. In 2015 a novel provision was added to the Constitution Act, providing that '[i]n cases brought before the courts, the courts have the power and obligation to review whether Acts and other decisions by the state authorities are contrary to the Constitution'.

In more general terms, the Norwegian system is seen as a combination of the robust US-style judicial review and the Nordic parliamentary-friendly approach. The Norwegian Supreme Court does not declare an act null and void but rather sets aside the provision in question. Moreover, Norway's approach to judicial review bears little resemblance to the European constitutional court approach because the Supreme Court eliminates the legal-normative power of a provision only in the actual concrete case before the Court, although its decisions can have the practical effect that the provision loses its authority in other cases too.

Sweden has five constitutional documents.[41] The Instrument of Government[42] contains the basic principles of the form of government, defining government functions, fundamental freedoms and rights and elections to the parliament (in Swedish '*Riksdag*'). In 1979, the Instrument of Government was reformed, and a cautious

[37] See in more detail Kierulf (2018).

[38] Kongeriket Norges grunnlov 1817 no 17.

[39] In contrast to Denmark, Finland and Sweden, Norway is not a European Union (EU) member.

[40] For more details see Husa et al. (2019).

[41] For a general overview, see Nergelius (2011).

[42] Riksdagsordning (2014:801).

form of judicial review was introduced as part of the written constitution. The relevant rule stated that a court could declare a provision of a parliamentary act or a government decree to be in violation of the constitution and thus inapplicable, but only if the error was of an 'evident' nature. However, this rule—which was worded similarly to Finland's—had very little practical effect on the behaviour of the courts.

Since 2011, an act no longer needs to be in 'evident' conflict with a constitutional rule in order to be set aside by a court or other public body. Thus, '[i]f a court finds that a provision conflicts with a rule of fundamental law or other superior statute, the provision shall not be applied…' However, this reform did not precipitate a dramatic change in the role of the Swedish parliament because the provision in question also contains a second part which states that: 'In the case of review of an act of law under paragraph one, particular attention must be paid to the fact that the Parliament (the '*Riksdag*') is the foremost representative of the people and that fundamental law takes precedence over other law.'

In other words, even while giving in to pressure for stronger judicial review, the Swedish system in fact sought to fuse together the traditional parliament-centred thinking and the more recent idea of separation of powers with a stronger judicial review approach. But even taking a more active role, judicial review may have less impact than advocates of these reforms might anticipate because Sweden's constitutional-political culture involving a strong role for the parliament also characterises its doctrine on sources of law. As noted, preparatory works (*travaux préparatoires*) to legislation are actively used by Swedish lawyers to obtain more information about the law – about the legislative will and the *ratio* (reasoning) for the rules under review.

The Finnish Constitution is written in a single act,[43] which entered into force in 2000.[44] This Constitution Act contains provisions about the principles for the exercise of public power, the organisation of the government and the relationships between the highest state organs. Additionally, the Act contains a catalogue of fundamental and human rights, which has had a great impact both in legal practice and in Finnish constitutional law scholarship.

In comparative analysis the most distinctive feature of the Finnish system is the way the constitutionality of legislation is safeguarded. The Constitution Act of 2000 empowered courts to perform judicial review of legislation. Moreover, the Act states that the courts and other public authorities are obliged to 'interpret legislation in such a manner that adheres to the Constitution, and to respect fundamental and human rights'. According to the Constitution Act (Article 106), when deciding a case the courts must give preference to the Constitution if applying a parliamentary act would be in 'evident conflict' with the Constitution Act.

Beginning in 2004, the courts have applied Article 106 in a handful of cases, but judicial review by the courts plays a minor role overall in terms of safeguarding the

[43] Suomen perustuslaki/Finlands grundlag 731/1999.

[44] See in more detail Husa (2011).

constitutionality of legislation. That said, certain signs are indicative of the gradually growing constitutional role of the judiciary.[45]

In practice, the constitutionality of laws is examined in advance, before an act enters into force. The key actor in this process is the Finnish parliament's Constitutional Law Committee. The function of such control is to prevent bills that conflict with the Constitution being enacted. From the constitutional point of view, the Committee's main function is to consider each bill and issue opinions on their constitutionality and bearing on human rights. Although it is comprised of ordinary parliament members, the Committee operates on a non-partisan basis (there is no party-political discipline) in reporting to the parliament on constitutionality.

Further, the Committee calls upon academic experts (on the basis of constitutional convention) to advise the Committee in its examinations of the constitutionality of each bill. The Committee's reports are official statements and are respected by the parliament and by the government, which seeks to redraft the provisions of any bill the Committee finds unconstitutional before the bill passes into law. If the unconstitutionality found is significant, the bill is, in practice, withdrawn, and the government must find a different way to proceed. The Constitutional Law Committee's official statements are published, and they enjoy a special status as legal sources. Additionally, the Committee follows its own 'precedents'.

All this results in a unique system for policing the constitutionality of legislation, which combines an abstract *ex ante* and concrete, case-bound *ex post* review. The role of the Constitutional Law Committee is a significant one, as is the role of the academic experts guiding the Committee's views. Professors and other leading constitutional law scholars are regularly invited to Committee hearings: it is not uncommon for a constitutional law professor to write (and then orally present) 40 to 60 opinions per a year, which must greatly impact the interpretation and application of the Constitution and fundamental rights.

The general European trend of constitutionalising,[46] as well as the strong European human rights approach, have also impacted the Nordic countries, both in legal practice and in legal scholarship.[47] These impacts have been especially apparent in Finland, where application and interpretation of the rules and principles of the new Constitution of 2000 have come under active discussion. Still, the notion of a constitutional court as guardian of the constitution and its institutions is foreign to the Nordic context. Until now, the democratic systems in the North have been based on a certain degree of social stability and on ideals of continuity and consensus. Imposing an outside legal institution on the Nordic environment could have unexpected and unwanted consequences not only on Nordic constitutional practice but also on the Nordic constitutional mind.

[45] See further Ojanen (2009).

[46] See e.g. Tuori (2015).

[47] See e.g. Krunke and Thorarensen (2018).

6 Nordicness: The Many Methods of Conflict Resolution

At the moment, a great variety of conflict resolution methods other than court litigation is in use in all Nordic countries. Similar trends towards alternative dispute resolution (ADR) are also visible in many other European countries. But the Nordic countries are atypical in the great variety of methods they employ, as well as the active role of their state institutions.

Legal advisory services broadly play an important role not only in preventing conflicts but also in resolving them. Legal advisory services are multifaceted; many of them are organised by state or municipal authorities, like public legal-aid offices and local-level consumer rights advisers, and funded by the public purse. Moreover, different boards issuing various types of recommendations, opinions, instructions or resolutions belong to the Nordic (lay and corporatist) legal tradition and occupy a central role in promoting access to justice. Boards are used, for instance, in insurance, labour, consumer and competition law disputes. The institution of ombudsman—including the Parliamentary Ombudsman, an institution with its origin in Sweden, and specialised ombudsmen—exists first and foremost for general oversight of legality but also plays a role in dispute resolution as well.

Today, there is a general trend toward increasing the incidence of conflict resolution outside the courts. This trend, however, can also be recognised in many other European countries, and different modes of ADR (alternative dispute resolution) are being promoted by the European Union as well. At the same time, there has been a transition in the Nordic countries from a system with numerous 'all-inclusive' local courts to a system of fewer but more rational and effective courts with specialist judges. Registration matters pertaining to real property have been transferred to administrative authorities, and undisputed money claims (summary matters) to enforcement authorities.[48]

In the Nordic courts, more emphasis has been placed on alternative procedures, while the personality and professional skills of judges and their personal responsibility for decisions have been accented. Moreover, the idea of procedural justice has been emphasised. One can speak of a client-centred approach, which emphasises the judge's communicative skills and the parties' subjective experience of (procedural) justice[49] as well as the interaction between the judge and the parties. Thus, important aspects of the perception of justice are not only the impartiality and the high professional and ethical standards of the judge but also the opportunity for the parties to 'participate' in the proceedings, and the manner in which they are treated during the court procedure.

While the Nordic countries use alternatives to ordinary (judicial) dispute resolution more often, the courts still play a prominent role in the interplay between ordinary dispute resolution and its alternatives. In the Nordic countries, it is often pointed out that a functioning court system secures the feasibility of alternative dispute resolution (ADR): the option to bring matters before a court informs commitment parties

---

[48]See further Linnanmäki (2021) and Jensen (2021).

[49]See e.g. Ervasti (2007), Vindeløv (2007).

make to achieve resolution by way of ADR. Hence, traditional court proceedings and ADR are not counterposed or mutually exclusive concepts, but function instead as complimentary, parallel systems.

Arbitration too has long been a typical dispute resolution method in business relations in the Nordic countries. Quite often civil cases are taken out of the courts and submitted to arbitration because court proceedings are perceived as too slow and devoid of expertise. The option of non-public proceedings plays an important role here too. At the same time, the use of conciliation and mediation has increased in both civil and criminal matters. This 'away from courts' trend is often explained by reference to broader movement toward individualisation and privatisation of societal and legal culture. It might also be seen as a reaction to the problems of court services, their low standard or narrow scope or the high costs and long duration of court proceedings.[50]

Mediation within the courts, discussed in Chap. 13, has become one of their central service functions, not merely a by-product of the traditional administration of justice. In fact, it can be understood as the courts' response to competition for clients as well as for legal power in society.

Overall, in the Nordic courts and elsewhere in the world, it remains important, for the position of courts in society as well as for development of the law, that courts still adjudicate a wide and comprehensive variety of disputes arising from every sector of society.

References

Björne L (2002) Den konstruktiva riktningen: den nordiska rättsvetenskapens historia 1871–1910. Institutet for Rättshistorisk Forskning, Lund

Boucht J (1999) De nordiska juristmötena och rättsgemenskapen i Norden. Defensor Legis 5:748–775

Bylander E (2013) Nordiska Föreningen för Processrätt och det tolfte nordiska processrättsmötet. Svensk Juristtidning, pp 337–342

Bylander E, Nylund A (2015) Inledning: Temanummer: Processrätt. Tidskrift utgiven av juridiska föreningen i Finland. Juridiska Föreningen i Finland, Helsingfors, pp 395–400

Bärlund J, Moegelvang-Hansen P (2019) Contracting with a social dimension. In: Letto-Vanamo P et al (eds) Nordic Law in European Context. Springer, Cham, pp 115–133

Carsten G (1973) Hundert Jahre Nordischer Juristentag: 1872–1972. Rabels Zeitschrift für Ausländisches und Internationales Privatrecht/Rabel J Comp Int Private Law 1:80–100

Carsten G (1993) Europäische Integration und nordische Zusammenarbeit auf dem Gebiet des Zivilrechts. Zeitschrift Für Europäisches Zivilrecht 2:335–348

Ervasti K (2007) Conflicts before the courts and court-annexed mediation in Finland. Scand Stud Law 186–199

Glenn HP (2005) On common laws. Oxford University Press, Oxford

[50] For instance, several cases against Finland Sweden and Norway in the European Court of Human Rights have dealt with the requirement of Article 6 of the European Convention on Human Rights that a court decision must be made within a reasonable time.

Husa J (2002) Nordic reflections on constitutional law: a comparative Nordic perspective. Peter Lang, Frankfurt am Main
Husa J (2011) The constitution of Finland: a contextual analysis. Hart, Oxford
Husa J (2019) Nordic constitutional mentality. In: Letto-Vanamo P et al (eds) Nordic law in European context. Springer, Cham, pp 41–60
Jensen C (2021) Small claims procedures in the Scandinavian countries. In: Ervo L et al (eds) Rethinking Nordic courts. Springer, Cham
Kierulf A (2018) Judicial review in Norway: A bicentennial debate. Cambridge University Press, Cambridge
Krunke H (2014) Constitutional identity seen through a Danish lens. Retfærd. Nordisk Juridisk Tidsskrift 4:24–40
Krunke H, Thorarensen B (eds) (2018) The Nordic constitutions: a comparative and contextual study. Hart, Oxford
Letto-Vanamo P (2010) Autonomy and heteronomy of judiciary: a historical approach. Oñati Socio-Legal Series no 1
Letto-Vanamo P (2014) Judicial dispute resolution and its many alternatives: the Nordic experience. In: Zekoll J et al (eds) Formalisation and flexibilisation in dispute resolution. Brill, Leiden, pp 151–164
Letto-Vanamo P, Tamm D (2016) Nordic cooperation in the field of law. In: Strang J (ed) Nordic cooperation: a European region in transition. Routledge, London, pp 93–108
Letto-Vanamo P, Tamm D (2019) Nordic legal mind. In: Letto-Vanamo P et al (eds) Nordic law in European context. Springer, Cham, pp 1–19
Linnanmäki K (2021) Mediation: a change in Finnish court culture? In: Ervo L et al (eds) Rethinking Nordic courts. Springer, Cham
Lund-Andersen I, Kronborg A (2019) Marriage and family relations. In: Letto-Vanamo P et al (eds) Nordic law in European context. Springer, Cham, pp 97–113
Modéer KÅ (1999) Den stora reformen: rättegångbalkens förebilder och förverkligande. Svensk juristtidning, pp 400–427
Mäenpää O, Fenger N (2019) Public administration and good governance. In: Letto-Vanamo P et al (eds) Nordic law in European context. Springer, Cham, pp 163–178
Nergelius J (2011) Constitutional law in Sweden. Kluwer, Alphen van den Rijn
Niemi J (2019) Promoting gender equality. In: Letto-Vanamo P et al (eds) Nordic law in European context. Springer, Cham, pp 79–95
Nylund A, Sunde JØ (2019) Courts and court proceedings. In: Letto-Vanamo P et al (eds) Nordic law in European context. Springer, Cham, pp 201–213
Ojanen T (2009) From constitutional periphery toward the center: transformations of judicial review in Finland. Nordic J Hum Rights 2:194–207
Petersen JH (2019) Nordic model of welfare states. In: Letto-Vanamo P et al (eds) Nordic law in European context. Springer, Cham, pp 21–39
Stenius H (2013) A Nordic conceptual universe. In: Haggren H et al (eds) Multi-layered historicity of the present: approaches to social science history. University of Helsinki, Department of Political and Economic Studies, Helsinki, pp 93–104
Sunnqvist M (2014) Konstitutionellt kritiskt dömande: Förändringar av nordiska domares attityder under två sekel. Institutet för rättshistorisk forskning, Stockholm
Sunnqvist M (2021) The changing role of Nordic courts. In: Ervo L et al (eds) Rethinking Nordic courts. Springer, Cham
Tamm D (1984) The Danish code of 1683: an early European code in an international Context. Scandinavian studies in law, pp 163–180
Tamm D, Slottved E (2009) The University of Copenhagen: a Danish centre of learning since 1479. University of Copenhagen, Copenhagen
Tamm H (1972) De nordiske juristmøder 1872–1972: Nordisk retssamvirke gennem 100 år. Nyt nordisk Forlag Arnold Busck, Copenhagen
Tuori K (2015) European constitutionalism. Cambridge University Press, Cambridge

Vindeløv V (2007) Mediation: a non-model. Djøf, Copenhagen
Wilhelmsson T (1987) Social civilrätt: om behovsorienterade element i kontraktsrättens allmänna läror. Lakimiesliiton kustannus, Helsinki
Wind M, Føllesdal A (2009) Nordic reluctance towards judicial review under siege. Nordic J Hum Rights 2:131–141

Courts, Law, Language and Culture

Ditlev Tamm

Abstract This article deals with some questions of legal language in the Nordic countries. It stresses the fact that, while there is no common legal language among these countries, there is still a strong common understanding even though each language (i.e., Danish, Norwegian and Swedish; Finnish is a different language) has also developed its own terminology. Nordic legal language has its roots in the first written form of the law in the years before and after 1200. Later, legal language was influenced by the German language, and, to some degree, more recently by English. The language of Nordic courts was always the vernacular. At the university, Latin was used until the eighteenth century (in dissertations still in the first part of the nineteenth century), but today studies of law are carried out in Nordic languages. There remains a great need for scholarly works on Nordic law in Nordic languages at a time when the balance between international orientation and the necessity of producing scholarly works in the national language is an issue to be discussed.

1 Introduction

There exists neither a common Nordic legal language nor a Nordic common law.[1] Around 1900, when Germany adopted its new civil code, Nordic voices were speaking in favour of a Nordic civil code common to all Nordic countries, but that remained a vision.[2] Each country still has its own legal system and its own language. All statutes or court decisions are written in the national language: Danish, Finnish, Icelandic, Norwegian or Swedish.

[1]Regarding this, see Letto-Vanamo et al. (2019).

[2]The most important example being a lecture from 1899 by the Danish professor Julius Lassen, in which he discusses the necessity for a new Danish Code and refers to the possibility that such a code could develop into a Nordic civil code.

D. Tamm (✉)
University of Copenhagen, Karen Blixens Plads 16, 2300 København S, Denmark
e-mail: ditlev.tamm@jur.ku.dk

L. Ervo et al. (eds.), *Rethinking Nordic Courts*, Ius Gentium: Comparative Perspectives on Law and Justice 90, https://doi.org/10.1007/978-3-030-74851-7_3

However, Nordic lawyers mostly do—or at least at official Nordic lawyers' meetings are supposed to—understand each other when they speak or write in their own language.[3] This is true for Danish, Norwegian and Swedish, whereas Finnish and Icelandic are rightly considered languages so different from the Nordic *lingua franca* that lawyers from these countries must use one of the other Nordic languages (or English) when meeting to discuss legal issues. Indeed, they meet in quite high numbers at the triennial Nordic Lawyers' Meeting or in other associations and gatherings among specific groups of lawyers such as judges and law professors. 'Speak your own language!' once was considered the rule, but this is no longer maintained with rigour. English often is used among law students and as the language of presentations among younger scholars and by lawyers who do not have a background in Scandinavian languages, such as Finnish lawyers. Sometimes Nordic lawyers may joke about specific legal terms which are unfamiliar to lawyers from other Nordic countries,[4] and often meaning is lost if a speaker does not speak in a very clear way, using terms that are familiar to most Scandinavians.

Despite these issues, however, there is no movement toward harmonising Nordic legal languages. Just as Nordic law itself is not in general a unified system, legal language also has its peculiarities specific to each Nordic country.[5] However, it should be noted that other Nordic languages are not considered foreign languages. There is a presumption among lawyers that they should understand each other and should be capable of reading a legal text in the language of another Nordic country.

Even if Nordic languages are similar, they do belong to two different groups within Nordic languages, an East and a West Nordic group. Denmark and Sweden belong to the Eastern group, Norway, Iceland and the Faroe Islands to the Western. However it is more complicated. Denmark and Norway from 1380–1814 were in a union, developed a common legal science since the eighteenth century and therefore shared for a long time common legal terms as did also Sweden and Finland. Thus as to legal language Danish and Norwegian lawyers will have more in common as to terms and difficulties of understanding will be more on a Swedish-Danish line. For a Dane or respectively a Swede understanding legal language of the other country will sometimes need specific knowledge of terms which cannot be deciphered without studying the other system. The legal concepts will often be the same but the terms can be so different, that they are not transparent. As mentioned, the duty not to participate in a decision if you due to family or other relations can be considered partial, in Danish or Norwegian is *inhabilitet,* and in Swedish *jäv.* Old Danish words as *tinglysning* is still in use, when Swedish lawyers would talk of *registering*, registration, when it comes to the protection of rights over real estate, which in Danish is *ejendom* and in Swedish a *fastighet*. A Danish layer would normally feel more or less a home in

[3]Nordic legal cooperation is based on a common understanding of Danish, Norwegian and Swedish. Finnish is a Finno-Ugrian language and Icelandic is a Nordic language but not commonly understood by other Nordic lawyers.

[4]Example, the concept of disability or partiality is known in Denmark as *inhabilitet* and in the Swedish legal language as *jäv*.

[5]Regarding legal language, see Mattila (2013).

Swedish private law, whereas the procedural system and public law and public law terms would look more different and also here both concepts and those terms will be found that are really different. In these fields lawyers have to be more careful as differences in terms may also indicate differences in the way a concept should be understood, e.g. an *ombudsmand* can have different functions in the respective countries and in penal law even words who look alike like Danish *ran* and Swedish *rån* may indicate different crimes and different ways of structuring the penal system.

2 The Roots of Nordic Law and Legal Language

The creation of a Nordic legal language went hand in hand with writing down the law in the Nordic countries, which occurred in the Middle Ages in the years after 1100. The age of some parts of the older Icelandic and Norwegian laws written in the vernacular is still a matter of dispute. With regard to Denmark and Sweden, the situation is more transparent. In Denmark, the first more general writing of the specific law of a region happened in the province of Scania (Skåne, since 1658 a part of Southern Sweden) shortly after 1200 and was followed by codes in the other two provinces (Sealand and Jutland) in the following century.[6] These laws were written down at a time, when no Danish written language was available. The old laws are thus the first texts of some substance written in the Danish language. We may therefore say, that Danish legal language is actually the basis of—and to some degree created—written Danish language. In principle, these old codes are written down in a clear and understandable language and only occasionally include words that do not stem from ordinary language.[7] The written laws include a series of old Danish words is used to denominate specific economic relations in the family household, transfer of property, division of land in the village, how to pay compensation in a case of manslaughter or to denominate certain crimes. Thus, some ideas of a legal language must have existed before the writing down of the law.[8]

However, the way in which the law in Denmark presents itself as rather well systematised and in a fluent language could suggest as the author someone with a background in studies of the learned language of the Middle Ages: Latin. Many articles in these laws are clearly influenced by the learned law of the time.[9] We may suspect that it was the wish to codify of the learned Archbishop of Scania, Anders

---

[6]The best-known of these codes is the Law of Jutland, dated 1241. See Tamm and Vogt (2016).

[7]This is especially the case for new concepts introduced in the law on division of a family estate. The word 'capital lot' (*hovedlod*) was thus used for the ideal part of any partner in a family community.

[8]Such words are especially mentioned and kept in their old Danish version by Anders Sunesen in the Latin work on the law of Scania, mentioned below.

[9]The topics of such articles include, e.g., how to perform baptism, peacekeeping, testaments and succession.

Sunesen,[10] that shortly after 1200 led to the codification of the local law in Danish at a time when the language used for drafting both royal and private documents was still Latin. Thus, the Danish legal language started out—as in the other Nordic countries—in the vernacular. Even if we may suspect that those who created Nordic medieval law knew Latin, they translated legal concepts into a Nordic language. In Norway, Denmark and Sweden, as in Iceland, law was handled by the local courts in the language understood by local people.[11]

There is a long and unbroken Nordic tradition of using the spoken language as a basis for proceedings in court. In old Anglo-Saxon England before 1066, there was a similar tradition of writing down the law in the English language. However, the later introduction of Law French as legal language complicated the English legal language in a way which has no parallel in the Nordic countries.

3 Germanic and Romanistic Law

The old dichotomy between what is seen as law of Germanic origin and what is seen as having roots in Roman law has for a long time divided legal historians, especially German historians. There used to be a tradition of speaking of Germanic law as being opposed to Romanistic law.[12] Germanic law was law as might be found in the old laws of Germanic peoples, such as Goths, Lombards, Franks, Burgundians, Frisians, Anglo-Saxons and other tribes from the North or East which invaded the Western Roman Empire in the fifth century or settled in that area. This so called Germanic group of law[13] also included medieval Nordic law and, as it was written in the vernacular (other laws were redacted in Latin), was seen as especially pure Germanic law.

It should be understood from what is said here about Nordic law that we cannot draw any clear distinction between Germanic and Roman/Canon law (or *ius commune*). When Nordic law was written down—this is perhaps especially the case for Danish, and later Swedish law—Canon law and Roman law were studied at universities in southern Europe, and both systems, especially Canon law, influenced the way Nordic law was put into writing. If, however, we identify Romanistic law with an in-depth study and understanding of the law based on Roman law sources, we are far from such an approach to the law in the medieval Nordic countries.

---

[10] Anders Sunesen, Archbishop of Scania 1201–1223 was educated in Paris and probably also Bologna. Using terminology from Roman law, he wrote a Latin version of the local law of Scania. See Tamm (2017).

[11] See the series of essays in Österberg and Bauger Sogner (2000).

[12] Romanistic law is in principle based on and takes its origin from Roman law.

[13] In Germany there is still talk of '*Germanenrechte*' even if the value of such a concept and the existence of sufficient common features to make it a group is highly doubted today.

4 Roman Law and Canon Law

In the Middle Ages in particular, the Law of the Church—that is, Canon law—had a great impact on Nordic law and Nordic legal language. The basic institutions of Canon law were created in the Middle Ages and became part of Nordic law. Family law, especially the law of marriage, was governed by Canon law on marriage; indeed, terms from Canon law have become part of family law terminology. And as already noted, the idea of writing down local law and the creation of a somewhat coherent system, as we find it in those laws, may go back to redactors educated in Canon law.

The history of the influence of Roman law and Roman law terminology in the Nordic countries is different from most of the rest of Europe complicated. Roman law never was considered in a Nordic country to be part of Nordic law, nor could it be quoted as such. Students from the Nordic countries studied at other European universities, such as Paris for theology and Bologna for the law and later mostly at German universities. They brought back with them knowledge of the learned '*ius commune*',[14] but such learned law was not implemented in the Nordic countries as it was in Germany. This meant that, in Germany, legal thinking and writing, as well as legal terminology based on Latin developed much earlier than in the Nordic countries. Later in history, but only since the eighteenth century, the impact of German learned law became very important for the education of Nordic lawyers and the making of Nordic legal literature. However, this happened at such late date in legal history that Nordic law was resistant to many concepts and ways of thinking in Roman law and thus kept its basis in the old laws.[15] This basis in old medieval law combined with later cooperation in the field of law is the main reason for considering Nordic law a 'legal family' of its own.[16]

5 The Language in Nordic Courts

Court procedures in the Nordic countries were carried out in the local language, and thus the law was essentially accessible to everyone, with no barrier in the form of a complicated legal language or foreign terms. An exception was the then-eastern part of Sweden, which we today know as an independent Finland. As Finland was the eastern part of Sweden, courts in Finland used Swedish rather than Finnish, whereas Finnish language was used by the majority of the population, mostly ignorant of

[14]'Ius commune' is the term used for Roman and Canon law as distinguished from local law, 'ius proprium', which could only be used when documentation of such a rule was produced before the court.

[15]This is the general explanation for the fact that Roman law was not recognised as the law of the land in the Nordic countries. Roman law, however, played an important role in the education of lawyers and has been a subject taught at the Faculty of Law at the University of Copenhagen since 1479.

[16]See, e.g., Zweigert and Kötz (1998).

Swedish and therefore in need of translation. Since 1863, both Swedish and Finnish have been official languages in Finland and been used by the courts.[17] Thus, a Finnish judge today is expected to understand both languages and to be able to conduct court proceedings in both Finnish and Swedish.[18] In Denmark and Norway, there is an uninterrupted tradition of orality in the Supreme Court, as well as of keeping all proceedings in the national language.

Nordic legal language was created in close connection with ordinary language and thus should be understood by—or understandable to—ordinary people.[19] In early modern times in the Nordic countries, the so-called '*ting*' or assembly was the place to make legal decisions. Evidently, however, many cases remained without a decision, while references to a particular statute or law are few, and this institution (held weekly in Denmark but often less frequently in other Nordic countries) institution to a high degree served as a place where controversies could be discussed and compromises or solutions found which were not directly based on written law. The courts thus played a minor role in law-making, and it was only after the establishment of a Royal appeal Court in Sweden[20] in 1614 and a Supreme Court in Denmark in 1661[21] that conditions were present for the courts to influence law-making.

In Denmark and Norway, modern codes were issued in 1683 and 1687, while in Sweden a new code was issued in 1734.[22] These codes did not contribute much to the development of legal language. In particular, the Danish and Norwegian codes relied heavily on older law, and thus old terms were still used, however in a modernized form. An example from the Danish code is the law of torts. No general concepts of liability were developed such as the Roman '*iniuria*' or '*culpa*'. The code would still use medieval terms in matters of torts, and it was only in the eighteenth century that the Supreme Court started to discuss '*culpa*' when referring to Roman law as a useful term in Danish law as well to describe the fundamental conditions for liability.

6 Europeanisation of Nordic Legal Language

It was only in the eighteenth century that Nordic legal language took a turn towards a more professional vocabulary. In Europe at that time, the study of Roman law was fundamentally changed by the introduction of the so-called '*usus modernus pandectarum*', which was a new and systematised way of introducing those parts of

---

[17] The Swedish language, however, dominated in legal scholarship and the higher courts until the beginning of the twentieth century. In 1902 Finnish and Swedish were recognised as having equal status in Finland.

[18] See Mortensen et al. (2019), p. 71.

[19] Even the critical British ambassador to Denmark at that time, Robert Molesworth, recognised the value of the Danish Code being accessible to all due to its style and language; see his (1694) Account of Denmark as it was in the Year 1692. London.

[20] See Korpiola (2014).

[21] Christensen et al. (2015).

[22] See about these codes Tamm (1984).

Roman law which were considered living law. An example is the elementary book known as the introduction to Roman law by J.G. Heineccius according to the so-called 'Institution' system of the Roman lawyer Gaius.[23] In legal studies Roman law was supplemented by great books on so-called Natural Law, which was free from Roman law but still inspired by Roman law in its description of those rules which should govern human society. The main authors, such as Hugo Grotius, Samuel Pufendorf, Christian Thomasius, Christian Wolff and Emer de Vattel, were widely read in the Nordic countries, and corresponding books in Danish could profit from the many new legal concepts found in these books.

Thus, what we might call Nordic legal science was developing based on a foreign model. The Institutes of Gaius, with their division of legal matters into persons, things and actions (*personae, res et actiones*), supplied the basic structure in manuals of Danish and Swedish law. We may say that it was the influence of Roman law terminology, Natural law structures combined with the law found in national codes that formed the foundations on which to build a new Nordic law. It was not an attempt to create a Nordic approach to the law, however, but was rather a 'Europeanisation' of the way to handle the old law which constituted a first step towards modern law in the Nordic countries. Germany, the German universities and German methods of studying both Roman law and natural law became extremely important for the new, more theoretical way of studying the law of the Nordic countries.

There was not much professional intercourse between the numerally still rather few Nordic lawyers. Influences and inspiration came from Germany and German legal thinkers. To the degree to which we might speak of a Nordic legal science, it was not created by a common effort but as a result of influence from reading the same 'international bestseller' law books and studying at the same universities. Roman law and Roman legal terminology were at this time introduced into Nordic law, but Roman law itself was not implemented as law by the courts. This meant that the Nordic legal systems were still rather simple in their structure and the legal language was accessible, even if some new concepts needed explanation.[24] The law of the Nordic countries was far from being any kind of 'civil law' based on a Romanistic tradition, but it was moving in that direction much more than could in any way be compared with English common law and its concepts based on the practice of the English courts.

[23]The best-known of these 'Institutionenlehrbücher' was probably Johann Gottlieb Heineccius, Elementa iuris civilis secundum ordinem institutionum: commoda auditoribus methodo adornata, published in several editions since 1723 (Heineccius 1723).

[24]The first, to write about the Natural law more extensively was the professor and author Ludvig Holberg, who in 1714/15 published a book in Danish on natural law mainly following the system of Pufendorf; see Koch (2016).

7 Nordic Cooperation in the Field of Law

A new epoch in the Nordic countries started after 1872, when any idea of a political union between the Nordic countries was given up.[25] Nordic cooperation in the field of law was a substitute in a more restricted area for more ambitious plans for a future Nordic union.[26] The common basis of this cooperation was a common Nordic tradition of a less theoretical and rather pragmatic approach to the law. The best way of achieving a more solid Nordic law based on statutes, especially within the law of commerce, and not just on unwritten principles was seen as passing single acts on different subject matters (e.g., the law of sale and contracts) rather than through a complete code. In the years after 1900, Nordic law-making was intense, and new legal concepts had to be developed in common.

This work was highly successful and gave Nordic lawyers a common platform of concepts and ways of legal reasoning, especially within private law in a broad sense, including family law, the law of obligations, insurance and company law and in other fields. A basic concept in the law of contracts is '*retshandel*', which stems directly from German '*Rechtsgeschäft*'. The Nordic law of obligations is deeply indebted to the German *Pandektenwissenschaft* and the concepts found in the German Civil Code.[27] However, other branches of the law such as property law and public law still differ considerably from each other in the Nordic countries.

8 Language and Style in Nordic Courts Today

The languages of Nordic courts are the Nordic languages. The style of Nordic courts in terms of drafting of decisions is different in each country. Since the enactment of a new Code of Procedure from 1919, Danish courts have been heavily dependent on the principle of orality. All proceedings and all documentation are, in principle, to be presented orally in court. Decisions, on the other hand, are often rather short in their argumentation or reasoning. This is also true for the Danish Supreme Court, which, however, adapts its style of writing to expectations of decisions which are clear as to grounds on which the decision is made. In the Norwegian Supreme Court, the judges in principle have their conclusions stated individually, whereas the Swedish and Finnish Supreme Courts issue longer decisions based on written procedure.

---

[25] Since the 1820s, the so-called Scandinavian movement aimed at creating a Nordic political union. After the Danish war with Prussia and Austria in 1864, this idea was abandoned as unrealistic due to the lack of support from other Nordic countries.

[26] See Letto-Vanamo and Tamm (2016).

[27] The German civil code (BGB) – the result of the work of several commissions – was based on the leading German school of Roman law at that time, which took its name from Justinian's Pandects. The most important lawyer of this school was Bernhard Windscheid, who wrote a manual of the law of the Pandects, which was also influential in the Nordic countries.

In Nordic courts, one will not find attempts at more personal descriptions of the circumstances as one sometimes finds in British or American superior courts. The language of decisions can normally be characterised as precise and professional but without over-use of legal terminology or in any way attempting a style similar to the brevity of the French *Cour de cassation* or the extensive argumentation of the European Court of Justice. However, no attempt is made to coordinate the style of Nordic courts.

None of the Nordic countries has adopted the system of constitutional courts. Several reasons can be pointed out for this being rooted in Nordic legal culture, with its respect for parliaments and a deep-seated tradition of law-making not by the courts but by the parliament. There is a continuous democratic tradition in the twentieth century, and no need is felt for constitutional courts as guardians of the constitution.[28] This does not mean that constitutional review is unknown, but Nordic courts have been restrictive in this respect and have not felt any necessity for specific constitutional courts as in countries with a more blurred democratic past.

9 Recent Developments

Since the 1980s, human rights and human rights terminology have played an increasing role in Nordic law. Nordic legal language has become richer in recent years, and new terms are being adapted from international law and American law. A new discussion is arising in academia with regard to balancing the need for legal education with a broader international outlook on the one side with the in-depth study of national law on the other side, which is greatly needed by the courts and also by practicing lawyers.

Actually, the legal language as such of the Nordic countries does not seem at the moment endangered. Since the Middle Ages, there has been a tendency to incorporate terms from foreign law and use them alongside older Nordic terms. Sometimes, one might even feel that the Nordic countries are going too far in maintaining their own terms at the cost of international understanding. Legal Latin is only kept in a few expressions.[29] As certain Latin words and expressions are common to lawyers in both continental Europe and the Anglo-Saxon world, the ignorance of Latin terms makes the understanding of terms of foreign law more difficult for Nordic students than for students from countries in which knowledge of Latin terms is upheld.

A possible danger for the future development national legal language, however, is the extensive use of English for academic purposes. Articles in English published in a recognised foreign law review are usually ranked higher in the academic evaluation systems than books on national law aimed at ordinary Danish or Finnish lawyers,

---

[28] See Husa et al. (2019), pp. 41–60 and Letto-Vanamo (2021).

[29] E.g., *culpa* for fault, *mora* for delay, *condictio indebiti, litis pendens* and other expressions from procedural law.

who normally will not read articles in English language reviews.[30] This may also lead to a neglect of national law by leading academic lawyers and thus a lower quality of literature on national law and in national languages. However, Nordic legal language does not seem to be under pressure. In Finland, an increasing number of academic works are written in English, while in other Nordic countries the tendency is also towards internationalisation of academic life at the law faculties. Big law firms will also often conduct international relations in English, but there remains a great need for national legal scholarship conducted in the national languages aimed at courts and such legal proceedings, which—as the great majority—are basically conducted in a Nordic language. Seen from this last perspective, even if Nordic legal languages as such do not seem endangered, they may become impoverished if too many Nordic scholars choose to publish only in foreign languages.

References

Christensen JP, Erichsen J, Tamm D (2015) The supreme court of Denmark. Gyldendal, Copenhagen

Heineccius J (1723) Elementa iuris civilis secundum ordinem institutionum: commoda auditoribus methodo adornata

Husa J (2019) Constitutional mentality. In: Letto-Vanamo P et al (eds) Nordic law in European context. Springer, New York, pp 41–60

Koch S (2016) Moralske Kierne eller Introduction til Naturens- og Folkerettens Kundskab, 1716, Ludvig Holberg (1684–1754). In: Martyn G (ed) The formation and transmission of western legal culture. Books that made the law in the western world. Springer, New York, pp 249–252

Korpiola M (2014) the svea court of appeal in the early modern period: historical reinterpretations and new perspectives. Institutet för Rättshistorisk Forskning, Stockholm

Letto-Vanamo P (2021) Courts and proceedings: some Nordic characteristics. In: Ervo L et al (eds) Rethinking Nordic courts. Springer, Cham

Letto-Vanamo P, Tamm D (2016) Cooperation in the field of law. In: Strang J (ed) Nordic cooperation: a European region in transition. Routledge, London, pp 93–108

Letto-Vanamo P, Tamm D (2019) Nordic legal mind. In: Letto-Vanamo P et al (eds) Nordic law in European context. Springer, New York, pp 1–19

Mattila H (2013) Comparative legal linguistics: language of law, Latin and modern lingua francas. Routledge, London

Molesworth R (1694) Account of Denmark as it was in the Year 1692. London

Mortensen B, Suksi M (2019) Respecting autonomies and minorities. In: Letto-Vanamo P et al (eds) Nordic law in European context. Springer, Cham, pp 61–77

Österberg E, Bauge Sogner S (2000) People meet the law: control and conflict-handling in the courts in the Nordic countries in the post-reformation and preindustrial period. Scandinavian University Press, Oslo

Tamm D (1984) The Danish code of 1683: an early European code in an international context. Scand Stud Law 28:163–180

Tamm D (2017) The liber legis Scaniae: Latin text with introduction, translation and commentaries. Brill, London

Tamm D and Vogt H (2016) The Danish medieval laws: the laws of Scania, Zealand and Jutland. Routledge Medieval Translations, London

[30] For more details, see van Gestel and Lienhard (2019).

van Gestel R, Lienhard A (2019) Evaluation academic legal research in Europe. Edward Elgar, London
Zweigert K, Kötz H (1998) An introduction to comparative law. Clarendon Press, London

The History of Nordic Legal Culture and Court Culture: The Story of What Should not Have Been, but Still Came to Be

Jørn Øyrehagen Sunde

Abstract The story of the making of a Nordic legal culture and court culture appears, at first glance, to be a story of what should not have been. Culture is about commonalities arising from common experiences. However, the similarities between the Nordic countries' political history are limited, with no common institutions before the late nineteenth century, large language similarities but no common legal language, and—most importantly—no common legal procedure. Still, the natural conditions in the very north of Europe came to shape the political and legal systems in similar ways, stimulating the desire to create a Nordic legal culture in the second half of the nineteenth century, with the Nordic Meeting for Lawyers playing a crucial role. Hence, law in the Nordic countries shares several characteristics today: a strong legislative tradition and strong courts with lay participation, accessible legal language in legislation and court decisions and orality in legal procedure, a small number of legal professionals and a small and pragmatic legal science. These characteristics can be viewed as building blocks in an overarching characteristic of Nordic legal culture and court culture: dialogue.

1 How to Approach Legal Culture

The Norwegian ambassador to Stockholm, former Prime mister Francis Hagerup, declared himself an advocate for a Nordic legal culture in 1916.[1] The Swedish Prime minister Carl Gustav Ekman spoke in 1928 on the necessity of a Nordic legal culture.[2] The Norwegian Minister of Justice Asbjørn Lindboe spoke of a Nordic legal culture at the Nordic meeting for heads of police in Oslo in 1932.[3] In Danish newspapers in

[1] *Stavanger Aftenblad* 8 November 1916.

[2] *Bergens Tidende* 20 July 1928.

[3] *Nordisk Politichef-konferanse,* 1932, p. 6.

J. Ø. Sunde (✉)
Department of Public and International Law, University of Oslo, Postboks 6706 St. Olavs plass, Oslo, Norway
e-mail: j.o.sunde@jus.uio.no

L. Ervo et al. (eds.), *Rethinking Nordic Courts*, Ius Gentium: Comparative Perspectives on Law and Justice 90, https://doi.org/10.1007/978-3-030-74851-7_4

1933, during the Greenland conflict between Norway and Denmark, it was claimed that Norway was a disgrace to the Nordic legal culture,[4] and at the meeting of the Nordic branches of the International Council on Social Welfare in 1934 a Nordic legal culture was again referred to as a fact.[5] The notion of a Nordic legal culture evolved quickly from something to be established to an established fact in the interwar period.

However, was this just a notion, or is there really a Nordic legal culture and even a Nordic court culture? If you ask a Nordic judge with international experience, he or she will confirm that the Nordic judges in international meetings often have the same viewpoints and take the same stands, as well as that they often socialise in the evening when the meeting is over. A Nordic prosecutor would confirm that this is also the case for Nordic lawyers, and for politicians the same would apply; in fact, people in all Nordic countries feel related and seek each other's company when staying outside their region in Europe. This very simple observation shows that there is a notion of Nordicness among Nordic lawyers and judges, as there is in general in the Nordic countries.[6] We are not only talking of a Nordic court culture, but a notion of a legal culture and Nordic culture in general.[7]

There are even empirical data that support this notion of Nordicness. If we apply the cultural model developed by Geert Hofstede for comparing national cultures, the Nordic countries display fairly high commonalities. The model measures power distance,[8] individualism versus collectivism,[9] masculinity versus femininity,[10] uncertainty avoidance,[11] long-term versus short-term orientation,[12] and indulgence versus

[4] *Morgenavisen* 9. February 1933.

[5] *Forhandlingene under Nordisk socialt møte 17–18 September* 1934, p. 56.

[6] On Nordicness, see Letto-Vanamo et al. (2019) for investigations of Nordicness and a Nordic legal culture.

[7] On a Nordic legal family and a Nordic legal culture, see Husa et al. (2007), Nylund (2010) and Letto-Vanamo et al. (2019).

[8] 'People in societies exhibiting a large degree of Power Distance accept a hierarchical order in which everybody has a place and which needs no further justification. In societies with low Power Distance, people strive to equalise the distribution of power and demand justification for inequalities of power'; https://hi.hofstede-insights.com/national-culture. Accessed 25 May 2020.

[9] 'The high side of this dimension, called Individualism, can be defined as a preference for a loosely-knit social framework in which individuals are expected to take care of only themselves and their immediate families. Its opposite, Collectivism, represents a preference for a tightly-knit framework in society in which individuals can expect their relatives or members of a particular ingroup to look after them in exchange for unquestioning loyalty'; https://hi.hofstede-insights.com/national-culture. Accessed 25 May 2020.

[10] 'The Masculinity side of this dimension represents a preference in society for achievement, heroism, assertiveness, and material rewards for success. Society at large is more competitive. Its opposite, Femininity, stands for a preference for cooperation, modesty, caring for the weak and quality of life. Society at large is more consensus-oriented'; https://hi.hofstede-insights.com/national-culture. Accessed 25 May 2020.

[11] 'The Uncertainty Avoidance dimension expresses the degree to which the members of a society feel uncomfortable with uncertainty and ambiguity. (…) Countries exhibiting strong UAI maintain rigid codes of belief and behaviour, and are intolerant of unorthodox behaviour and ideas. Weak UAI societies maintain a more relaxed attitude in which practice counts more than principles'; https://hi.hofstede-insights.com/national-culture. Accessed 25 May 2020.

[12] 'Every society has to maintain some links with its own past while dealing with the challenges of the present and the future. (…) Societies who score low on this dimension, for example, prefer to

restraint.[13] According to this model, the Nordic countries are generally characterised by a mentality of equality, collectivism, cooperation, stability, strong social norms, and a balance between past and future orientations.[14] If we compare with the Baltic states, Estonia, Latvia and Lithuania, we find that they score similarly to the Nordic countries, but they are more focused on the future and have much weaker social norms.[15] When comparing with the United Kingdom, France, Belgium, the Netherlands and Germany, we can see that in general especially the desire to cooperate, to seek stability and to focus on the future rather than the past is higher in the Nordic countries.[16] If we then compare with Portugal, Spain, Italy and Greece, we see that similarities are only coincidental.[17]

According to this model, then, there is a Nordic culture in general, both because the Nordic countries have common features and because they share more common features with each other than with other countries. However, can we also speak of a Nordic legal culture and a Nordic court culture more scientifically and not only as a notion? This question will be investigated in this chapter after we have defined and explained legal culture theoretically and have investigated how different kinds of interrelations are decisive for the making of legal culture. What we will see is that the history of Nordic legal culture and court culture is the story of what should not have been, but still came to be.

2 Legal Culture Defined and Explained

Legal culture has been defined in different ways. Lawrence M. Friedman, a pioneer within legal-cultural studies, defines legal culture in *The Legal System* (1975) as comprising the 'ideas, values, attitudes and beliefs of a specific group of people

maintain time-honoured traditions and norms while viewing societal change with suspicion. Those with a culture which scores high, on the other hand, take a more pragmatic approach: they encourage thrift and efforts in modern education as a way to prepare for the future'; https://hi.hofstede-insights.com/national-culture. Accessed 25 May 2020.

[13] 'Indulgence stands for a society that allows relatively free gratification of basic and natural human drives related to enjoying life and having fun. Restraint stands for a society that suppresses gratification of needs and regulates it by means of strict social norms'; https://hi.hofstede-insights.com/national-culture. Accessed 25 May 2020.

[14] See https://www.hofstede-insights.com/country-comparison/denmark,finland,norway,sweden/ and https://www.hofstede-insights.com/country-comparison/iceland/. Accessed 25 May 2020. See Husa et al. (2007), p. 28.

[15] See https://www.hofstede-insights.com/country-comparison/estonia,latvia,lithuania/. Accessed 25 May 2020.

[16] See https://www.hofstede-insights.com/country-comparison/france,germany,the-netherlands,the-uk/ and https://www.hofstede-insights.com/country-comparison/belgium/. Accesed 25 May 2020.

[17] See https://www.hofstede-insights.com/country-comparison/greece,italy,portugal,spain/. Accessed 25 May 2020.

towards law'.[18] This definition can be taken as representative of a whole tradition within legal-cultural research, where the emphasis is on mentality and what we can call ideas and expectations of law.[19] Differing from this tradition, John Bell claims that '[T]he law is something more than simply a system of rules or legal standards. Those rules operate in a context of institutions, professions and values that form together a "legal culture".'[20] Legal culture is, according to Bell, not merely a question of ideas and expectations of law but also of the institutional practices that constitutes law. However, Bell overemphasises the latter when he claims that 'the institutional systems and practices precede the ideas'.[21] Hence, we will take a middle way and define legal culture as ideas and expectations of law made operational by institutional practices.[22]

Even when defined, legal culture can still seem to be more a notion than a fact. There is a long and rather varied tradition of splitting legal culture into elements to make it more manageable as an analytical tool. In a pioneer article on 'Foundations of European Legal Culture' published in 1985, Franz Wieacker investigates (1) personalism, (2) legalism, and (3) intellectualism with regard to the European legal culture.[23] Mark van Hoecke and Mark Warrington, in their article 'Legal Cultures, Legal Paradigms and Legal Doctrine: Towards a New Model of Comparative Law' from 1998, investigate legal cultures using the elements of (1) concept of law, (2) legal sources, (3) legal method, (4) argumentation, (5) legitimation, and (6) ideology.[24] John Bell, in his *Judiciaries of Europe* (2006) applies a personal, institutional and external perspective on the judiciary to reveal its character in France, Germany, Spain, Sweden and England. In practice, he investigates (1) the organisational setting and the judicial career, (2) history and values, (3) the judicial role, (4) professional judges and the legal community, (5) lay judges and (6) professional judges. We have chosen a different approach, as we split legal culture into institutional and intellectual structure and six elements, all together making up the legal cultural model. Under the institutional structure, we find there are two elements to be investigated when exploring legal cultures: (1) conflict resolution and (2) norm production. Under the intellectual structure, we find four more legal-cultural elements to be explored: (3) idea of justice, (4) legal method, (5) professionalisation, and (6) internationalisation.[25]

The institutional structure of a legal culture is, in short, that of institutions wherein law is shaped through different practices. Since the High Middle Ages, the main practices for shaping law in the Nordic countries have been court decisions and legislation. The intellectual structure consists of, in short, the ideas and expectations of law that influence the different practices shaping law. Court decisions and legislation are made

---

[18]Friedman (1975), p. 223.

[19]See the discussion in Cotterrell (2019), pp. 720–724.

[20]Bell (2006), p. 6, which is the definition he also uses in Bell (2001).

[21]Bell (2006), p. 7.

[22]Sunde (2010), p. 20, Sunde (2011), p. 51, Sunde (2014), p. 231 and Sunde (2020), p. 27.

[23]Wieacker (1990), p. 1.

[24]Hoecke and Warrington (1998), p. 495.

[25]Sunde (2020), pp. 33–34.

according to an idea of what is just and fair, and they come with a legal method that ensures that the applied law fulfils the ideas and expectations with regard to justice and fairness. What is considered just and fair might vary among professional lawyers and laypeople, and hence the level of professionalisation in the legal system is of importance with regard to what the ideas and expectations of the law will be. The international influence on the law also influences the ideas and expectations of the law, and hence it is among the legal-cultural elements under the intellectual structure.

We will investigate the Nordic legal culture and court culture by the above-presented definition of legal culture and the legal-cultural model. The investigation will include both legal culture and court culture, since they are highly intertwined in the Nordic countries. However, first we have to explain how we can speak of a Nordic legal culture and court culture as something more than a sense of Nordicness. After all, the Nordic countries have only limited commonalities in their political history, no common institutions before the late nineteenth century, large language similarities but no common legal language, and no common legal procedure.

3 The Interactions that Shape a Legal Culture

The are many definitions of culture. For our purpose, it is sufficient to state that culture is a product of human interaction; that is, it is through interaction in different social settings that shared ideas and expectations emerge. This is how a common understanding of words, sentence structure, and grammar is created, upheld, changed and finally lost. This is also what governs the life cycle of conflict resolution and norm production, ideas of justice, legal methods, level of professionalisation and internationalisation. In this context, interaction is to be understood more like communication, since it includes all kinds of information transfer and is not dependent on people actually being in the same place at the same time, observing and participating in the same events.[26]

The shared ideas and expectations of law are strongest between those who interact most often, whereas they weaken as the degree of interaction decreases until they are finally entirely lost. There are four modes of interaction that are interesting when studying legal culture and court culture. The first mode of interaction is between people sharing the space of the world with each other, the second is between people now and in the past, the third is between people and institutions, and the fourth is between people and nature. It is in the crossroads between these four modes of interaction that ideas and expectations of law are shaped through institutional practices.

It is fairly obvious that interactions between people sharing the world shape legal culture and court culture. Meetings between judges in court buildings, meetings of presidents of administrative courts or of the Consultative Council of European Judges, or the Nordic Lawyers Meeting are all events that at different levels contribute to

[26] See Kvam (2010), pp. 183–183.

creating common ideas and expectations of law. However, we must not get lost in the internal legal interactions. In addition to the internal legal culture, which is the legal culture shared by lawyers, there is also an external legal culture.[27] The external legal culture is not much investigated in legal literature, but it is the lay or popular legal culture[28] shared by the legal subjects. Especially the Nordic court culture, with its tradition of lay participation,[29] has been and partly is shaped by the interaction with the ideas and expectations of law in society more widely. However, we must also not forget that law is not a closed system in relation to the society it regulates,[30] and discussions on law in media, ordinary conversations, and so on also contribute to the interaction shaping the ideas and expectations of law.

It is obvious that history plays a role when shaping the ideas and expectations of law. No language speaker starts from scratch when making sense of and speaking a language, because we inherit the use of the language of previous users. This path dependency also applies to legal culture and court culture.[31] This does not mean that all Nordic lawyers at all times have shared the same ideas and expectations of courts. Rather, it only implies that there are always existing ideas and expectations with which new ideas and expectations must interact. While Sweden and Finland have a well-established system of administrative courts, Iceland, Norway and Denmark have no separate administrative court or chambers for administrative cases in general courts, and it is hard to see any other reason than history for this distinction.[32]

It is less obvious that the communication between different institutions and between institutions and people also must be taken into consideration as a separate kind of interaction. This is because institutions are not actors but rather consist of people who act on their behalf and in their name. However, institutions are different from groups of people in general. Social, ethnic and religious groups are often organised, but organisation is not their primary objective. An institution consists of a group of people with the primary objective of being sufficiently organises to be able to perform specific tasks with efficiency. Law-making and -applying institutions like Parliaments, Departments of Justice and the judiciary hence shape our ideas and expectations of the law to a much larger extent than the interactions of people. This said, we must not forget that the interactions of and with institutions have less effect when they do not correspond with the existing ideas and expectations. Hence, institutions are forceful but also are in a dialogue and have their ideas and expectations shaped through the interactions in which they take part.

The importance of the nature for legal culture has long been stressed. In the seventh century, Isidor of Seville, a bishop on the Iberian Peninsula, noted that good laws were those adjusted to local conditions and customs: 'A law should be honourable,

---

[27]See briefly Friedman (1975), pp. 223–224, but also Gibson and Caldeira (1996), p. 58.

[28]See Cotterrell (2019), p. 718.

[29]On lay participation in Nordic courts, see Letto-Vanamo (2021).

[30]Eckhoff and Sundby (1991), p. 45.

[31]See Husa et al. (2007), pp. 10–13.

[32]See Difi-notat 2012:3 Forvaltningsdomstoler i Norge? Kort gjennomgang av begreper og synspunkter. Direktoratet for forvaltning og IKT, Oslo, pp. 15–16.

just, feasible, *in agreement with nature*, in agreement with the custom of the country, appropriate to the time and place'.[33] The same idea was later expressed in *De l'esprit des lois*, published by Charles Montesquieu in 1748, in which he, like Isidor, advised the lawmaker to make law in accordance with the local natural and cultural conditions:

> They [the laws] should be in relation to *the climate of each country, to the quality of its soil, to its situation and extent,* to the principal occupation of the natives (...) they should have relation to the degree of liberty which the constitution will bear; to the religion of the inhabitants, to the inclinations, riches, numbers, commerce, manners, and customs.[34]

Historically, the interaction with nature has been very important as a precondition for survival. This is less the case for many people today. However, as we have seen, historical interactions shape ideas and expectations of law just like contemporary interactions do. Hence, we still have to take into consideration the interaction with nature as a framework for all other interactions that shape ideas and expectations of law.

We have above considered the four different modes of interaction that shape legal culture and court culture. We will now apply them actively to identify and explore crucial factors in a Nordic legal culture and court culture.

4 A Nordic Legal Culture and Court Culture

4.1 The Interaction of Nature and History

We have seen that Charles Montesquieu was of the opinion that 'the climate of each country, to the quality of its soil, to its situation and extent' was important to take into consideration when making laws.[35] This climate theory was as important to Western legal development as the theory of the three branches of government, since it was decisive for the popularity of the idea of national law as good law. However, by the second half of the eighteenth century it was already controversial. Still, as explained above, there are good reasons for a modest use of this perspective.[36] When it comes to the Nordic countries, we should keep in mind that the relationship between geography on one hand and governance on the other is vital due to the Nordic states' vast territories with small populations.[37]

The Nordic countries' vast territories can be difficult to traverse. Historically, this was even more the case.[38] In the High Middle Ages, Norway ruled Orkney, Shetland, the Faeroe Islands, Greenland and Iceland in addition to mainland Norway. The

---

[33] *The Etymologies of Isidor of Sevilla* (2006), p. 121 no. xxi (italics mine).

[34] Montesquieu (2001), p. 23 (italics mine). See also p. 246.

[35] See Shackleton (1955), pp. 317–32.

[36] See Lando (2001), p. 6.

[37] With Denmark as an exception.

[38] For a short introduction to the Nordic realms in the Middle Ages, see Korpiola (2018), pp. 378–381.

Swedish realm included Finland, and Norway was ruled by the Swedish king from 1319 until 1397. From then until 1523, the Scandinavian kingdoms were joined under one queen or king. Later Denmark, Norway, Iceland and the Faeroe Island made up the Western Scandinavian realm,[39] and Sweden and Finland the Eastern Scandinavian realm. In the seventeenth century, Sweden would also rule the Baltic States and territories stretching far down into the European continent, while Denmark would acquire small colonies in India, Africa and the Caribbean. In 1811, Finland became a grand duchy under the rule of the Russian Czar. Three years later, the Swedish king possessed the Norwegian crown in a political union between the two countries. Norway gained its independence in 1905, Finland gained independence in 1917 and Iceland became an independent republic in 1944.[40]

A vast territory is difficult to control. However, control is essential to establish authority to tax and, in so doing, to establish the economic foundation for a state. How does one exert control when communication possibilities are limited and the territory one wants to control is vast? Very generally speaking, we can say that one instrument to strengthen central power in the Middle Ages, when the foundation of the modern state was made, was, paradoxically, to establish a decentralised feudal system of power. This system of power aimed at making sure that central power through vassals as agents reached out to every corner of the realm. Another instrument was—again very generally speaking, and paradoxically—to encourage the establishment of towns with a large degree of internal self-rule to attract trade and, hence, to be able to target taxation.[41]

In most of the Nordic countries, these two strategies were less suitable. Large parts of the Nordic countries were forested, were dominated by mountains or had a rugged coastline. Hence, it was hard for knights in castles with their soldiers to achieve military control. Moreover, it was in the hard-to-control areas that the natural resources[42] that were popular on the European market were found, like fish, walrus tusks, falcons, cairn cat (ermine) fur, and so on. At the same time, most Nordic towns stayed rather small until the nineteenth century. Hence, a model very different from feudalism and urbanisation had to be developed in the Nordic countries for control, enabling taxation, state formation and growth[43]—one of cooperation with the local peasantry and their popular assemblies.[44] This would prove most important for the development of a Nordic legal culture.[45]

---

[39]The Orkney Islands and Shetland were mortgaged to Scotland in 1468 and 1469, and control of governance was lost step by step until 1611, when the islands definitely were included in the Scottish realm when Norwegian law was replaced with Scottish.

[40]For a short introduction to the Nordic countries in the Early Modern Period, see Pihlajamäki (2018), p. 807. It can also be noted that Denmark lost Schleswig and Holstein in 1850 and 1864 and that Finland lost its parts of Karelia in 1940.

[41]See the analysis of Sassen (2006), pp. 31–61.

[42]On the role of controlling access to natural resources and markets, see Iversen (2020), pp. 297–298.

[43]On feudal structures and urbanisation in the Nordic countries, see Pihlajamäki et al. (2018), pp. 808–811 and 821–822.

[44]Iversen (2016), pp. 124–135.

[45]See analysis in Bagge (2010), pp. 379–387.

In Nordic regions and localities there were popular assemblies. The origin of these assemblies is uncertain; the only major popular assembly whose origin we know with certainty is the annual Icelandic Alþingi meeting at Þingvellir that began in 930. It was established by the elite of Iceland as a popular assembly and instrument of governance. For the other Nordic countries, we can say that the king and the church—as the two parts of state power in the Middle Ages—took an interest in the assemblies and reorganised them to suit their purpose—that is, as an instrument for interaction and governance.

Popular assemblies were in no way unique to the Nordic countries. Rather, this was a rather universal instrument for governance. However, with state formation, popular assemblies easily lose power to the sovereign and the ruling elite.[46] This is also the case in the Nordic countries, but to a far lesser degree.[47] The popular assemblies, reshaped by royal power, were necessary as a place where royal and local authorities could interact for governance purposes in the absence of feudal lords and towns. The popular assemblies thus became a birthplace for a system of interaction making shared authority and governance possible.[48]

4.2 Interaction of People and History

Without going into detail, it became the prerogative of the king and church in the Nordic realms in the High Middle Ages to legislate, with the legislation being valid from the promulgation at the assembly. It is a common trait among all the Nordic realms that they used this technique of governance very soon after it was developed in the study of Roman and Canon law from the middle of the twelfth century. The code of law, Liber Augustalis, issued by King Fredric II of Sicily in 1231, can be seen as the first extensive and cohesive legislative effort in Europe in the High Middle Ages.[49] King Valdemar I of Denmark issued a code of law for Jutland in 1241; King Magnus VI of Norway issued a code of law for the realm in 1274, a code for the towns in 1276 and a code of law for Iceland in 1281; and King Magnus IV of Sweden did the same in his realm around 1350.[50] These were not singular events but established legislation as an instrument for governance.[51] Hence, singular statutes amending the codes of law were issued in all Nordic realms throughout the Middle Ages and into the Early Modern Period starting with the Reformation. In 1683 and 1687, the Danish King Christian V issued new codes of law for Denmark and Norway, respectively, while Iceland kept their medieval code from 1281 up to the present day. In 1734,

[46] Iversen (2013), pp. 5–17.

[47] See Husa et al. (2007), p. 15.

[48] See Bagge (2010), p. 226.

[49] Wolf (1996), pp. 47–48.

[50] On legislation in the Nordic realms in the Middle Ages, see Korpiola et al. (2018), pp. 385–388.

[51] See Husa et al. (2007), p. 15.

Fredric I of Sweden issued a code for his Swedish realm, including Finland.[52] Thus, the Nordic countries have a long tradition of governance through legislated law.[53] However, none of the Nordic countries has a code of law in the modern sense, which has given leeway for the legal pragmatism that we will deal with later.[54]

Making codes of law as an instrument of governance does not mean that one actually governs. Law in book and law in action do not have to correspond, and throughout most of legal history the correspondence between the two has in general been weak. The interaction between governing institutions and the governed has hence been equally weak. However, the number of preserved copies of the medieval codes for Jutland, Norway, Iceland and Sweden with Finland indicates that the codes were effectual instrument of interaction.[55] This was not due to the codes themselves but, rather, to their application, which to some extent took the interaction from command to dialogue. Lay participation in courts lasted longer in the Nordic countries than in most other European countries[56] (with the exception of the British Isles)—long enough to enjoy the revitalisation of lay judges with the French revolution. However, from the Early Modern Period, lay participation in Nordic courts was only found in the first-level courts. In the state hierarchy, these courts are subject to higher courts and hence are the courts with the least power to influence the shaping of law. At the same time, it was the first-level courts that decided the large majority of cases. Still, the continuous use of lay judges in Nordic courts is less important than the notion of lay judges being a Nordic legal feature to be restored in the nineteenth and early twentieth century, as the effect of actual and desired continuity is often much the same.

A long tradition of lay participation in courts, a long tradition of legislation, the use of the courts as a place for dialogue between sovereign and subjects, and the application of law as an act of dialogue would not have been possible without a tradition for using the vernacular language in a legal context.[57] With the exception of Denmark, Nordic legislation and legal documents have primarily been in the vernacular language.[58] Roman and Canon law, which was the learned law studied at universities from the middle of the twelfth century, was written and taught in Latin. Latin would also, to a large degree, become the legal language in Western Europe in the Middle Ages and onwards to the seventeenth and eighteenth centuries.[59] Hence, the legislation in the Nordic countries sprung from a learned law tradition totally dominated by Latin, in a cultural sphere where Latin in general was the primary

---

[52] Pihlajamäki et al. (2018), pp. 812–814.

[53] See Letto-Vanamo (2021) on the role of legislation in the Nordic countries.

[54] See Husa et al. (2007), pp. 18–20; see also p. 23.

[55] *Danmarks gamle landskapslove med kirkeloverne*, Jónsson (2004), p. 26, and *Samlig af Sweriges Gamla Lagar* Schlyter (1982), pp. I-LXI.

[56] Husa et al. (2007), pp. 15–17. For France and Germany, see Dawson (1960), pp. 69–83 and 109–112.

[57] On law and language, see Tamm (2021).

[58] Mattila (2006), p. 131.

[59] Mattila (2006), pp. 126–131.

legal language. However, the legislation enacted in the Nordic countries was in the vernacular language. This was not due to a lack of knowledge of learned law or Latin.[60] For instance, as early as 1163 or 1164 we find the first adaptation of Roman law in Norwegian law,[61] only decades after the study of Roman law emerged as a subject taught at universities. In general, Roman and Canon law's influence on Nordic law was quite substantial in Nordic legislation. From this perspective, abandoning Latin as a legal language was not an obvious choice and, hence, must have been done deliberately. However, taking into consideration the model of governance, with the public assembly as a place for dialogue, using the vernacular as legal language was a natural choice. Hence, this was a result of the governance model chosen in the Nordic countries. This also had an effect on the legal profession.

The universities of Uppsala and Copenhagen were established in 1477 and 1479 and offered lectures in law.[62] For members of the upper strata of society, it was not unusual to go abroad to study law before taking a seat in the higher courts or in chambers overseeing legislation.[63] However, a legal education was not a requirement for actors within the legal systems in the Nordic countries before 1736 for the Danish-Norwegian realm, nor before 1749 for the Swedish realm including Finland. Hence, it was not until the beginning of the nineteenth century that Nordic judges, prosecutors and judges all had a legal degree. This means that the Nordic legal and court culture was first fully professionalised at the time when lay participation in Western Europe was revitalised after the French revolution. The introduction of the jury system was a major instrument for making courts an arena for dialogue between legislators and legal subjects. During the nineteenth century, increased lay participation in courts would crash with the increase in the legal profession ultimately reversing and thus preserving this ancient dialogic feature of Nordic law.

Orality in court procedure is closely linked to lay participation.[64] As has been stressed above, lay participation in courts is a general feature in Nordic courts, and lay participation has favoured an oral procedure; listening to claims and the presentation of evidence are more effectual with lay judges than passing around written documents, and vice versa.[65] This is also why written documents play a more prominent role in the Nordic Supreme Courts, which have never had any lay participation, than in lower courts. The historical situation has slightly changed, since Iceland today has no lay participation in courts, and Finland has had few lay judges since a reform in 1993.[66] However, few European countries have more lay judges in relation to professional judges than Finland, with a ratio of 1.7 lay judges per 1 professional

[60] On excess of learned law in Nordic realms, see Korpiola et al. (2018), pp. 390–394; on application of learned law in the political sphere, see Korpiola et al. (2018), pp. 396–399.

[61] Sunde (2019), pp. 151–152.

[62] Pihlajamäki et al. (2018), p. 823.

[63] See Husa et al. (2007), p. 17, which briefly deals with this for Sweden and Finland.

[64] On orality and legal procedure, see Hjort (2021).

[65] The exception is Iceland, which has an oral procedure but no lay judges in the courts today.

[66] See p. 3 at https://finlex.fi/sv/esitykset/he/2014/20140004.pdf and at https://finlex.fi/sv/esitykset/he/2008/20080085.pdf. Accessed 25 May 2020.

judge.[67] This leaves Finland as number 12 of 20 European countries (out of the total of 48) that have lay judges at all. The top four countries in Europe with the largest number of lay judges compared to professional ones are Norway (78:1), Denmark (29:1), the UK (9.3:1) and Sweden (7.6:1).[68] The UK also has a long history of oral procedure, which strengthens the assumption that there is, in general, a relation between orality and lay participation.

The use of vernacular language and the orality of legal procedure must not only be seen in light of lay participation in courts but must also be related to the legislative tradition. Since the Middle Ages, the Nordic legislation has aimed at the general public and not at a class of learned lawyers (which, in any case, did not exist). Since the legislation was aimed at the general public and not trained lawyers, the legislative language was straightforward and close to the everyday language used in society. This is, of course, relative: the legislative language, like the language used in courts and court decisions, has been criticised both in the Nordic countries and in general for being overly complicated and dependent on alienating terminology. However, compared to the legal language in comparable countries in Western Europe, the Nordic legal language has been relatively accessible and the legislation possible to read and understand, albeit not at the level of detail that only legal interpretation can explore. When orality is a dominant legal characteristic in general,[69] the legislative language will be brought closer to everyday language. This has to been seen in light of the dialogue perspective that has already stressed several times: if the legislator and the courts with the lay judges are in a dialogue, the legislative language has to promote and not disrupt the dialogue. This will also pull the legislative language towards the everyday language.

When a legal profession with trained lawyers emerged and became a factor in the legal system, the legal language should have changed and become more professional as well. At least for the Danish-Norwegian realm, this was the case in the second half of the eighteenth century, with, for instance, a notable increase in the use of Latin legal terminology in legal practice. However, during the nineteenth century, legislative technique changed and preparatory work, often written by or with the participation of legal scholars, accompany the legislation. In the preparatory work, we find more detailed and sophisticated legal discussion, making it possible to keep the legal language rather straightforward and close to everyday language. This is one reason why preparatory work is a legal source in all Nordic countries.[70]

The late professionalisation of Nordic law and courts is linked to the late growth of legal science in this northern region of Europe. Without students attending lectures in

---

[67] These countries are Belgium (2.3:1), the Czech Republic (2:1), Estonia (2.1:1), France (3.7:1), Germany (4.7:1), Monaco (4:1), Slovenia (3.9:1) and the UK (9.3:1); European Commission for the Efficiency of Justice, 'European judicial systems—Efficiency and quality of justice', *CEPEJ Studies*, no. 26 2018, p. 103. Available at https://rm.coe.int/rapport-avec-couv-18-09-2018-en/16808def9c. Accessed 22 May 2020.

[68] European Commission for the Efficiency of Justice 2018, p. 103. Available at https://rm.coe.int/rapport-avec-couv-18-09-2018-en/16808def9c. Accessed 22 May 2020.

[69] Nylund (2010), pp. 177–178 and Nylund et al. (2019), pp. 208–209.

[70] Husa et al. (2007), p. 34 and Nylund (2010), p. 174.

law, there was no need for more than a handful of professors in the subject, for legal literature and legal journals. In all these aspects, Nordic law was not in sync with the rest of Western Europe.[71] It can be argued that a legal science to be reckoned with in the legal system first emerged in the nineteenth century. Legal science hence did not become a go-between between legislator and court before the American, French, and subsequent revolutions made the democratic idea popular and an effective force in society. On one hand, it took the entire nineteenth century to develop the Nordic democracies. The Norwegian constitution of 1814 introduced a radical democracy, but it was no longer up to date with Western European democratic development after 1848. Denmark and Iceland, Sweden and the grand duchy of Finland were still lurking behind and did not catch up with Norway before the First World War. On the other hand, the democratic idea, implying that the people constituted the legislator, still made it difficult for the legal science to become too much of a filter in the dialogue between legislator and courts.

The dominating legal theoretical tradition in the Nordic countries is one that we can label Scandinavian legal pragmatism. Lars Björne finds there is a long tradition of the present legal method in the Nordic countries that gives room for legal pragmatism in Nordic law.[72] This pragmatic tradition has dominated in the Nordic countries since the emergence of legal science in the eighteenth century, partly due to the weak position of legal science. In Norway, for instance, the number of ordinary professors in law was not greater than the 18 Supreme Court justices before in the 1980s. This meant that legal science was not in a position to push a legal theory or a legal method that would have a normative effect on the well-established and strong court and legislative traditions. Instead of becoming a go-between, legal science instead became a dialogue smoother, pushing a legal theory emphasising both law and legal practice and creating an instrument to harmonise the two. As Lars Björne has shown, the instrument to achieve this harmony was to operate with a wide range of legal sources that were less structured in a hierarchy than levelled. Not only did this approach make it possible to harmonise the apparent legal dichotomy of legislation and practice, but the harmonisation of a multitude of legal sources gave leeway for pragmatic considerations in legal practice as a glue holding the different pieces together. This fit well with lay participation, orality and the late emergence of professional lawyers and legal science. This can also be claimed to be the essence of Scandinavian legal realism,[73] but more generally it describes the core of the theory and method of law in the Nordic countries.

Thus far, we have seen how the natural conditions of the Nordic countries influence the model of governance chosen, as well as how this model is linked to several characteristics of Nordic legal culture and court culture that have been developed throughout history. These characteristics include a strong legislative tradition and strong courts with lay participation, accessible legal language in legislation and court decisions and orality in legal procedure, a small number of legal professionals and a

---

[71] See Husa et al. (2007), p. 17.

[72] Björne (1991), pp. 218–225.

[73] See Husa et al. (2007), pp. 32–33.

small and pragmatic legal science. These characteristics can be viewed as building blocks in an overarching characteristic of Nordic legal culture and court culture: dialogue.

Up till now, we have examined the interactions between nature and people and between history and people. These interactions prepare for the rather late interactions between people sharing the world together and between institutions and people that would be decisive for taking these characteristics and transforming them to a Nordic legal culture and court culture.

4.3 Interaction of People and Institutions

As we have seen, the Nordic countries were tied together in one political union from 1397 to 1523. More than 125 years of common political history is, on one hand, not insignificant. On the other hand, we are only referring to a personal union, with each country having their own political institutions, and a union that was superseded with a period of almost 300 years with a Danish-Norwegian Western Scandinavian realm including Iceland and a Swedish Eastern Nordic realm including Finland. These two realms were frequently at war with each other until the end of the Great Nordic War in 1720. However, in the second half of the nineteenth century, a pan-Scandinavian movement emerged. With it came a desire to identify, highlight and develop commonalities. As we have seen, such commonalities could also be found within law, and lawyers were not indifferent to these changes. This is the backdrop for the first Nordic Meeting for Lawyers in 1872.[74]

The common features of the legal cultures and court cultures developed through the interactions between nature and people and between history and people explain why the Nordic Meetings for Lawyers could become important. The meetings take place only every third year and last for a couple of days. Such short and periodic meetings might not be expected to contribute much to the shaping of a Nordic legal culture and court culture. However, the experience of shared common legal characteristics also had the effect that the Nordic Meeting for Lawyers de facto gave birth to a much more intensive and decisive interaction between institutions and people, as well as to institutional practices.

A series of common Nordic legislation has been produced since 1880. The legislative cooperation was very important until the 1960s[75] but was later made less relevant because of legislative cooperation within the EEA and EU.[76] However, the cooperation between legislative institutions is still important, even though it does not produce statutes enacted in all Nordic countries.

Firstly, meetings are still held between the Departments of Justice in the Nordic countries to mend existing legislation, to discuss new legislation, and to establish a

[74] See Boucht (1999), pp. 748–775.

[75] Nylund (2010), pp. 172–176.

[76] In Backer (2018), p. 18.

common front regarding EU legislation.[77] Secondly, some of the individuals engaged in these meetings are also engaged in the Nordisk Administrativt forbund (Nordic Administrative Association) established in 1918.[78] Most of their meetings are held nationally by each national branch, but they hold their own Nordic meetings.[79] Since 1920, they have published their own Nordic journal,[80] withholding the Nordic focus and strengthening the institutional cooperation by pulling together the individuals acting on behalf of the institutions.

The Nordic Lawyers' Meetings also came to be the first move towards other kinds of legal cooperation. Since 1888, *Tidsskrift for rettsvitenskap* (*Scandinavian Journal of Law*) has been published, targeting Nordic lawyers.[81] Even before the journal, there was already Nordic cooperation within legal science. However, the journal, with board members for the different Nordic countries, advanced this cooperation. At the university level, there are meetings and cooperation between Nordic legal scholars in the different fields of law, including criminal law, law of obligations, procedural law and legal history. This cooperation has also created a market for other Nordic law journals, like the journal *Nordisk tidsskrift for international ret* (*Nordic Journal for International Law*) from 1930[82] and *Retfærd,* published from 1976.[83]

At times, this kind of informal and individual cooperation has overlapped with the formal legislative cooperation. An example is the Nordic journal for criminal law (*Nordisk tidsskrift for Strafferet*) from 1912,[84] which must be seen as a backdrop for the meeting of criminal lawyers from 1948, which again is an important backdrop for the standing Nordic committee for criminal law (*Nordisk strafferetskomité*) from 1960,[85] and active for over 30 years. This blurred line between interactions between people and institutions is in general a characteristic of the interactions that have been important in shaping not only a Nordic legal culture but also a Nordic court culture.

The cooperation between courts and judges has been less intense and extensive than that related to legislation and legal science. The main meeting place for Nordic judges has continued to be the Nordic Meeting for Lawyers. However, since 1958, a Nordic collection of judgements (*Nordisk Domssamling*) has been published twice a year as an addition to *Tidsskrift for rettsvitenskap.*[86] From the early 1990s, the presidents of the Nordic Supreme Courts have met socially, and from the early 2000s they have instead met with some of their justices at a seminar.[87] The Nordic court

[77] Backer makes a vague reference to this practice (2018), pp. 19–20 and 26.

[78] See https://www.nafnet.no/. Accessed 22 May 2020.

[79] Björne (2007), p. 27.

[80] See https://www.djoef-forlag.dk/openaccess/nat/index.php. Accessed 22 May 2020.

[81] See https://www.idunn.no/tfr?languageId=2#/about. Accessed 22 May 2020.

[82] Björne (2007), p. 27.

[83] See https://www.jus.uio.no/forskning/publikasjoner/retferd/. Accessed 24 May 2020.

[84] Greve (2013), p. 1.

[85] See Waaben (1969), p. 102–103.

[86] See https://www.idunn.no/nd#/about. Accessed 22 May 2020.

[87] Sunde (2017), p. 56.

culture is hence less a product of the interaction between judges than a result of other kinds of Nordic legal interaction between institutions and people that have shaped a Nordic legal culture, which also have had consequences for a Nordic court culture.

5 The Essence of a Nordic Legal Culture and Court Culture

Above, we have used a theory of interaction to detect and systematise the communication processes that have shaped a Nordic legal culture and court culture. To do so, we have linked the processes to a series of factors. These factors are not randomly chosen but rather are the factors that make up the legal cultural model. The aim of the model is to make legal cultural analyses and comparison possible by identifying the factors that are influenced by the interaction and then shape legal culture. The model does not aim at identifying all relevant factors but only the factors that in general are the most important and that, hence, a legal-cultural analysis should start with. As mentioned previously, these factors are (1) conflict resolution, (2) norm production, (3) idea of justice, (4) legal method, (5) professionalisation and (6) internationalisation. However, the legal-cultural model is just a starting point for a legal-cultural analysis and has to be adjusted and supplemented in accordance with the subject analysed. Hence, we started the historical investigation by looking at the model of governance and the public assemblies (conflict resolution), legislation (norm production), Scandinavian legal pragmatism (idea of justice and legal method), professional lawyers and legal science (professionalisation). We treated idea of justice and legal method as one unit, and the same with professionalisation and internationalisation, and we spent quite some time on lay judges, orality, legal language and preparatory work as sub-categories under conflict resolution and norm production. We found that the crucial element is the model of governance and its dependency on interaction between legislation and courts, as well as the late professionalisation. Orality, legal language and pragmatic law are results of and also strengthen this interplay.

The commonalities and interaction strictly linked to judges are not decisive for shaping a Nordic court culture. Rather, the court culture must be seen in light of the general legal culture of the Nordic countries. This legal culture is based on commonalities that emerged from shared natural conditions and the political choices made from the state formation in the Nordic countries from the High Middle Ages. This again gave a reason for the decisive desire to strengthen the Nordic legal commonalities in the second half of the nineteenth century. Beginning in 1872, the Nordic Meeting for Lawyers served as a catalyst in the process of making a Nordic legal culture and court culture. However, this development was not purely legal but had political backing, as we have seen from the statements made by Francis Hagerup and Carl Gustav Ekman in the early twentieth century. The history of a Nordic court culture is hence rather complex, and it is the history of what should not have been, but still came to be.

References

Backer I (2018) Styrket nordisk lovsamarbeid: muligheter og Utfordringer. Report to the Nordic Council of Ministers, København

Bagge S (2010) From Viking Stronghold to Christian Kingdom – State Formation in Norway, c. 900-1350. Museum Tusculanums Forlag, Copenhagen

Bell J (2001) French legal cultures. Butterworths, London

Bell J (2006) Judiciaries within Europe. Cambridge University Press, Cambridge

Björne L (1991) Nordisk Rättskällelära: Studier i rättskälleläran på 1800-talet. Institutet for rättshistorisk forskning, Lund

Björne L (2007) Realism og Skadinavisk realism: Den nordiske rättsvetenskapens historia Del IV: 1911–1950. Institutet for rättshistorisk forskning, Lund

Boucht J (1999) De Nordiska juristmöterna och rättsgemenskapen i Norden. Defensor Legis 5:748–775

Brøndrun-Nielsen J, Jørgensen P (eds) (1933) Danmarks gamle landskapslove med kirkeloverne, vol II: Jyske Lov. Gyldendalske boghandel, Copenhagen

Cotterrell R (2019) Comparative law and legal culture. In: Reimann M, Zimmermann R (eds) The Oxford handbook of comparative law. Oxford University Press, Oxford, pp 710–733

Dawson J (1960) A history of lay judges. Harvard University Press, Cambridge

Eckhoff T, Sundby N (1991) Rettssystemet: Systemteoretisk innføring i rettsfilosofien. Tano Aschehoug, Oslo

European Commission for the Efficiency of Justice (2018) European judicial systems: Efficiency and quality of justice. Council of Europe, Strasbourg

Friedman LM (1975) The legal system: A social science perspective. Russel Sage Foundation, New York

Gibson J, Caldeira G (1996) The legal cultures of Europe. Law and Society Review 1:55–86

Greve V (2013) Systematisk register til Nordisk tidsskrift for kriminalvidenskab 1983–2012. The Danish Royal Library, Copenhagen

Hjort MA (2021) Sources of inspiration of Nordic procedural law: Choices and objectives of the legal reforms. In: Ervo L et al (eds) Rethinking Nordic courts. Springer, Cham

Husa J, Nuotio K, Pihlajamäki H (2007) Nordic law: between tradition and dynamism. In: Husa J et al (eds) Nordic Law: between tradition and dynamism. Intersentia, Antwerpen, pp 1–39

Isidor (2006) The etymologies. Cambridge University Press, Cambridge

Iversen F (2013) Concilium and Pagus: Revisiting the Early Germanic Thing System of Northern Europe. Journal of the North Atlantic 5:5–17

Iversen F (2016) Huseby and the Scandinavian taxation model. In: Anne Pedersen; Lisbeth Eilersgaard Christensen & Thorsten Lemm (eds.), Husebyer – status quo, open questions and perspectives. University Press of Southern Denmark, 121–138

Iversen F (2020), Between Tribe and Kingdom: People, land, and law in Scandia AD 500-1350. In Rulership in 1st to 14th century Scandinavia royal graves and sites at Avaldsnes and beyond, Dagfinn Skre (ed.), De Gruter, Berlin, pp. 245–304

Jónsson M (2004) Inngangur, Jónsbók. Lögbok Islendinga, Reykjavik

Korpiola M (2018) High and late medieval Scandinavia: codified vernacular law and learned legal influences. In: Pihlajamäki H et al (eds) The oxford handbook of European legal history. Oxford University Press, Oxford, pp 378–404

Kvam B (2010) Communication and technology as agents of legal change. In: Sunde JØ, Skodvin KE (eds) Rendezvous of European legal cultures. Fagbokforlaget, Bergen, pp 183–193

Lando O (2001) Nordic countries, a legal family? A diagnosis and a prognosis. Global Jurist Advances 2:1–15

Letto-Vanamo P (2021) Courts and proceedings: Some Nordic characteristics. In: Ervo L et al (eds) Rethinking Nordic courts. Springer, Cham
Letto-Vanamo P, Tamm D (2019) Nordic legal mind. In: Letto-Vanamo P et al (eds) Nordic law in European context. Springer, Cham, pp 1–19
Mattila H (2006) Comparative legal linguistics. Ashgate Publishing, Aldershot
Montesquieu C (2001) The spirit of the laws. Batoche Books, Ontario
Nylund A (2010) Mixing past and future: The making of a Nordic legal culture 1850–2050. In: Sunde J, Skodvin K (eds) Rendezvous of European legal cultures. Fagbokforlaget, Bergen, pp 167–181
Nylund A, Sunde J (2019) Courts and court proceedings. In: Letto-Vanamo P et al (eds) Nordic law in European context. Springer, Cham, pp 202–213
Pihlajamäki H (2018) Scandinavian law in the early modern period. In: Pihlajamäki H et al (eds) The Oxford handbook of European legal history. Oxford University Press, Oxford, pp 806–830
Rindal M, Spørck B (2018) Kong Magnus Håkonsson Lagabøtes landslov: Norrøn tekst med fullstendig variantapparat 1. Bind. Arkivverket, Oslo
Sassen S (2006) Territory, Authority, Rights. From Medieval to Global Assemblages, Princeton University Press, Princeton N.J.
Schlyter C (ed) (1982) Samlig af sweriges gamla lagar, vol X: Konung Magnus Erikssons Landslag. Berglingska boktryckeriet, Lund
Shackleton R (1955) The evolution of Montesquieu's theory of climate. Revue Internationale De Philosophie 33(34):317–332
Sunde JØ (2010) Champagne at the funeral: An introduction to legal culture. In: Sunde J, Skodvin K (eds) Rendezvous of European legal cultures. Fagbokforlaget, Bergen, pp 11–28
Sunde JØ (2011) Legal cultural changes in Europe: Teaching future prospects on the basis of legal history and comparative law. In: Modéer K, Nilsén P (eds) How to teach European comparative legal history. Lund University Press, Lund, pp 47–57
Sunde JØ (2014) Live and let die—an essay concerning legal-cultural understanding. In: Adams M, Hairbaut D (eds) The method and culture of comparative law—essays in honour of Mark van Hoecke. Oxford University Press, Oxford, pp 221–234
Sunde JØ (2017) From courts of appeal to courts of precedent: Access to the highest courts in the Nordic countries. In: van Rhee C, Fu Y (eds) Supreme courts in transition in China and in the West. Springer, Cham, pp 53–76
Sunde JØ (2019) 'Aldeles berøvet Forstandens brug': Konedrap i Møllendal i 1798 og psykisk sjuke i norsk rettshistorie. In: Matningsdal M, Strandbakken A (eds) Integritet og ære: Festskrift til Henry John Mæland. Gyldendal, Oslo, pp 143–157
Sunde JØ (2020) Managing the unmanageable. In: Koch S et al (eds) Comparing legal cultures. Fagbokforlaget, Bergen, pp 23–40
Tamm D (2021) Courts, law, language and culture. In: Ervo L et al (eds) Rethinking Nordic courts. Springer, Cham
van Hoecke M, Warrington M (1998) Legal culture, legal paradigms and legal doctrine: Towards a new model for comparative law. Int Comp Law Q 3:495–536
Waaben K (1969) Retssammenligning og retsfællesskab i nordisk strafferet. Svensk Juristtidning 1:102–112
Wieacker F (1990) Foundations of European legal culture. Am J Comp Law 1:1–29
Wolf A (1996), Gesetzgebung in Europa 1100-1500 - zur Entstehung der Territorialstaaten, Beck'sche Verlagsbuchhandlung, München

Sources of Inspiration of Nordic Procedural Law: Choices and Objectives of the Legal Reforms

Maria Astrup Hjort

Abstract This article is based on the following question: does Nordic procedural law exist? Procedural law is often regarded as a national matter, and, unlike in many other legal disciplines, there has not been any official Nordic legislative collaboration in this field. Whether one can refer to procedural law as Nordic or not also has an impact on our perception of procedural law as part of a Nordic community. One way of examining the 'Nordic-ness' of procedural law is to examine the sources of inspiration used when reforming procedural codes and acts. These sources are found in the preparatory works to the legislation. This article surveys the sources that have been used to reform the procedural codes and acts in the Nordic countries over the last three centuries and shows how the objects for the procedural reforms have an impact on the choice of sources of inspiration. The survey also shows that the object for the reforms changes over time, and this influences the choice of sources of inspiration. Further, the use of the sources found in the preparatory works is discussed, and this brings us back to the starting point—namely whether, based on the use of the sources of inspiration, the procedural law in the Nordic countries can be described as Nordic.

1 Introduction

Is there such a thing as Nordic procedural law? Procedural law is traditionally recognised as a national matter, and one might argue that similarities in different countries' procedural law have either a historical explanation or are due to the fact that another country's procedural law has been used as a source of inspiration for reforming this country's procedural law. A method to survey the 'Nordic-ness' of the Nordic countries' procedural law is to examine what sources the countries have used when reforming their procedural law. In the Nordic countries, the preparatory works are an important legal source, and, in addition to being a factor in interpretation of the legislation, the preparatory works usually also contain statements on sources of inspiration for changes in the legislation. The basis for this article is the preparatory works

M. A. Hjort (✉)
University of Oslo, Karl Johans gate 47, 0162 Oslo, Norway
e-mail: m.a.hjort@jus.uio.no

L. Ervo et al. (eds.), *Rethinking Nordic Courts*, Ius Gentium: Comparative Perspectives on Law and Justice 90, https://doi.org/10.1007/978-3-030-74851-7_5

to Nordic procedural acts and codes the last three centuries, and the question is what sources of inspiration the Nordic countries have used in designing their procedural law and how this use fits with the idea of a Nordic procedural law.

2 Legislation and Society

All modern societies have legislation that regulates the citizens' rights and obligations and how the citizens can claim these rights and obligations. The legislator will always try to adapt the legislation to the society in which it operates, and this strong connection between the legislation and the society has significance in several contexts.[1]

First, the connection between the legislation and the society explains why societies that are similar politically, geographically and culturally often have legislation with many common features. The Nordic countries share—among other things—a common view on democracy, welfare, social security and equality.[2] The five countries also shares a common history. Unions in different constellations have led to common legislation in periods,[3] or legislation designed separately for the individual countries of the union but by the same legislator.[4] The shared history explains the similarities in the societies and, at the same time, gives the Nordic countries a common legal platform to develop their legislation.

Second, the connection between legislation and society has an impact when one of the two elements changes. Changes in society lead to a need for changes in legislation, and changes in legislation change society. As both society and ideas on improvement of the legislation are constantly evolving, there will regularly be a need and desire to make changes in or reforms to the legislation. The question is how these changes should be designed and in what direction the changes are going. Legislators will practically never draft new legislation without looking at how other jurisdictions regulate the issue. The design of the changes comes down to the issue of sources of inspiration.

---

[1]See, e.g., Knoph (1998), p. 1 and Mathiesen (2011), pp. 26 ff.

[2]Backer (2018), p. 14.

[3]Such as for Sweden and Finland in the period of 1154–1809.

[4]As in Norway and Iceland in the period 1260–1450, see Sigurðsson (2015), p. 17, and Denmark-Norway in the period 1660–1814.

3 Objectives of the Procedural Reforms

3.1 *First Wave of Reforms: Establish a Justifiable Basis for the Judgment*

Before initiating a procedural reform, the legislator must be clear about the objectives of the reform. The goals of the Nordic procedural reforms have varied throughout history. Many of the reforms have also had several objectives.[5] The survey of procedural reforms in the Nordic countries shows that the objectives of the reforms coincide, and over time simultaneously change. In the further analysis, it will continuously be examined which sources of inspiration were the basis for the changes in the litigation.

The Nordic reforms of procedural law from modern history can roughly be divided into three periods: one in the beginning of the twentieth century, one at the turn of the twenty-first century, and one at the beginning of the twenty-first century. In the first wave of Nordic procedural reforms, at the beginning of the twentieth century, there were two objectives explicitly stated. The first objective was to obtain a procedural arrangement that established a justifiable basis for the decisions, and the second was to reduce the processing time. The court proceedings in all five Nordic countries were based on three codes: Christian V's Danish and Norwegian Codes from 1683 and 1687 and the Swedish Code of 1734. Finland was in union with Sweden when the Code of 1734 was passed, and thus the code became applicable in Finland as well. Iceland was part of Norway when Norway entered into union with Denmark in 1660, and the rules of procedure of Christian V's Norwegian Code of 1687 became applicable to Iceland.[6] The three codes contained older practices and provisions and represented regulation from the 'Ancient Regime'.[7]

Denmark, Norway and Sweden all made attempts to reform the procedural law during the nineteenth century, but, except from the Norwegian Criminal Procedure Act from 1887, none of the attempts succeeded.[8] The Norwegian Criminal Procedural Act succeeded probably due to the political desire to introduce the jury system.[9] The jury system was sourced from England and partly Scotland, and important elements in the new procedure included orality, immediacy, free assessment of evidence, the introduction of a prosecution authority and separation of the executive and the judiciary authority.[10]

---

[5] Uzelac provides an overview of basic objectives for civil procedure; see Uzelac (2014), p. 5.

[6] See Arnesen (1762), p. 23. King Fredrik the Fourth's order was announced at the Icelandic parliament in 1719.

[7] Kekkonen (2009), p. 5. See also Robberstad (1971), p. 117 and Andersen (2019), p. 13.

[8] Hjort (2021), Sects. 2.1, 2.2 and 2.4 give a fuller description.

[9] Hjort (2021), Sect. 2.2 gives a fuller description.

[10] Bilag III to Dok. no. 1 (1885), p. 467. The changed view of the assessment of evidence is further discussed in Skyberg (2019).

Finland also drafted several proposals for reform of the procedural law, and some were adopted. None of these, however, changed the overall problems in the procedure.[11] There were several reasons why the legislative processes were stranded, but the main problems were lack of faith in the radical changes of the existing procedures, questions on financing and how the transition from the old to the new legislation should be conducted.[12]

At the end of the nineteenth century, the situation became more and more critical. The reform committee to the Norwegian Civil Procedure Act stated that a 'main shortcoming of our procedural system is its imperfect ability to bring about the true matter of the case'.[13] A pervasive problem with the litigation was the use of writing.[14] The decisions were subject to a written examination, which meant that all testimonies had to be protocolled. Questions to the witnesses had to be prepared in advance, and there was no possibility to ask follow-up questions without calling the witness again. As a result, ambiguities and an increased risk of a defective decision base could easily arise.

To establish a justifiable basis for the decisions, the solution to fulfil the first reform objective was to introduce oral proceedings. The Norwegian Criminal Procedure Act was the first modern Nordic act based on oral proceedings, and it was an important source of inspiration for the following acts in Nordic countries. This was mainly due to the fact that the Norwegian Criminal Procedure Act had already been enacted in 1887 and that the legal solutions in this act were a novelty.[15] The wave of procedural reforms came at the beginning of the twentieth century: the Norwegian Civil Procedure Act was passed in 1915; the Danish Code of Judicial Procedure followed in 1916 and the Swedish Code of Judicial Procedure was enacted in 1942.

The change from written proceedings to oral proceedings with immediate submission of evidence was primarily sourced from the German and Austrian procedural legislation in Denmark, Sweden and Norway.[16] Both the Norwegian Civil Procedure Act and the Danish Code of Judicial Procedure were enacted before the First and

[11] Hjort (2021), Sect. 2.5 gives a fuller description.

[12] Regarding Norway, see Hearing in Odelstinget 5–7 July 1915, pp. 1451–1499 and Hjort (2007), pp. 30 ff., regarding Sweden, see SOU 1944:10, pp. 28 ff., regarding Denmark, see Bilag VII Retspleje-Reformen. En Oversigt (1901), pp. 3217–3226.

[13] Ot.prp. no. 1 (1910), p. 9 (My translation). For a corresponding view in the Danish preparatory work, see Bilag VII Retspleje-Reformen. En Oversigt (1901), pp. 3231–3232.

[14] This applies at least for Denmark, Norway, Sweden and Finland. Unfortunately, it has not been possible to find more detailed information about Iceland's procedural law in the nineteenth century and the beginning of the twentieth century; however, since Iceland was governed by Denmark for a large part of this period, it is natural to assume that Icelandic procedural law had some of the same problems as in Denmark.

[15] See the Norwegian criminal procedure highlighted in Danish preparatory works: Bilag VII Retspleje-Reformen. En Oversigt (1901), pp. 3235–3236, questions regarding processing of the Police Affairs, pp. 3317–331, and Excerpt from the Norwegian criminal procedure statistics, pp. 3343–3352.

[16] Denmark: see for example Bilag II to Udkast til Lov om den borgerlige Retspleje (1901), pp. 2725, 2729, 2731, 2734, 2751, 2785, 2800–2801, 2806–2807 and 2809, Sweden: see SOU 1926:33, pp. 7 ff. and pp. 18 ff., Norway: see Udkast (1908) Bilag III to Ot.prp. 1 (1910), p. 79. Three major acts

Second World Wars. The Swedish Code of Judicial Procedure was enacted in 1942, in the middle of the Second World War, and having German and Austrian legislation as sources of inspiration was perceived as problematic.[17] Attempts were therefore made to tone down the importance of the German and Austrian influence in the legal literature.[18]

Iceland and Finland did not reform their procedural law during this first wave of procedural reforms. Finland was part of Russia from 1809 to 1917, and after the Second World War, the financial resources needed to modernise the judicial procedure were absent.[19] Iceland became fully independent in 1944, but even though the civil procedure was reformed in 1936 and the criminal procedure in 1951, this did not meet the legislative needs. In the following decades, Iceland continued to reform their procedural acts.[20]

Oral proceedings were also the answer to the second objective of the procedural reforms, so as to reduce the processing time. In the eighteenth and nineteenth centuries, the Nordic countries had court proceedings that took a disproportionately long time.[21] This was mainly because of written proceedings,[22] as it was time-consuming to write down the basis for the judgment. With the transition from written to oral proceedings, this improved significantly.[23] In Sweden, the oral proceedings was a remedy for the constant need for adjournment. In civil cases and criminal cases brought by an individual party, there were hardly any preparations made in the cases before the main hearing, except for the statements of claim being submitted, which were often incomplete.[24] The Swedish reform committee, The Judicial Procedure Commission, stated that the solution was a public procedure based on orality and immediacy, and with free evaluation of evidence.[25]

An interesting observation is that the solutions were sourced from the same jurisdictions. In addition to examining the development of procedural law in the other Nordic countries, both German and Austrian procedural law became important sources of inspiration for the development of new Nordic procedural law. German law was an important source of inspiration in several areas of law and a channel for the influence of Roman Law-based terminology and systematisation.[26] However,

---

were adopted simultaneously in 1915: The Civil Procedure Act, the Courts of Justice Act and the Enforcement of Claims Act.

[17]Bellander (2017), pp. 52 ff.

[18]See Gärde (1931), p. 3 and Schlyter (1934), p. 530, among others.

[19]Letto-Vanamo (2012), p. 91.

[20]Hjort (2021), Sect. 2.3 gives a fuller description.

[21]Regarding Finland, see Kekkonen (2009), pp. 5 and 12. Regarding Norway, see Ot.prp. no. 1 (1910), p. 7.

[22]Regarding Denmark, see Bilag VII Retspleje-Reformen. En Oversigt (1901), pp. 3261–3262.

[23]Regarding Sweden, see SOU 1926:32, pp. 15–23.

[24]SOU 1926:31, p. 21. See also Hjort (2021), Sect. 2.4.

[25]SOU 1926:31, pp. 15–26 and SOU 1926:32, pp. 18–22. Björne (1998), pp. 415 ff. also addresses the Swedish debate on free assessment of evidence.

[26]Letto-Vanamo (2012), p. 90.

the choice of German and Austrian procedural law as sources of inspiration for the Nordic procedural reforms probably has a more concrete explanation. The Nordic countries had identified the problems they were facing in this area, and German and Austrian procedural law could point to reforms that offered solutions to those particular problems. The results of Franz Klein's civil procedure reform in Austria in 1895 must have seemed convincing in Norway, Denmark and Sweden, and the use of a jury made it necessary to have oral procedure in criminal cases as well. The Nordic countries thus moved in the same direction, not because it was a common Nordic idea of how procedural law could be developed but because they faced the same problems and looked to the same sources of inspiration in the process of solving them.

3.2 Second Wave of Reforms: Secure a Fair Trial

The second wave of procedural reforms took place at the turn of the twenty-first century and was an adjustment of the effects of the first reforms. The proceedings were still oral and immediate, but the view of these principles became more nuanced, and new elements were adapted to the procedure. It appeared to be a common goal in the Nordic countries to achieve efficient proceedings, but not to the detriment of a fair trial. The Convention for the Protection of Human Rights and Fundamental Freedoms was enacted in 1950 and entered into force in 1953, but it was not until the 1980s and 1990s that the Nordic countries realised that the Convention set the framework for procedural legislation through Article 6 on the right to a fair trial. The convention had an impact on the objectives for the reforms and how the procedural litigation was designed.[27]

As mentioned, the Norwegian criminal procedure was enacted in 1887, and the need for reform arose earlier than with the other Nordic procedural acts. A reform committee was set up in 1957, and thus the reform of the criminal procedure in Norway was ahead of the second wave of Nordic procedural reforms. The mandate pointed out several issues that the committee should address.[28] Like the procedural reforms in the second wave of reforms, the reform committee stated that the procedure should continue to be oral and immediate. The main question was whether Norway should continue with a system including lay judges.[29] After a comprehensive reform process, a new Criminal Procedure Act with jury trials was passed in 1981.[30]

Finland and Iceland joined the second wave of procedural reforms at the turn of the twenty-first century, but with a different starting point than the other Nordic countries. The two countries had a goal of establishing a procedure that was both efficient and fair, but in addition, the procedural legislation had to fulfil the objectives

[27]The best example is probably the first article in the Norwegian Dispute Act stating the purpose of the act. The article has many similarities to Article 6 in the Convention.

[28]NUT 1969:3, p. 71.

[29]NUT 1969:3, p. 81 and Ot.prp. no. 35 (1978–79), p. 7 and pp. 13 ff.

[30]Hjort (2021), Sect. 3.6 gives a fuller description.

that the other three Nordic countries had established many decades earlier. Although Iceland regularly had made changes in legislation, the need for a pervasive reform was still present at the end of the twentieth century. A case for the Court of Human Rights in 1987 gave Iceland a push to reform their procedural law, and in 1989, Iceland's parliament appointed a reform committee.[31] The result was a complete review and reform of both civil and criminal procedure with acts from 1989 and 1991.[32] The Criminal Procedural Act from 1991 has already been reformed, and the current Criminal Procedural Act was passed in 2008, followed by an act on the special prosecuting authority.[33]

Finland based their proceedings on the old rules in the Code of 1734 with an 'oral-documentary' procedure until the 1990s,[34] when comprehensive legislation was made to meet today's expectations. The procedure in the lower courts was reformed in 1993 and 1997 for civil and criminal cases, respectively. In 1998, the appeal court was reformed in the same line.[35] All the reforms were made within the framework of the Code of 1734, and the similarity to Swedish legislation was thus still striking. Just as in Iceland, Finland had a need for adjustments of their reforms, and improved procedural litigation was enacted in 2003 and 2006.[36] Most Finnish preparatory work refers to foreign law, especially Swedish, Norwegian and Danish law. Sometimes it refers to English, German and French law,[37] but the 'template' seems to be based on Nordic procedural law.[38]

Sweden, Denmark and Norway followed closely after Iceland and Finland, and the three countries all set up reform committees in 1998 and 1999. For Norway, this was only a matter of reforming the civil procedure, since the criminal procedure had already been reformed, ahead of the second wave of reforms. Sweden implemented several reforms after the entry into force of the Swedish Code of Judicial Procedure in 1942 and these reforms put Sweden ahead of the second wave of procedural reforms in many ways.[39] Still, all three committees were instructed to examine how oral and written proceedings should be weighed against each other to make the procedure more efficient, while still ensuring that it would satisfy current rule of law requirements.[40]

[31] Case of Jón Kristinsson v. Iceland, no. 12170/86, Commentary to Act. No. 92/1989. Hjort (2021), Sect. 3.2 gives a fuller description.

[32] See Commentary to Act No. 92/1989, Commentary to Act No. 19/1991 and Commentary to Act 91/1991.

[33] See Act No. 88/2008 and Act No. 135/2008.

[34] Ervo (2009), p. 55.

[35] See L 1056/1991, L 689–690/1997 and L 165/1998.

[36] See L 768/2002, L 381/2003 and L 244/2006.

[37] See for example RP 190/2017, pp. 10–12 and RP 32/2001, pp. 13–14.

[38] Hjort (2021), Sect. 3.3 gives a fuller description.

[39] Hjort (2021), Sect. 3.4 gives a fuller description.

[40] See SOU 2001:103, pp. 384–385, SOU 2003:74, pp. 55 ff., SOU 2005:117, pp. 43 ff., Justitsministeriet (1998), pp. 1–3 and NOU 2001:32, p. 140–141. See also Lindblom (2000).

The efficiency object led to several changes. One common change was an increased use of written elements in the proceedings. In the reforms from the beginning of the twentieth century, the requirement of orality was introduced almost without exceptions to ensure the transition from written to oral proceedings. In the second wave of reforms, the legislatures could allow themselves to open up for some written elements without a fear of relapse back to written proceedings. One implication of this was a change in the presentation of written evidence in court. Whereas previously there had been a requirement for written evidence to be read in the oral hearings, following the change it was sufficient to point out what the evidence should prove.[41]

Another change was the shift to a focus on a more flexible procedure. More flexible procedural rules provide proceedings that are more efficient, because the proceedings can be adapted to the individual case. In Denmark, this resulted in a proposed scheme where the procedure contained a number of standard elements that could be combined according to the individual case's needs.[42] Another way of making the procedure more flexible is to establish different procedural tracks. Both Denmark and Norway introduced a simplified procedure for cases with a claim of limited value.[43] The small claims track is less expensive than the general track and thus allows for judicial proceedings of cases that were previously resolved outside the court system. The flexibility in the procedural rules requires active judges who adapt the proceedings to the individual case. In both Denmark and Norway, the importance of active case management was emphasised in the preparatory works.[44] The Norwegian committee referred to Denmark and Sweden as important sources of inspiration for drafting the Dispute Act,[45] but the Norwegian survey differs from the other Nordic countries' procedural reforms by clearly emphasizing England as an important source of inspiration.[46] Still, the main objectives coincide.

A third common change was the increased use of technology. Like Finland, all three countries opened, *inter alia*, the possibility of remote interrogations and main hearings through video conferencing.[47] However, the main rule was still that parties should be present or represented physically during the main hearing. Opening up the

---

[41] See SOU 2001:103, p. 183, NOU 2001:32, pp. 758 and 978, and KBET 2001 no. 1401, pp. 293 ff.

[42] KBET 2001 no. 1401, p. 271.

[43] The limit for using this simplified procedure is, however unequal in the two countries. In Denmark, the small claims procedure is offered for claims less than 50,000 DKK (app. 6 700€), while the Norwegian limit is set at 250,000 NOK (~25,000 €).

[44] NOU 2001:32, pp. 238 ff., KBET 2001 no. 1401, pp. 269 and 315 ff. Denmark has produced several preparatory works in connection with procedural reforms. Hjort (2021), Sect. 3.5 gives a fuller description.

[45] The Danish consideration KBET 2001 no. 1401 is mentioned in NOU 2001:32, pp. 135, 295, 682 and 841. Other Danish considerations are also pointed out in the Norwegian consideration; see NOU 2001:32, pp. 327–330.

[46] NOU 2001:32, pp. 181–184 and pp. 330–332.

[47] Finland: RP 83/2001, pp. 15–20, Denmark: KBET 2001 no. 1401, p. 61 and pp. 363–368, Sweden: SOU 2001:103, pp. 83 ff. and Norway: NOU 2001:32, pp. 242–243 and p. 608.

possibility of handling the case without all actors being physically present required the installation of necessary technical equipment. Nevertheless, the Nordic courts took their first steps towards a legal procedure based on modern ICT. Sweden was ahead of the other Nordic countries with the recording of all testimonies from the district courts for use in a possible appeal.[48]

3.3 Third Wave of Reforms: Adapt the Proceedings to the Individual Case

Sweden, Norway and Denmark had their reformed procedural legislation passed in, respectively, 2005, 2005 and 2006.[49] By 2008, these reforms were all in force, and at that point, all the Nordic countries had reformed their procedural legislation. One might think that the Nordic countries then would not do changes in their procedural legislation for a while, but in reality, the opposite occurred. The procedural rules have already undergone another procedural reform after the reforms at the turn of the twenty-first century. By adapting the procedural law to social development and the use of technological tools, the Nordic countries have taken a further step towards an ideal balance between fairness and efficiency in trials.

Sweden evaluated its reform from 2005 in 2011–2012 and concluded that the use of technology in courts had been a success.[50] The legislator decided to make further use of the court's audio and video recording by not only recording testimonies during the main hearing but also taking evidence outside the court session. *Inter alia*, this would be convenient in cases when the main hearing is postponed and parties and witnesses have appeared to provide testimonies.[51] Several preparatory works have been conducted to survey the possibility of making the procedure more effective and flexible.[52]

Iceland has not initiated any major reform efforts that have led to new acts, but, like both Finland, Sweden and Denmark, a number of amending laws.[53] Regarding use of audio and video recordings, Iceland has followed Sweden's example, and amendments were introduced in the Icelandic Criminal Procedure Act and the Civil Procedure Act in 2019, regulating the use of recordings from the district courts.[54]

---

[48] Prop. 2004/05:131, p. 105. See also SOU 2008:93. In Sweden, the use of ICT started already during the second wave of procedural reforms. Hjort (2021), Sect. 3.4 gives a fuller description.

[49] Regarding Sweden, see Lag 2005:683; regarding Norway, see Lov-2005-06-17-90; regarding Denmark, see Lov 2006-06-08 no. 538.

[50] SOU 2012:93, p. 265, Prop. 2015/16:39, pp. 20 ff.

[51] Prop. 2015/16:39, p. 39. Hjort (2021), Sect. 4.2 gives a fuller description.

[52] See f.ex. SOU 2013:17 and SOU 2018:44.

[53] Hjort (2021), Sect. 4.4 gives a fuller description.

[54] Lög no. 76 25. júní 2019, in force 5 July 2019.

In Denmark, the Court Administration adopted the Danish Court's digitisation strategy in 2014, with the expressed goal of being able to handle the whole proceeding in civil cases digitally.[55] Paper vouchers and postal mails in civil proceedings disappeared as early as in 2016. Today, through a digital self-service portal, one can file a case, pay court fees, get information and guidance through a new text library and communicate with others.[56] In Norway, the Norwegian Courts Administration established a web portal for the exchange of case information and documents in disputes, judgments, and filing fees in both civil and criminal cases.[57] However, compared to Denmark, Norwegian procedural legislation is a bit behind on this point.[58] The Norwegian Criminal Procedure Act from 1981 is about to be reformed, and the proposals for a new criminal procedure act will modernise the criminal justice system, but the committee has a somewhat more cautious approach in digitizing the procedure compared to, for example, Sweden.[59]

Finland has had 41 major and minor amendments related to the Code of 1734 since the last criminal procedure reform came into force in 2006.[60] These changes can be said to fit one of two purposes; changes made to structure and clarify the legislation, or changes made to make the procedure more flexible and better adapted to a constantly evolving society.[61] As part of the latter purpose, technological changes like serving by telephone and the use of video links as a substitute for physical presence result in a more efficient procedure.[62] Digital submission of statements of claim is also mandatory in Finland in civil cases, and in criminal cases the ability to use video links at the hearings was expanded in 2018.[63] The defendants now have the opportunity to follow the whole hearing via video link and participation via video link is equal to physical presence. All these changes are made to adapt the proceedings to the individual case and thus make the proceedings more efficient, and technological tools are frequently used in this respect.

The goals a country sets for its procedural reform represent a way to settle its status. They communicate how far the country has developed its procedural law and in what direction the country wants to develop. Although it is a gradual transition, a procedure that establishes a justifiable decision base in the case can be considered a first-generation goal, while real access to court litigation for small claims is a typical second-generation goal. Making use of digital technology to make proceedings even more efficient and streamlined is a goal of a third-generation procedure

---

[55] LFF-2015-10-07 no. 22 General remarks Sect. 2.

[56] LFF-2015-10-07 no. 22 General remarks Sect. 2. Hjort (2021), Sect. 4.3 gives a fuller description.

[57] So far, the portal is only accessible to attorneys and courts.

[58] The Dispute Act was evaluated in 2013, and the efficiency and productivity of the courts was examined. No amendments were proposed based on the evaluation report; see Report (2013).

[59] NOU 2016: Sect. 4.5 gives a fuller description.

[60] L 244/2006. Search at finlex.fi accessed 28.5.2020.

[61] Hjort (2021), Sect. 4.1 gives a fuller description.

[62] L 362/2010 and L 422/2018.

[63] Finland: RP 190/2017, p. 26 and RP 200/2017, p. 29 (The latter amendment came into force 1.6.2018).

reform, and time will tell whether the corona pandemic has acted as a catalyst for a fourth generation of procedural reforms. Some objectives, in particular the desire for time-efficient proceedings, continue as goals in all generations, but the instruments used change. Central to this article is the fact that the goals set for procedural reforms also are crucial for the choice of sources of inspiration.

4 Choice of Sources of Inspiration

Procedural law is often viewed as a national matter, and legislative committees preparing considerations and act proposals in procedural law are not obligated to survey foreign law for potential sourcing. Nevertheless, this is common, especially in considerations with overall importance. Presenting foreign law implies an appraisal of which country's legislation it is of interest to survey. Several factors can be decisive.

One important factor is the similarity between the legal system potentially sourced from and the legal system to be reformed. It is common to look to countries with similarities, which in practice are countries within the same legal tradition.[64] The Nordic countries are often considered a separate legal family, and this itself gives a law committee in a Nordic country a reason to survey the other Nordic countries in drafting an act proposal. The Nordic legal family is limited in size, and if one adhered strictly to the categories established in comparative law theory, access to sources of inspiration would be narrow. However, the Nordic countries have similarities with both common law and civil law. Traditionally, the Nordic legal family is considered to be closer to civil law than common law, and the discussion above clearly shows a tendency to both refer to and make use of foreign law from civil law countries rather than common law countries. An example is Franz Klein's Austrian procedure reform from 1895, which was an important source of inspiration for several of the Nordic countries.[65] Presumably, repeated use of sources of inspiration from the same legal family strengthens the connection with this family. This is perhaps why reactions arose when elements of English law were used as a central source for the Norwegian Dispute Act, without examining the relevant civil law countries more thoroughly.[66]

However, the choice of sources of inspiration is not limited to countries in legal-family relationship, and there are many historical examples of law being sourced without any legal connection between the two legal systems. The reason is often

[64] This again assumes that this is a voluntary reception.

[65] Regarding Denmark, see Bilag II to Udkast til Lov om den borgerlige Retspleje (1901), p. 2725; regarding Sweden, see SOU 1926:33, pp. 45–47 and pp. 99–101; and regarding Norway, see Utkast (1908) Bilag III to Ot.prp. 1 (1910), p. 79. Based on Norwegian preparatory work, it seems that Finland's proposal for reform of the judicial system from 1901 has used Austrian procedural law as a source of inspiration.

[66] Robberstad (2004), pp. 585 ff.

that the recipient country has not chosen this sourcing itself.[67] Even law introduced with force will also, over time, attach itself locally and interfere with local law. Two descriptive examples are the influence of Canon and Roman law in most of Europe. In Nordic countries in modern times, however, the choice of sources of inspiration and reception of foreign law is based on the legislator's own preference.

Even based on voluntariness, sources of inspiration are not chosen solely on the basis of legal family relationships. In consideration of the Norwegian Civil Procedure Act of 1915, the committee clearly expressed another important factor:

> In developing the draft of a new procedure act for Norway, there must of course be a question of seeking a model in foreign procedural acts and drafts, and of utilizing the experience gained in other countries. Without being bound to commit to a certain foreign legislation, the Committee has—like in Denmark and Finland—sourced inspiration where one has previously had a similar condition as us, and where the new acts have substantially pursued the same legal tendencies as those leading this draft act. This especially applies to the German and Austrian Civil Procedure Acts, and the draft of a new procedure act for Norway has preferably joined the Austrian model because it largely avoids the disadvantages that have been shown to adhere to the French and German procedural law and, in general, seems to show extremely favourable practical results.[68]

The above quote explains why Austrian law was an important source of inspiration. Klein's reform replaced a written and highly formalised procedure with an oral and immediate procedure based on free assessment of evidence.[69] As described above, this led to the court having a more justifiable basis for its decisions. Another effect of the procedural reform was increased efficiency.[70] Klein's reform was a solution to problems with which many procedural schemes in Europe struggled, and it became an important source of inspiration in many countries.[71]

The choice of Austria as a source of inspiration in the beginning of the twentieth century was a simple choice. The two main objectives for the Nordic reforms were to achieve procedural legislation that established a justifiable basis for the decisions and to reduce the processing time. Austrian procedural rules could fulfill both these objects. In addition, Austria was a jurisdiction with features that the Nordic countries could recognise. Being a jurisdiction from the civil law tradition, Austria had courts similar to the Nordic, and the similarities made it easier to convince critics that the great upheaval of the procedural legislation was feasible.

There are examples of choices of sources of inspiration across legal cultures and families, but there are also challenges associated with such choices.[72] A procedural solution that works well in one country can have a completely different effect in a country with a different legal culture, even if the rules are concurrent. As described

---

[67]Mousourakis (2013), p. 225. Mousourakis mentions several reasons for reception of foreign law; e.g., because of conquest, colonial expansion or the political influence of the state whose law is adopted.

[68]Udkast (1908) Bilag III to Ot.prp. 1 (1910), p. 79, my translation.

[69]Hagerup (1899), p. 241.

[70]Hagerup (1899), pp. 305–306.

[71]Uzelac (2014), p. 6.

[72]Mattei (1994), p. 6.

in the introduction, there is a strong connection between legislation and society, and different societies can respond differently to the same rules. Therefore, it is safer to source inspiration from countries with common legal features.[73]

In the legal literature, it is argued that the choice of sources of inspiration can be made based on which procedural scheme gives the best efficiency. Mattei defines efficiency as the rules that gives the lowest transaction costs at all times, and it is emphasised that although legal systems have different rules, this difference does not necessarily have to mean a difference in efficiency.[74] Different legal systems can develop alternative solutions to the same legal problem, and the solutions can be equally efficient. Efficiency is, as I discussed in Sect. 3.3, a fundamental goal repeated in all generations of procedural reforms, but the assessment that Mattei puts forward probably fits best in the second and third generation of procedural reforms. Moreover, although Mattei talks about legal transplant on a very general basis, it may seem that he is primarily aiming at substantive legal rules.[75] It remains, therefore, to be seen whether this legal economic reasoning can also be brought forward in the context of procedural law.

As a general summary, the Nordic countries seems to have chosen their sources of inspiration based on two principles: countries with which it is natural to compare and countries that can demonstrate good solutions to the procedural problems that need to be solved. The principles are often used in combination. On a Nordic level, I find it difficult to point to a certain displacement of sources of inspiration over time, but as a general observation, German-speaking countries seems to be less often used. This may be due to political reasons or lack of knowledge of the German language and legislation, or it may simply be because good solutions are found in other places. In any case, a trend that has persisted over time is the Nordic countries' choice to refer to each other.

5 Use of Sources of Inspiration

The Nordic countries nearly always consider the other Nordic countries' procedural law in the preparatory work to their procedural reforms.[76] The review of the Nordic countries' procedural law is often followed by additional selected countries. However, the fact that the preparatory works include a review of foreign procedural

---

[73]Watson (1974), p. 17 emphasise the importance of good systematic knowledge of foreign law before sourcing from it: 'A rule of Swedish law which is successful at home might be a disaster in the different circumstances existing in Scotland; a rule of French law which there works badly might provide an ideal rule for Scotland.'.

[74]Mattei (1994), pp. 11 and 19.

[75]Watson (2001), p. 87 also mentiones the efficiency argument related to amending substantive provisions.

[76]This applies to Danish, Norwegian, Finnish and Swedish preparatory work. The Icelandic preparatory work does not seem to have a tradition of presenting foreign law in a separate chapter. Sources of inspiration will appear in the discussion in the preparatory work.

law is not equivalent to the use of these procedural rules as source of inspiration for developing own procedural rules. A test to examine the actual use of certain foreign rules could be to see if the committee has also referred to the relevant foreign rules in the specific motives for the proposal. There is no guarantee that one will find such references. The question then is what use the Nordic law committees make of the review of foreign procedural law. Is it actually a presentation of sources of inspiration, or are there other reasons for the committee to present such a review?

One explanation may be that it has become a tradition to present a review of foreign legislation in the preparatory work to large procedural reforms and that the committee presents the review on a routine basis to meet this expectation.[77] However, the review of the Nordic preparatory works gives the impression that the review has a purpose. Although it may seem like a routine, the committee has actively chosen the countries represented and elucidated certain elements from their procedural rules. To argue that the review is only a compulsory item in the consideration and has no intrinsic value would be to underestimate the review.

Another explanation may be that the presentation of foreign law legitimises the committee's suggestions. Instead of using the foreign law as a source of inspiration, the committee can point out the strengths and weaknesses of the solutions chosen in the neighbouring country and, on this basis, justify a proposal. Thus, the foreign law will serve as a basis for comparison.

A third explanation may be that a review of foreign law is presented to put one's own procedural rules into context. Based on the review of preparatory work from the Nordic countries, it may appear that the presentation of procedural law in the Nordic countries is primarily intended for this purpose.[78]

There are certainly examples of law committees being inspired by other Nordic countries and that the committees have used procedural law from other Nordic countries explicitly as a source of inspiration.[79] However, the main impression is that the review of the Nordic countries' procedural law is primarily made to place one's own legislation in a procedural landscape. The preparatory work does not give the impression that this is being done to explicitly point out a Nordic procedural law community. The basis for the use of inspiration from other Nordic countries simply seems to be the assumption that the other Nordic countries face the same problems as one's own and that one can therefore source from the experiences these countries have gained. Although the Nordic countries are not explicitly used as sources of inspiration, the significance of such contextualisation should not be underestimated. The Law Committee raises awareness of solutions in the Nordic countries, and this may have an impact on the solutions the Committee itself proposes.

---

[77] According to Letto-Vanamo and Tamm (2019), p. 7 a review of the Nordic countries' law 'forms part of the preparatory procedure for new laws in Finland'.

[78] Icelandic preparatory works differ on this point, because they do not give a review of foreign law, but rather mention foreign law where it is explicitly used.

[79] Examples are the reference to Danish and Norwegian legislation in Icelandic preparatory work, see Commentary to Act No. 88/2008, p. 85; the reference to Swedish legislation in Finnish preparatory work, see RP 83/2001, p. 19; and the reference to Danish and Norwegian rules on criminal proceedings in SOU 1926:33, f. ex. pp. 32–33 and pp. 145–146.

So far, I have surveyed the use of sources of inspiration by reviewing foreign legislation in the preparatory works, and this may serve as a base. However, the actual use of sources of inspiration may be far more complex. On one hand, the Law Committee will hardly ever have carte blanche to propose whatever changes they like. The Committee's mandate will usually address a problem to be solved or even a type of solution preferred. These limitations may well affect from which countries it is possible to draw inspiration. On the other hand, the Law Committee does not always address the origin of the source of inspiration, and the source could be more than one solution or a combination of solutions in several countries. When writing the preparatory works, the Law Committee's priority is not necessarily to highlight the origin of the source of inspiration. Moreover, the more complex is the background for the source, the more difficult it is to reveal the 'real' source of inspiration.

All these factors affect the picture the preparatory works give concerning the use of sources of inspiration, making it difficult to draw clear conclusions from the use of sources of inspiration regarding the question of whether Nordic Procedural Law exists as a phenomenon. The introduction of class action rules in Norwegian law may serve as an example of mixed sources of inspiration. The Norwegian Civil Procedure Committee's mandate clearly stated that one of the Committee's tasks was to study and submit proposals for rules on class actions. At that point, Sweden was preparing to adopt rules on class actions, and the Norwegian preparatory works present the Swedish solution. Even though American legislation was the original source, the Swedish solution was of decisive importance for the final design of the Norwegian rules.[80] One may argue that the Norwegian rules were inspired by the US rules on class actions and that this indicates an open approach to the use of sources of inspiration. However, the same example may be used to argue for a Nordic consciousness when implementing legal elements from non-Nordic countries. The key point in this context is to emphasise that there are many nuances in the use of a source of inspiration, and the Nordic countries' use of sources of inspiration does not necessarily give a clear answer to the question of whether Nordic Procedural Law exists.

6 The 'Nordic-Ness' in the Nordic Procedural Law

Political and cultural ties bind the Nordic countries together and form the basis for the extensive legal cooperation within the Nordic countries.[81] Over more than 100 years, joint Nordic acts have been made in fields like purchases, agreements, money claims, intellectual property rights, torts, citizenship and several parts of family law. The Nordic countries also signed the Helsinki agreement in 1962, in which one of the

---

[80] Ot.prp. no. 51 (2004–2005), pp. 320 ff.

[81] Letto-Vanamo and Tamm (2019), pp. 2–5 discusses this topic.

main objectives was a 'wish to implement uniform provisions in the Nordic countries in as many respects as possible'.[82]

Procedural law has, however, been regarded as a national matter, and history shows only a few examples of legal cooperation.[83] There was a modest attempt at legal cooperation in 1830, when the Norwegian law committee drafting a criminal procedure act went to Stockholm to discuss the topic with the Swedish law committee drafting a similar act. The Norwegian committee returned home and imparted that the meeting had been successful, stating that '[b]oth sides have communicated to each other several remarks that will be of considerable use during the future processing of the draft'.[84] However, the meeting did not result in any further cooperation, and neither of the drafts from the committees resulted in a new procedural act or amendments to the current legislation.

In modern times, legislative cooperation in the field of procedural law has been limited to joint meetings of law committees that happen to be working on similar reforms at the same time. For example, the Norwegian Civil Procedure Committee, the Danish Judicial Council and the Swedish Law Committee met in the period of 1999–2001 while they were all working to reform the procedural law.[85] The Norwegian Justice Department's law department also organised a two-day seminar with participation from all five Nordic countries and from England (Lord Woolf).[86] However, these meetings seem to have led to nothing more than knowledge of what the other law committees were working on.

Regarding Nordic legislative cooperation, Backer states that it is of great importance whether the EU has competence on the issue or whether the issue falls outside the competence of the EU.[87] Procedural law falls within the competence of the EU but outside the scope of the EEA Agreement, and therefore a Western-Nordic cooperation could be envisaged (i.e., between Iceland, Norway and Denmark).[88] However, the conclusion so far is clear: the Nordic legislative cooperation is no source for inspiration of Nordic procedural law.

Without legislative cooperation and with varying use of the other Nordic countries' procedural law as a source of inspiration in the formulation of procedural reforms and major legislative changes, cf. previous chapter, one can wonder if there is a Nordic community within the procedural law at all. Is the 'Nordic model' covering the procedural law?

The review of legislation in the five Nordic countries shows that procedural law in the Nordic countries has many common features, but common historical, cultural

---

[82]LOV-1962–03-23 no. 2, preamble.

[83]Letto-Vanamo and Tamm (2019), p. 10 argues that the lack of legislative cooperation in procedural law is due to the fact that the legislation is formed as a code.

[84]Departements-Tidende (1830), p. 573.

[85]NOU 2001:32, p. 85.

[86]NOU 2001:32, p. 85.

[87]Backer (2018), p. 37.

[88]Criminal law and procedural law are covered by the Danish reservation. Backer (2018), p. 37.

and social features can explain this.[89] It is not surprising that countries with many similarities choose the same solution when reforming their legislation. But is the similarity an active and conscious attitude towards the Nordic countries as a legal community?

Backer describes the Nordic model as follows:

> Value-sharing and similarities in social and natural conditions in the Nordic region help to form the platform for a Nordic model for how society should be organized. Fundamental to the Nordic countries is a system of governance [including elements] such as democracy and the rule of law. Each individual must be equal. Freedoms and rights for the individual are combined with community solutions that express solidarity in society and with measures to protect weak groups. The Nordic model also allows for variations and nuances between the different countries, and this is expressed in different ways, both in legal thinking and legislation and in working life and leisure in the Nordic countries.[90]

The Nordic countries' basic common features and common historical starting point prepare the ground for similar legislation. When choosing sources of inspiration for drafting new legislation, this review shows that sourcing from the other Nordic countries is of first preference. This tendency is pervasive in preparatory work to procedural legislation in all the Nordic countries. In my opinion, this is not because the Nordic countries 'happen to' have many similarities, but because these countries are legally entitled as a family. Only after presenting a review of the solutions in the Nordic legal family do the committees survey other countries, primarily in Europe.

Furthermore, although the importance of the other Nordic countries is not always visible in the specific motives for proposal, this does not mean that the other Nordic countries have lost their position as central sources of inspiration for Nordic countries' procedural law. The use of other Nordic countries as a source of inspiration can also take place in less visible forms. By being aware of the solutions chosen in the other Nordic countries and the experiences they have gained, the reforming country is able to place itself in a procedural landscape, without explicitly expressing this in the preparatory work for the specific provisions. Joint meetings and seminars with the other Nordic countries, like those mentioned above, are efficient tools to source inspiration in a more informal way. However, from an academic point of view, this procedure is challenging because the source of inspiration is difficult to trace.

Another challenge when researching the 'Nordic-ness' in the Nordic procedural law is that of the obvious differences and variations between the procedural systems and choice of sources of inspiration. However, as Backer emphasises, the Nordic model allows for variations and nuances between the Nordic countries. Thus, non-traditional choices, such as the use of England and the United States as sources of inspiration for the Norwegian Dispute Act, do not undermine the family ties between the Nordic countries. Both the linguistic and the cultural community contribute to strengthening the relation, and this community does not disappear because of sourcing outside the Nordic region.

---

[89] Nylund and Sunde (2019) elaborates on this topic.

[90] Backer (2018), p. 14, my translation.

The Nordic perspective in procedural law also appears in other ways. Through Nordic forums, representatives from the Nordic countries meet regularly and maintain the community through academic lectures and discussions.[91] In the context of research, a Nordic community is visible through doctoral dissertations in Nordic languages, where a representative from another Nordic country participates in the dissertation committee. Moreover, in assessments for academic positions, it is common to include a representative from another Nordic country in the assessment committee. The Nordic procedural law community is also visible in the law itself. In case law, there are many examples of bringing in procedural views from the other Nordic countries when national legal sources fall short,[92] and in the procedural literature there are references to legal solutions in other Nordic countries.[93] Not least, several publications present comparative discussions on Nordic procedural law, and this interest in the Nordic commonalities within procedural law is in itself a manifestation of Nordic procedural law as a community. This book also strengthens this impression.[94]

References

Aarli R, Hedlund M-A, Jebens SE (2015) Bevis i straffesaker: utvalgte emner. Gyldendal Juridisk, Oslo

Andersen P (2019) Processen i Danske Lov. In: Bang-Pedersen UR, Baumbach T, Scharf O and Stevnsborg H (eds) Retsplejeloven 100 år, DJØF Forlag, København

Arnesen J (1762) Historisk Indledning til den gamle og nye Islandske Rættergang. Trykt hos Joh. Boppenhausen, Kiøbenhavn

Backer IL (2018) Styrket nordisk lovsamarbeid: muligheter og utfordringer. Nordisk ministerråd, Denmark

Bellander H (2017) Rättegångskostnader: om kostnadsbördan i dispositiva tvistemål. Iustus förlag, Uppsala

Björne L (1998) Brytningstiden: Den nordiske rättsvetenskapens historia. Rättshistoriskt bibliotek vol. LVIII. Institutet för rättshistorisk forskning, Lund

Bylander E, Lindblom PH (2005) Muntlighet vid domstol i Norden. Iustus förlag, Uppsala

Departements-Tidende (1830)

Ervo L (2009) Characteristics of procedure. In: Ervo L (ed) Civil justice in Finland, Nagoya University comparative study of civil justice, vol 2. Jigakusha Publishing, Tokyo, pp 55–100

[91] An example is the Nordic Procedural Law Conference, which is held every third year under the direction of the Nordic Association for Process Law.

[92] Some examples: From Denmark: U.2019.3878, which refers to Swedish and Norwegian law. From Norway: HR-2019–1954-A, where the Supreme Court refers to Swedish law, and Rt. 2008 p. 1730, where the Supreme Court refers to both Swedish and Danish law. From Sweden: NJA 2008 p. 733, which refers to Danish and Norwegian law. From Finland: KKO:2005:34, which refers to Swedish law. Icelandic case law has unfortunately not been available.

[93] Two of many possible examples: The Danish book Gomard and Kistrup (2007), where reference is made to Swedish law on page 226, and the Norwegian book Aarli, Hedlund and Jebens (2015), where reference is made to Danish law on pp. 421, 592 and 625.

[94] Korpiola (1999), Bylander and Lindblom (2005) and Heivoll and Flaaten (2017) could also be mentioned, among other publications.

Gärde N (1931) Rättegångsreformen: några synpunkter. SvJT 1931:1–16
Gomard B, Kistrup M (2007) Civilprocessen. Thomson, København
Hagerup F (1899) Den nye østerrigske civilproces. Tidsskrift for Retsvidenskap 1899:241–314
Heivoll G, Flaatten S (2017) Rettslige overgangsformer: Politi- og kriminalrett i nordisk rettsutvikling. Akademisk publisering, Oslo
Hjort MA (2007) Muntlighetsprinsippet i sivilprosessen: Fra klubbeslag til tastetrykk. Institutt for offentlig retts skriftserie, Oslo
Hjort MA (2021) Development of the Nordic procedural law. Forthcoming article in Oslo Law Review
Justitsministeriet (1998) Justitsministeriets kommissorium av 19. januar 1998
Kekkonen J (2009) Roots of civil procedure in Finland from the point of view of modernity. In: Ervo L (ed) Civil justice in Finland, Nagoya university comparative study of civil justice. Jigakusha Publishing, Tokyo, pp 3–16
Knoph R (1998) Knophs oversikt over Norges rett, 11th Ed. by Kåre Lilleholt. Universitetsforlaget, Oslo
Korpiola P (1999) Nordic perspectives on medieval canon law. Matthias Calonius Society, Helsinki
Letto-Vanamo P (2012) Finnish law in European perspective. In: Nuotio K, Melander S, Huomo-Kettunen M (eds) Introduction to Finnish law and legal culture. Forum Iuris, Publications of the Faculty of Law University of Helsinki, Helsinki
Letto-Vanamo P, Tamm D (2019) Nordic legal mind. In: Letto-Vanamo P, Tamm D, Mortensen BOG (eds) Nordic law in European context. Springer, Cham, pp 1–19
Lindblom PH (2000) Civilprocessens grundprinciper de lege ferenda: synspunkter i anslutning till det aktuella civilprocessuella reformarbetet i England, Danmark, Finland, Norge och Sverige. In: Lindblom PH, Progressiv process: spridda uppsatser om domstolsprocessen och samhällsutvecklingen. Iustus förlag, Uppsala
Mathiesen T (2011) Retten i samfunnet: en innføring i rettssosiologi. Pax forlag, Oslo
Mattei U (1994) Efficiency in legal transplants: an essay in comparative law and economics. Int Rev Law Econ 14:3–19
Mousourakis G (2013) Legal transplants and legal development: a jurisprudential and comparative law approach. Acta Juridica Hungaria 54:219–236
Nylund A, Sunde JØ (2019) Courts and court proceedings. In: Letto-Vanamo P, Tamm D, Mortensen BOG (eds) Nordic law in European context. Springer, Cham, pp 201–213
Robberstad K (1971) Rettssoga I. Universitetsforlaget, Oslo
Robberstad A (2004) Utenlandske sivilprosessforbilder: for Francis Hagerup og Tvistemålsutvalget (NOU 2001: 32). In: Andersson, Lindell (eds) Festskrift til Per Henrik Lindblom. Iustus förlag, Uppsala, pp 575–588
Schlyter K (1934) Högtidssammankomst å riddarhuset den 13 december 1934 ägnad 1734 års lag. Hälsningstal. SvJT 1934:529–531
Sigurðsson JV (2015) Kongemakt og lokalsamfunn på Island ca. 1260–1450. Heimen 52:17–24
Skyberg LF (2019) Prinsippet om fri bevisbedømmelse i et komparativt rettshistorisk og psykologisk perspektiv. TfS 2019:237–257
Uzelac A (2014) Goals of civil justice and civil procedure in the contemporary world. global developments: towards harmonisation (and back). In: Uzelac A (ed) Goals of civil justice and civil procedure in contemporary judicial systems. Springer, London, pp 3–31
Watson A (1974) Legal transplants, an approach to comparative law. Scottish Academic Press, Edinburgh
Watson A (2001) Society and legal change. Temple University Press, Philadelphia, USA

Culture and Mentality in East-Nordic Courts

Laura Ervo

Abstract In this chapter, the East-Nordic, that is Finnish and Swedish, court culture and mentality and its historical, cultural and societal roots are explored. The objective of the chapter is to uncover the mechanisms underlying the East-Nordic court mentality and the hallmarks of Swedish and Finnish court culture, as well as to identify how these processes influence adjudication. Emphasis is put on the historical development of these countries, since Finland was part of Sweden until 1809. After Finland became an autonomous Grand Dutchy of the Russian Empire, it suffered under Russification, whereas Sweden was still part of the western sphere. Even after Finland gained independence in 1917, the history of the two countries has differed to some extent. Therefore, it is interesting to explore the manner in which the differences in history are manifested in contemporary court proceedings. This study is based mainly on comparative and historical resources.

1 Starting Points

The term legal culture often refers to a particular legal tradition, a set of legal institutions that has evolved with historical development, and the way in which justice is practiced. Legal culture has been examined, for example, in terms of the number of trials, attitudes towards legal institutions, legal rhetoric and legal ideology. Expressions such as European legal culture, Nordic legal culture and national legal culture are also often used.[1]

Legal culture can be further divided into two sub-areas. Namely, it is possible to refer in a more elitist way to the legal profession and their activities or in a more popular way to the people´s perceptions of the justice, courts and law. Therefore, legal culture can mean the way in which law is practiced or how people react to it. Legal culture can also include legal practitioners, like judges, prosecutors, attorneys

[1] Ervasti (2005), p. 352.

L. Ervo (✉)
School of Law, Psychology and Social Work, Örebro University, 701 82 Örebro, Sweden
e-mail: Laura.ervo@oru.se

L. Ervo et al. (eds.), *Rethinking Nordic Courts*, Ius Gentium: Comparative Perspectives on Law and Justice 90, https://doi.org/10.1007/978-3-030-74851-7_6

and so on, as well as their practices. Also, the specific language constituting legal concepts and terms and legal procedures at the courts are included into the legal culture. As part of a legal culture, there is often talk of a court culture. In the broadest sense, legal culture refers to the whole legislation, judiciary and legal conditions of a state or group of states. If understood in this way, legal culture is one part in the concept of culture as a whole.[2]

As mentioned above, court culture is a part of legal culture. It refers to the culture of courts, including procedures and professions. In turn, court mentality is a part of court culture. It consists of a judge's mental set of tools, those psychological instruments and habits with which he or she fulfils his or her professional duties and acts as a citizen in society. The judge's characteristics, education, environment and worldview are included in this set as well.[3] The court mentality can therefore be summarised as a judge's psychological toolbox.

Whenever legal decisions are made, decision makers' personal ways of thinking as well as their ideology are in play. It must be admitted that adjudication is not an exact science or a strictly technical subject. Courts' objectivity and judges' impartiality are, of course, very fundamental legal principles and the starting point of the whole adjudication as such. Still, the mentality including, for instance, judges´ ideology cannot be totally avoided. The significance of these types of factors in the decision making should be taken seriously.[4] They cannot be totally avoided even if a judge is well educated and working in a very professional way. This is why it is important to research the court culture including court mentality and how it affects decision making.

In this article, the East-Nordic court culture and mentality as well as reasons for them are researched and compared with each other. The reasons are sought mainly in the history. The objective of the chapter is to find out how the East-Nordic court mentality works and what kinds of ingredients are included in the Swedish and Finnish court culture. Subsequently, the findings should help to illustrate how everything described above all this affects the adjudication. However, it has not been the aim to research how court culture or judges' mentalities affect decision making in single cases but rather research the phenomenon as such and in general. Therefore, no empirical studies are conducted, and the traditional legal method is used. What the behaviour and mentality are concerned, also the auto ethnography is used.[5] The references consist mainly of resources of comparative law and legal history.

As a starting point, the investigation uses the concept of Nordic law, which forms a legal family despite civil law and common law distinctions. According to Husa, the most relevant similarities do not concern formal legal rules but rather the legal mentality in the Nordic countries.[6] Also Letto-Vanamo and Tamm talk about the

---

[2]Ervasti (2005), p. 352.

[3]Kemppinen (1992) and Yrttiaho (2000), p. 292.

[4]Hautamäki (2004), pp. 133.

[5]The author has quite a long working experience in both countries in question.

[6]Husa (2010), p. 6.

Nordic mind or 'Nordic-ness' instead of the Nordic law.[7] This is because certain basic values concerning social justice, social ethics and law in general are similar in the region. Because of the close relationship of Nordic jurisdictions and their common stylistic hallmarks, they form a special legal family.[8]

2 Reasons in History

2.1 Swedish Origins

The earliest substantial Swedish law texts are the provincial laws, which were the means of law-holding in Sweden during the Middle Ages. Around 1200, the laws began to be transferred to written form. This was probably due to clerical influences. The oldest of the Swedish provincial laws is the *Västgötalagen*, which was used in the west part of Sweden. Around 1350, the Swedish provincial laws were replaced by the Magnus Eriksson country law.[9]

Mostly three factors, namely societal development, Christianity and the reception of the foreign law have affected the development of the Swedish legal culture.[10] Also, the German-Roman tradition had an important influence on the Swedish legal system. A comprehensive Swedish code was enacted in 1734. This code, known as The Code of 1734, was divided into the following sections: The Books on Marriage, Inheritance, Land, Building, Commerce, Crimes, Judicial Procedure and the Book on Execution of Judgements. This structure can still be found in the Swedish law book. In addition, there are some later codes, namely, the Parental Code (1949), the Environmental Code (1998) and the Social Insurance Code (2010).[11]

During the seventeenth century, Sweden emerged as a great power by taking direct control of the Baltic region. Sweden's role in the Thirty Years' War determined the political and religious balance of power in Europe. In 1721, Russia and its allies won the war against Sweden, marking an end to the Swedish superpower in Europe. Sweden joined in the Enlightenment and, between 1570 and 1800, experienced two periods of urban expansion.[12]

Sweden's last war was the Swedish–Norwegian War in 1814. Sweden won the war, and, as a result, Norway formed a union with Sweden that lasted until 1905. Since 1814, Sweden has been at peace, adopting a non-allied foreign policy in peacetime and neutrality in wartime. During World Wars I and II, Sweden remained neutral. Additionally, Sweden attempted to stay out of alliances and remain officially neutral

[7]Letto-Vanamo and Tamm (2019), pp. 1 and 9.

[8]Husa (2010), p. 6.

[9]Inger (2011), p. 13–17.

[10]Inger (2011), p. 9.

[11]Ortwein (2003), p. 411.

[12]Inger (2011), p. 75 and 78.

during the entirety of the Cold War. The social democratic party held the government for 44 years (1932–1976).[13]

2.2 Sweden-Finland and Its Effects

As explained above, the East-Scandinavian countries, namely Sweden and Finland, have a common history. From the 1200s onwards, Finland constituted the eastern part of Sweden, a status that continued until 1809. Before the Swedish period, there was no state or central power in Finland. Centralised power and nationwide legislation started to develop simultaneously during the Swedish period.[14] Therefore, both countries share the same origins in terms of the legal system and principles.

Due to this common history, and especially the common legislative tradition which survived in modern-day Finland for quite a long time, the prerequisites for common court culture are quite unique. The fact that legal systems, with their main principles, are still rooted in the same formal basis provides a guarantee that key legal concepts and principles are in fact understood in a similar way in both countries. Thanks to the shared religion, the value base is shared as well. This common morality affects the legal interpretations despite the fact that both countries are rather secularised.[15] Values of honesty and a strong work ethic are among the fruits of that Lutheran morality.[16]

2.3 Finland as Autonomous Grand Duchy of the Russian Empire and Russification

In 1809, Finland became an autonomous part of Russia; even then, however, Swedish laws remained in force and continued to be valid throughout the whole Russian period. Indeed, the Russian legal system did not have much of an effect in Finland, where the Swedish model remained prevalent up to and including the establishment of Finland as an independent country in 1917.[17]

More generally speaking, Finland is said to be the border between the West and East due to the fact that, both geographically and historically, Finland is located between Sweden and Russia. The religions of the regions differ (Orthodox in Russia and Lutheran in Sweden and Finland), and thus the values and ways of thinking differ as well. These differences can be seen in the local culture, which varies between the western and eastern parts of Finland. Eastern Finland, which is closer to the Russian

[13]Inger (2011), p. 307.

[14]Ervo (2014b), pp. 386–390.

[15]Ervo (2014a).

[16]More about this see Husa et al. (2007), pp. 23–24.

[17]Ervo (2014b), p. 250.

border, shows more similarities with the Russian lifestyle. For instance, there is an Orthodox religious minority in the eastern part of Finland.

It is difficult to ascertain without comprehensive empirical studies whether this border situation affects the court culture. Therefore, it is also impossible to say whether and how these cultural differences between the eastern and western parts of Finland as such could affect the court culture, which is legally bound and based on common statutes. At first glance, such differences might be assumed to be very small, due to the fact that court culture is a professional culture and therefore it is consisting partly of legally bound parts—in the other words, it is not only about culture but also about professional duties My experience—after working quite a long time in both named countries—and answer is that the Finnish court culture is very western due to the Swedish origins and the country's current situation as one of the Nordic countries. It can also be said that there are no great difference in the court culture between the western and eastern part of Finland, because the question relates to a professional and legally bound culture at courts. Still, the Finland's position as a borderline and its potential effects on the court culture is interesting and should be researched further.[18] However, let´s return to the historical development again.

From 1890 onward, a policy of 'Russification' was introduced, and this era is therefore sometimes called the period of oppression. The policy's aim was arguably to make Finland more Russian. However, whenever certain Russian exceptions were made in the field of legislation, the Finnish legal services protested widely, and the new system was never fully followed. Notably, these exceptions made in the field of legislation still only covered some aspects of the legal system, while other aspects were still officially and formally legislated by the Finnish (formerly Swedish) laws only.[19]

The Code for Juridical Procedure, for instance, has been valid without any breaks from 1734 until today,[20] despite the historical vicissitudes wherein Finland was a part of Sweden, an autonomous part of Russia and an independent state, respectively.[21] Seldom is one code so sustainable that it stays valid through three different empires. Despite of the reforms in contents, the same structure is mainly followed even today. The reason for this must be in the deep correspondence of the code´s contents with

[18] Still, there are many comparative studies between Finland and Sweden. For instance, in Karonen and Östberg (2018) Finland and Sweden have been compared with each other from historical and political perspectives. There are also some comparisons based on geography or geopolitics. Karonen and Östberg (2018), pp. 433–434. However, the pure cultural aspects do not play a big role in this research. Also, for instance Niemi and Kiesiläinen (2007) and Niemi (2018) has compared Sweden and Finland from the legal perspective. She pays attention especially in the legal theory point of view. Niemi and Kiesiläinen (2007), pp. 89–108 and Niemi (2018), pp. 230–244. Closest with the similar perspective comes Husa et al. (2007), pp. 1–36. Also there the legal situations in Finland and Sweden are compared with the historical and cultural points of view.

[19] Ervo (2014b), p. 250.

[20] This does not mean that the contents were not reformed and updated. However, the code as such has never been abolished but the reforms have always updated the contents bit by bit. Therefore, for instance, the structure is still mainly the same.

[21] Ervo (2014b), p. 250.

the local values (i.e., morality) and the way of thinking (i.e., mentality) and therefore culture (i.e., the context of morality and mentality together).

During the autonomous period, legislative reforms were not easy to realise in Finland. Therefore, the Finnish legislation was for some time static and not subject to development. The Russian period and its challenges led to rapid developments in independent Finland and to some flexibility in applying and interpreting laws to correspond with the demands in the current society. It is said that since then, legal reforms have usually been realised quickly without wide societal discussion. One of the main goals has been effectiveness.[22] The other effect from the Russian period is that of easily adopted new interpretations in the case law whenever needed, if the legislator has not reacted to current needs in the society. This makes flexibility, creative solutions and common-sense trademarks of the Finnish legal culture, which from the more careful Swedish perspective could even be described imaginative.[23]

Especially in Finland, legal problems which are not covered by a specific statutory provision are often solved by applying analogical principles expressed in the other statutes or by supplementing case law. Additionally, in the uncodified or only insufficiently codified areas, legal doctrine plays an important role.[24] This is especially true in Finland.

It has been argued that especially this part of the Finnish history—the period of autonomy and ensuing legislative challenges—have marked Finnish legal culture and made it what it is today. Moreover, Russification caused an emphasis on legality[25] to take root among civil servants, and this culture of legality still affects the current system.[26] However, not all scholars share this explanation. Björne, for example, is of the opinion that the passive resistance of the Finnish civil servants and the countermeasures made against the nationwide (Russian) legislation did not have much to do with the legalism as such but were more based on the will to interpret laws as the interpreter desired. Björne also discusses the Finnish legalism further and illustrates his opinion that the legalism is just a myth with a number of sad historical examples, like trials after the civil war.[27]

---

[22]Kekkonen (1998a), p. 936 and Saarnilehto (2003), p. 74. In the latter source it is said that those problems were solved between 1917 and 1995.

[23]Sallila (2011), p. 466. Nylund and Sunde have described the Nordic court culture in general as pragmatic and creative. Nylund and Øyrehagen Sunde (2019) p. 201. It is for sure true. It is up to which one is comparing. At large and compared with other countries, the Nordic culture as such is creative and pragmatic. However, when compared single Nordic countries with each other, some differences at this inside level can be found. Also, in Letto-Vanamo and Tamm (2019) the Nordic legal culture as such is described as pragmatic and uncomplicated. Letto-Vanamo and Tamm (2019), p. 9.

[24]Bernitz (2007), p. 20.

[25]According to the Oxford English Dictionary, legality refers to the quality or state of being in accordance with the law.

[26]Aalto (1976), pp. 40–42, Jussila (2004), p. 254, Kekkonen (1998b), pp.162–163 and Kemppinen (1999) and Virtanen (1974), pp. 11–410.

[27]Björne (2012), pp. 149–152. Compare for instance with Letto-Vanamo and Tamm (20f19), pp. 7–8 where Finland is named as a more legalistic country than the other Nordic countries.

However, these types of tragedies linked with wars and other exceptional circumstances, like trials after the civil war or the war-responsibility trials in Finland after the Second World War, cannot be used as daily-life examples. They are of a political nature, and therefore neither the legalism nor the legal protection was fully (or even partially) realised. Of course, the depth of the legalism and the legal protection of the society will be tested under exceptional circumstances, and if the practice will stand even then, then legalism and the legal protection can be said to be fully in force. Usually, the legalism will work during good times, but whenever societal (political) problems arise, the violations unfortunately start to become more common.

The role of legality can also be challenged in Finland today. Of course, in both Sweden and Finland legality is highly appreciated as one of the most important principles in legal democracy and rule of law. Still, the notion that legality plays a bigger role in Finland compared with Sweden or other Nordic countries can be argued to be a myth. I would say that the myth is the role of the legality in Finland as such, not its background and reasons for it. I would also argue that there are not major differences in experiencing and realizing legality in the Nordic countries. It is a basic tenet in the Nordic law as a matter of fact. Perhaps the situation would have be different in Finland earlier, such as at the beginning of the country's independence, when the signs of Russian period still were in people's minds and had a greater effect than they do today.

Also, the judicial activism as well creative and instrumentally acting courts and judges in Finland are facts which tells us that in a very pedant way interpreted legality is probably not the most important aim. If the legality were taken in a very strict and formal way, there would not be much space for judicial activism or creative, practical solutions. However, these above-named effects; creative interpretations and respect of legality do not directly correspond with each other but in fact are quite opposite tools to handle difficult and undesirable political situations.

Reality and daily life at courts looks very different today than in the early 1920s. There are new challenges like multiculturalism and globalisation thanks to which clients at courts represent many different cultures and speak many different languages. At the end of 2019, there were about 19.56% foreign inhabitants (born abroad) in Sweden[28] whereas the same figure for Finland in 2018 was 7%.[29] At the same time, cases are more international as well. Both criminality and business are no longer confined by state borders but have an international and cross-border character. Therefore, judges need to know how to tackle these types of cultural differences and language problems and how to decide cases which are not based only on the national law. In this modern context, the strict respect of legality or origins to that type of previous legal culture in Finland seem no longer to be current issues. The daily-life situations show that many other problems and values have become more current by time.

---

[28] https://www.scb.se/hitta-statistik/statistik-efter-amne/befolkning/befolkningenssammansattning/befolkningsstatistik/. Accessed 14 June 2020.

[29] https://www.tilastokeskus.fi/tup/maahanmuutto/maahanmuuttajat-vaestossa/ulkomailla-syntyneet.html. Accessed 14 June 2020.

2.4 The Main Cornerstones in Recent History Until Today

When the Finnish Parliament adopted the Declaration of Independence of Finland on the 6th of December 1917, the new state thus already had a rich national culture and centuries of experience in managing its own affairs. As explained above, the makings of the independent nation stem partly from the times of Swedish rule (from the thirteenth century until 1809) and especially from the period when Finland was an autonomous Grand Duchy of the Russian Empire (1809–1917).

Extra flavour was added to this cultural soup by the Finnish civil war in 1918 and its consequences, as well as by the Second World War and the war-responsibility trials, which were of an accentuated political nature. The latter incidents may likely have resulted in increased demands on democracy, the rule of law and legal protection.[30] In the 1970s, unemployment caused a deep crisis in Finland, as did the economic depression in the beginning of the 90s; such periods have cultural and mental effects,[31] not only in general but also specifically in the court culture. With these two and other potential crises still in their minds, the general audience and professional groups like judges and legislators are more sensitive when faced with difficult situations and the associated risks. It is easy to remember what things were like during times of crisis, and it is not forgotten that new crisis are still possible in the future. There is no belief that happy days will last forever.[32]

In Sweden, there have been no wars and more need for workers than unemployment; even the economy has consistently been relatively buoyant, at least compared with many other countries. The current COVID-19—crisis is the biggest crisis in the last 200 years.

In Sweden, the ideology of *folkhemmet*[33] well illustrates recent Swedish societal history. It still profoundly affects the self-image[34] of Swedes today. Nothing similar has occurred in Finland, even though both countries are welfare states. The idea of *folkhemmet* strongly affects Swedish culture and the Swedish way of living, especially with regard to social connections like working environment and labour law. It highlights the importance of group participation in decision-making (e.g., in the

---

[30] Kekkonen (1998a), p. 936.

[31] According to Lehtinen et al. (1995), the economic depression increased metal problems in Finland, pp. 323–329, whereas according to Viinamäki et al. (1997) the correlation is unclear. Still, in the latter study economic factors also seem to correspond with mental problems, p. 1689.

[32] See, for instance, Kiander (2001), pp. 131, where the results of a research program on the "1990s economic depression" of the Finnish Academy is presented. Also, Kekkonen pays attention to how economic depressions and other crises affect legal culture. See Kekkonen (1999), pp. 51, 88 and 93. How societal changes affect courts has been discussed in Tuomioistuinlaitoksen kehittämiskomitean välimietintö (committee report) 2003, pp. 18.

[33] *Folkhemmet* is a political concept that played an important role in the history of the *Swedish Social Democratic Party* and the Swedish welfare state. The core of the *folkhem* vision is that the entire society ought to be like a small family where everybody contributes. See more about the concept in, e.g., Dahlqvist (2002), pp. 445–465.

[34] Bertilsson (2010), p. 28.

workplace). This social way of thinking arising from the *folkhemmet* ideology is very widespread throughout Swedish society.

This mindset affects legal culture as well, including the ways in which legal tools are used and laws are interpreted. The differences in juridical law-making can be explained by these societal reasons, which have led to two different court mentalities in the East-Nordic countries.

The discussion on legality, described above, its origins and meaning in daily life and during the exceptional circumstances, is current also today. The legality is not working in the same way during the exceptional times than in the normal daily life. It has been evident, for example, during the current COVID-19 period, when the government in Finland has given false information on the valid restrictions, most likely to make people more compliant. It has not clearly informed on the difference between recommendations and obligations. Because the parliament and government decided to implement emergency legislation, this type of unclear information has been deeply misleading. Under normal conditions, people can more easily estimate what is and is not legal, but a general audience cannot know the contents and limits of emergency legislation. For instance, Finnish citizens were not told that they could still come and go over the border based on their fundamental rights despite the emergency legislation.[35] Only since the legal scholars started to pay attention to this lack in information, the written instructions were changed and for instance, ministers started to stress this in an oral way too. Still, I argue that it is not entirely appropriate to use exceptional political trials as daily-life examples. How the law should be interpreted and applied in daily life in routine cases should be researched as well. The situation as a whole should then be compared with the research target, like legality. Only if the legality is interpreted and followed strictly both in the daily life as well as during the exceptional circumstances, it is possible to draw conclusions which describe the local attitudes in general. The cases with political value are usually exceptional, and sadly often tragic, examples. Therefore, I would like to sum up that what Russification affected into the Finnish legality is no longer very current. The value of legality has become lower. Additionally, it must be stressed that the above described traditional effects from the periods of Russification are in contrast. On the one hand, legality is underlined in this context. On the other hand, the rapid reforms and creative case-law as a solution are mentioned too.

---

[35] For instance, the official newssheets on the website of the Finnish border guard https://www.raja.fi were misleading during the early stage of the pandemic. After the media and some professors debated the issue, they were adjusted and now it clearly whether the instructions are merely recommendations, or whether they are enforceable rules, and whether the restrictions apply only to foreigners, or also to Finnish citizens.

See for instance, https://yle.fi/uutiset/3-11487500, https://www.uusisuomi.fi/uutiset/apulaisprofessori-loytaa-useita-ongelmia-suomen-koronatoimista-ratkaisujen-tekeminen-on-karannut-osin-pois-eduskunnan-kasista/1a415363-b0e5-46c0-8629-e0b1fd30a5de, https://svenska.yle.fi/artikel/2020/05/07/manniskorattsprofessor-martin-scheinin-man-har-ansett-att-det-bara-ar-diktaturer, https://perustuslakiblogi.wordpress.com/2020/03/ and https://sverigesradio.se/artikel/7468102. Accessed 11 Feb 2021.

3 Sweden as a Role Model

The attitude towards the Swedish legal system has been extremely positive in Finland. Especially in the legislative culture, Sweden is usually seen as a good model which can safely be followed. Still, the Swedish model is not directly copied; instead, the Finnish legislator often is careful and waits for more thorough evaluation based on the Swedish experience before the Swedish model is followed in legislative reforms. By doing so, the Finnish legislator often uses Sweden as a test lab. This method is easy due to the common background and similarities in jurisdiction. Both East-Nordic countries belong to the same Scandinavian legal family and additionally have a common history. This means that the legal system, legal principles and the court system are, if not identical, very similar to each other. Additionally, the surrounding society and the mentality of people is—at least at the macro level—very similar. This facilitates legal transplants. Actually, Swedish models or experiences are not even perceived as legal transplants in Finland but rather are seen more as a 'domestic product'.[36] Based on the common history of Sweden and Finland, this is understandable. Still, much has happened in Finland since the Swedish period. Therefore, the common history cannot explain everything, but the main reasons for having Sweden as a role model, must be in the common culture, which still has effects due to geographical and mental similarities. This is why the Swedish transplants feel home-made.

Another reason for easily adopting Swedish reforms and learning from the Swedish experience, is the strong common East-Scandinavian jurist identity, which is built mostly by regular Nordic contacts and co-operation in practice.[37] In daily life, Nordic lawyers and researchers frequently keep in touch, especially with their Swedish colleagues. Especially in Finland, the Swedish case law and scientific literature are carefully followed, referenced and used in the Finnish research but also, for instance, at courts by judges and attorneys. In Sweden, this tradition is less common due to the language barrier. All Finns can understand Swedish, but most Swedes cannot understand Finnish. The Finnish scientific literature written in Swedish language and court cases in Swedish are the clear minority even though Finland has two national languages, Finnish and Swedish. Therefore, the Finnish legal discussion is more difficulty followed in Sweden than the Swedish discussion in Finland.

All of the above is very true with regard to the legislative culture as well as scientific research and legal education at universities. Still, the daily life in adjudication differs more than the well working collaboration at the legislative field.[38] The reason for this is that the toolboxes of Swedish and Finnish judges are not identical. Whenever a new interpretation is needed due to the new practical circumstances and needs, if the legislator has not yet reacted with amendments, the Finnish courts normally interpret the valid sections of a law in an instrumental way to reach the best working

[36] See for instance Ervo (2015), p. 136.

[37] Sallila (2011), p. 457.

[38] See for instance Letto-Vanamo and Tamm (2019), pp. 2–5 and 14–17.

solution in a new situation. This type of common sense belongs in the toolbox of Finnish judges and is not found to be generally speaking illegal or risky[39] to do so.[40] However, this is not the case in Sweden. Especially before joining in the EU in 1995 Swedish courts were very careful and extremely bound to travaux preparatoires and wordings.[41] Thanks to Europeanisation, this has changed somewhat since the early 2000s. Still, the difference between the neighboring countries is significant in this sense. The more creative Finnish way of interpreting and applying valid sections of laws is strange to Swedish judges. They have not traditionally used these types of creative instruments to interpret in their adjudication, even though recently the Swedish case law has grown more important and judges have become more creative and willing to solve problems within the court.[42]

4 Main Differences Between East-Nordic Countries

4.1 Discuss and Run—Cultural Differences in Reacting

Some key differences between the Finnish and Swedish legal cultures do exist.[43] Among these are the differences in efficiency and speed of reforms, in addition to the above-mentioned courts' power to create justice. The Swedish legislative culture is quite dialogic compared with the Finnish one. For instance, travaux preparatoires—like SOU-reports—are very comprehensive and well prepared. It is also typical that a wide societal discussion precedes planned reforms.[44]

This difference concerns not only the legislative culture but the culture as a whole. It is a notorious fact that the Swedish decision-making which aims to achieve consensus is time-consuming, and there are several long-lasting meetings and comprehensive discussions before the final decision. In those occasions, all actors may attend discussions and offer their opinions.[45] From the Finnish perspective, this kind of decision making is time consuming and not effective.[46] In Finland, the result is generally more appreciate than the method by which it is achieved.

[39]Nor the general audience or guardians of law and order normally find it to be allowed to do so.

[40]Still, this type of Finnish court culture has even been criticised as too passive despite this instrumental approach. Määttä (2011), pp. 207–225.

[41]See for instance Letto-Vanamo and Tamm (2019), p. 7.

[42]Bertilsson (2010), pp. 29–31, Fura-Sandström (2004), pp. 264–265.

[43]Niemi has compared Sweden and Finland and the named similarities and differences in her article from the legal theory perspective. See Niemi (2018).

[44]Ervo (2015), pp. 144–145 and Kekkonen (1998b), p. 936.

[45]See for instance, https://ruotsi.rajaneuvonta.fi/company/alku/liikekulttuuri-ruotsissa/. Accessed 14 June 2020.

[46]Watch for instance a TV program on the named differences: https://areena.yle.fi/1-1164648. Accessed 14 June 2020.

The Finnish way to 'run things', or to *do* instead of to *discuss* (or reflect or analyze), is the main difference between the Finnish and Swedish cultures, and this can be seen very prominently in the legal culture.[47]

4.2 Judicial Law-Making

The above-mentioned cultural difference can be one reason for differences in judicial law-making as well, because the common atmosphere and traditions are reflected in courts and affect the work done in them. The decision-making procedures at courts when adjudicating or in the legislature when legislating naturally follow the common culture.

Namely, the court mentality is one crucial factor in so-called judicial activism or judicial law-making and in its opposite—that is, judicial self-restraint. These concepts refer to judges´ activity in creating new interpretations and, in difficult cases, even new solutions to problems. Judges can be like passive civil servants who just apply the law more or less technically, or they may closely resemble political actors when they actively create law and up-date interpretations.[48]

The precedents play a significant but practical role in Nordic legal systems. The way in which Nordic law normally tends to identify precedents is highly informative. The Nordic attitude toward precedent describes very well how in the Nordic legal culture the role of the courts and the accompanying role of the legislator are found to be at least partly parallel.[49] This reveals something potentially important with regard to the Nordic spirit of law,[50] particularly in Finland as compared to Sweden.

Swedish courts and judges are more bound to the wordings of rules as well as travaux préparatoires compared with their Finnish colleagues, who can make quite finalistic interpretations to find practical and well-functioning solutions, especially in situations where the older legislation does not correspond to the current societal needs and the legislator has not yet reacted.[51] A search using the term 'fair trial' among the precedents of the Finnish Supreme Court yielded six examples of this, of which five included this type of creative interpretation, especially in the lower courts.[52] Especially lower courts, and sometimes the minority at the Supreme Court, seem to have a tendency to interpret law quite widely and in an instrumental way. Still, the Supreme Court and especially its majority are still more bound to the wordings of sections of laws.

---

[47]Ervo (2015), p. 145.

[48]Ervo (2015), p. 149 and Hautamäki (2003), p. 171.

[49]Husa (2010), p. 6.

[50]Simoni and Valguarnera (2008), p. 97.

[51]Ervo (2015) p. 145.

[52]The identified cases were The Supreme Court 2016: 98, 88, 85, 84, 76 and 45, of which cases 96, 88, 84, 76 and 45 were interesting in this sense.

In the literature, Siltala has stressed that there are two different 'trends' in the Finnish adjudication: namely, the legalistic one and the more creative one. The latter is used especially when European legislation has to be applied to find the more similar interpretation between Finnish and European rules.[53] Hautamäki is of the opinion that judicial activism is increasing in Finland due to more open norms which delegate more discretion to the courts.[54] Tuori shares the opinion of Hautamäki and Siltala, saying that activism is increasing and affecting especially EU legislation.[55]

There are also dissenting opinions in the literature. For instance, Mattila wrote in 1998 that judges in Finland and Sweden see themselves as executors of the legislator.[56] Husa shared the same opinion in 2010 but added that activism in the Nordic countries is increasing. According to him, the role of precedent has also been remarkably weak in the formal and doctrinal sense. One crucial factor the different legal activism between the neighboring countries, is the Finnish and Swedish legal-cultural attitude, according to which moral questions should be left to national Parliaments, not to courts of law, as Husa noted in 2010.[57]

I think that the reason to these different kind of opinions in the legal literature is that the authors do not compare judicial activism with the same standards. It is clear that both Swedish and Finnish courts and judges are careful in a broad sense; they are professional and follow legislation in a respectful way. The amount of offences in office are at a low level, and corruption is not a problem. In addition, there are high levels of control. For instance, ombudsmen are common in both countries, and the threshold to contact them is at a low level because there are not many formalities related to do so and the information is easily at hand. From that perspective, legalism is at a high level in both East-Nordic countries.[58]

Still, at the micro level the difference is essential.[59] If we compare only Finland and Sweden with each other, we can see that judicial activism does not traditionally exist in Sweden. The requirements of Europeanisation have changed this domestic situation quite comprehensively, but still the activism is limited to those situations where there are no other changes to react to but where courts and judges need to find a harmonious interpretation to follow not only the Swedish national laws but also the demands of the European law.[60] With regard to judicial self-restraint, it is a question of the level of restraint. It might still be true today that courts are self-restrained in both countries to some degree, but despite this fact there are differences in the Finnish and Swedish mentality in this respect.

---

[53] Siltala (2003), p. 294.

[54] Hautamäki (2003), p. 172.

[55] Tuori (2000), p. 1051.

[56] Mattila (1998), p. 706.

[57] Husa (2010), pp. 7–8.

[58] Ervo (2013a, b), pp. 117–132.

[59] Also, Letto-Vanamo and Tamm have underlined the differences between the single Nordic countries. Letto-Vanamo and Tamm (2019), pp. 1–2.

[60] Bertilsson (2010), pp. 29–31, Fura-Sandström (2004), pp. 264–265.

What was described above is at the same time connected to the sources of law. In Finland, judges use their discretion much more than their colleagues in Sweden do. The differences in culture and mentality lead to a situation in which individual solutions are rare in Sweden and courts wait for the legislator's reaction whenever new solutions are needed.[61] In Finland, it is not considered risky to make fair and rational decisions in a situation where the law seems to be old-fashioned or otherwise lacking. The same is true in situations where the wording of provisions include the possibility for discretion. In those situations, judges do react and find a solution which works well in practice. They have an instrumental mentality, in which a quick and practical solution is appreciated. It is considered fair to react as a court to solve a problem when the legislator has not yet done so or when the legislator has delegated that power to courts by open and goal-aimed norms.[62] Often, the Nordic law has been generally found to be practical and concrete, rather than theoretical and abstract, in nature.[63] Despite these characteristics there are practical and 'more practical' jurisdictions among the Nordic countries. When Sweden and Finland are compared with each other, Finland is clearly the more practical jurisdiction.

In Sweden, on the other hand, these type of situations are normally found as gaps in the legislation, and those gaps in a democracy should be filled by legislative power, not by judicial activism.[64] However, this is not due only to the different understanding of democracy but also to the common culture which is discursive and communal in Sweden. Legislative procedure corresponds with that type of national culture much better than juridical activism do. Therefore, judicial activism does not fit well into the Swedish court culture and the mentality of judges. Also judges are 'children' of their time and their surrounding society and therefore affected by it. Despite of the education and profession they are affected the more common lifestyle and world view in the society as such.

5 The Current Situation

Today, the Finnish legal culture is still characterised by quick solutions and rapid reforms, which can be realised whenever needed through new interpretations in the case law if the legislator has not reacted to relevant new and current needs in the society. This makes flexibility, creative solutions and common sense trademarks of the Finnish legal culture, which has can be illustrated as 'folksy'; in the other words down-to-earth, practical and flexible.[65] In addition, discretion has in many cases

---

[61] See, for instance, Tuori (2000), pp. 1049–1050. Also, Husa has paid attention to a big role of the parliament in Sweden from the perspective of the constitution. Husa (2019), p. 41.

[62] Ervo (2020), p.

[63] Husa (2010), p. 5.

[64] Holland (1991), p. 2.

[65] Letto-Vanamo and Tamm describe the Nordic legal culture as pragmatic, uncomplicated and realistic. There does not exist unnecessary formality and an uncomplicated and understandable legal

been delegated from the legislator to the adjudicator in the form of open norms and concepts in laws to guarantee flexible solutions in new situations of application. The reasons for this can be found in history. In particular, the periods of Russification have been said to affect the legal culture in a way which still can be seen today.[66] I have partly challenged this approach above, but there might be some truth in it still today.

However, the mentality in general varies between Swedes and Finns. Finns are more individual and direct. They are straightforward and enjoy realizing plans, whereas Swedes find more enjoyment in making plans together. Long-lasting discussions with all actors before making a plan or realizing it are trademarks of the Swedish culture as such. This is true in general and not only with regard to the legal culture. This fact probably offers much more clarification than the already quite archaic explanations of Russification and the other historical reasons which were presented above.[67]

The other question is why Swedes are more communal, social, and collaborative compared with the more individualistic Finns.[68] In Sweden, for instance, the workplace culture is from the bottom up, whereas in Finland it is still more hierarchical, though less so than in the past.[69] If we do not focus on the DNA and origins of those two people but try to find the societal reasons and explanations, the Swedish '*folkhemmet*'-movement can be one explanation. Still today, this ideology of folkhemmet is affecting deeply and in a comprehensive way the Swedish way of thinking and running issues. This difference in cultures can be seen everywhere in the society. Legal culture and court culture are not exceptions to but good examples of these cultural differences and varying ways of thinking.

Some practical differences in national situations also cause cultural differences. As explained above, Swedish society is more multicultural than Finnish society. Almost 20% of Sweden's inhabitants were born abroad, a rate which is and must be seen in daily-life culture as well. The corresponding number in Finland is 7%, which is much lower but not insignificant. How this significant proportion of foreign-born residents affects the court culture is an interesting question. In fact, its impacts are visible in daily life, such as in court proceedings where foreigners are parties and should be treated in the same way as native-born citizens. As a matter of fact, its impacts are visible in daily life, such as in court proceedings where foreigners are parties and should be treated in the same way as Swedes. How to reply to this

style is characteristic like transparency, equality, and avoidance of extremes too. Letto-Vanamo and Tamm (2019), p. 9.

66 Ervo (2015), pp. 143–144 and Sallila (2011), p. 466.

67 See for instance, https://finlandrelocation.com/en/naapurisopu-suomi-ja-ruotsi/. Accessed 14 June 2020 and https://www.infofinland.fi/fi/elama-suomessa/tyo-ja-yrittajyys/suomalainen-tyokulttuuri. Accessed 14 June 2020.

68 See for instance, https://finlandrelocation.com/en/naapurisopu-suomi-ja-ruotsi/. Accessed 14 June 2020.

69 See, e.g., Bernitz (2018), p. 386 and Isaksson (2008), pp. 16, 20 and 39.

challenge in practice, is one of current questions.[70] In addition, there might be latent effects, for instance in the form of stereotypes.[71] Finland shares the same challenges but so far at a lower level compared with Sweden.

These differences at the micro level, however, do not inhibit Nordic collaboration, for instance in legislative matters.[72] Due to quite uniform legislation, the court culture is also more or less uniform, but only at the macro level. As explained above, there are some differences in the way of thinking and especially in the way of acting which are important to understand in order to get the correct impression of current East-Nordic court cultures (sic, plural). At the macro level, there is only one East-Nordic court culture, but at the micro level there are both Finnish and Swedish court cultures, which do vary.

References

Aalto T (1976) Kansakunnan historia 4: Kansakunta kerää voimia 1855–1890. Werner Söderström Osakeyhtiö, Helsinki

Bernitz U (2007) What is Scandinavian law? Concept, characteristics, future. Scand Stud Law 50:13–29

Bernitz U (2018) Nordic law: position and possibilities. Tidskrift utgiven av Juridiska Föreningen i Finland 5:385–391

Bertilsson B (2010) Förändringstendenser i svensk rättskultur: rättskipningens funktion och domarens roll. SvJT 1:23–32

Björne L (2012) Suomalainen legalismi: tarua vai totta? Lakimies 1:146–152

Dahlqvist H (2002) Folkhemsbegreppet: Rudolf Kjellén vs Per Albin Hansson. Historisk Tidskrift 3:445–465

Ervasti K (2005) Tuomioistuinkulttuurin kehityslinjoja. Oikeus 2005:352–375

Ervo L (2013a) Liability and social control of Scandinavian judges. In: Giżyńska M, Piszcz A (eds) Liability of public officers: selected issues. Oficyna Wydawnicza Szkoły Wyższej im. Pawła Włodkowica, Plock, pp 117–132

Ervo L (2013b) Between legal and social control: Scandinavian ombudsmen. In: Annual conference of British institute for international and comparative law. The British Institute for International and Comparative Law

---

[70]https://www.domstol.se/globalassets/filer/gemensamt-innehall/styrning-och-riktlinjer/strategier-och-riktlinjer/bemotandestrategi-for-sveriges-domstolar.pdf. Accessed 14 June 2020 and Ökat förtroende för domstolarna—strategier och förslag—Betänkande av Förtroendeutredningen Stockholm 2008, SOU 2008:106, p. 62.

[71]Torstensson (2010), pp. 95–100.

[72]The Nordic Council, established in 1952, fosters co-operation among parliamentarians from its member nations, Denmark, Finland, Iceland, Norway and Sweden, and autonomous territories, Faroe Islands, Greenland and Åland. The Nordic Council of Ministers, created in 1971, promotes cooperation among government officials. The Nordic Council and its committees tackle, for instance, topics in legislation where the Nordic countries might wish to coordinate their policies. See, e.g., https://nordics.info/show/artikel/nordic-council-and-nordic-council-of-ministers/, https://www.norden.org/en both accessed 14 June 2020 and Nordic programme for co-operation on legislative affairs (2015–2018)

Ervo L (2014a) Religious affects in civil procedure = Влияние религии на гражданский процесс: East-Scandinavian perspective = восточноскандинавская перспектива. Herald of civil procedure = Vestnik Grazdanskogo Protsessa 4:35–50
Ervo L (2014b) Nordic court culture in progress: historical and futuristic perspectives. In: Ervo L, Nylund A (eds) The future of civil litigation. Access to courts and court-annexed mediation in the Nordic countries. Springer, Cham, pp 383–407
Ervo L (2015) Comparative analysis between East-Scandinavian countries. Scand Legal Stud 61:135–152
Ervo L (2020) Group actions in the East-Nordic legal culture. In: Uzelac A (ed) Class actions: the holy grail or a wrong trail? Springer, Cham
Fura-Sandström E (2004) Rättsbildning i en ny miljö: hur har domstolarnas roll och betydelse förändrats? Domstolarnas roll då, nu och sedan. SvJT 3:263–269
Hautamäki VP (2003) Tuomioistuin Aktivismi Tutkimuskohteena. Oikeus 2003:170–180
Hautamäki VP (2004) Teleologisk tolkningsinställning och judiciell aktivism – några teoretiska synpunkter. Tidskrift utgiven av Juridiska Föreningen i Finland 2:133–150
Holland KM (1991) Introduction. In: Holland KM (ed) Judicial activism in comparative perspective. Palgrave Macmillan, London, pp 1–11
Husa J, Nuotio K and Pihlajamäki H (2007) Nordic law—between tradition and dynamism. In: Husa J, Nuotio K, Pihlajamäki H. (eds) Nordic law—between tradition and dynamism . Intersentia, pp. 1–36
Husa J (2010) The stories we tell ourselves—about Nordic law in specific. Isaidat Law Rev 1:1–17
Husa J (2019) Constitutional mentality. In: Tamm D, Mortensen BOG (eds) Letto-Vanamo P. Nordic law in European context. Springer, Cham, pp 41–60
Inger G (2011) Svensk rättshistoria. Liber, Stockholm
Isaksson P (2008) Leading companies in a global age: managing the Swedish way. Vinnova Report VR 2008:14. Vinnova, Stockholm
Jussila O (2004) Suomen suuriruhtinaskunta 1809–1917. Werner Söderström Osakeyhtiö, Helsinki
Karonen P, Östberg K (2018) Avslutning. In: Meinander H, Karonen P, Östberg K (eds) Demokratins drivkrafter: kontext och särdrag i Finlands och Sveriges demokratier 1890–2020. Skrifter utgivna av Svenska Litteratursällskapet i Finland, Helsinki, pp. 423–435, 492–493
Kekkonen J (1999) Suomen oikeuden historiallisia kehityslinjoa. Helsingin ylipiston oikeustieteellisen tiedekunnan julkaisut, Helsinki 1999
Kekkonen J (1998a) Suomen oikeuskulttuurin historiaa ja paikannusta. Lakimies, pp 929–936
Kekkonen J (1998b) Suomen oikeuskulttuurin suuri linja 1898–1998. Suomalainen Lakimiesyhdistys 100:1–183
Kemppinen J (1992) Tätä kaikki asianomaiset noudattakoot: korkein oikeus, ihmiset ja yhteiskunta 1918–1990
Kemppinen J (1999) Oikeuskulttuuri, in Encyclopædia Iuridica Fennica. Suomalainen lakimiesyhdistys, Helsinki
Kiander J (2001) 1990-luvun talouskriisi Suomen Akatemian tutkimusohjelma: Laman opetukset. Suomen 1990-luvun kriisin syyt ja seuraukset. Valtion taloudellinen tutkimuskeskus, Government Economic Research Center Helsinki 2001
Lehtinen V, Lindholm T, Puukka P, Moring J, Veijola J, Väisänen VE (1995) Onko lama lisännyt mielenterveyshäiriöiden esiintyvyyttä? Duodecim 111:323–329
Letto-Vanamo P, Tamm D (2019) Nordic legal mind. In: Tamm D, Mortensen BOG (eds) Letto-Vanamo P. Nordic law in European context. Springer, Cham pp 1–19
Mattila HES (1998) Pohjoismainen oikeus, in Encyclopædia Iuridica Fennica. Suomalainen Lakimiesyhdistys 1998:706
Määttä T (2011) Lainsäätäjän kunnioittamisasenne, tavoitteellinen laintulkinta ja lakien tavoitesäännökset vallitsevassa tuomarinideologiassa. In: Pakarinen A et al. (eds) Lainvalmistelu, tutkimus yhteiskunta Jyrki Talan juhlakirja. Turun yliopisto, Oikeustieteellinen tiedekunta, pp 207–225

Niemi J (2018) Challenges in legal argumentation: A Swedish-Finnish perspective. In: Dahlberg M (ed) Law and society. De Lege: Juridiska Fakulteten i Uppsala Årsbok 2018. Iustus förlag, Uppsala, pp 227–249
Niemi J, Kiesiläinen J (2007) Comparing Finland and Sweden: the structure of legal argument. In: Husa J, Nuotio K, Pihlajamäki H (eds) Nordic law—between tradition and dynamism. Intersentia, pp 89–108
Nordic programme for co-operation on legislative affairs 2015–2018. The Nordic Council of Ministers 2015. https://norden.divaportal.org/smash/get/diva2:799191/FULLTEXT01.pdf.
Nylund A, Øyrehagen Sunde J (2019) Courts and court proceedings. In: Letto-Vanamo P, Tamm D, Mortensen, BOG (eds) Nordic law in European context. Springer, Cham, pp 201–213
Ortwein BM (2003) The Swedish legal system: an introduction. Ind Int Comp Law Rev 2:405–445
Saarnilehto A (2003) Kansallisen oikeuskulttuurin uhat. Lakimies 1:74
Sallila J (2011) Eurooppalainen oikeuskulttuuri, pohjoismainen perinne ja juristi-identiteetti. Oikeushistoria Suomen oikeustieteellisissä aikakauslehdissä n. 1945–1970. Oikeus 4:457–475
Siltala R (2003) Oikeustieteen tieteenteoria. Suomalainen Lakimiesyhdistys, Helsinki
Simoni A, Valguarnera F (2008) La tradizione giuridica dei Paesi nordici. Giappichelli, Torino
Torstensson N (2010) Judging the immigrant accents and attitudes. Umeå Universitet, Department of Language Studies, Umeå
Tuomioistuinlaitoksen kehittämiskomitean välimietintö. Komiteanmietintö 2003:1
Tuori K (2000) Tuomarit ja tuomioistuimet suomalaisessa oikeuskulttuurissa. Lakimies 7–8:1049–1050
Viinamäki H et al. 1997.Viinamäki H, Kontula O, Hintikka J, Niskanen L, Koskela K (1997) Laman vaikutus suomalaisten mielenterveyteen. Lääkärilehti 1997(4):1689
Virtanen K O (1974) Ahdistettu kansakunta 1890–1917. Kansakunnan historia 5. Werner Söderström Osakeyhtiö, Helsinki
Yrttiaho E (2000) Tuomarimentaliteteti ja kansan oikeustaju. Oikeudenkäytön representaatiot suomalaisessa kaunokirjallisuudessa ja mediassa käytävässä oikeudenmukaisuuskeskustelussa. Lapin yliopisto, Rovaniemi

Europeanisation, Globalisation and Nordic Courts

Europeanisation of Nordic Civil Procedure: Does the Map Match the Terrain?

Anna Nylund

Abstract EU law has a tangible influence on the civil procedure law in the Nordic countries. This chapter explores how EU civil procedure law is practised and perceived in the Nordic countries. First, a brief account of the manifold levels and types of EU civil procedure law is given. The extent to which Nordic legal academics, judges and legal counsel make use of and discuss EU civil procedure law is analysed. A key question is whether lawyers appear to have a relatively superficial knowledge of EU law (i.e., they identify only central issues) or whether they have acquired profound skills (i.e., they are able to identify and address complex issues). Third, the transposition of EU hard law and case law into national civil procedure law in the Nordic countries is examined. The Nordic countries generally implement EU hard law diligently, at least formally. Nevertheless, it will be argued that the quality of implementation is sufficient and that case law-based rules are often inadequately transposed. Finally, the consequences of a superficial approach to EU civil procedure law in the Nordic countries are discussed.

1 Introduction to Europeanisation of Civil Procedure

1.1 Introductory Remarks

Since the 1990s, European law has continuously shaped Nordic civil procedural law. Three waves of Europeanisation can be identified. The first wave was the requirements of a fair trial and other human rights enshrined in the European Convention on Human Rights (ECHR) that have been transmitted through the case law of the European Court of Human Rights (ECtHR). This wave brought procedural human rights

---

A. Nylund (✉)
UiT, The Arctic University of Norway, Hansine Hansens veg 18, 9037 Tromsø, Norway
e-mail: anna.nylund@uit.no

L. Ervo et al. (eds.), *Rethinking Nordic Courts*, Ius Gentium: Comparative Perspectives on Law and Justice 90, https://doi.org/10.1007/978-3-030-74851-7_7

to the forefront of Nordic law, making the ECHR an integrated part of Nordic procedural law.[1] The second wave, or rather a set of waves, emanates from European Union law, and comes in various forms: 'constitutional' law, regulations, directives, case law, soft law and international conventions regulating proceedings with cross-border elements, or that are designed to improve the enforcement of central EU policies, such as consumer and competition law. The third wave consists of networks, training, rankings, information portals and so forth, mainly within the domain of EU but also through the Council of Europe and other organisations.[2]

The first wave was an earthquake for criminal procedure. Additionally, it caused palpable changes to civil procedure argumentation because it highlighted the role of legal principles embodying various aspects of fair trial rights in legal argumentation, particularly in legal scholarship.[3] In contrast, the second wave of European law has been creeping in more gradually: the legislation is voluminous and omnipresent, and yet many lawyers working in the field of procedural law are oblivious to it, or at least underestimate the magnitude of it, and its far-reaching implications. This chapter will explore the paradoxes of mismatching perceptions and realities of the nature and impact of EU procedural law in the Nordic countries. The study is limited to civil procedural law, since also covering criminal procedure would be both beyond the scope of this chapter and at least partly redundant, as some of the basic mechanisms apply there as well.

In this chapter, the nature and amount of EU law with relevance for civil procedure is briefly discussed in Sect. 2. Section 3 explores the Nordic response to EU civil procedure law among various stakeholders: scholars, judges and practitioners. Thereafter, transposition of EU hard law and case law in Nordic civil procedure law is analysed in Sect. 4. In the final Sect. 5, the ramifications of the discrepancies between the level of EU influences and Nordic perceptions of, and reactions to, EU civil procedure law are discussed.

1.2 The Nordic Countries, the EU and the EEA Agreement

In the area of Justice and Home Affairs, the Nordic countries have chosen different approaches to EU law. Finland and Sweden are bound by all EU law, whereas Denmark has an exemption from Justice and Home Affairs, as a result of the 1993 referendum where the Danish people rejected the Maastricht Treaty. Hence, EU law enacted to improve judicial cooperation in civil matters is not applicable in Denmark unless Denmark has used its right to opt in. In contrast, EU civil procedure

[1] See, e.g., Bang-Pedersen et al. (2017), pp. 67 ff., Bylander (2017), Frände et al. (2012), pp. 214 ff., Skoghøy (2011), pp. 4–24 and Ervo (2005).

[2] Storskrubb (2019a).

[3] Examples of doctoral disseratiotions from this period in the field of civil procedure where selected aspects of the European Convvention on Human Rights art. 6 is discussed in detail are Bernt (2011), Bylander (2006), Knuts (2006) and Ervo (2005).

law, emanating from the duty to provide effective and equivalent protection of rights derived from EU law, efficient enforcement of EU consumer law and so forth, applies in Denmark.

Although Iceland and Norway are not EU Member States, the Agreement on the European Economic Area (EEA) extends a major part of EU law directly or indirectly to EEA/EFTA states.[4] Iceland and Norway are not EU Member States but rather are bound by the EEA Agreement, which extends the single, internal market to the EEA states. The EEA Agreement is limited to the four freedoms of the Single Market (i.e., free movement of goods, capital, services and labour); consequently, Justice and Home Affairs are not included in it. The EEA Agreement contains a mechanism for incorporating EU law into the agreement, which creates an obligation for EEA states to implement EU law. Moreover, the EFTA Surveillance Authority (ESA) mirrors the EU Commission, and the EFTA Court has the role of the CJEU. EEA states are obliged to ensure homogenous application of EU law across the EU and EEA states. Courts in EEA countries have the right, but not a duty, to request Advisory Opinions from the EFTA Court on interpretation of EU law.[5]

Although the EEA Agreement as such does not cover Justice and Home Affairs, EEA states have by no means escaped Europeanisation. Firstly, the duty to effective and equivalent protection of rights derived from EU law applies in EEA states in the same manner as in EU Member States.[6] Second, the EFTA Court has found that although the EU Fundamental Rights Charter has not been formally incorporated into the EEA Agreement, it is part of the general principles of law.[7] Third, substantive law (e.g., consumer and competition law) sometimes has implications for procedural law and, hence, is applicable in the EEA states. Fourth, the Lugano Convention serves in practice as an extension of the Single Market, creating free movement of judgments. The Convention mirrors the Brussels I *bis* Regulation. Fifth, EEA states regularly implement EU procedural law voluntarily to ensure effective and equal protection of rights across the Single Market. For example, Norway has implemented the Intellectual Property Rights Enforcement Directive[8] in the Dispute Act,[9] even though the Directive has not been incorporated into the EEA Agreement.[10]

Interestingly, sometimes EEA states would like to participate in EU civil justice but are barred from doing so. The Unified Patent Court system is the paramount example,

---

[4]Nylund (2016, 2020), Fredriksen and Strandberg (2018) and Fredriksen (2008). For Iceland and Norway, the term EU/EEA law, and sometimes EU/EEA/Lugano or EU/EEA/EFTA law would be more accurate than EU law, but for simplicity EU law is used to refer to all categories.

[5]See, e.g., Fredrisken (2018), Poulsen (2016) and Fenger et al. (2012).

[6]E.g., Nylund (2020), Franklin (2018), Fredriksen and Strandberg (2018), Lang (2017), Fredriksen and Franklin (2015), Fredriksen (2010, 2012) and Temple Lang (2012).

[7]Spano (2017) and Björgvinsson (2014).

[8]Parliament and Council Directive 2004/48/EC of 29 April 2004 on the enforcement of intellectual property rights O.J. L157/48 (2004).

[9]Act relating to mediation and procedure in civil disputes (The Dispute Act) Lov om mekling og rettergang i sivile tvister (tvisteloven) of 17 June 2005 no. 90.

[10]See, e.g., Nylund (2020) and Fredriksen and Strandberg (2018).

where the CJEU Opinion 1/09[11] has been interpreted to preclude non-Member States from participating.[12]

The Nordic countries are a paramount example of multi-speed integration in judicial cooperation, with varied approaches to EU civil procedure law. The EEA Agreement adds a layer of complexity, since the Agreement might modify the application of EU law, or EU law may not be applicable at all. Similarly, some of the EU law on judicial cooperation in civil matters, such as the Brussels I *bis* Regulation, apply in Denmark. Despite these differences among the Nordic countries, the similarities are more striking than the differences, and many differences are more a matter of nuance than fundamental differences.[13]

2 The Variegated European Civil Procedure Landscape

The landscape of EU civil procedure law has been described and analysed in detail elsewhere[14]; thus, painting the landscape with a broad brush suffices here. Europeanisation exists on several levels.[15]

The first level consists of EU constitutional law, particularly article 47 of the EU Charter of Fundamental Rights,[16] which includes the right to a fair trial. Additionally, the basic principles of EU law, primarily the principle of effective judicial protection, form part of EU constitutional law. The second level is EU hard law—directives and regulations, which come in many forms. Some of them have an overt civil procedure content that regulates mainly cross-border cases, such as the Brussels I *bis* Regulation[17] on jurisdiction and the recognition and enforcement of judgments in civil and commercial matters. Other EU regulations create distinct European procedures for cross-border cases that parallel national procedures such as the European Small Claims Regulation.[18] A notable part of procedural hard law, however, is found in instruments with a primarily substantive content or instruments aiming for efficient enforcement of a particular type of rights, such as intellectual property rights or consumer rights. The third level of EU civil procedure law consists of Court of Justice of the European Union (CJEU) case law, in which the court develops procedural rules and doctrines, such as the requirements of effective and equivalent

[11]Opinion 1/09 of 8 March ECLI:EU:C:2011:123.

[12]For a discussion on the role of the Unified Patent Courts, see Petersen and Schovsbo (2018).

[13]Nylund (2020). Adler-Nissen (2015) argues that the Denmark and Norway are in very similar positions regarding legislation on the Area of Freedom, Security and Justice.

[14]E.g., Storskrubb (2019a) and Storskrubb (2008).

[15]Krans (2015).

[16]Charter of Fundamental Rights of the European Union O.J. C326/391 (2012).

[17]Regulation (EU) No 1215/2012 of the European Parliament and of the Council of 12 December 2012 on jurisdiction and the recognition and enforcement of judgments in civil and commercial matters O.J. L351/1 (2012).

[18]Regulation (EC) No 861/2007 of the European Parliament and of the Council of 11 July 2007 establishing a European Small Claims Procedure O.J. L199/1 (2007).

protection of rights arising from EU law.[19] Another example is the duty for courts to apply selected parts of EU consumer law on their own motion. Soft law, such as various recommendations, constitutes the fourth level. Finally, international treaties entangled in EU law, such as the 2007 Hague Convention on International Recovery of Child Support and other Family Maintenance, constitute the fifth level.[20]

The impact EU law asserts on national law is partly overt and direct.[21] The requirement of effective and equivalent protection of rights emanating from EU law is generally recognised as a doctrine with direct implications for national civil procedure law.[22] In cross-border cases, national courts must clearly adhere to the EU rules on cross-border taking of evidence and service of documents. The duty to implement collective redress mechanisms for private enforcement of competition law and alternative dispute resolution mechanisms in consumer cases is also indisputable.

Nevertheless, part of the impact of EU civil procedure law is less manifest. Several factors contribute to reducing the visibility of the potential impact on national law, among others the fact that the procedural rules are embedded in EU law seemingly regulating substantive law. For instance, regulations concerning, for instance, consumer and competition law include rules on the burden and standard of proof. The procedural content risks being neglected or considered accessory: regulations are often transposed in statutory law regulating the specific subject area and not integrated in the rules of civil procedure. Moreover, EU law is sometimes considered merely 'technical' in nature, with few, if any, long term ramifications for national law.[23]

Case law-based rules also run the risk of remaining hidden in legislation-based legal cultures, since lawyers could be oblivious to the existence or implication of the rules, because they do not actively follow, or they misinterpret, CJEU case law.

EU civil procedure law has innate, covert features with potentially highly disruptive power. The criteria determining the identity of a case or the classification of a case, such as a family maintenance case or a labour case, could be discordant with national law.[24] The classification and identity of a case have profound implications on several aspects of civil procedure law, such as the power and obligation of the court to act on its own motion and the rules on *lis pendens* and *res judicata*. Therefore, differences between national law and EU law could result in a need for significant modifications of national law.

If the interconnections and potential tensions between national law and European law are not made explicit, European civil procedure law risks becoming a jack-in-the-box that surfaces unexpectedly and uncontrollably. Thomas Wilhelmsson argued in the mid-1990s that the piecemeal, sectoral approach of EU law, where the

---

[19]Example, Prechal and Cath (2014), Bobek (2010), Storskrubb (2008), p. 15, and Dougan (2004), pp. 28–34.

[20]Nylund and Strandberg (2019a).

[21]Krans (2020).

[22]Example, Krans and Nylund (2020a, b), Bobek (2010), Storskrubb (2008) and Dougan (2004).

[23]E.g., Galič (2020) and Ervo (2020).

[24]E.g., Nylund (2017b), pp. 355–356.

focus is on enforcing certain policies rather than on maintaining law as a coherent system, markedly increases the indeterminacy of law.[25] EU law does not aspire to a coherent, hierarchical structure and lacks legal cultural roots, yet it is integrated into national law and legal culture that endeavours to be coherent. These 'hidden' elements in EU civil procedure law surface in a Member State at irregular intervals. Avoiding surprising encounters with EU law requires vigilance on the part of the legal community: policymakers, legislators, judges, legal counsel and academics. The question is how the Nordic legal community perceives and adapts to the European legal landscape.

3 The Nordic Map of EU Civil Procedural Law

3.1 EU Civil Procedure in Legal Scholarship

Based on Nordic research on Europeanisation of civil procedure published in English, the level of interest in the topic is high.[26] Eva Storskrubb could be characterised as a trailblazer in building the foundations of European civil procedure law as a separate subfield of law situated at the crossroads of EU law and civil procedural law.[27]

There is also a considerable body of research that has been conducted in Nordic languages.[28] Torbjörn Andersson was one of the pioneers of the field when he authored a two-volume dissertation in the mid-1990s on the influence of EU law on how competition law cases are handled in Swedish procedural law.[29] Erik Werlauff explored the impact of EU law on Danish civil procedure in 1997.[30] Halvard Haukeland Fredriksen's comparative study on the impact of requests for preliminary rulings on German civil procedure and the impact of requests for advisory opinions on Norwegian civil procedure was seminal, although due to the fact that it was written in German, it has reached a smaller Nordic audience.[31] The considerable academic interest in the topic raises the question of whether the academic discussions translate into a high level of understanding among lawyers, judges and lawmakers.

---

[25] Wilhelmsson (1997).

[26] E.g., Nylund (2016, 2020), Nylund and Strandberg (2019b), Šadl and Wallerman (2019), Wallerman (2018, 2019a, b), Storskrubb (2018, 2019a, b), Franklin (2018), Fredriksen and Strandberg (2018), Petersen and Schovsbo (2018), Wind (2018), Storskrubb and Wallerman (2017), Derlén and Lindholm (2017a, b),Hess et al. (2016), Petersen (2016), Wallerman (2016a, b) and Linna (2015).

[27] Storskrubb (2008).

[28] E.g., Storskrubb (2017a, b), Lindfors (2017), Fredriksen (2011, 2016), Linna (2016) and Wallerman (2015).

[29] Andersson (1997).

[30] Werlauff (1997).

[31] Fredriksen (2009).

3.2 Courts and Judges Applying EU Law

Courts constitute an important player in the Europeanisation of procedural law in at least two ways. First, national courts contribute to shaping EU law by requesting preliminary rulings. Second, national courts enforce EU law and hence play a pivotal role in the application of EU law and in making national law conform to the requirements of EU law.

The number of references for preliminary rulings from Nordic, in particular Swedish, courts has been debated. The EU Commission has investigated Finnish and Swedish courts for failure to refer cases.[32] At the end of 2020, Danish courts had made a total of 144 references, Finnish courts 127 and Swedish courts 150. Icelandic courts have made 35 requests for advisory opinions and Norwegian courts 64 requests. Considering the more limited scope of the EEA Agreement and the more limited jurisdiction of the EFTA Court, it is hardly surprising that courts in EEA countries make fewer requests than courts in EU Member States do. Additionally, the population sizes explains some of the differences among the Nordic countries. In recent years, the number of requests from Norwegian courts has increased compared to earlier years, with an annual average of 3.6 requests for advisory opinions.

Several commentators, among others Halldóra Thorsteinsdóttir in this volume,[33] have spotted at least some hesitation among Nordic courts in referring cases to the CJEU.[34] However, based on an quantitative analysis of *inter alia* the number of incoming civil cases, population size and size of the economy, Morten Broberg and Niels Fenger argue that the number of requests for preliminary rulings is neither high nor low.[35] The alleged disinclination of Nordic courts to request preliminary rulings could stem from many factors and should not be as such taken as a sign of Euroscepticism. The Nordic legal method entails harmonising arguments derived from different sources, which makes courts comfortable with conducting an independent analysis of the content of EU law and aligning national law with EU law through interpretation.[36]

Referring cases to the CJEU is akin to judicial review of statutory law in light of the constitution. In both cases, courts question whether statutory law should be disregarded due to the fact that it is incompatible with law of a higher rank. The fact that the historical attitude towards judicial review has been ambivalent except for review of formal aspects of statutes could explain a certain self-restraint both in the

---

[32] Miettinen (2019) and Bernitz (2012).

[33] Thorstensdóttir (2021).

[34] Miettinen (2019), Bernitz (2012, 2018), Derlén and Lindholm (2017b), Rytter and Wind (2011), Martinsen and Wind (2010), Wind (2009) and Wind et al. (2009). For Iceland and Norway, see Fredriksen (2016), Poulsen (2016), Barnard (2014), Magnússon (2014), Sigurbjörnsson (2014) and Hreinsson (2012).

[35] Broberg and Fenger (2013, 2015). For related arguments regarding Icelandic courts, see Björgvinsson (2007) and Örlygsson (2007).

[36] Bernitz (2018), p. 31. For an account of the Nordic legal methods, see, e.g., Helland and Koch (2014) and Boucht (2014).

propensity to refer cases to the CJEU and in the form and content of the references made.[37] The early 1990s mark a clear shift in attitudes towards constitutional review, and today judicial review is acknowledged as a task of (at least) the Supreme Courts in all Nordic countries.[38] As a consequence of more active judicial review nationally, the threshold for making request could decrease over time.

Mastering the art of framing the request for a preliminary ruling in a manner that makes sense to the CJEU is a prerequisite for getting a useful answer. Identifying the more complex issues of EU law and issues arising at the crossroads of national and EU law necessitates a profound knowledge of EU law. The same applies to exploiting the opportunities to contribute to the development of EU law through preliminary references. Several commentators have questioned whether Nordic judges possess the skills necessary to conduct a fertile dialogue with the CJEU.[39]

With regard to national courts applying EU law, Nordic courts do apply EU law. However, several authors have argued that while Nordic courts apply EU law diligently when EU law is clearly applicable and the requirements it poses are unambiguous, they fail to recognise more intricate and less obvious issues.[40]

In matters concerning civil justice, by the end of 2020, Nordic courts had made a total of 20 requests for preliminary rulings. Finnish courts had made eight requests,[41] Swedish courts seven,[42] and Danish courts five requests.[43] The Nordic courts had

---

[37]Bernitz (2018) pp. 31 –33, Wind (2010, 2018),Sunnqvist (2014) and Martinsen and Wind (2010).

[38]Example, Sunnqvist (2021), Husa (2000, 2019), Helgadóttir (2011), Nergelius (2009), Ojanen (2009), Sand (2009) and Schaumburg-Müller (2009).

[39]Wallerman (2016b, 2018), Wind (2018), Derlén and Lindholm (2017a, b) and Jääskinen (2005).

[40]Wallerman (2016b, 2018), Wind (2018), Derlén and Lindholm (2017a, b), Sunnqvist (2014) and Hreinsson (2012). See also Leijon and Karlsson (2013).

[41]Case C-435/06 *C* ECLI:EU:C:2007:714, Case C-523/07 *A* ECLI:EU:C:2009:225, Case C-4/14 *Christophe Bohez v Ingrid Wiertz* ECLI:EU:C:2015:563, Case C-310/14 *Nike European Operations Netherlands BV v Sportland Oy, in liquidation* ECLI:EU:C:2015:690, Case C-521/14 *SOVAG—Schwarzmeer und Ostsee Versicherungs-Aktiengesellschaft v If Vahinkovakuutusyhtiö Oy* ECLI:EU:C:2016:41, Case C-605/14 *Virpi Komu, Hanna Ruotsalainen, Ritva Komu v Pekka Komu, Jelena Komu* ECLI:EU:C:2015:833, Case C-88/17 *Zurich Insurance plc, Metso Minerals Oy v Abnormal Load Services (International) Ltd* ECLI:EU:C:2018:558, Case C-433/18 *ML v OÜ Aktiva Finants still pending.*

[42]Case C-98/06 *Freeport plc v Ole Arnoldsson* ECLI:EU:C:2007:595, Case C-68/07 *Kerstin Sundelind Lopez v Miguel Enrique Lopez Lizazo* ECLI:EU:C:2007:740, Case C-111/08 *SCT Industri AB i likvidation v Alpenblume AB* ECLI:EU:C:2009:419, Case C-147/12 *ÖFAB, Östergötlands Fastigheter AB v Frank Koot, Evergreen Investments BV* ECLI:EU:C:2013:490, Case C-445/15 *PPU P v Q* ECLI:EU:C:2015:763, Case C-554/17 *Rebecka Jonsson v Société du Journal L'Est Républicain* ECLI:EU:C:2019:124, Case C-198/18 *CeDe Group AB v KAN sp. z o.o., in liquidation* ECLI:EU:C:2019:1001.

[43]Case C-341/93 *Danværn Production v Schuhfabriken Otterbeck* ECLI:EU:C:1995:239, Case C-18/02 *Danmarks Rederiforening, acting on behalf of DFDS Torline A/S v LO Landsorganisationen i Sverige, acting on behalf of SEKO Sjöfolk Facket för Service och Kommunikation* ECLI:EU:C:2004:74, Case C-39/02 *Märsk Olie & Gas v Firma M. de Haan en W. De Boer* ECLI:EU:C:2004:615, Case C-49/12 *The Commissioners for Her Majesty's Revenue & Customs v Sunico ApS, M & B Holding ApS, Sunil Kumar Harwani* ECLI:EU:C:2013:545, Case C-368/16 *Assens Havn v Navigators Management (UK) Limited* ECLI:EU:C:2017:546.

requested the CJEU to opine on the Brussels I *bis* Regulation and its predecessors 13 times,[44] the Brussels II *bis* Regulation[45] and its predecessor five times,[46] the insolvency proceedings regulation[47] and its predecessor twice[48] and the European Small Claims Regulation once.[49] Of the four Regulations, only the Brussels I Regulation applies in Denmark. Thus, it is hardly surprising that the number of requests for preliminary rulings is lower from Danish courts. Since the EFTA Court does not have the power to interpret the Lugano Convention, Icelandic and Norwegian courts cannot request advisor opinions. Therefore, there are no such cases for the EEA countries.

Analysing requests for preliminary rulings and advisory opinions for procedural questions in other areas of law is beyond the scope of this chapter. However, an in-depth analysis of possible procedural aspects included in requests concerning other areas of law could give additional insight.

[44]Case C-98/06 *Freeport plc v Ole Arnoldsson* ECLI:EU:C:2007:595, Case C-111/08 *SCT Industri AB i likvidation v Alpenblume AB* ECLI:EU:C:2009:419, Case C-49/12 *The Commissioners for Her Majesty's Revenue & Customs v Sunico ApS, M & B Holding ApS, Sunil Kumar Harwani* ECLI:EU:C:2013:545, Case C-147/12 *ÖFAB, Östergötlands Fastigheter AB v Frank Koot, Evergreen Investments BV* ECLI:EU:C:2013:490, Case C-4/14 *Christophe Bohez v Ingrid Wiertz* ECLI:EU:C:2015:563, Case C-521/14 *SOVAG — Schwarzmeer und Ostsee Versicherungs-Aktiengesellschaft v If Vahinkovakuutusyhtiö Oy* ECLI:EU:C:2016:41, Case C-605/14 *Virpi Komu, Hanna Ruotsalainen, Ritva Komu v Pekka Komu, Jelena Komu* ECLI:EU:C:2015:833, Case C-368/16 *Assens Havn v Navigators Management (UK) Limited* ECLI:EU:C:2017:546, Case C-88/17 *Zurich Insurance plc, Metso Minerals Oy v Abnormal Load Services (International) Ltd* ECLI:EU:C:2018:558, Case C-433/18 *ML v OÜ Aktiva Finants still pending.*

[45]Council Regulation (EC) No 2201/2003 of 27 November 2003 concerning jurisdiction and the recognition and enforcement of judgments in matrimonial matters and the matters of parental responsibility, repealing Regulation (EC) No 1347/2000. O.J. L338/1 (2003).

[46]Case C-435/06 *C* ECLI:EU:C:2007:714, Case C-68/07 *Kerstin Sundelind Lopez v Miguel Enrique Lopez Lizazo* ECLI:EU:C:2007:740, Case C-523/07 *A* ECLI:EU:C:2009:225, Case C-4/14 *Christophe Bohez v Ingrid Wiertz* ECLI:EU:C:2015:563, Case C-445/15 *PPU P v Q* ECLI:EU:C:2015:763.

[47]Regulation (EU) 2015/848 of the European Parliament and of the Council of 20 May 2015 on insolvency proceedings *O.J. L141/19 (2015).*

[48]Case C-310/14 *Nike European Operations Netherlands BV v Sportland Oy, in liquidation* ECLI:EU:C:2015:690, Case C-198/18 *CeDe Group AB v KAN sp. z o.o., in liquidation* ECLI:EU:C:2019:1001.

[49]Case C-554/17 *Rebecka Jonsson v Société du Journal L'Est Républicain* ECLI:EU:C:2019:124.

3.3 Lawyers Make EU Civil Procedure Law Come Alive, or not?

The role of EU law in the legal landscape depends partly on whether lawyers actually use EU law to argue their cases. The European Enforcement Order (EEO) Regulation[50] illustrates the fact that the discreet EU procedures for cross-border cases are seldom used. In a study on cross-border cases in the EU, the Finnish legal professionals interviewed had never come across an EEO despite the fact that the interviewees were selected among persons with expertise in cross-border proceedings.[51] The European small claims proceedings and payment order proceedings are also little used.[52]

The number of lawyers who are well-informed of EU civil procedure is low in the Nordic EU countries. In the aforementioned study on cross-border cases, a lawyer working in a law firm serving the business community explained that the firm always contacts a partner firm in the country concerned rather than using EU instruments in cross-border cases.[53] Unfamiliarity with the discrete EU procedures results in few lawyers using them. The lack of use becomes self-perpetuating—why use a process when nobody else uses it? Some of the judges interviewed in the study lamented that only a small group of judges attend trainings on EU civil procedure and that many attendees already have previous experience working with EU law, while judges with limited knowledge and skills in EU law, who hence need training, do not attend. The trainings could thus contribute to increasing the knowledge gap among judges. Except for cross-border service and taking of evidence, judges and lawyers seldom encounter EU civil procedure law; thus, they think of EU civil procedure law as something that is 'technical' and useful only for a few lawyers specialising in cross-border litigation. This contributes to a perception that EU law is almost irrelevant in the domain of civil justice.

3.4 Conclusions on EU Law and Nordic Lawyers

Nordic lawyers are aware of the basic instruments and characteristics of EU law and utilise them when they consider them appropriate and relevant. It is clear that Nordic court culture has become Europeanised and that Nordic courts apply European substantive law regularly. Nonetheless, the general level of knowledge is superficial and is limited to the most commonly used instruments and situations where the dissonance between national law and EU law is clear. Still, we should not infer that Nordic courts apply EU law less efficiently than do courts in other European

---

[50] Regulation (EC) No 805/2004 of the European Parliament and of the Council of 21 April 2004 creating a European Enforcement Order for uncontested claims O.J. L143/1 (2004).

[51] Gascón Inchausti et al. (2017).

[52] Ervo (2019), pp. 88–90.

[53] Gascón Inchausti et al. (2017).

countries. On the contrary, there is reason to believe that judges across Europe have limited knowledge of EU law and that their encounters with EU law are scarce.[54]

The high interest in EU civil procedure among legal academics has not translated into a high level of knowledge among lawyers and judges. One reason for this discrepancy could be that a significant portion of the writings are in English and the intended audience is international, while Nordic lawyers seldom read English language texts. Handbooks and commentaries, where lawyers and judges would find information related to the specific hard law provisions or specific CJEU rulings in Nordic languages, could enable judges to access information more efficiently. Mainstreaming European civil procedure law in textbooks on civil procedure could also be helpful.

4 Transposing of EU Civil Procedure in Nordic Law

4.1 Implementation of EU Hard Law in Nordic Legislation

Although Nordic legislators implement EU law loyally, the quality of implementation does not always suffice. EU procedural law that is fragmental, is sectoral or contains concepts and ideas that are not fully concordant with national law necessitates careful analysis before it is transposed into law, so as to uphold the coherence of national law.

In the Nordic countries, the method of implementation of EU law is often haphazardly chosen. For instance, the rules on disclosure of evidence in actions for infringement of intellectual property rights are incorporated in the Norwegian Dispute Act, while corresponding rules for competition law will be implemented in the Competition Act.[55] The preparatory works do not provide reasons for selecting a specific method of implementation.[56] Although the rules on disclosure for competition and intellectual property rights are not identical, transposing them in different ways augments the existing disconnection between them by reducing links between them.[57] Since the context influences interpretation, the rules on disclosure for intellectual property rights cases are likely to be construed in the light of the general rules of civil procedure, whereas the rules on competition law will be read in the light of substantive competition law.[58] The result is an atomisation of civil procedure law

[54]E.g., Krans and Nylund (2020b), Andrews (2016), Galič (2016), Krans (2016), Piszcz (2016) and Nowak et al. (2011).

[55]*Act on competition between undertakings and control with concentrations* (Competition Act) Lov om konkurranse mellom foretak og kontroll med foretakssammenslutninger (konkurranseloven) 5 March 2004 no 12.

[56]Hjort (2019).

[57]Petersen (2016), pp. 19–20.

[58]Petersen (2016), pp. 24–25.

where rules applicable only for a specific type of case increasingly reduce the role of general procedural rules.

The rules of evidence are central: They determine *inter alia* whether or not witnesses must be heard orally and or in written form, the standard of proof and the burden of evidence.[59] In the Nordic countries, the general rules of evidence apply to all cases, unless special rules have been enacted for a specific type of case. However, EU law does not have a doctrine of evidence; that is, there is no clear baseline definition of the standard of proof, nor a shared idea of how evidence should be presented.[60] This should be taken into account when implementing EU evidence law in national law.

For instance, the Antitrust Damages Directive[61] that regulates actions for infringement of competition law contains numerous rules on evidence, including rules on the standard of proof. When these rules are transposed, the legislator should, when applicable, use national terminology rather than the terminology used in the Directive to describe the standard of proof. In the event that the standard of proof does not have an equivalence in national law, new standards of proof that are intelligible to national lawyers should be crafted. None of the legislation implementing the Directive in the Nordic EU Member States[62] includes any reference to the standard of proof. The Finnish implementing act even makes a reference to the general rules on evidence in the Code of Judicial Procedure. In the absence of specific rules on the standard of proof, Nordic lawyers will most likely apply their national rules and doctrines. The transposing legislation mentions other aspects of evidence, such as disclosure, but evidence is not comprehensively regulated. Since EU law is implemented as if there was a single European doctrine of evidence and as if the national doctrine fully corresponds to it, discrepancies are likely to be overlooked, and judges and lawyers will be unlikely to detect them. National evidence law will influence the type and amount of admissible evidence as well as the form (i.e., oral or written) in which the evidence is presented, which will consequently impact the outcome of the case.

Nordic cooperation could improve the quality of implementation of EU hard law. The basic tenets of procedural law are similar in the Nordic countries to provide a fertile ground for analysing possible discrepancies between national law and EU law and finding the most appropriate method of implementation. Cooperation does not necessitate all five countries embracing identical solutions; rather, the aim should be to provide a sound basis for decision-making. Furthermore, active cooperation could

---

[59]For an overview of the standards of evidence in Nordic law, see Strandberg (2019).

[60]Example, the Brussels I *bis* Regulation O.J. L351/1 (2012), Payment Order Regulation O.J. L399/1 (2006), and the Damages Directive O.J. L349/1 (2014). For a more detailed discussion, see Hau (2020).

[61]Directive 2014/104/EU of the European Parliament and of the Council of 26 November 2014 on certain rules governing actions for damages under national law for infringements of the competition law provisions of the Member States and of the European Union O.J. L349/1 (2014).

[62]The Danish Act on Actions for Infringement of Competition Law (Lov om behandling af erstatningssager vedrørende overtædelser af konkurrenceretten no. 1541 af 12/12/2106), the Finnish Act on Damages in Competition Law (Laki kilpailuoikeudellisista vahingonkorvauksista 2016/1077) and the Swedish Competition Damages Act (Konkurrensskadelag 2016:964).

also result in the Nordic countries detecting potential weaknesses and pitfalls during the drafting of EU law and, hence, give them the opportunity to address the issues before the legislation is enacted.

4.2 Transposition of Case Law Based Civil Procedural Law

Part of EU civil procedure law is based almost exclusively on case law. The doctrine of procedural autonomy[63] and the duty of courts to apply EU consumer law on their own motion[64] are paramount examples. Case law-based procedural law is unfamiliar to Nordic lawyers, except for Norwegian lawyers: Nordic courts make law only when the new rules can be derived directly from statutory law or fundamental legal principles. The innate nature of case law is to take two steps forward and one step back, resulting in gradual development and a partly disjointed line of argumentation, which in the context of procedural law is unfamiliar to Nordic lawyers. Furthermore, courts respond to the particular legal and factual issues in each case rather than taking a principled, general approach, resulting in considerable opacity and a need for further clarification. Hence, determining the scope of the obligations on national civil procedure law arising from CJEU case law is rather onerous.

If national statutory law is incompatible with EU law, courts must strive to interpret the national rule in a manner that renders it compatible with EU law. When interpretation does not yield satisfactory results, courts are obliged to give primacy to EU law. Several examples where Nordic courts have failed to align national rules with EU law through interpretation, although such an interpretation is feasible, can be found. Norwegian rules for demanding a security for the liability of costs constitute one example. The Norwegian Dispute Act section 20–11 stated that a party domiciled outside Norway could be required to provide a security unless it would be contrary to Norway's international obligations, but it did not mention the EEA Agreement specifically. Technically, the provision was concordant with EU law, because it clearly included the EEA Agreement. However, Norwegian lower courts regularly required claimants domiciled in EEA countries to provide a security, and they continued to do so even after the Supreme Court[65] found the practice unlawful. Finally, the EFTA Surveillance Authority demanded that the provision should be amended to explicitly include parties from EEA States. The Norwegian government complied and amended the law.[66]

Another example is the duty of courts to apply EU consumer law on their own motion. Nordic courts already have the power, and partly also a duty, to exercise active judicial guidance.[67] Hence, one could conclude that judicial guidance as is it

[63] Krans and Nylund (2020a, b).

[64] Example, Wallerman Ghavanini (2020) and Andersson (2019).

[65] HR-2014–377-U.

[66] Hjort (2019), pp. 114–116.

[67] E.g., Wallerman Ghavanini (2020), Andersson (2019) and Fredriksen and Strandberg (2019).

is regulated in Nordic procedural law fulfils these obligations. However, there are several caveats. First, most consumer cases are dealt with outside the courts or in simplified proceedings, such as orders for payment proceedings. In these proceedings, the case documents are not available to the court. This could be problematic, particularly in the wake of the CJEU ruling in the *Bondora* case.[68] Second, the fact that the consumer remains passive in most cases, which hinders the court from giving active guidance, entails a further complication in many consumer cases.[69] Third, even when both parties are active, the duty to judicial guidance based on EU law probably exceeds the minimum requirements of national law, at least in some situations. However, judges appear to lack awareness of possible differences between national law and EU law,[70] in the same way as in the Norwegian case on a security for legal costs. Thus, resorting to judicial guidance is not a panacea; rather, the Nordic legislators should assess whether current legislation complies with the obligations under EU law.[71]

In consumer cases, vigilant staff handling simplified cases and judges supervising them are pivotal, as the Finnish Supreme Court ruling KKO 2015:60[72] illustrates. In the case, a consumer credit company filed a simplified claim against a consumer. The consumer did not file a statement of defence, although the late payment interest rate was 118% and the terms for determination of the rate were unclear. The district court rejected the late payment interests, since the terms of the interest were not compliant with the Unfair Terms Directive.[73] The consumer credit company appealed, first to the Court of Appeals and then to the Supreme Court, while the consumer remained passive. The Supreme Court held for the consumer: it obligated courts to analyse the case file in their own motion. However, this case is likely to be exceptional, both since the court spotted the unfair term and since the consumer credit company persistently pursued the case. Although the ruling entails clarification of some issues, many other issues remain unresolved.

Despite the challenges that CJEU case law has caused for consumer cases, Nordic lawmakers have not been inclined to explore the problems and weaknesses of their current systems. As Anna Wallerman Ghavanini has noted, complex issues are left to the courts to solve despite the fact that the workload prevents judges from actively

---

The Nordic rules on judicial guidance are similar to the German rules on die materielle Prozessleitung.

68 Joined Cases C-453/18 and C-494/18 *Bondora AS v Carlos V. C. and XY*, Judgment of the Court of 19 December 2019, ECLI:EU:C:2019:1118.

69 Andersson (2019).

70 Wallerman Ghavanini (2020).

71 Wallerman Ghavanini (2020), Andersson (2019), Fredriksen and Strandberg (2019) and Nylund (2019).

72 See also Mäenpää (2016).

73 Council Directive 93/13/EEC of 5 April 1993 on unfair terms in consumer contracts O.J. L95/29 (1993).

searching for unfair terms and that problems arise from institutional structures and regulation rather than how work is organised within courts.[74]

4.3 Conclusions on the Transposition of EU Civil Procedure Law

The Nordic countries implement EU law diligently and, in the case of Norway (and Iceland), sometimes opt to implement EU law even when they have no formal obligation to do so.[75] Consequently, the problem is the mode and quality of implementation, particularly with regard to the fact that much of the adaptation is left to the judiciary. While Nordic judges are accustomed to flexible norms and to weighing, balancing and harmonising principles and rules, the marked differences in approach between EU law and national civil procedure law are not easily bridged through interpretation alone. Makeshift implementation adds up to a patchwork that erodes the system from within. Systematic changes could be put in place to reduce the number of times the jack-in-the-box of EU law pops up and to help retain comprehensive, coherent Nordic court cultures. However, one should not infer that the quality of implementation of EU law is solely Nordic problem: on the contrary, it appears to be omnipresent.[76]

5 Navigating When the Map and the Terrain Do Not Match

5.1 Lost Opportunities for Developing Nordic Civil Procedure Law

Overlooking the density and potential impact of European civil procedural law has several detrimental consequences related to the development of national law.

EU law contains several procedural innovations, such as court-connected mediation, disclosure of documents, and collective redress, that should be regarded as potential benchmarks. For example, court-connected mediation was introduced in Finland partly as a result of the Civil Mediation Directive.[77] Steps had already been taken to enact rules on court-connected mediation, and EU law served as an additional argument to propel the reform. Although the Directive only mandates providing court-connected mediation in cross-border cases, Finland—and many

---

[74] Wallerman Ghavanini (2020).See also, e.g., Andersson (2019), Fredriksen and Strandberg (2019), Rudanko (2016) and Savola (2016).

[75] Nylund (2020).

[76] Krans and Nylund (2020b).

[77] Directive 008/52/EC of the European Parliament and of the Council of 21 May 2008 on certain aspects of mediation in civil and commercial mattersO.J. L136/1 (2008).

other Member States—opted to extend mediation to all civil cases. The impact on Finnish court proceedings and court culture has been palpable, as Kirsikka Linnanmäki demonstrates in her chapter in this volume.[78]

However, there are numerous examples of lost opportunities of benchmarking. For example, the Norwegian government did not use the Civil Mediation Directive to assess its court-connected mediation regime. One probable reason for this is that the Dispute Act had been adopted a few years earlier, and thus the time was not ripe for revising the rules. Still, any amendments resulting from benchmarking could have been enacted a few years later simultaneously with other changes. Unlike in EU Member States, agreements to mediate a dispute before litigation are not enforceable in Norway. Furthermore, out-of-court mediation does not influence limitation and prescription periods in Norway, which could deter the parties from attempting to mediate before starting court proceedings.[79] Thus, out-of-court mediation is less favourably treated in Norway than in many other European countries.

The European Payment Order Procedure[80] and the European Small Claims Procedure are other examples of lost opportunities to improve national legislation. Despite the fact that Finnish law does not have fully-fledged payment order proceedings and has no small claims proceedings at all, the European procedures were not used to discuss whether Finnish procedural rules should be coordinated with EU procedures and whether EU procedures had any tangible advantages *vis-à-vis* national procedures. Non-harmonisation, as well as harmonisation, should ensue from a deliberate choice and comparison of the rules: it should not be the result of a haphazard process.

5.2 The Missing Nordic Input in the Development of EU Civil Procedure Law

The magnitude of the Europeanisation of civil procedure law should induce national governments to act proactively by attempting to influence the content of EU civil procedure law at an early stage (i.e., before rules are enacted).[81] Several methods could be used, often in parallel. Whitepapers, green papers and other policy documents should be scrutinised to recognise issues that are pertinent from a Nordic perspective. The Nordic governments could consequently argue why a solution on the EU level is redundant, why a different solution would be superior to the one proposed by the EU, why some solutions are problematic for Nordic law, or any combination of these. The Nordic countries could also position themselves as innovators by strategically enacting innovations.

[78]Linnanmäki (2021).

[79]E.g., Nylund (2017a) and Bernt (2015).

[80]Regulation (EC) No 1896/2006 of the European Parliament and of the Council of 12 December 2006 creating a European order for payment procedure O.J L399/1 (2006).

[81]Stadler (2018), p. 777.

Nordic cooperation is the key to increasing the quality of implementation and the quality of EU civil procedure law. It is unfeasible for a single Nordic country to be proactive in multiple legal fields. Therefore, the Nordic countries should join forces to detect potentially problematic issues early, advance Nordic viewpoints and, when necessary, lobby for specific solutions. Additionally, formal Nordic cooperation in the field of civil procedure could make the Nordic countries a powerhouse of innovation. Pilot projects could be designed across the countries; for example, one country could pilot one model and another country could pilot another model. The results could then be contrasted to optimise one or both models. As a result, Nordic countries could be a European trailblazer, and Nordic innovations could serve as a blueprint for EU law.

5.3 Nordic Cooperation as a Method of Improving Quality

EU civil procedure law exerts substantial influence on Nordic civil procedure law and Nordic court culture. Europeanisation does not abolish the need for Nordic cooperation; in fact, the opposite is true. Nordic cooperation, both formal and informal, at all stages of the process of Europeanisation could enable us to foresee and prepare for the challenges that lie ahead by influencing EU law.[82] It could also enable us to ameliorate problems arising from Europeanisation and to reduce the tensions between Nordic law and legal culture and European law. The first step should be to recognise that our map does not fit the terrain and to take Europeanisation seriously.

References

Adler-Nissen R (2015) Through the EU's front and back doors: the selective Danish and Norwegian approaches in the area of freedom, security and justice. In: Grøn CH, Nedergaard P, Wivel A (ed) The Nordic Countries and the European Union: still the other European Union? Routledge, Abingdon, pp 212-229

Andersson T (1997) Rättsskyddsprincipen. Iustus förlag, Uppsala

Andersson T (2019) *Ex officio* application of the unfair terms directive cases against consumers: a Swedish perspective. In: Nylund A, Strandberg M (eds) Civil procedure and harmonisation of law: the dynamics of EU and international treaties. Intersentia, Cambridge, pp 153–170

Andrews N (2016) European influences upon English civil justice: tempests or gentle breezes? The European Union and national civil procedure. In: Nylund A, Krans B (eds) The European Union and National Civil Procedure. Intersentia, Cambridge, pp 31–46

Bang-Pedersen UR, Christensen LH, Petersen CS (2017) Den civile retspleje. Hellerup, Pejus

Barnard C (2014) Reciprocity, homogeneity and loyal cooperation: dealing with recalcitrant national courts? In: The EFTA Court (ed) The EEA and the EFTA courts. Decentered integration. Hart, Oxford, pp 151–168

[82] Leino-Sandberg and Leppävirta (2018).

Bernitz U (2012) Preliminary references and Swedish courts: what explains the continuing restrictive attitude? In: Cardonnel P, Rosas A, Wahl N (eds) Constitutionalising the EU judicial system. Essays in honour of Pernilla Lindh. Hart, Oxford, pp 177–187
Bernitz U (2018) Preliminary rulings to the CJEU and the Swedish judiciary: current developments. In: Derlén M, Lindholm J (eds) The court of justice of the European Union: multidisciplinary perspectives. Hart Publishing, Oxford, pp 17–34
Bernt C (2011) Meklerrollen ved mekling i domstolene. Fagbokforlaget, Bergen
Bernt C (2015) Mediation of legal disputes in Norway. Institutionalized, pragmatic and increasingly popular. In: Esplugues C, Marquis L (eds) New developments in civil and commercial mediation. Springer, Cham, pp 511–545
Björgvinsson DT (2007) Application of article 34 of the ESA/Court Agreement by Icelandic courts. In: Monti M, von und zu Liechtenstein PN, Vesterdorf B, Westbrook J, Wildhaber L (eds) Economic law and justice in times of globalisation. Festschrift for Carl Baudenbacher. Nomos Verlag, Baden-Baden, pp 37–50
Björgvinsson DT (2014) Fundamental rights in EEA law. In: The EFTA court (ed) The EEA and the EFTA courts. Decentered integration. Hart, Oxford, pp 263–280
Bobek M (2010) Why there is no principle of procedural autonomy of the member of states. RRDE 36
Boucht J (2014) Introduction to Finnish and Swedish legal method. In: Helland I, Koch S (eds) Nordic and Germanic legal methods. Mohr Siebeck, Tübingen, pp 165–187
Broberg M, Fenger N (2013) Variations in member states' preliminary references to the court of justice: are structural factors (part of) the explanation? Eur Law J 19(4):488–501
Broberg M, Fenger N (2015) Förhandsavgöranden från svenska domstolar: Är svenska domstolar väsentligt mindre benägna att begära förhandsavgöranden än domstolar i andra medlemsstater? Europarättslig Tidskrift 18(4):769–790
Bylander E (2006) Muntlighetsprincipen: en rättsvetenskaplig studie av processuella handläggningsformer i svensk rätt. Iustus förlag, Uppsala
Bylander E (2017) Regeringsformens krav på alla rättegångars genomförande rättvist och inom skälig tid. Svensk Juristtidning 102(5–6):370–398
Derlén M, Lindholm J (2017a) Från Champagne till Ramlösa: EU-domstolens rättspraxis i svenska underinstanser. Europarättslig Tidskrift 4: 695–716
Derlén M, Lindholm J (2017) Serving two masters: CJEU case law in Swedish first instance courts and national courts of precedent as gatekeepers. In: Derlén M, Lindholm J (eds) The court of justice of the European Union: multidisciplinary perspectives. Hart Publishing, Oxford, pp 79–100
Dougan M (2004) National remedies before the court of justice: issues of harmonisation and differentiation. Hart, Oxford
Ervo L (2005) Oikeudenmukainen oikeudenkäynti. WSOY, Vantaa
Ervo L (2019) Harmonisation or fragmentation of national law? An East Nordic perspective. In: Nylund A, Strandberg M (eds) Civil procedure and harmonisation of law: the dynamics of EU and international treaties. Intersentia, Cambridge, pp 77–98
Ervo L (2020) The Finnish way of understanding procedural autonomy: a practical approach to implementing EU civil procedural law. In: Krans B, Nylund A (eds) Procedural Autonomy across Europe. Intersentia, Cambridge, pp 57–80
Fenger N, Rydelski MS, van Stiphout T (2012) European Free Trade Association (EFTA) and European Economic Area (EEA). Wolters Kluwer, Alphen aan den Rijn
Frände D, Havansi E, Helenius D, Koulu R, Lappalainen J, Lindfors H, Niemi J, Rautio J, Virolainen J (2012) Prosessioikeus. SanomaPro, Helsinki
Franklin CNK (ed) (2018) The effectiveness and application of EU and EEA law in national courts: principles of consistent interpretation. Intersentia, Cambridge
Fredriksen HH (2008) Tvisteloven og EØS-Avtalen. Tidsskrift for Rettsvitenskap 121(3):289–359
Fredriksen HH (2009) Europäische Vorlageverfahren und nationales Zivilprozessrecht: eine Untersuchung der Vorlageverfahren an den EFTA-Gerichtshof und den EuGH als Bestandteile des norwegischen bzw. des deutschen Zivilprozesses. Mohr Siebeck, Tübingen

Fredriksen HH (2010) One market, two courts: legal pluralism vs. homogeneity in the european economic area. Nordic J Int Law 79(4):481–499

Fredriksen HH (2011) EU/EØS-rett i norske domstoler. Europautredningen. Utvalget for utredningen av Norges avtaler med EU, Oslo

Fredriksen HH (2012) Bridging the widening gap between the EU Treaties and the agreement on the European economic area. Eur Law J 18(6):868–886

Fredriksen HH (2016) Høyesterett som EØS-domstol. In: Skoghøy JEA, Øie TM, Matningsdal M (eds) Rettsavklaring og rettsutvikling - Festskrift til Tore Schei. Universitetsforlaget, Oslo, pp 438–464

Fredriksen HH (2018) The EFTA court. In: Howse R, Ruiz-Fabri H, Ulfstein G, Zang MQ (eds) The legitimacy of international trade courts and tribunals. Cambridge University Press, Cambridge, pp 138-181

Fredriksen HH, Franklin CNK (2015) Of pragmatism and principles: the EEA agreement 20 years on. Common Mark Law Rev 52:629–684

Fredriksen HH, Strandberg M (2018) Norwegian civil procedure under the influence of EU law. In: Uzelac A, van Rhee CHR (eds) Transformation of civil justice: unity and diversity. Springer , Cham, pp 41–62

Fredriksen HH, Strandberg M (2019) *Ex officio* application of EU consumer protection law in Norwegian courts. In: Nylund A, Strandberg M (eds) Civil procedure and harmonisation of law: the dynamics of EU and international treaties. Intersentia, Cambridge, pp 171–191

Galič A (2016) Slovenian civil procedure and the transformative power of the EU. In: Nylund A, Krans B (eds) The European Union and national civil procedure. Intersentia, Cambridge, pp 131–146

Galič A (2020) Procedural autonomy between EU law and the Slovenian law of civil procedure. In: Krans B, Nylund A (eds) Procedural autonomy across Europe. Intersentia, Cambridge, pp 165–182

Gascón Inchausti F, Hess B, Cuniberti G, Oberhammer P, Reqejo Isidro M, Weitz K, Storskrubb E, Kramer X (2017) An evaluation study of national procedural laws and practices in terms of their impact on the free circulation of judgments and on the equivalence and effectiveness of the procedural protection of consumers under EU consumer law. Strand 1: mutual trust and free circulation of judgments. Brussels, European Commission

Hau W (2020) Who is afraid of European civil procedure? A German perspective on the waning procedural autonomy of the member states. In: Krans B, Nylund A (eds) Procedural autonomy across Europe. Intersentia, Cambridge, pp 81–100

Helgadóttir R (2011) Nonproblematic judicial review: a case study. Int J Const Law 9(2):532–547

Helland I, Koch S (2014) Introduction to Norwegian legal method. Nordic and Germanic legal methods: contributions to a dialogue between different legal cultures, with a main focus on Norway and Germany. In: Helland I, Koch S (eds) Nordic and Germanic legal methods. Mohr Siebeck, Tübingen, pp 99–140

Hess B, Bergström M, Storskrubb E (eds) (2016) EU civil justice: current issues and future outlook. Swedish studies in European law. Hart, Oxford

Hjort MA (2019) The EU's Iinfluence on Norwegian civil procedure through national substantive law. Civil procedure and harmonisation of law. In: Nylund A, Strandberg M (eds) Civil procedure and harmonisation of law: the dynamics of EU and international treaties. Intersentia, Cambridge, pp 111–124

Hreinsson P (2012) The interaction between Iceland courts and the EFTA court. In: The EFTA Court (ed) Judicial protection in the European economic area. German Law Publishers, Stuttgart, pp 90–99

Husa J (2000) Guarding the constitutionality of laws in the Nordic countries: a comparative perspective. Am J Comparat Law 48(3):345–381

Husa J (2019) Constitutional mentality. In: Letto-Vanamo P, Tamm D, Mortensen BOG (eds) Nordic law in European context. Springer, Cham, pp 41–60

Jääskinen N (2005) Internationella normer i nordisk rätt. Europarättslig tidskrift (3):520–531

Knuts G (2006) Förfarandegarantier vid domstolsanknuten medling. Suomen lakimiesyhdistyksen kustannus, Helsinki
Krans B (2015) EU law and national civil procedure law: an invisible pillar. Eur Rev Private Law 23(4):567–587
Krans B (2016) The impact of EU law on Dutch civil procedure law. In: Nylund A, Krans B (eds) The European Union and national civil procedure. Intersentia, Cambridge, pp 89–100
Krans B (2020) Procedural autonomy in the Netherlands: a fading relic? In: Krans B, Nylund A (eds) Procedural autonomy across Europe. Intersentia, Cambridge, pp 101–118
Krans B, Nylund A (2020) Aspects of Procedural autonomy. In: Krans B, Nylund A (eds) Procedural autonomy across Europe. Intersentia, Cambridge, pp 1–11
Krans B, Nylund A (2020) Comparative insights on procedural autonomy. In: Krans B, Nylund A (eds) Procedural autonomy across Europe. Intersentia, Cambridge, pp 227–244
Lang JT (2017) The principle of sincere cooperation in EEA Law. In: Baudenbacher C (ed) The fundamental principles of EEA law. Springer, Cham, pp 73–89
Leijon K, Karlsson C (2013) Nationella domstolar som politiska aktörer: främjare av rättslig integration eller försvarare av nationella intressen? Statsvetenskaplig Tidskrift 115(1):5–34
Leino-Sandberg PSM, Leppävirta LH (2018) Does staying together mean playing together? The influence of EU law on co-operation between EU and non-EU States: the Nordic example. Eur Law Rev 43(3):295–312
Lindfors H (2017) Poistuvan eksekvatuurin aika ja sen vaikutukset Bryssel Ia-asetuksen oikeussuojajärjestelmään. In: Riekkinen J (ed) Oikeutta oikeudenkäynnistä täytäntöönpanoon: Juhlajulkaisu Tuula Linna. Helsinki, Alma Talent, pp 209–220
Linna T (2016) Bryssel I-asetuksen ja välimiesmenettelyn suhde. Defensor Legis 97(2):178–185
Linna TH (2015) Actio pauliana and res judicata in EU insolvency proceedings. J Private Int Law 11(3):568–584
Linnanmäki K (2021) Mediation: a change in Finnish court culture? In: Ervo L, Letto-Vanamo P, Nylund A (eds) Rethinking Nordic Courts. Springer, Cham
Mäenpää K (2016) Kuluttajaluoton koron kohtuullisuus ja tuomioistuimen tutkimisvelvollisuus—KKO 2015:60. Lakimies 114(2):336–343
Magnússon S (2014) Efficient judicial protection of EEA rights in the EFTA pillar: different role for the national judge? In: The EFTA court (ed) The EEA and the EFTA courts. Decentered integration. Oxford, Hart, pp 117–132
Martinsen DS, Wind M (2010) When national courts go to Europe: reluctant or active players in the integrationsprocess? In: Koch H, Hagel-Sørensen K, Haltern U, Weiler JHH (eds) Europe. The new legal realism. Essays in honour of Hjalte Rasmussen. DJØF Publishing, Copenhagen, pp 479–500
Miettinen S (2019) Duties to refer duties: the commission investigates whtether Finnish supreme courts failed to refer tax cases to the court of justice. Europarättslig tidskrift (2):245–260
Nergelius J (2009) Judicial review in Swedish law: a critical analysis. Nordic J Hum Rights 27(2):142–159
Nowak T, Amtenbrink F, Hertogh M, Wissink M (2011) National judges as European Union judges: knowledge, experiences and attitutdes of lower court jduges in Germany and the Netherlands. Eleven International Publishing, Den Haag
Nylund A (2016) Norway: an insider outside—or an outsider inside—European civil justice. In: Nylund A, Krans B (eds) The European Union and national civil procedure. Intersentia, Cambridge, pp 101–114
Nylund A (2017a) Civil procedure Norway. Kluwer Law International, Alphen aan den Rijn
Nylund A (2017) Sak samma om det är samma sak? Tidskrift Utgiven Av Juridiska Föreningen i Finland 153(2–4):345–359
Nylund A (2019) Comparing the efficiency and quality of civil justice in Scandinavia: the role of structural differences and definitions of quality. Civ Just Q 38(4):427–439

Nylund A (2020) Procedural autonomy, the EEA agreement and Norwegian law: the art of bridging a gap and maintaining it too. In: Krans B, Nylund A (eds) Procedural autonomy across Europe. Intersentia, Cambridge, pp 119–138

Nylund A, Strandberg M (2019) Introduction. In: Nylund A, Strandberg M (eds) Civil procedure and harmonisation of law: the dynamics of EU and international treaties. Intersentia, Cambridge, pp 1–10

Nylund A, Strandberg M (2019) Conclusions on civil procedure and harmonisation of law. In: Nylund A, Strandberg M (eds) Civil procedure and harmonisation of law: the dynamics of EU and international treaties. Intersentia, Cambridge, pp 231–242

Ojanen T (2009) From constitutional periphery toward the center: transformations of judicial review in Finland. Nordic J Hum Rights 27(2):194–207

Örlygsson T (2007) Iceland and teh EFTA court: twelve years of experience. In: Monti M, von und zu Liechtenstein PN, Vesterdorf B, Westbrook J, Wildhaber L (eds) Economic law and justice in times of globalisation. Festschrift for Carl Baudenbacher. Nomos Verlag, Baden-Baden, pp 225-242

Petersen CS (2016) Danish civil procedure and the internal market: impact and challenges of sectoral harmonisation. In: Nylund A, Krans B (eds) The European Union and national civil procedure. Intersentia, Cambridge, pp 17–30

Petersen CS, Schovsbo JH (2018) Decision-making in the unified patent court: ensuring a balanced approach. In: Geiger C, Nard CA, Seuba X (eds) Intellectual property rights and the judiciary. Edward Elgar Publishing, Cheltenham, pp 37–57

Piszcz A (2016) Polish civil proceedings: how much Europeanised? In: Nylund A, Krans B (eds) The European Union and national civil procedure. Intersentia, Cambridge, pp 115–130

Poulsen TC (2016) Norwegian courts. In: Baudenbacher C (ed) The handbook of EEA law. Springer, Cham, pp 257–275

Prechal S, Cath K (2014) The European acquis of civil procedure: constitutional aspects. Uniform Law Rev 19(2):179–198

Rudanko M (2016) Kohti kuluttajaprosessioikeutta: kuluttajaluottojen korot ja tuomioistuinten tutkintavalta. Lakimies 114(6):879–906

Rytter JE, Wind M (2011) In need of juristocracy? The silence of Denmark in the development of European legal norms. Int J Const Law 9(2):470–504

Šadl U, Wallerman A (2019) 'The referring court asks, in essence': Is reformulation of preliminary questions by the court of justice a decision writing fixture or a decision-making approach? Eur Law J 25(4):416–433

Sand IJ (2009) Judicial review in Norway under recent conditions of European law and international human rights law-a comment. Nordisk Tidsskrift for Menneskerettigheter 27:160–169

Savola P (2016) Hylätään selvästi perusteettomana: tuomioistuimen tutkimisvallasta erityisesti kuluttaja-asioissa. Lakimies 114(1):53–76

Schaumburg-Müller S (2009) Parliamentary precedence in Denmark: a jurisprudential assessment. Nordisk Tidsskrift for Menneskerettigheter 27:170–184

Sigurbjörnsson M (2014) To refer or not to refer? In: The EFTA court (ed) The EEA and the EFTA courts. Decentered Integration. Hart, Oxford, pp 101–106

Skoghøy JEA (2011) Dommerrollen gjennom de siste 50 år: noen utviklingstrekk. Lov og Rett 50(01–02):4–24

Spano R (2017) The EFTA court and fundamental rights. Eur Const Law Rev 13(3):475–492

Stadler A (2018) Book review: the European Union and national civil procedure. Rabels Zeitschrift Für Ausländisches Und Internationales Privatrecht 81:773–777

Storskrubb E (2008) Civil procedure and EU law: a policy area uncovered. Oxford University Press, Oxford

Storskrubb E (2017) Några tankar om hur EU-rättens tentakler genomtränger processrätten. Tidskrift Utgiven Av Juridiska Föreningen i Finland 153(2–4):360–383

Storskrubb E (2017b) Tillit mellan rättssystemen i EU: det civilrättsliga perpektivet. In: Bakardjieva Engebrekt A, Michalski A, Oxelheim L (eds) Tilliten i EU vid ett vägskäl. Santerus Academic Press, Falun

Storskrubb E (2018) Mutual trust and the dark horse of civil justice. Camb Yearb Eur Leg Stud 20:179–201

Storskrubb E (2019) EU civil justice at the harmonisation crossroads? In: Nylund A, Strandberg M (eds) Civil procedure and harmonisation of law: the dynamics of EU and international treaties. Intersentia, Cambridge, pp 11–34

Storskrubb E (2019b) Mutual trust in civil justice cooperation in the EU. In: Bakardjieva Engebrekt A, Bremberg N, Michalski A, Oxelheim L (eds) Trust in the European Union in challenging times. Palgrave Macmillan, pp 159–180

Storskrubb E, Wallerman A (2017) Judicial cooperation in civil matters: coming of age? In: Servent AR, Trauner F (eds) The Routledge handbook of justice and home affairs research. Routledge, Abingdon, pp 203–214

Strandberg M (2019) Standards of evidence in Scandinavia. In: Tichý L (ed) Standard of proof in Europe. Mohr Siebeck, Tübingen, pp 135–159

Sunnqvist M (2014) Konstitutonellt kritiskt dömande. Förändringen av nordiska domares attityder under två sekel. Jure, Stockholm

Sunnqvist M (2021) The changing role of Nordic courts. In: Ervo L et al (eds) Rethinking Nordic Courts. Springer, Cham

Temple Lang J (2012) The duty of national courts to provide access to justice in the EEA. In: The EFTA Court (ed) Judicial protection in the European economic area. German Law Publishers, Stuttgart, pp 100–135

Thorsteinsdóttir H (2021) Globalisation and court practice in Iceland: new case law of the Supreme Court in relation to the EEA Agreement and European Convention on Human Rights. In: Ervo L et al (eds) Rethinking Nordic Courts. Springer, Cham

Wallerman A (2015) Om fakultativa regler. En studie av svensk och unionsrättslig reglering av skönsmässigt beslutsfattande i processrättsliga frågor. Iustus förlag, Uppsala

Wallerman A (2016) The curious incident of the dog in the night-time: Europeanisation of civil procedure in Sweden. In: Nylund A, Krans B (eds) The European Union and national civil procedure. Intersentia, Cambridge, pp 147–160

Wallerman A (2016) Towards an EU law doctrine on the exercise of discretion in national courts? The Member States' self-imposed limits on national procedural autonomy. Common Mark Law Rev 53(2):339–360

Wallerman A (2018) Referring court influence in the preliminary ruling procedure: the Swedish example. In: Derlén M, Lindholm J (eds) The court of justice of the European Union: multidisciplinary perspectives. Hart Publishing, Oxford, pp 153–170

Wallerman A (2019a) Can two walk together, except they be agreed? Preliminary references and (the erosion of) national procedural autonomy. Eur law Rev 2:159–177

Wallerman A (2019) Who is the national judge? A typology of judicial attitudes and behaviours regarding preliminary references. In: Rauchegger C, Wallerman A (eds) The eurosceptic challenge national implementation and interpretation of EU law. Hart Publishing, Oxford, pp 155–174

Wallerman Ghavanini A (2020) Manouvering procedural autonomy in Sweden. In: Krans, B, Nylund A (eds) Procedural autonomy across Europe. Intersentia, Cambridge, pp 203-226

Werlauff E (1997) Fælleseuropæisk procesret: europaretlige krav til dansk retspleje. København, Jurist- og Økonomforbundets Forlag

Wilhelmsson T (1997) Jack-in-the-box theory of European Community Law. In: Krämer L, Micklitz HW, Tonner K (eds) Law and diffuse intersts in the European legal order: Liber Amicorum Norbert Reich. Nomos, Baden Baden, pp 177–194

Wind M (2009) When parliament comes first: the Danish concept of democracy meets the European Union. Nordisk Tidsskrift for Menneskerettigheter 27(2):272–288

Wind M (2010) The Nordics, the EU and the reluctance towards supranational judicial review. J Common Mark Stud 48(4):1039–1063

Wind M (2018) The Scandinavians: the foot-dragging supporters of European law? In: Derlén M, Lindholm J (eds) The court of justice of the European Union: multidisciplinary perspectives. Hart Publishing, Oxford, pp 191–210

Wind M, Martinsen DS, Rotger GP (2009) The uneven legal push for Europe questioning variation when national courts go to Europe. Eur Union Polit 10(1):63–88

Nordic and European Judicial Cooperation in Criminal Matters

Dan Helenius

Abstract Judicial cooperation in criminal matters between the Nordic states has traditionally been extensive. This cooperation has included matters of extradition, legal assistance in regard to evidence, transfer of the enforcement of punishments and transfer of criminal proceedings and criminal jurisdiction. Since the late twentieth century and the early twenty-first century, the Nordic cooperation agreements have to a rather significant degree been replaced or complemented by EU legislation. Nevertheless, the Nordic agreements continue to be of relevance in many aspects, which gives rise to a rather complicated system of interwoven legal frameworks. This contribution aims to point out legal similarities and differences as well as overlaps between these frameworks, but also to elaborate on the characteristics of the Nordic cooperation as compared to the EU regulated cooperation system. It is specifically argued that the reason for the success of the Nordic cooperation is the mutual trust that the Nordic states share. However, this trust differs somewhat from the trust that is presumed to exist also between the EU Member States.

1 Introduction

Within the EU—a form of regional cooperation itself—there have historically existed two regions with an even closer regional—or sub-regional—cooperation, namely the Benelux states and the Nordic states. This regional cooperation has also concerned criminal and criminal procedural matters.[1] In this chapter, I will focus on matters of judicial cooperation in criminal matters between the Nordic states. By this, I mean cooperation through different means with the aim of facilitating transnational criminal law enforcement. A systematic examination of the core areas of judicial cooperation and their regulation in the Nordic states is given. Today, these areas are to a significant degree regulated by EU law, but to a large extent they are also

[1] See Lahti and Träskman (1994), pp. 251–252 and Thunberg Schunke (2004), p. 49.

D. Helenius (✉)
University of Helsinki, Yliopistonkatu 3, 00101 Helsinki, Finland
e-mail: dan.helenius@helsinki.fi

L. Ervo et al. (eds.), *Rethinking Nordic Courts*, Ius Gentium: Comparative Perspectives on Law and Justice 90, https://doi.org/10.1007/978-3-030-74851-7_8

regulated by regional Nordic agreements. The Nordic framework is compared to the corresponding EU legal framework throughout the text. The aim is not only to point out legal similarities and differences as well as overlaps between these frameworks but also to elaborate on the characteristics of the Nordic cooperation as compared to the EU regulated cooperation system. Specifically, I will discuss whether the mutual trust on which the Nordic cooperation is based is comparable to the mutual trust that is presumed to exist between the EU Member States.

I will mainly use Finnish legislation to exemplify the national implementation of Nordic cooperation agreements. This is done with the full understanding that the legal provisions in other Nordic states may differ in certain specific regards. References are, however, occasionally also made to the legislation of other Nordic states. Since the Nordic legal framework in this area is largely based on inter-Nordic agreements, national legislation is to a large degree comparable. My aim is not to conduct an in-depth comparison between specific legal provisions of the Nordic states but to highlight features that are common for all of these states.

2 Judicial Cooperation in Criminal Matters Between the Nordic States

Judicial cooperation in criminal matters between the Nordic states has traditionally been extensive. Perhaps unlike the cooperation between the Benelux states, the Nordic cooperation has not decreased with time, at least not significantly, although it has to a rather significant degree been replaced or complemented by EU cooperation since the late twentieth century and the early twenty-first century.[2] Nevertheless, inter-Nordic agreements are in many respects still relevant. This gives rise to a rather complicated system that is not always easy to grasp, since several inter-related legal frameworks have to be taken into consideration. The answer to the question of whether the Nordic cooperation has acted as a concrete inspiration and ideal model for the current EU cooperation based on the principle of mutual recognition does not seem to be unequivocally clear, but there does seem to be consensus that this is almost certainly the case.[3]

As a starting point, cooperation between the Nordic EU states of Denmark, Finland and Sweden is based on EU legislation, while cooperation between these countries and Norway and Iceland is based on inter-Nordic agreements. However, EU legislation takes precedence only so long as the Nordic countries have not introduced legislation of their own that allows cooperation to be "extended or enlarged" and helps to "simplify and facilitate further the procedures" dealt with by EU law and

[2]See Thunberg Schunke (2004), pp. 49–50. See generally on the historical development of the EU regulated judicial cooperation in criminal matters, Klip (2016), pp. 374–380.

[3]See, e.g., Strandbakken (2009), p. 364, Mathisen (2010), p. 11 and Elholm and Feldtman (2014), p. 151.

"provided that the level of safeguards set out" in EU law is respected.[4] This circumstance calls for due care, since authorities in the Nordic states have to keep different legal regimes in mind with regard to matters of judicial cooperation.[5]

The Nordic cooperation in criminal matters intensified after the Second World War and especially during the 1960's, when several agreements on cooperation were adopted.[6] The general framework for this cooperation was based on the so-called Helsinki Treaty of 1962, which included provisions on, *inter alia*:

- equal treatment of Nordic citizens in the drafting of laws and regulations (art. 2).
- establishing uniform rules relating to criminal offences and penalties. With regard to criminal offences committed in one Nordic country, all other Nordic countries should as far as possible be able to investigate and prosecute such offences (art. 5).
- ensuring that decisions by a court of law or other public authority in one Nordic country can also be executed in the other Nordic countries (art. 7).
- ensuring that public authorities in the Nordic countries may correspond directly with one another (art. 42).

Since the 1960s, the main forum for furthering cooperation has been the Nordic council of ministers. In addition, the Nordic Criminal Law Committee—a body consisting of civil servants with expertise in criminal law—has also been of great importance through its legislative draft reports.[7]

There are, of course, many reasons why the Nordic states have chosen to cooperate so closely with each other and why this cooperation has proven so successful.[8] First of all, the Nordic countries have a long history of cooperation in legal matters in general. The common history between the Nordic countries has led to similar legal traditions and similarities in economic, social and cultural development, as well as common approaches to crime control and human rights policies. Much has been written on the largely common penal policy of the Nordic states. This policy is commonly characterised by a low level of penal repression. Another joint feature is the traditionally welfarist view on criminality, which considers crime to be foremost a social problem that should be dealt with not only by means of criminal law. Needless to say, these features amount to a certain degree of common understanding on how

[4] Most EU instruments explicitly allow such further integration; see, e.g., art. 34.3 of directive 2014/41/EU of the European Parliament and of the Council regarding the European Investigation Order in criminal matters O.J. L130/1 (2014).

[5] Additionally, there are also separate agreements between Norway and Iceland and the EU (excluding the Nordic EU countries); e.g., the Agreement on the surrender procedure between the Member States of the European Union and Iceland and Norway O.J. L292/1 (2006). See further on this matter Suominen and Kvam (2009).

[6] See, e.g., Lahti and Träskman (1994), p. 256.

[7] On the history of Nordic cooperation in criminal matters, see, e.g., Lahti and Träskman (1994), p. 256 and Melander (2007), pp. 111 ff.

[8] See generally Lahti and Träskman (1994), pp. 256–257.

criminality should be managed.[9] Still today, the Nordic states often look to each other for possible solutions when deliberating on legal amendments.[10]

These factors, in turn, have fostered a strong mutual confidence or trust between the Nordic countries, which can be regarded as a pre-requisite for a well-functioning cooperation. This mutual trust has, in turn, enabled a more effective cooperation due to the fact that the Nordic states have been able to agree upon common principles and procedural rules governing such cooperation. As is well known, the current cooperation in the EU, based on the principle of mutual recognition, is specifically presumed to require a sufficient degree of mutual trust among the Member States.

According to the Court of Justice of the European Union (ECJ), the principle of mutualrecognition by necessity implies that the Member States have mutual trust in their criminal justice systems and that each of them recognises the criminal law in force in the other Member States even when the outcome would be different if its own national law were applied.[11] The principle of mutual recognition is said to be founded on the mutual confidence between the Member States that their national legal systems are capable of providing equivalent and effective protection of the fundamental rights recognised at EU level.[12] This presumption of mutual trust in turn requires that each Member State consider all the other Member States to be in compliance with EU law and particularly with the fundamental rights recognised by EU law.[13]

This legal structure is said to be based on the fundamental premise that each Member State shares with all the other Member States, and recognises that they share with it, a set of common values on which the EU is founded. This premise implies and justifies the existence of mutual trust between the Member States that those values will be recognised and, therefore, that the law of the EU that implements them will be respected.[14] Consequently, the EU *prima facie* demands of its Member States that they trust each other in the name of effective cooperation.

However, as the recent development with regard to upholding human rights and the rule of law within the EU has shown, trust is not something that can be simply be presumed and taken for granted.[15] According to the ECJ, limitations of the principles of mutual recognition and mutual trust between Member States can be made 'in exceptional circumstances'.[16] Judicial cooperation through mutual recognition can function to different degrees, depending on how far the states are willing to go. This

---

[9]See, e.g., Melander (2007) and Lappi-Seppälä and Nuotio (2019), pp. 194–197.

[10]See Letto-Vanamo and Tamm (2019), p. 7 and Lappi-Seppälä and Nuotio (2019), p. 181.

[11]Joined cases C-187/01 *Gözütok* and C-385/01 *Brügge*, Judgment of the Court of 11 February 2003, ECLI:EU:C:2003:87, para. 33.

[12]Joined cases C-404/15 *Aranyosi* and C-659/15 *Căldăraru*, Judgment of the Court (Grand Chamber) of 5 April 2016, ECLI:EU:C:2016:198, para. 77.

[13]Opinion 2/13 of the ECJ, ECLI:EU:C:2014:2454, para. 191. Further on this presumption, see Sicurella (2018), pp. 309–312.

[14]Opinion 2/13 of the ECJ, ECLI:EU:C:2014:2454, para. 168.

[15]See in depth Satzger (2018a).

[16]Opinion 2/13 of the ECJ, ECLI:EU:C:2014:2454, para. 191 and joined cases C-404/15 *Aranyosi* and C-659/15 *Căldăraru*, Judgment of the Court (Grand Chamber) of 5

in turn depends on the level of trust the states have in each other: the more trust, the farther recognition may be taken. The number of limitations the states place on cooperation indicates the character and degree of mutual recognition they are willing to accept.[17]

The Nordic states have abolished—or at least alleviated—several of the traditional obstacles to judicial cooperation in criminal matters, simplified the procedures for cooperation and even harmonised parts of their national criminal procedural legislation. The Nordic states were also forerunners in allowing direct communication between competent authorities (prosecutors, courts) in matters of judicial cooperation—without involvement of central authorities such as the ministries of justice—even before this model was adopted in the cooperative framework of the EU and the Council of Europe.[18]

One of the fundamental initial ideas behind applying mutual recognition in criminal matters in the EU was that cooperation should be possible despite differences in substantive and procedural law.[19] Mutual recognition was regarded as a less intrusive method: instead of harmonising the laws of the Member States, the Member States should simply accept and disregard legal differences and recognise each other's judicial decisions. However, the cooperation between the Nordic states seems to have functioned so well precisely because these areas of law do not differ very much between them. It should be noted, however, that the legal similarities between the Nordic States have not simply come about by coincidence but are also a result of conscious measures. For instance, the Nordic council endeavoured to harmonise the criminal and procedural legislations of the Nordic states during the latter half of the twentieth century. This precondition of legal similarity has gradually also become clear at the EU level: mutual recognition is not feasible without some degree of harmonisation of both substantive criminal law and criminal procedural law.[20] However, it should also be pointed out that the criminal legislations in the Nordic states are far from completely identical. One area in which the solutions differ quite radically is prostitution. Prostitution is legal in Denmark and Finland, whereas Norway, Iceland and Sweden have criminalised the purchase of sexual services.[21] It is certainly not inconceivable that such differences might have a negative impact on the possibilities of cooperation.[22]

Also, it should not be forgotten that the inter-state movement between the Nordic states has traditionally been relatively intense. This has, among other things, been

April 2016, ECLI:EU:C:2016:198, para. 82. See most recently, Case C-128/18 *Dorobantu* ECLI:EU:C:2019:857, para. 47.

[17] Satzger (2019), p. 54. See also Asp (1998), p. 36 for a similar argument in regard to the Nordic states.

[18] Thunberg Schunke (2004), p. 177.

[19] See, e.g., Communication from the Commission to the Council and the European Parliament—Mutual recognition of Final Decisions in criminal matters (COM/2000/0495 final), p. 4 and Satzger (2019), p. 45.

[20] See, e.g., Thunberg Schunke (2013), p. 8.

[21] See further Träskman (2009), pp. 296–301 and Toftegaard Nielsen et al. (2017), pp. 402–403.

[22] Cf Mathisen (2010), p. 25.

due to the countries' geographical proximity and flexible migration rules.[23] Among the individual criminal cases with foreign elements, many contain elements (e.g., the nationality of the offender or victim) that pertain to other Nordic countries. These circumstances in turn, have made effective cooperation in criminal matters more or less a necessity among the Nordic states.[24]

Below, I will give an account of the main forms of judicial cooperation in criminal matters, which include: extradition, legal assistance in regard to evidence, transfer of the enforcement of punishments and transfer of criminal proceedings and criminal jurisdiction.[25] The Nordic agreements will be reflected against the EU framework throughout the text.

3 Extradition

Extradition between the Nordic states was initially based on bilateral treaties during the early twentieth century. However, cooperation gradually became increasingly informal and detached from these treaty obligations.[26] In a sense, trust grew naturally out of this perceived well-functioning and effective cooperation.

Following this early period, the Nordic countries agreed upon substantially identical legislation on extradition in the 1950s and 1960s.This agreement did not take the form of an international convention, which is something that overall has been characteristic for the Nordic cooperation.[27] Cooperation has often been based not on officially binding conventions but, rather, on 'informal' agreements on harmonisation and a willingness to assist one another. A certain reluctance towards over-formalisation and an emphasis on pragmatical solutions can clearly be perceived.[28] In fact, the mutual trust between the Nordic states may initially have led to the notion that cooperation did not require binding agreements, since this trust rendered cooperation possible on its own.[29] This type of cooperation is strikingly different from the EU cooperation, where trust has formally been declared and demanded of the Member States by way of binding instruments in order to achieve effective cooperation.

In a way, Nordic cooperation during this era did indeed signify a form of mutual recognition. However, the system was in fact based on facultative cooperation and

[23]See Tolttila (2011), pp. 369–370.

[24]Lahti and Träskman (1994), p. 257.

[25]On different forms of judicial cooperation in criminal matters, see, e.g., Satzger (2018b) pp. 4–6.

[26]Strandbakken (2009), p. 368 and Tolttila (2011), p. 373.

[27]See Lahti and Träskman (1994), p. 271 and Mathisen (2010), p. 5.

[28]Melander (2007), pp. 113–115 calls this type of cooperation 'soft harmonisation'. Voluntary and informal cooperation due to practical needs has been characteristic in regard to not only criminal but also civil matters; see Smits (2007), pp. 63–64 and Letto-Vanamo and Tamm (2019), pp. 9–12.

[29]See Melander (2007), p. 115 and Tolttila (2011), p. 375.

did not explicitly require any recognition at all.[30] The formal requirement to cooperate and the institutionalisation of mutual recognition only came later due to EU obligations. Thus, one could say that the Nordic system does not require mutual recognition, but that it nevertheless functions in the same way as a mutual recognition based system due to a strong degree of mutual trust and willingness to cooperate.

The Nordic extradition regime functioned in parallel with the extradition framework of the Council of Europe and the EU during the latter half of the twentieth century. In 2003, the framework decision on the European arrest warrant (EAW) was adopted in the EU.[31] This was the first instrument based on the principle of mutual recognition in criminal matters. The idea behind the EAW as well as the principle of mutual recognition was to simplify judicial cooperation in criminal matters and make it more effective by removing several of the legal obstacles that had traditionally made such cooperation cumbersome and time-consuming.

However, it did not take long for the Nordic countries to update their own extradition framework. The Nordic ministers of justice had already concluded in 2002 that the Nordic extradition regime should be revised.[32] In 2012, the Convention on surrender on the basis of an offence between the Nordic states finally entered into force. This convention is generally referred to as the 'Nordic arrest warrant' (NAW).[33]

To take Finland as an example, this situation entails that the authorities have to operate with three different extradition regimes, depending on which country is involved in the extradition procedure. The Act on Extradition between Finland and Other Nordic Countries (1383/2007) specifically applies to surrender procedures between Finland and other Nordic countries. If surrender is to take place between Finland and another EU country that is not a Nordic country, the Act on Extradition on the Basis of an Offence Between Finland and Other Member States of the European Union (1286/2003) applies. To make things even more complicated, if surrender is to take place between Finland and a state that is neither an EU nor a Nordic state, the so-called General Extradition Act (456/1970) applies. This means that three different extradition regimes apply depending on the nature of the country involved in the extradition procedure.[34]

As already mentioned, the premise within both the EU and the Council of Europe has been that regional cooperation is allowed and even desirable, as long as this cooperation goes further than the existing European regulations. According to the EAW framework decision (art. 31.2), 'Member States may conclude bilateral or multilateral agreements or arrangements [...] in so far as such agreements or arrangements allow the prescriptions of this Framework Decision to be extended or enlarged and help to simplify or facilitate further the procedures for surrender of persons'.

---

[30]Mathisen (2010), p. 16.

[31]Council framework decision (2002/584/JHA) of 13 June 2002 on the European arrest warrant and the surrender procedures between Member States O.J. L190/1 (2002).

[32]Mathisen (2010), p. 17.

[33]See generally, e.g., Suominen (2014).

[34]The situation would also seem to be similar in the other Nordic countries. See, e.g., Strandbakken (2009), p. 367.

The NAW, in many ways, goes further than the EAW in simplifying the extradition procedure and making it more effective.[35] Perhaps one of the greatest divergences between the EAW and the NAW is that the NAW does not require double criminality under any circumstances; rather, it only requires that the offence in question must have a more severe punishment than fines. If all legal systems were identical, the requirement of double criminality would essentially lose its significance. Although far from completely identical, the Nordic systems are still so similar that requiring double criminality has been considered redundant.[36] However, it should be noted that the abolishment of the double criminality requirement did not come about with the NAW. Rather, this requirement had already been abolished in the previous legal framework for extradition between the Nordic countries from the 1960s.[37]

Another change that came with the EAW was the obligation for Member States to surrender their own nationals.[38] As is well known, states traditionally do not surrender their own nationals.[39] If the EAW has been issued for the purposes of execution of a custodial sentence or detention order, surrender may be refused if the executing Member State undertakes to execute the sentence or detention order in accordance with its domestic law, provided that the requested person is staying in, or is a national or a resident of, the executing Member State (art. 4.6). Furthermore, if the EAW has been issued for the purpose of conducting a criminal prosecution and the person who is the subject of the EAW is a national or resident of the executing Member State, the executing Member State may make surrender subject to the condition that the person is returned to the executing Member State in order to serve his or her sentence (art. 5.3).

The Nordic states have also acted as forerunners in this regard. The extradition regime preceding the NAW already allowed for the surrender of nationals to other Nordic countries, albeit with certain additional requirements.[40] The abolishment of these requirements can, again, be regarded as a sign of mutual trust between the Nordic states.

Interestingly, the Nordic states have abolished several grounds for refusal that still persist within the EU cooperation regime, whereas they have preserved grounds for refusal that have been difficult for the EU to accept. According to ch. 2, sec. 4.6 of the act on Extradition between Finland and Other Nordic Countries, extradition shall be refused if there are justifiable grounds to suspect that the requested person is threatened by capital punishment, torture or other degrading treatment or that he or she would be subjected to persecution due to, *inter alia*, his or her religion, beliefs or political opinions. The same also applies if there is justifiable cause to assume that he

---

[35]For an in-depth analysis of the differences between the EAW and the NAW, see Mathisen (2010).

[36]See Asp (1998), p. 11. However, the territoriality exception may still apply. According to Finland's 'Nordic' extradition act, double criminality is required when the act in question is deemed to have been committed in Finland or on board a Finnish vessel.

[37]Lahti and Träskman (1994), p. 274.

[38]Suominen (2011), p. 129.

[39]See, e.g., Mathisen (2010), p. 13 and Suominen (2011), pp. 127–129.

[40]See further Lahti and Träskman (1994), p. 275 and Mathisen (2010), p. 10.

or she would be subjected to a violation of his or her human rights or constitutionally protected due process, freedom of speech or freedom of association.

The question of refusal to surrender due to potential human rights violations has been highly topical in regard to the EAW during the last few years. The threat of persecution or other human rights violations is an established ground for refusal in the traditional system of extradition as well as other forms of judicial cooperation in criminal matters.[41] However, when the EAW framework decision was adopted, no such ground for refusal was explicitly included in the instrument. This was largely the case because such a ground for refusal would intrinsically seem to be contradictory to the whole idea of mutual recognition and mutual trust. If there is a presumption of trust, then Member States should in principle also have faith that human rights are respected in all other Member States. It was not until 2016 that the EU Court of Justice explicitly confirmed that a risk of human or fundamental rights violations in the requesting state may act as a ground for refusal, albeit under 'exceptional circumstances'.[42]

When Finland implemented the EAW framework decision in Finnish legislation, it was nevertheless decided that threats of persecution or other human rights violations should be included as a mandatory ground for refusal. According to the Finnish government, this ground for refusal could be derived from the general wording of the framework decision as well as Finland's other international human rights obligations.[43] The same solution was also adopted in several other Member States.[44]

If we consider mutual trust to inherently require that the human rights standards of other states should never be questioned, it would seem natural that the Nordic states would not apply such a ground for refusal. However, this assumption was evidently not regarded as a problem when the NAW was implemented in Finland, as well as in the other Nordic states, even though the NAW convention does not explicitly contain such a ground for refusal.[45] According to the Finnish government, the obligation to respect human rights, and consequently the obligation to refuse extradition when these rights are threatened, can be derived from the purpose of the convention as well as the Finnish constitution.[46] This clearly demonstrates that mutual trust does not require blind trust in other states' abilities to invariably uphold human rights guarantees. Trust can be conditional even between states that are as closely interconnected and confident in each other's legal systems as the Nordic states.[47]

---

[41] See, e.g., Lahti and Träskman (1994), pp. 279–280.

[42] See joined Cases C-404/15, *Aranyosi* and C-659/15 PPU, *Căldăraru*, Judgment of the Court (Grand Chamber) of 5 April 2016, ECLI:EU:C:2016:198. See further on this topic, e.g., Satzger (2018a), Bárd and Ballegooij (2018) and Helenius (2019).

[43] Finnish Government Bill HE 88/2003 vp, p. 22.

[44] See Suominen (2011), p. 307.

[45] See Suominen (2011), pp. 204–218.

[46] Finnish Government Bill 51/2007 vp, p. 18.

[47] Similarly also Suominen (2011), p. 220.

4 Legal Assistance in Regard to Evidence

A treaty on mutual legal assistance in criminal matters was adopted among the Nordic states in 1974.[48] This treaty mainly concerns mutual legal assistance through service and taking of evidence. For instance, it enables the hearing of witnesses to be conducted in another Nordic state.[49]

The treaty was implemented in Finland through a Decree (470/1975) but also partly through a separate Act on the obligation in certain cases to appear before a court in another Nordic country (349/1975). According to this Act, a person who has reached the age of 18 years and who permanently resides in a Nordic country has an obligation to appear before a court in another Nordic country to be heard as a witness, taking into account the importance of such a hearing and possible inconveniences that may be caused by it. This obligation concerns not only witnesses but also parties in criminal cases (secs. 1 and 9).

In addition to this Nordic agreement, the general act on International Legal Assistance in Criminal Matters (4/1994) applies in Finland. This act concerns most forms of legal assistance, except, *inter alia*, extradition and transfer of the enforcement of punishments (sec. 1 and 2). It is applied parallel to the above-mentioned Nordic agreement, insofar as the same forms of legal assistance are concerned. However, the Nordic agreement allows for more extensive communication between competent authorities and also makes it possible to communicate in Danish and Norwegian, in addition to Finnish and Swedish.[50]

On the EU level, directive 2014/41/EU of the European Parliament and of the Council regarding the European Investigation Order (EIO) in criminal matters was adopted on 3 April 2014. The directive makes it possible for a Member State to have one or several specific investigative measures carried out in another Member State to obtain evidence. It also concerns evidence that is already in the possession of the competent authorities of the executing State (art. 1). With regard to the relationship between Finland and the other EU Member States, the general act on International Legal Assistance in Criminal Matters applies only to measures that are not regulated by the EIO directive (sec. 1.3). However, since Denmark does not take part in the EIO (p. 45 of the directive's preamble), previous agreements—including Nordic ones—on legal assistance will continue to apply in regard to Denmark.[51] Naturally, Norway and Iceland also do not take part in the EIO. It should also be noted that the EIO directive, in the same way as the EAW framework decision, allows for bilateral and multilateral agreements, 'insofar as these make it possible to further strengthen the aims of this Directive and contribute to simplifying or further facilitating the procedures for gathering evidence' (art. 34.3).

[48] Treaty of 26 April 1974 between Finland, Denmark, Iceland, Norway and Sweden on mutual assistance through service and taking of evidence.

[49] See Lahti and Träskman (1994), p. 282.

[50] See further on this matter, Finnish Government Bill 61/1993 vp, pp. 11–12, 26, 28 and 34.

[51] Finnish Government Bill 29/2017 vp, p. 90. See also Espina Ramos (2019), p. 55.

Again, we can see that inter-Nordic agreements are not completely replaced by EU legislation but continue to apply and to be of practical relevance. However, it must be said that things are not made easy for the legal authorities, since these again have to keep in mind several different, inter-related legal frameworks. To some degree, more far-reaching obligations than those between the EU Member States seem to be rendered possible between the Nordic states specifically due to their close geographical proximity. This especially concerns the obligation to appear before other Nordic courts to be heard as a witness.[52]

5 Transfer of the Enforcement of Sentences

In the 1960s, an agreement was concluded between the Nordic States on transferring of the enforcement of a sentence from one Nordic country to another. In Finland, the Act on cooperation between Finland and the other Nordic states on the enforcement of criminal sentences was adopted in 1963 (326/1963).

This form of cooperation, among other things, makes it possible to transfer the enforcement of fines, confiscations, conditional and unconditional prison sentences, conditional release from prison and community service sentences from one Nordic country to another. Such transfer of enforcement can be deemed appropriate especially when the sentenced person is a citizen of a Nordic state other than the one that imposed the sentence, or when he or she has his or her permanent residence or has resided for a long time in such a state. After the transfer, the punishment is enforced largely in accordance with the law of the enforcing state.[53]

Like extradition and legal assistance in regard to evidence, this form of cooperation also takes place alongside the EU framework on the transfer of criminal sentences. At the EU level, there are four instruments that deal with transfer of enforcement. Specifically, these concern financial penalties,[54] confiscation,[55] probation measures and alternative sanctions[56] and custodial sentences.[57] When these instruments were implemented in Finland, it was concluded that the Nordic enforcement act should continue to apply between Finland and the Nordic EU Member States (i.e., Denmark

[52]See Asp (1998), pp. 27 and 37.

[53]Lahti and Träskman (1994), p. 284.

[54]Council framework decision 2005/214/JHA of 24 February 2005 on the application of the principle of mutual recognition to financial penalties O.J. L76/16 (2005).

[55]Council framework decision 2006/783/JHA of 6 October 2006 on the application of the principle of mutual recognition to confiscation orders O.J. L328/59 (2006).

[56]Council framework decision 2008/947/JHA of 27 November 2008 on the application of the principle of mutual recognition to judgments and probation decisions with a view to the supervision of probation measures and alternative sanctions O.J. L377/102 (2008).

[57]Council framework decision 2008/909/JHA of 27 November 2008 on the application of the principle of mutual recognition to judgments in criminal matters imposing custodial sentences or measures involving deprivation of liberty for the purpose of their enforcement in the European Union O.J. L327/27 (2008).

and Sweden), since this act essentially helps to simplify and further facilitate the procedures regulated by the EU instruments. Here, again, all the EU instruments in question allow for more far-reaching cooperation. Denmark and Sweden have also declared that they will continue to apply the Nordic arrangements.[58]

6 Criminal Jurisdiction and Transfer of Criminal Proceedings

In 1970, the chief prosecutorial authorities of the Nordic countries concluded an agreement on the transfer of criminal proceedings in certain cases. The agreement essentially consolidated practice that had been common among the Nordic police and prosecutorial authorities since the 1940s.[59] Like many other Nordic agreements, this agreement does not have the nature of an official treaty and has not been implemented as such in the Nordic states. In practice, however, it has nevertheless been applied as an official treaty.[60] The agreement also does not impose any legal duties on the states per se but, rather, is a practical agreement between the prosecutorial authorities of the states.[61] Here, again, we can see that informal cooperation is the key feature, which is made practically functional due to mutual trust.

The aforementioned agreement makes it possible for charges for an offence that has been committed in one Nordic state to be brought in another Nordic state, if the suspect resides in the latter state and the act in question is also punishable in that state. Under certain conditions, charges may also be brought in the state where the suspect is found instead of in the place where the act was committed. When choosing the proper forum for prosecution, both the interests of the suspect and the possibilities of an effective investigation of the matter should be taken into consideration.[62] Prosecution is then transferred following a request of the competent authority (i.e., a prosecutorial authority) in the Nordic state where the act was committed. The aim is essentially to enable a 'proper administration of justice' that renders it possible to take into account all circumstances that have a bearing on the matter when deciding where to prosecute.[63]

---

[58]See Finnish Government Bills HE 142/2006 vp, pp. 8–9, 25 and 28; HE 47/2007 vp, pp. 11–12 and 40–44; HE 10/2011 vp, pp. 33, 51–52, 62 and 66; and HE 97/2014 vp, p. 7.

[59]Asp (1998), p. 17.

[60]Lahti and Träskman (1994), p. 283.

[61]See Strandbakken (2009), p. 371.

[62]Lahti and Träskman (1994), pp. 283–284.

[63]See Vander Beken et al. (2002), p. 25 and Helenius (2014), p. 135. Cf. also Explanatory report (Basic Solutions) to the European Convention on the Transfer of Proceedings in Criminal Matters (CETS No. 73): 'The transfer of proceedings may take place in respect of any offence which may be prosecuted in the requesting State and in respect of which the condition of dual criminal liability is fulfilled, if such a transfer is in the interests of a proper administration of justice.' It should be noted that among the Nordic States, Finland has not signed the European Convention on the Transfer

In ch. 1 of the Finnish Criminal Code (39/1889), concerning the scope of application of Finnish criminal law (i.e., Finland's criminal jurisdiction), this agreement can be seen firstly in the provision on offences committed by Finns (sec. 6). According to this provision, Finnish law applies to offences committed outside of Finland by Finnish citizens. The provision further states that 'a person who was apprehended in Finland and who at the beginning of the court proceedings is a citizen of Denmark, Iceland, Norway or Sweden or at that time is permanently resident in one of those countries' is deemed equivalent to a Finnish citizen. This means that charges can be brought in Finland against a resident of another Nordic country, even if the only connection to Finland is that the person in question was apprehended in Finland. Consequently, from a jurisdictional perspective, all Nordic citizens are treated equally, with the additional requirement that they are apprehended in the forum state. Today, all Nordic states have a corresponding jurisdictional provision on Nordic residents.[64] Here, one can speak of a 'Nordic' principle of active personality in combination with a principle of apprehension.[65]

The agreement between the Nordic prosecutors can also be seen in the Finnish criminal code's provision on the requirement of a prosecution order by the Prosecutor General (ch. 1, sec. 12). The point of departure of this provision is that offences committed outside Finland may not be investigated or prosecuted in Finland without a separate prosecution order by the Prosecutor General. The idea behind the provision is that the Prosecutor General should make an assessment of whether or not it is appropriate that the case be handled in Finland, taking into consideration both the interests of the suspect and those of other states that might be better suited to deal with the matter. In the same way as mentioned above, this mechanism enables a proper administration of justice in cases of concurrent criminal jurisdiction.[66]

However, an order by the Prosecutor General is not required if the offence was committed in one of the other Nordic countries and the competent public prosecutor of the place of commission has requested that the offence be tried in a Finnish court. In this case, a request of transfer from one Nordic prosecutor to another is sufficient. Since the Nordic agreement on transfer of criminal proceedings is intended to facilitate flexible cooperation between the Nordic prosecutors, the requirement of a separate prosecution order by the Prosecutor General would be contradictory to this purpose.[67] The competent Nordic prosecutors are thus authorised to handle the question of where to prosecute among themselves, without the involvement of any higher prosecutorial authorities.

of Proceedings in Criminal Matters of 1972 (ETS No.073). Iceland has signed the treaty but not ratified it.

[64] Helenius (2014), p. 241 and Elholm and Feldtman (2014), pp. 149–150. The Norwegian criminal code previously did not include such a provision, but today it is found in sec. 5.2.

[65] Helenius (2014), p. 241. 'Active personality' here refers to both the nationality and the domicile of the person, since both connections constitute sufficient grounds for jurisdiction.

[66] See Helenius (2015), pp. 43–47.

[67] Finnish Government Bill HE 1/1996 vp, p. 27.

This form of Nordic cooperation is perhaps the most far-reaching one in comparison to the EU level. In 2009, several Member States put forward an initiative for a framework decision on the transfer of proceedings in criminal matters.[68] The objective of the framework decision would have been to 'increase efficiency in criminal proceedings and to improve the proper administration of justice within the area of freedom, security and justice by establishing common rules facilitating the transfer of criminal proceedings between competent authorities of the Member States, taking into account the legitimate interests of suspects and victims'. However, the framework decision was never adopted due to the entry into force of the Lisbon Treaty, and no similar proposal has been put forward since then.[69] From a jurisdictional perspective, the populations of the EU Member States are not treated as EU citizens but rather as citizens of each Member State. In contrast to the Nordic States, the EU is apparently not yet ready for such a level of mutual trust and profound cooperation.

7 Conclusion

Nordic cooperation is still very much alive in practice, although common legislative efforts (e.g., by the Nordic Criminal Law Committee) have decreased since the 1980's.[70] The latest large-scale common project was the NAW. However, despite EU instruments replacing several of the former Nordic agreements, the Nordic states still continue to apply their own regional framework in many areas.

A few years before the EU cooperation in criminal matters seriously took off in the early 2000s, it was explicitly stated that the Nordic states should endeavour as far as possible to create a 'borderless area for cooperation in criminal matters'.[71] Here, parallels can clearly be drawn to the idea of the EU as a 'single judicial area'. In such an area, not only would judgments and other judicial decisions ideally move freely, but also it would not be of relevance where an offence was committed, since all states would have jurisdiction over all offences committed within the common area. Law enforcement authorities would also be able to move freely and apply coercive and other measures irrespective of national borders.[72] Although the Nordic states cannot yet be said to constitute a 'single judicial area' of their own, one can see that

---

[68] Initiative of the Kingdom of Belgium, the Republic of Bulgaria, the Czech Republic, the Kingdom of Denmark, the Republic of Estonia, the Hellenic Republic, the Kingdom of Spain, the French Republic, the Republic of Latvia, the Republic of Lithuania, Republic of Hungary, the Kingdom of the Netherlands, Romania, the Republic of Slovenia, the Slovak Republic and the Kingdom of Sweden for a Council Framework Decision 2009/…/JHA of … on transfer of proceedings in criminal matters O.J. C219/7 (2009).

[69] On the added value of transfer of criminal proceedings within the EU, see Klip (2016), pp. 533–534.

[70] See Melander (2007), p. 112 and Lappi-Seppälä and Nuotio (2019), pp. 181–182.

[71] See Swedish Government Bill 1999/2000:61, p. 61.

[72] See especially the ideals expressed in Wersäll (2006).

the Nordic cooperation relatively consistently goes deeper than the EU cooperation does.

On the other hand, EU legislation should not necessarily be regarded as something negative that has only encroached upon the 'good old' Nordic cooperation. Simplification and pragmatism are certainly desirable, as long as they do not bring about legal uncertainty or disadvantages for the individual persons involved.[73] EU legislation in the field of judicial cooperation in criminal matters has perhaps resulted in more strictly prescribed formalities, but it has likely also strengthened the procedural rights of suspects, defendants and victims.[74]

Whatever the reasons are for the success of the Nordic cooperation within the area of judicial cooperation in criminal matters, there seems to be agreement that this success is due to one key feature: mutual trust.[75] The foundation for this trust is obviously more solid than that between the EU Member States for several reasons, including legal, political and otherwise societal similarities. However, the characterisation of this trust is also different from that of the EU. Nordic cooperation initially grew out of a perceived practical need for fewer formalities and greater efficiency. This is certainly also true for the development of the EU cooperation, but the Nordic cooperation has not been as ideologically coloured as the EU cooperation. While mutual trust among the EU Member States was more or less declared and demanded, trust among the Nordic states developed naturally and organically: the Nordic states were never required to trust each other but simply decided to jointly do so, because it was perceived as practically feasible.[76] However, even between the Nordic states, trust does not imply blind trust, as is indicated by the retention of a human and fundamental rights clause in regard to cooperation. As has been pointed out many times, the mere fact that trust is declared does not mean that it actually exists.[77] Trust needs to be fostered in order to develop and persist. The Nordic states have strived to do this, not only through common legal solutions but also by learning from each other's legal experiences. There is doubtless still much for the EU to learn from the Nordic states.

[73] See Asp (1998), pp. 34–37 for certain misgivings regarding the Nordic cooperation during the late twentieth century.

[74] On EU measures regarding fundamental and procedural rights, see, e.g., Mitsilegas (2016), pp. 124–211 and Satzger (2018b), pp. 165–169.

[75] See, e.g., Lahti and Träskman (1994), p. 259 and Strandbakken (2009), p. 364.

[76] Cf. Satzger (2019), p. 46.

[77] See, e.g., Suominen (2011), pp. 47–48.

References

Asp P (1998) Nordic judicial co-operation in criminal matters. Uppsala University and Swedish Society for European Criminal Law, Uppsala

Bárd P, van Ballegooij W (2018) Judicial independence as a precondition for mutual trust? The CJEU in minister for justice and equality v. LM. New J Eur Crim Law 3:353–365

Elholm T, Feldtman B (2014) Nordic trends of jurisdiction: an international perspective. In: Elholm T, Feldtman B (eds) Criminal jurisdiction: a Nordic perspective. Djøf Forlag, Copenhagen, pp 149–182

Espina Ramos JA (2019) The European investigation order and its relationship with other judicial cooperation instruments: establishing rules on the scope and possibilities of application. Eucrim 1:53–60

Helenius D (2014) Straffrättslig jurisdiktion. Suomalainen Lakimiesyhdistys, Helsinki

Helenius D (2015) The if, how, and when of criminal jurisdiction: what is criminal jurisdiction anyway? Bergen J Crim Law Crim Just 1:22–47

Helenius D (2019) Mänskliga rättigheter som hinder för överlämning inom EU: en granskning av senaste tids rättspraxis. In: Frände D et al (eds) Juhlajulkaisu Kimmo Nuotio 1959-18/4-2019. Unigrafia, Helsinki, pp 53–75

Klip A (2016) European criminal law: an integrative approach. Intersentia, Cambridge

Lahti R, Träskman PO (1994) Finland: the regionalization of international criminal law and the protection of human rights in international cooperation in criminal proceedings. Int Rev Penal Law 1–2:251–287

Lappi-Seppälä T, Nuotio K (2019) Crime and Punishment. In: Letto-Vanamo P, Tamm D, Mortensen BOG (eds) Nordic law in European context. Springer, Cham, pp 179–199

Letto-Vanamo P, Tamm D (2019) Nordic legal mind. In: Letto-Vanamo P, Tamm D, Mortensen BOG (eds) Nordic law in European context. Springer, Cham, pp 1–19

Mathisen G (2010) Nordic cooperation and the European arrest warrant: intra-Nordic extradition, the Nordic arrest warrant and beyond. Nordic J Int Law 1–33

Melander S (2007) Nordic criminal justice policy: single path or separate ways? In: Husa J, Nuotio K, Pihlajamäki H (eds) Nordic law: between tradition and dynamism. Intersentia, Antwerp, Oxford, pp 109–124

Mitsilegas V (2016) EU criminal law after Lisbon. Hart, Oxford and Portland, Oregon

Satzger H (2018a) Mutual recognition in times of crisis—mutual recognition in crisis? An analysis of the new jurisprudence on the European arrest warrant. Eur Crim Law Rev 3:317–331

Satzger H (2018b) International and European criminal law. Nomos, Beck, Hart, München, Oxford, Baden-Baden

Satzger H (2019) Is mutual recognition a viable general path for cooperation? New J Eur Crim Law 1:44–56

Sicurella R (2018) Fostering a European criminal law culture: in trust we trust. New J Eur Crim Law 3:308–325

Smits J (2007) Nordic law in a European context: some comparative observations. In: Husa J, Nuotio K, Pihlajamäki H (eds) Nordic law: between tradition and dynamism. Intersentia, Antwerp and Oxford, pp 55–64

Strandbakken A (2009) Extradition between the Nordic countries, and the new Nordic arrest warrant. In: Keijzer N, van Sliedregt E (eds) The European arrest warrant in practice. TMC Asser Press, The Hague, pp 363–376

Suominen A (2011) The principle of mutual recognition in cooperation in criminal matters: a study of the principle in four framework decisions and in the implementation legislation in the Nordic member states. Intersentia, Cambridge

Suominen A (2014) The Nordic arrest warrant finally in force. Eur Crim Law Rev 1:41–45

Suominen A, Kvam B (2009) Skjær i sjøen for Norges strafferettslige samarbeid med EU. Lov og Rett, pp 478–492

Thunberg Schunke M (2004) Internationell rättslig hjälp i brottmål inom EU: Effektivitet v. rättssäkerhet. Iustus, Uppsala
Thunberg Schunke M (2013) Whose responsibility? A study of transnational defence rights and mutual recognition of judicial decisions within the EU. Intersentia, Cambridge, Antwerp, Portland
Toftegaard Nielsen G, Elholm T, Jakobsen MN (2017) Kommenteret straffelov: Speciel del. Jurist- Og Økonomforbundets Forlag, København
Tolttila K (2011) The Nordic arrest warrant: what makes for even higher trust? New J Eur Crim Law 4:368–377
Träskman PO (2009) Purchase of a sexual service: a lawful private delight or an offence? A study of criminal legislation in the Nordic countries. Scand Stud Law 290–301
Vander Beken T, Vermeulen G, Steverlynck S, Thomaes S (2002) Finding the best place for prosecution: European study on jurisdiction criteria. Maklu, Antwerpen, Apeldoorn
Wersäll F (2006) Straffrättsligt samarbete i ett gränslöst Norden. Nordisk Tidsskrift for Kriminalvidenskab 2:122–126

Globalisation and Court Practice in Iceland: New Case Law of the Supreme Court in Relation to the EEA Agreement and European Convention on Human Rights

Halldóra Thorsteinsdóttir

Abstract This article examines the status of international treaties in Iceland law and how Icelandic court practice has developed in recent years in that area. With regard to the relationship between domestic law and international law, Iceland adheres to the principle of dualism. This means that international law does not come into force as Icelandic law unless implemented by the legislator. As a result, Icelandic Courts will not, in general, apply provisions of international treaties unless they have been incorporated into Icelandic statutory law. However, this does not mean that international obligation are not fulfilled, as Icelandic Courts will seek to interpret domestic law in line with international obligation to the extent possible. If an international treaty has been implemented into Icelandic law, its provisions are binding like other domestic law. With regard to the EEA Agreement, Icelandic Courts will seek to interpret national law in accordance with EEA obligations and follow the judgments of the EFTA Court if the Icelandic provision in question is open to such an interpretation. With regard to the European Convention on Human Rights, Icelandic Courts will even go a step further, as recent judgments show that Icelandic Courts tend to interpret the human rights provisions of the Icelandic Constitution in line with interpretation laid down by The European Court of Human Rights, even in cases where such an interpretation does not exactly fit within the direct wording of the provision in question. This is due to a special connection between the human rights chapter of the Icelandic Constitution and the Convention, as one of the legislators' main goals when amending the Constitution in 1994 was to bring the human rights chapter more in line with the Convention.

H. Thorsteinsdóttir (✉)
Department of Law, Reykjavik University, Menntavegur 1, 101 Reykjavik, Iceland
e-mail: halldorath@ru.is

L. Ervo et al. (eds.), *Rethinking Nordic Courts*, Ius Gentium: Comparative Perspectives on Law and Justice 90, https://doi.org/10.1007/978-3-030-74851-7_9

1 Introduction

Like other Nordic countries, the Icelandic legal system has experienced rapid changes due to the development of international law in recent years, and an increasingly large proportion of national law is rooted in international agreements the Icelandic state has signed. Icelandic Courts have also been subject to these changes and have had to answer questions regarding the relation between domestic law and international law and the effects of international treaties when interpreting Icelandic statutory law.

The aim of this article is to shed light on the impact of the most important international treaties Iceland has signed on the Supreme Court's case law in recent years. Emphasis will be placed on the European Convention on Human Rights (ECHR) and the EEA Agreement, as these are undoubtedly the international agreements that have had most impact on the Icelandic legal system in recent years.

2 The Status of International Law in Iceland

With regard to the relation between domestic law and international law, Iceland adheres to the principle of dualism. Ratified international treaties therefore do not assume the force of domestic law, as they are only binding according to international law.[1] In other words, domestic law and international law are two separate legal systems, and the rules of international law will not be part of national law without being implemented into national law by the Icelandic Parliament.[2] As a result, individuals and legal persons are unable to invoke directly the international provisions before Icelandic courts. This is in contrast to monistic systems, where international law is seen as an integral part of the national legal system and indeed often prevails in the event of conflict between international law and national law.[3] On the other hand, following the transformation of international legislation into domestic law, international provisions are no longer considered international law in the application of the legislation on the domestic level and will be applied equally to domestic law.

Looking at court practice in Iceland, where international law has been referred to or applied, it is clear that there are many examples of judgments where the courts, by reference to the principle of dualism, have refused to give effect to unincorporated treaties. An example is Case No. 23/1974 of 18 June 1975, which went to trial before the ECHR became a part of domestic law. The case was about lawsuit filed by E against the city of Reykjavík on the grounds that regulations prohibiting him from keeping a dog were contrary to Article 8 of the ECHR. The Supreme Court of Iceland held that the rules in question were not to be disregarded on the grounds that they

[1] Tryggvadóttir and Ingadóttir: Online article: https://www.nyulawglobal.org/globalex/Iceland1.html.

[2] Björgvinsson (2014), p. 26.

[3] Wallace (2005), p. 37.

were contrary to the aforementioned Article, but also pointed out that the Convention had not acquired the status of law in Iceland.[4]

Another example is Case No. 77/1985 of 25 November 1985. The case concerned Mr. Kristinsson conviction for a traffic offence by a district criminal court where the deputy judge who heard the case was also a deputy chief of police. Before the Supreme Court, the defendant, claimed that the judgment should be annulled on the grounds that a judge that else served as a chief of police could not be impartial. He maintained that the double role exercised by the judge while handling his case violated the principles enshrined in Articles 2 and 61 of the Icelandic Constitution and Article 6 of the ECHR on the right to an impartial tribunal, but the latter was solely binding upon the Icelandic state as an international obligation. The Supreme Court stated that under the Icelandic judicial structure, judicial powers in district courts outside Reykjavik were in the hands of the town magistrates and district commissioners who served collaterally as chiefs of police. No specific facts had been demonstrated to establish the impartiality of the town magistrate or his deputy. The Court therefore dismissed Kristinsson's claim.[5] Even though it did not refer to the ECHR in its reasoning, the Court clearly affirmed its position that incorporation of the convention was needed before it could be applied in domestic law.[6]

This, however, does not mean that Icelandic Courts do not consider unimplemented international obligations. Although international treaties do not have the same status as domestic law without being implemented by the Parliament, Icelandic courts seek to interpret the national law in accordance with international obligations insofar as possible.[7] This is due to the principal rule that domestic law should be interpreted in accordance with international law insofar as possible.[8] On the other hand, as a general rule, the domestic rules prevail if there is a conflict between the rules in question.[9]

Despite this, there are judgments in which it might be said that Icelandic Courts have gone quite a long way in interpreting domestic law in accordance with international law. At least a few judgments exists, especially in the 1990s, in which the result is not easily reconciled with the dualist principle. An example is Case No. 494/1991 of 6 June 1992. It was a criminal case against a defendant who could not speak Icelandic. He was therefore assisted during the proceedings by a court interpreter. According to relevant domestic rules at the time, the cost of the work of court interpreters was to be counted as legal costs and should therefore by imposed on the defendant, if convicted. However, the Supreme Court of Iceland stated that the

[4]See also Case No 273/1986 of 10 March 1987.

[5]It should be noted that the European Commission of Human Rights held unanimously that the proceedings were in breach of Article 6 of the Convention.

[6]Hannesson (2011), p. 434.

[7]See for instance Case No 177/1998 of 4 February 1990 and Case No 120/1989 of 9 January 1990.

[8]Björgvinsson (2020), p. 103.

[9]Thorarensen (2017), p. 343.

relevant provisions should be interpreted in light of Article 6 of the ECHR and that the cost should therefore be paid by the State Treasury.[10]

In the Supreme Court's Case No 120/1989 of 9 January 1990, the Icelandic judicial structure was addressed again and a demand was made for the annulment of a district court judgment in a criminal case, on the grounds that the district court judge had not been impartial. However, this time the Court stated that changes had occurred in the particular Icelandic conditions that formed the background for the judicial structure. It then referred to the decisions of the ECHR Commission, which had concluded that the domestic proceedings in the aforementioned Kristinsson case had been in breach of Article 6 of the ECHR. The Commission had come to the conclusion that the fact that a judge in a criminal case was also a deputy chief was contrary to the aforementioned Article.

Many scholars have written about these judgments.[11] Regarding Case No. 494/1991 of 6 June 1992, many have addressed the fact that, as the Icelandic provisions in question were incompatible with the ECHR, not only was the domestic law interpreted as consistent with the ECHR provisions but in fact the latter was given primacy over conflicting statutory domestic law.[12] At the same time, it should be noted that the judgment was made in special circumstances, following the result from the European Commission on Human Rights regarding the Kristinsson Case No. 77/1985 of 25 November 1985, which is discussed above. In other words, Icelandic Courts were under pressure regarding Iceland's obligations according to the Convention.[13] In addition, the case was about defendants' constitutional rights in criminal cases and, therefore, about rights that were important from both international and national perspectives in relation to human rights. Finally, it should be mentioned that if a conflict occurs between domestic law and international law, Icelandic Courts will be more willing to apply interpretation more compatible with the international rule if the international commitment in question also affects interpretation of the Icelandic Constitution.[14] This is especially the case with the ECHR, as described later in this article.

Most international treaties or agreements Iceland has ratified have not been incorporated into the national system. They are therefore not a part of the domestic law. Examples include the Universal Declaration of Human Rights from 10 December 1948, the International Covenant on Civil and Political Rights and the Covenant on Economic, Social and Cultural Rights from 16 December 1966, the International Convention on the Elimination of All Forms of Racial Discrimination from 21 December 1965 and the Convention on the Elimination of all Forms of Discrimination against Women from 18 December 1979. However, the legislator has on many

[10] Björgvinsson (2015), p. 96.

[11] See for example Björgvinsson (2015), p. 99; Arnardóttir (2018), p. 16; and Aðalsteinsson (1990), p. 22.

[12] See for example Björgvinsson (2015), p. 99; Arnardóttir (2018), p. 16; and Aðalsteinsson (1990), p. 22.

[13] Thorarensen (2019), p. 84.

[14] Thorarensen and Leifsson (2011), p. 34.

occasions considered it necessary or desirable to incorporate treaties in order to give their provisions legal effect on the national level.[15] This was done, for instance, with the two most important and influential treaties Iceland has entered: the ECHR and the EEA Agreement. Of all of Iceland's international obligations, these two treaties are without doubt the ones that have had most impact in Iceland. The following sections will discuss the status of these agreements in Icelandic law and their effect on court proceedings.

3 The European Convention on Human Rights

3.1 The Status of ECHR in Icelandic Law

Iceland signed the ECHR in 1953, but it did not have the force of law in Iceland until 1994, when it was incorporated and given the status of statutory law by the ECHR Act.[16] Prior to the incorporation, Icelandic courts had stated that, as the ECHR did not have the status of law, courts would not rely on it if there was a conflict between the international obligation and national law. However, international obligations such as the ECHR were considered relevant when interpreting national rules governing similar rights. This could for example be seen in the Asmundsson case,[17] where the Supreme Court took Article 8 of the ECHR into account when stating that the National Audit Office access to medical records was in breach of the principle of privacy.[18]

Since its incorporation, the ECHR has had the status of statutory law. This was clearly stated in the ASÍ case,[19] where the District Court ruling, which was confirmed by the Supreme Court, said: 'The provisions of the ECHR do not enjoy the status of constitutional law.' However, there has been a tendency to consider it as having a special status in Icelandic law and Icelandic Courts tend to mention its provisions when referring to corresponding provisions of the Constitution.[20] This is, firstly, because of the nature of the rights guaranteed in the treaty as fundamental rights. Secondly, it has been mentioned that the ECHR's status has to be seen in the light of its international background, and the principle of interpreting national law in accordance with international law.[21] Thirdly, and perhaps most importantly, the ECHR has gained a special status in Icelandic law due to its direct connection to the Icelandic Constitution.[22] One of the primary goals in the Constitutional changes in 1995 by the

---

[15] Björgvinsson (2015), p. 64.

[16] Act No. 62/1994.

[17] Case no. 5/1989 from 20 January 1989.

[18] Thorarensen (2017), pp. 345–346.

[19] Case No. 167/2002 from 14 November 2002.

[20] See for example Case No. 65/1999 from 30 September 1999 and Case No. 214/2014 from 20 November 2014.

[21] Björgvinsson (2008), p. 312.

[22] Björgvinsson (2017), p. 66.

Constitutional Act No. 97/1995, which occurred shortly after the Act on the ECHR was implemented in Icelandic law, was to take into account the international obligations that Iceland had undergone through its membership in international human rights treaties and especially the ECHR.[23] The human rights chapter of the Constitution was thus linked directly to ECHR's provisions. In the Explanatory Report to the law, it is also stated that although the ECHR should not have the status of Constitutional law, and that its provisions did not change the Constitution, it had to be borne in mind that the main reason for implementing it in domestic law had been to increase human rights protection in Iceland and that implementing it would lead the Courts to be more willing to interpret the Constitution in accordance with the Convention.[24] Due to this, it has been said that the ECHR in fact has a special status in Icelandic.

3.2 The Status of the Judgments of the European Court of Human Rights

3.2.1 Formal Status

With regard to the effects of the judgments of the European Court of Human Rights (ECtHR) in Icelandic law, the principle of dualism applies. Article 2 of the Icelandic ECHR Act No. 62/1994 provides that the decisions of the European Commission of Human Rights, the ECtHR and the Committee of Ministers of the Council are not binding in Icelandic domestic law. In the Explanatory Report, it is also stated that the incorporation of the ECHR as statutory law does not automatically change the status of the decisions of the above-mentioned international institutions in the domestic system, since these decisions only concern the question of whether the Icelandic state has breached its obligations under the Convention.[25] The decisions are therefore only binding under international public law, and they cannot overturn or invalidate domestic legislation or judgments of the national courts.

This reflects the firm position of the legislature that, despite the incorporation of ECHR, the principle of dualism still applies with regard to the decisions of these institutions. This principle position is further reiterated in the Explanatory Report, where it is emphasised that these decisions do not acquire binding legal effect in the national legal system in the same way as the text of the ECHR. It is up to the national courts and authorities to interpret the provisions of the ECHR independently. It is further reiterated that the incorporation does not involve any transfer of judicial power. The Council of Europe and the ECtHR only have the power to declare whether the ECHR has been breached, and their decisions do not annul domestic judgments. Moreover, it is for the Icelandic authorities, which operate on the basis of Icelandic

[23] Parliamentary Reports, A, pp. 2073 and 2077–2081.

[24] Parliamentary Reports, A, p. 2080.

[25] Parliamentary Reports A 1992–1993, Doc. No. 1160, pp. 5847–5939. Björgvinsson (2015) p. 144.

law, to enforce the obligations established by the decisions of the ECtHR and other institutions.[26]

An example of this understanding is Case No. 371/2010 of 22 September 2010, where the Supreme Court clearly stated that the incorporation of the ECHR into Icelandic law did not change the principal rule of dualism in terms of the relationship between international law and domestic law. Another example is the Jóhannesson and Jónsson case,[27] in which the Supreme Court dismissed a case which had been reopened by a special committee on the grounds of a judgment in which the ECtHR had stated that a judgment of the Supreme Court had been in breach of the *ne bis in idem* rule. When dismissing the case, the Supreme Court stated that the rules did not include permission to reopen a case because of a judgment of the ECtHR which established a breach of the ECHR. It then said that, according to Article 2 of the ECHR Act,[28] the judgments of the ECtHR were not binding in Icelandic law and that the Explanatory Report following the bill stated explicitly that despite the incorporation of the Convention, the dualism doctrine still applied.

3.2.2 Indirect Binding Effect in Practice

Despite a few judgments in 1990–2000,[29] the implementation of the ECHR into Icelandic law did not seem to have the same effect on Constitutional interpretation as one might have expected. The Convention was indeed often mentioned in judgments of Icelandic Courts, but it did not seem to have much independent effect on the interpretation on the human rights provisions in the Constitution.[30] Nor did Icelandic courts put much emphasis on the judgments of the ECtHR when establishing the rights derived from the Constitution regarding human rights. They mentioned the relevant Article of the ECHR, but direct references to ECtHR judgments were rare. However, in recent judgments, the influence of ECtHR case law has been more noticeable.

Today, Icelandic courts tend to refer to ECtHR case law more often than before. It is also clear that although the courts do not consider the ECtHR judgments to be formally binding, the ECtHR case law affects the interpretation of the Convention in Icelandic law as well as the human rights provisions of the Constitution. This has been increasingly noticeable since 2010, and today it seems highly unlikely that a judgment is made in which the Constitution's human rights provisions are not put

[26]Björgvinsson (2015), pp. 144–145.

[27]Case No. 12/2018 from 21 May 2019.

[28]Act no. 62/1994.

[29]See, e.g., Case No. 167/2002 from 14 November 2002 and Case No 120/1989 from 9 January 1990. In the latter case, The Supreme Court of Iceland even interpreted a provision of the Constitution regarding eligibility of a judge in accordance with a provision of the Convention guaranteeing same rights. See also the interview with Róbert Ragnar Spanó ECHR justice in Kjarninn: https://kjarninn.is/frettir/2019-03-18-segir-tregdu-islenskra-domstola-ad-fylgja-domum-mde-vera-undanhaldi/.

[30]See, e.g., Case No. 475/2008 from 30 April 2009, Case No. 454/2009 from 11 March 2010 and Case No. 328/2008 from 5 March 2009.

into context with ECHR's provisions and the rules the ECtHR has laid down in its practice. Three examples are Case No. 215/2014 of 18 December 2014, Case No. 467/2015 of 13 August 2015 and Case No. 367/2016 of 30 March 2017. In the latter case, Article 71 of the Constitution on freedom of privacy was interpreted in accordance with comparable provision of Article 8 of the ECHR. With regard to the interpretation of Article 71 of the Icelandic Constitution on freedom of privacy, the Supreme Court held, after referring to the Case of Paradiso and Campanelli v. Italy of 24 January 2017 regarding family relationship and children born to surrogate mothers:

> According to Article 71 (1) everyone should enjoy freedom of privacy and family. Among things that have to be taken into account when interpreting the provision is how The European Court of Human Rights has interpreted a parallel provision in Article 8 (1) of the European Convention on Human Rights.[31]

This case is an example of how Icelandic Courts have become more willing to take into account the case law of the Court in Strasbourg and demonstrates that the ECHR is in fact an integral element when it comes to interpreting the human rights provisions of the Constitution.[32]

Another example is Case No. 283/2016 of 21 September 2017, in which the Supreme Court departed from previous judgments because of new judgments from the European Court of Human Rights regarding the rule of *ne bis in idem*.[33] In other words, the Strasbourg Court's judgments were considered de facto 'binding', despite the wording of Article 2 of law no. 62/1994. In addition, it might be mentioned that the case was decided by seven Supreme Court justices, something which is only done in particularly important cases.[34] The Appeal Court (Landsréttur) judgment in Case No. 209/2018 of 9 March 2018 is also a good example, as the Landsréttur interpreted provisions on cost insurance in a new way because of a certain ECtHR judgment regarding access to justice according to Article 6 of the ECHR.

In all of these cases, Icelandic Courts have taken a step further in interpreting the Icelandic Constitutional provisions on human rights in accordance with the ECHR and ECtHR case law. In other words, ECtHR case law was decisive in interpreting the interplay of the constitution and general provisions.[35]

In light of this, and despite what has previously been said about the formal status of the ECHR and ECtHR judgments in Icelandic law, it is safe to say that the effect of the ECtHR on court practice in Iceland is considerable, at least to the extent that Icelandic provisions are in parallel with those of the ECHR. If the ECtHR has interpreted the Convention in one of its rulings, Icelandic Courts will follow that interpretation insofar as possible when interpreting the human rights provisions of the Icelandic Constitution. This applies at least when the provision in the Constitution

[31] Author's translation.

[32] Spanó: Lunch meeting in Nauthóll, 2 November 2018.

[33] Spanó: Lunch meeting in Nauthóll, 2 November 2018.

[34] Arnardóttir (2018), p. 21.

[35] Interview with Róbert Ragnar Spanó, ECHR justice in Kjarninn.: https://kjarninn.is/frettir/2019-03-18-segir-tregdu-islenskra-domstola-ad-fylgja-domum-mde-vera-undanhaldi/.

mirrors a provision in the ECHR, and guard the same rights as the ECHR. This was specially stated in the abovementioned Case No. 371/2010 of 22 September 2010, in which the Supreme Court of Iceland emphasised that Icelandic courts would consider ECtHR's decisions when interpreting the ECHR when applied as a part of the domestic law. It is also clear that the Supreme Court will, when examining each case, consider whether the national authorities have sufficiently taken into account the principles flowing from its judgments.[36]

In relation to the effects of the ECHR on Icelandic Court procedures, it might also be mentioned that a new Court of Appeal, Landsréttur, started its work in Iceland on 1 January 2018, replacing the former two-tiered system with a three-tiered system. One of the aims of the establishment of this court, which is a second instance court handling cases between the District Courts and the Supreme Court of Iceland, was to fulfil ECHR obligations in relation to review before a higher court. At the moment of writing, a case concerning the appointment of judges at the new court is still pending before the Grand Chamber of the ECtHR. The case concerns the claim of Mr. A, who was convicted at a district court of driving without a valid license and of being under the influence of narcotics. He appealed the decision to the new Court of Appeal, in which one of the judges was Ms. E, one of the candidates whom the Minister of Justice had appointed to the court even though she was not among the 15 candidates initially selected by a special evaluation committee. By a judgment of 23 March 2018, the Court of Appeal upheld the District Court's judgment on the merits and that judgment was appealed to the Supreme Court. Before the Supreme Court the applicant insisted that the Court of Appeal's judgment be quashed and the case be remitted for retrial. His claims were based, *inter alia*, on the ground that the appointment of Ms. E. had violated the general principle that authorities should appoint the most qualified candidate for office. Therefore, Ms. E's appointment had not been in accordance with the law as required by Article 59 of the Constitution and Article 6 of the ECHR. This had also resulted in Mr. A not enjoying a fair trial before an independent and impartial tribunal as stipulated in Article 70 of the Constitution and Article 6 of the ECHR. By a judgment of 24 May 2018, the Supreme Court rejected the applicant's claims and upheld the judgment of the Court of Appeal. With regard to the complaint concerning the appointment of Ms. E, the Supreme Court held that although the appointment of the judges had not been fully in accordance with law, it had been a breach that did not have significance. The fifteen judges had been appointed in accordance with formal procedural rules of the Judiciary Act,[37] and it could not therefore be said that rulings of the Court of Appeal, which Ms. E delivered along with others, were on that ground a 'dead letter' as claimed by Mr. A. When it was assessed whether Mr. A had not enjoyed the right to a fair trial before an independent and impartial tribunal according to the Constitution and Article 6 of the ECHR, account had to be taken of the fact that the appointment of all fifteen of the judges had become a reality upon the signing of their letters of appointment and that they all fulfilled the requirement of the Judiciary Act to be appointed in the light of

[36]See, e.g., Case No. 33401/02 from 9 June 2009.

[37]Act No. 50/2016.

their professional experience and legal knowledge. They had independence in their judicial work but also a duty to perform it under their own responsibility, and the Constitution precluded them from being discharged except with judicial decision. Therefore, in spite of the flaws in the procedure by the Minister of Justice, it could not be said that there was sufficient reason to justifiably doubt that Mr. A had enjoyed a fair trial before independent and impartial judges. That decision was then brought before the European Court of Human Rights. In its Chamber judgment of 12 March 2019, the ECtHR held that there had been a violation of Article 6 as the bench at Landsréttur had not been established by law. At the time of this writing, that judgment is now under consideration at the Grand Chamber.

4 The EEA Agreement

4.1 The Status of the Agreement in Icelandic Law

As Iceland is not a member of the European Union (EU), its relation to the EU is mainly based on the EEA Agreement, which came into effect in 1994 and was incorporated by the EEA ACT.[38] The EEA Agreement unites the EU member states and the three EFTA/EEA states (Iceland, Liechtenstein and Norway) into a single market governed by the same basic rules. EEA law originates from EU law. As a matter of principle, the EU law rules concerning the single market have been transposed and are being transposed to the EEA legal order. According to the EEA agreement, the EFTA States are obliged to implement and apply EU legal acts that have been incorporated into the Agreement by the EEA Joint Committee.

All the relevant Internal Market legislation is integrated into the EEA Agreement so that it applies throughout the whole of the EEA. The core of the rules relates to the free movement of goods, capital, services and persons throughout the 31 EEA States – the 28 EU States and 3 of the EFTA States. In addition, the EEA Agreement covers horizontal areas such as social policy, consumer protection, environment, company law, statistics, tourism and culture. However, the common policies in the fields of agriculture, fisheries, taxation, foreign trade and currency are not part of EEA law.

4.2 The EFTA Surveillance Authority and the EFTA Court

The successful operation of the EEA depends upon uniform implementation and application of the common rules in all EEA States. The EFTA Surveillance Authority (ESA) monitors compliance with the EEA Agreement in the EFTA States in the same way that the EU Commission does in the EU Member States. In addition, the EFTA Court operates in parallel to the Court of Justice of the European Union, with a

[38] Act No. 2/1993.

jurisdiction with regard to EFTA States. The Court is mainly competent to deal with infringement actions brought by the ESA against an EFTA State with regard to the implementation, application or interpretation of EEA law rules, for giving advisory opinions to courts in EFTA States on the interpretation of EEA rules and for appeals concerning decisions made by the ESA.[39]

To this end, a two-pillar system of supervision has been devised: the EU Member States are monitored by the EU Commission and the EFTA States are party to the EEA Agreement by the ESA.

4.3 *Protocol 35 of the EEA Agreement*

From Article 7 EEA, it follows that EU secondary legislation will not become a part of the national legal order until specific measures have been taken to implement it. The direct applicability and direct effect of secondary legislation, including EU regulations, are therefore dependent on it having been incorporated in the national legal order in accordance with constitutional and other domestic legal standards. This clearly corresponds to the principle of dualism.[40]

However, the Icelandic state is bound by Protocol 35 of the EEA Agreement, whose aim is to help achieve a homogeneous EEA without requiring the states to transfer legislative powers to any institution of the EEA. The EFTA Court has also stated that national Courts need to interpret national law in accordance with EEA rules.[41] The Sole Article of Protocol 35 says:

> For cases of possible conflicts between implemented EEA rules and other statutory provisions, the EFTA States undertake to introduce, if necessary, a statutory provision to the effect that EEA rules prevail in these cases.[42]

Article 3 of the EEA Act in Iceland was meant to implement this rule. It says that domestic law and regulations shall be interpreted, to the extent appropriate, in accordance with the EEA Agreement and the regulations incorporated into the agreement. Accordingly Iceland has adopted a specific rule providing for consistent or friendly interpretation in line with the EEA commitments. However no clear-cut primacy rule has been implemented as would seem to be the requirement by the wording of Protocol 35.[43] It is also clear that article 35 only regulates the situation in which an implemented EEA rule conflicts with another statutory rule. It does not regulate the situation in which an EEA rule is not implemented.

It has therefore been debated whether Article 3 really provides for the primacy of EEA law as required by Protocol 35.[44] The explanatory notes refer to the Icelandic

---

[39] https://eftacourt.int/the-court/introduction/.

[40] Björgvinsson (2015), p. 70.

[41] Hreinsson (2014), p. 274.

[42] Article of Protocol 35.

[43] Björgvinsson (2015), p. 70.

[44] Pétursson (2017), p. 207; Björgvinsson (2006), p. 132; and Einarsdóttir (2007), pp. 25–35.

legal tradition that domestic law shall be interpreted in line with international obligations to the extent possible. It also refers to the legal tradition that law of the status of lex specialis prevails over other law and that an EEA rule would often be considered a rule of that type. The explanatory note then mentions that Article 3 provides that domestic law arriving from the EEA agreement will in general be considered a lex specialis rule with regard to younger law in conflict. The latter will therefore not prevail unless especially decided by the legislature.[45] However, this understanding is not in accordance with the direct wording of Article 3.

4.4 *Article 3 in Court Practice*

The first time the Icelandic Supreme Court interpreted Article 3 was in Case No. 477/2002 from 15 May 2003. Mr. E claimed that the State had breached Article 14 of the EEA Agreement by demanding higher taxes on books in foreign languages (24,5%) than on Icelandic books (14%). The Court referred to the explanatory notes previously mentioned and interpreted Article 14 of the EEA Agreement to be lex specialis that should prevail over the older tax rules in question.

This judgment led many to believe that the Supreme Court would interpret Article 3 in a way consistent with what was stated in the explanatory notes regarding EEA rules as a lex specialis.[46] However, another approach can be found in more recent judgments, where it is stated that, despite Article 3 and the fact that domestic law shall be interpreted in line with international obligations, an interpretation of any kind will not exceed the wording of written statutory law. In other words, an interpretation *contra legem* is not permitted.

This was for example stated in Case No. 79/2010 of 9 December 2010. The case concerned a vendor's and importer's liability for damages caused by candy it sold and imported. Iceland had implemented a directive on a product liability (85/373/EB) with Law No. 21/1991, but in addition to the manufacturer's and importer's liability the Icelandic provision made the distributor responsible as well. This went beyond the directive in question, and at the time the European Court of Justice had already determined that a similar provision in Danish law was not in accordance with the directive. Nonetheless, the Supreme Court of Iceland refused to set the wording of the Icelandic provision aside because of Article 3. It said:

> Article 3 of law No. 2/1993 states that statutes and regulations shall be interpreted in so far as appropriate in accordance with the EEA to accord with the EEA Agreement and the rules based thereon. According to this, the wording of domestic law will insofar as possible be interpreted in line with the EEA rules. It will not, however, lead to a result where the wording of domestic law is ignored.[47]

---

[45] Parliamentary Reports, A 1991–1992, p. 5922.

[46] See Líndal and Magnússon (2011), p. 176; Tynes (2002), pp. 494–495; and Pétursson (2017), p. 209.

[47] The law in question, Act No. 25/1991 on Product Liability, was subsequently amended in accordance with the EEA-rule and is now Act No. 3/2014.

The Supreme Court's Case No. 92/2013 of 13 October 2014 is another example where a clear and precise wording of domestic legislation stands in the way of EEA conformity. In this case, Mr. G wanted a tax decision deemed invalid, because he did not get a tax relief that he would have gotten if he had lived in Iceland instead of Denmark at a certain time. The Supreme Court concluded that Iceland had not implemented the relevant directive (the Citizenship Directive)[48] sufficiently. Therefore, Icelandic tax authorities could not have relied on the EEA rule in question in their decision because it was contrary to the clear and precise wording of a domestic rule. This is in accordance with the fact that Article 35 of the EEA Agreement does not regulate non-implementation.[49]

It follows that if the provisions of national law cannot be interpreted in accordance with the provisions of the EEA rule, the Icelandic law should apply, provided that the traditional Icelandic legal explanatory rules do not lead to a different conclusion. In other words, the implemented EEA rules will not prevail.[50]

On the other hand, if the wording of the Icelandic provision in question is in line with EEA law, Icelandic courts will seek to conduct EEA-consistent interpretation. The Supreme Court's Case No. 169/2011 from 17 January 2013 is a good example, as the Supreme Court interpreted the meaning of 'deposit' in accordance with the EFTA Court's advisory opinion on the matter.[51] Another example is the WowAir case,[52] in which the flight company WowAir claimed that another company, Icelandair, had a competitive advantage regarding time slots at the Keflavik airport. In reaching a conclusion, Icelandic courts interpreted domestic legislation in line with EEA law and in that connection mentioned the interpretation rule in Article 3.

According to the aforementioned judgments, it is clear that clear and precise wording of a domestic legislation prevents EEA-consistent interpretation if the provisions in question are in conflict. Recent judgments seem to exclude the possibility of a priority effect of implemented EEA rules when in conflict with younger domestic law. The Supreme Court seems to think of Article 3 as an interpretative method to be used when interpreting law arising from the EEA Agreement rather than as a rule prescribing the priority of implemented EEA rules.[53] Domestic law is only interpreted in accordance with EEA law to the extent possible within the wording of the national law. This is in line with the wording of Article 3 of Law No. 2/1993, although it is clear that the provision does not meet the obligations arising from Protocol 35.[54] This does not mean that individuals have no remedies to rely on in terms of wrongful

---

[48]Directive 2004/38/EC of the European Parliament and of the Council of 29 April 2004 O.J. L158/77 (2004).

[49]See also Case No. 160/2015 from 13 May 2015, Case No. 243/2015 from 26 November 2015 and Supreme Court Case No. 10/2013 from 24 January 2013.

[50]Einarsdóttir and Stefánsson (2020), p. 350.

[51]Case No. E-17/11, EFTA Ct. Rep. 2012s. 916.

[52]Case No. 95/2015 from 18 February 2015.

[53]Pétursson (2017), p. 207; Björgvinsson (2006), p. 132; and Einarsdóttir (2007), pp. 25–35.

[54]Pétursson (2017), p. 223.

implementation, as they may seek damages on that ground before Icelandic Courts.[55] The ESA can also bring an infringement action against the Icelandic State before the EFTA Court with regard to the implementation.[56] In light of this, it has been pointed out that the application of properly implemented EEA rules in Iceland hardly meets the requirement of Protocol 35, as the EEA rules do not have priority over incompatible Icelandic law. In light of the Supreme Court's ruling on the subject and the wording of Article 3 of the EEA Act, it seems clear that in order to fulfil that obligation it could be necessary to implement Protocol 35 in a way more in line with the aim of that protocol.[57]

5 Summary

It is safe to say that the relationship between Icelandic Courts and European law has improved significantly in recent years. Although some judgments may be indeed be found in which the Courts have been a bit hesitant in this regard, this only seems to be the case when the clear wording of the Icelandic provision in question does not leave room for the interpretation required by the international rule. Overall, numerous judgments show clear efforts to interpret domestic law in accordance with international law obligations, especially with regard to the EEA agreement and the ECHR. To some extent, the latter seems, at least in recent years, to have had a more direct effect on the Court practice, as Icelandic courts seem to be willing to give the human rights provisions of the Icelandic Constitution the same meaning as derived from the ECHR according to the ECtHR's case law. This is, among other things, due to the relationship between the Icelandic ECHR Act and the human rights chapter of the Icelandic Constitution, as addressed in Sect. 3. The EEA agreement in Icelandic law differs from ECHR, as the regulatory framework resulting from the contract is more complicated and complex, and the implementation into national law and the wording of the national rule following the implementation are not always exactly the same as laid down by the European law. According to a few judgments of the Supreme Court, that can be a problem, as the wording of a domestic legislation can prevent EEA-consistent interpretation if the provisions in question are in conflict.

References

Aðalsteinsson R (1990) Alþjóðlegir mannréttindasáttmálar og íslenskur landsréttur. Tímarit Lögfræðinga 1:3–27

Arnardóttir O (2018) Nálægðarregla, svigrúm til mats og samband Mannréttindadómstóls Evrópu við landsrétt. Bókaútgáfan CODEX, Reykjavík

[55] See, e.g., Case No. 236/1999 from 16 December 1999.

[56] Pétursson (2017), p. 222.

[57] Einarsdóttir and Stefánsson (2020), p. 353.

Björgvinsson D (2006). EES-réttur og landsréttur. Bókaútgáfan CODEX, Reykjavík

Björgvinsson D (2008) Lögskýringar. Kenningar, aðferðir og sjónarmið við skýringu og beitingu laga. Reykjavík

Björgvinsson D (2014) Staða dóma Mannréttindadómstóls Evrópu í íslenskum landsrétti. Tímarit Lögréttu 1:23–42

Björgvinsson D (2015) The intersection of international law and domestic law—a theoretical and practical analysis. Edward Elgar Pub, Cheltenham

Björgvinsson D (2016) The effect of the judgments of the ECtHR before the national courts—a nordic approach? Nord J Int Law 85:303–321

Björgvinsson D (2017) Mannréttindasáttmáli Evrópu. Meginatriði, skýring og beiting. Mannréttindasamningar Sameinuðu þjóðanna. Meginreglur, framkvæmd og áhrif á íslenskan rétt

Björgvinsson D (2020) Þjóðaréttur og landsréttur í dómum Hæstaréttar. Hæstiréttur í hundrað ár, pp 95–132

Einarsdóttir M (2007) Forgangsáhrif Réttilega Innleiddra EES-Reglna. Tímarit Lögréttu 1:29–34

Einarsdóttir M and Stefánsson S (2020) Beiting innlendra EES-reglna í íslenskum rétti í ljósi bókunar 35. Hæstiréttur í hundrað ár, pp 341–357

Hannesson Ó (2011) The status of non-implemented EEA law in Iceland: lessons from the judicial reactions of the supreme court to international law. Nordic J Int Law 80:425–458

Hreinsson P (2014) Samræmd EES-Túlkun. Tímarit Lögfræðinga 3:273–307

Líndal S, Magnýsson S (2011) Réttarkerfi Evrópusambandsins og Evrópska efnahagssvæðisins. Hið íslenska bókmenntafélag, Reykjavík

Pétursson G (2017) Forgangur EES-reglna. Hvað er að frétta af bókun 35?. Fullveldi í 99 ár. Safn ritgerða til heiðurs dr. Davíð Þór Björgvinssyni sextugum. Reykjavík

Thorarensen B (2017) Staða og áhrif Mannréttindasamninga Sameinuðu þjóðanna í íslenskum rétti. Mannréttindasamningar Sameinuðu þjóðanna. Meginreglur, framkvæmd og áhrif á íslenskan rétt, pp 339–381

Thorarensen B (2019). Stjórnskipunarréttur – Mannréttindi. Bókaútgáfan Codex, Reykjavík

Tryggvadóttir R, Ingadóttir Þ.: Online article, https://www.nyulawglobal.org/globalex/Iceland1.html

Thorarensen B and Leifsson P (2011) Þjóðaréttur. Bókaútgáfan Codex, Reykjaví

Tynes D (2002) Ys og þys út af engu? Hugleiðingar um bókun 35 við samninginn um Evrópska efnahagssvæðið. Úlfljótur 3:473–496

Wallace R (2005) International law, 5th edn. Sweet & Maxwell, London

The Changing Role of Nordic Courts

Martin Sunnqvist

Abstract The Supreme Courts in all the Nordic countries reserve, and exercise, the power to set aside unconstitutional laws. In this way, they protect the rule of law and the human rights that are enshrined in their national constitutions. However, they go about this in different ways and treat different constitutional rights in ways distinct from one another. In this chapter, I discuss the development of the diversified judicial review of legislation in the Nordic countries. I also discuss the independence of their judiciaries in the light of the latest developments in Europe. Finally, I discuss the importance of developing standards for the interpretation of case law on these constitutional issues. Recent development brings with it two consequences for Nordic courts: the task of assessing the independence of judiciaries in other EU states, and questions about how the rule of law and the independence of the judiciary can be strengthened at home.

1 Introduction

According to theories of separation of powers, courts serve an important role in deciding whether legislation falls within the boundaries defined by constitutions, especially as regards the protection of human rights and fundamental freedoms. In the Nordic countries, the role of the courts has been evolving since the early nineteenth century. The courts originally concentrated exclusively on applying law to criminal and civil cases and distributing justice to the citizens. But, at different times in the nineteenth and twentieth centuries, they have also found themselves competent to determine whether state authorities are acting within their constitutional boundaries, and whether legislation has respected human rights and fundamental freedoms. I will discuss this development briefly in this section. I will also discuss the courts' constitutional relationship to international documents such as the European Convention on Human Rights (ECHR), and whether the courts have granted a 'preferred position' to some constitutional rights.

M. Sunnqvist (✉)
Faculty of Law, Lund University, Box 207, 22100 Lund, Sweden
e-mail: martin.sunnqvist@jur.lu.se

L. Ervo et al. (eds.), *Rethinking Nordic Courts*, Ius Gentium: Comparative Perspectives on Law and Justice 90, https://doi.org/10.1007/978-3-030-74851-7_10

The roles of Nordic courts have not only changed in terms of the intensity of constitutional review—through a recent, still ongoing change, national courts in one EU member state are called upon to assess the independence of courts in another EU state. This change was effected by threats against the independence of the judiciary in Poland, among other countries. Thus, ample reason exists to discuss the common principles for institutional judicial independence.

As regards this latter development, it is crucial that judgments be well-reasoned and conclusive. Even though the EU institutions have some power to put legal pressure on countries whose governments fail to respect the rule of law and judicial independence, persuasive pressure directly from legal actors is also important. I will therefore discuss the interpretation of precedents, focusing on Nordic constitutional cases.

2 Constitutional Roles of Nordic Courts

There are important differences between the court systems of the Nordic countries. The eastern Nordic countries, Sweden and Finland, have separate systems of administrative courts, leaving only criminal and civil cases to the general courts. In the western Nordic countries, Denmark, Norway and Iceland, administrative cases are brought before the general courts. Conversely, the absence of constitutional courts is a feature common to all the Nordic countries. Thus, the Supreme Courts (and in Sweden and Finland also the Supreme Administrative Courts) are the highest courts deciding cases wherein constitutional issues are at stake.[1]

The development of constitutions in each country has been different. Whereas the modern Norwegian state was established through a constitution (fundamental law, *grunnlov*) adopted during the gap in 1814 between the Danish and Swedish ruling kings of Norway, the Swedish constitution (instrument of government, *regeringsform*) of 1809 and the Danish constitution (fundamental law, *grundlov*) of 1849 were designed to replace largely absolutist rule with a system that distributed powers between king, parliament and courts. In Finland, the old Swedish constitutional acts from 1772 and 1789 remained valid during the period of Russian rule, but a new constitution (instrument of government, *regeringsform*) was adopted in 1919. Further, every Nordic country has instituted several constitutional amendments over the years, most importantly Sweden and Finland, where the constitutions were totally re-written through the instrument of government (*regeringsform*) of 1974 and the fundamental law (*grundlag*) of 1999, respectively.[2]

The constitutional role of the courts, and the courts' role in ensuring that the legislature and the public authorities keep within the bounds of their decision-making

---

[1] See e.g. Bull (2018) pp. 61–64, Smith (2018) pp. 109 and Nylund and Sunde (2019) pp. 201–213.

[2] See e.g. Suksi (2018) pp. 9–42 and Husa (2019) pp. 41–60.

power, have developed at different times in the Nordic countries.[3] The Norwegian Supreme Court was the first Nordic supreme court to apply the constitution in its decision making. It did this as early as the early nineteenth century, whereas the supreme courts of Denmark, Sweden, and Iceland were very reluctant to apply their own constitutions until the late twentieth century, even though there were cases in the early-twentieth-century where the possibility of constitutional review of statutes was presupposed. This difference is, I believe, explained by the fact that the modern Norwegian state was established through the adoption of the constitution, similar to the way the union of the United States was established through its federal constitution. Indeed, in one 1866 case, Norwegian Supreme Court Chief Justice Lasson used in his judgment phrases reminiscent of Chief Justice Marshall's in the 1803 case *Marbury* v. *Madison*.[4]

In Finland, the historical development has been unique because the courts guarded the old Swedish constitutional laws from the eighteenth century, still valid in Finland after 1809, against pressure from Russian authorities in the late nineteenth and early twentieth century.[5] This development came about because the Finnish state was established through the old constitutions together with the promise by the Russian Emperor, in his capacity as Grand Duke of Finland, to respect them.[6] After the adoption of the constitution in 1919, the Finnish courts became institutions very loyal to the legislative function of the parliament, a characteristic that only began to change with the enactment the new fundamental law of 1999, which paved the way for a more constitutional role for the courts. According to Sect. 106 of Finland's constitution, Finnish courts can set aside statutory provisions which are 'obviously' contrary to the constitution.

The obviousness requirement was taken from the Swedish instrument of government (*regeringsform*), adopted in 1974 but amended in 1980 with a provision that confirmed the right of the courts to set aside unconstitutional statutes but required the unconstitutionality to be obvious (Chap. 11 Sect. 14). In 2010 this requirement was abolished and replaced with a clause reminding the courts that parliament is the premier representative of the people and that constitution is above law.[7]

The important changes, however, came in case law at different times in each country. In Norway, the Supreme Court was rather reluctant to exercise its competence to review legislation in the 1950s and 1960s but did exercise it in a case in 1976.[8] The court's competence in this arena was confirmed in an amendment to the constitution in 2015 (Sect. 89). In the other countries, some cases demonstrate

---

[3]See, generally, as regards Sect. 2 of this chapter for a much more detailed discussion Sunnqvist (2014a). For a very good overview of the history of constitutionalism and judicial review, see Halpérin (2019). An overview in English over the development in Norway is provided by Kierulf (2018), and a Nordic comparison in English by Smith (2018) pp. 107–132. The development of judicial review in Iceland is analysed by Helgadóttir (2009).

[4]Sunnqvist (2014a) pp. 246–255 with references, esp. Smith (1990) p. 430.

[5]Sundberg (1983).

[6]Sunnqvist (2014a) pp. 1023–1027.

[7]Sunnqvist (2014a) pp. 742–750, 912–914.

[8]Rt. [Retstidende] 1976 p. 1.

extraordinarily clearly that the courts consider themselves competent to act as constitutional courts; examples to that effect occurred in the year 1999 for Denmark,[9] 2013 for Sweden[10] and 2014 for Finland.[11] The judgments from 1976 (Norway) and 1999 (Denmark) were based on the countries' respective national constitutions, but in the judgments from 2013 and 2014, the Swedish and Finnish courts, respectively, invoked instead the EU Charter of Fundamental Rights and the ECHR. This also indicates the Europeanisation of judgments concerning fundamental rights issues.

Thus, each of the Nordic countries' supreme courts safeguard the rule of law and the human rights enshrined in the constitutions. They do so, however, in different ways. Not only do they treat different constitutional rights differently,[12] they also have different ways of understanding the relationship between rights guaranteed in national constitutions and similar rights in international documents such as the ECHR.

3 Variations of Judicial Review

In the aforementioned 1976 case, the Norwegian Supreme Court not only took the lead again among the Nordic countries in the arena of judicial review, it also spearheaded an interesting development regarding different standards of review for different constitutional rights. In so doing, the Court relied on a 1952 case but developed it further.

In the 1952 case, the Supreme Court differentiated between constitutional rights which directly protect individual citizens and constitutional rules that distribute powers between the parliament and the government. If the parliament had delegated powers to the government, the judgment held, courts should show restraint in their judicial review, since parliament could itself act if the government used the delegated powers in a way that infringed the parliament's rights.[13]

In the 1976 case, the Norwegian Supreme Court further developed the reasoning in the case from 1952 by dividing judicial review of legislation into three categories: constitutional rules about freedom and security of the individual, economic rights of the individual and the relationship between the branches of government. The last category is to be supervised the least strictly, while individuals' constitutionally guaranteed freedom and security receive the highest level of protection. The individuals' economic rights should be in an intermediate position. In the event that there are

[9]UfR [Ugeskrift for Retsvæsen] 1999 p. 841.

[10]NJA [Nytt Juridiskt Arkiv] 2013 p. 502 and HFD [Högsta förvaltningsdomstolens årsbok] 2013 ref. 71.

[11]KKO [Korkein Oikeus] 2014:67.

[12]See for a more detailed discussion Sunnqvist (2014a) pp. 1059–1070 and Sunnqvist (2015).

[13]Rt. 1952 p. 1089. See Sunnqvist (2014a) pp. 525–528 for a more detailed discussion.

doubts about whether a rule is in contradiction to the constitution, the courts should interpret it in a way that does conform with the constitution.[14]

This development coincided with writings in Danish legal literature that suggested that the freedom of speech should have a preferred position in relation to other constitutional rights.[15] This perspective has then been further developed in Denmark[16] as well as in Norway.[17]

Following this development in the other Nordic countries, when, in 2010, the Swedish constitution was to be amended, it was suggested in the *travaux préparatoires* that central parts of the constitutionally guaranteed rights and freedoms should be supervised more strictly by the courts than other constitutional norms.[18]

Despite these parallel developments, there is no commonly accepted view on whether different constitutional rights should be divided into different categories at all, or, if so, how such categories should be organised. I have suggested[19] that cases from, above all, the Norwegian, Danish and Swedish Supreme Courts from the nineteenth and twentieth centuries can form a basis for arranging the issues into seven categories.

Especially noteworthy, I find reason to place one category highly in the hierarchy of the intensity of judicial review: the responsibility of judges to ascertain fair trial and due process of law.[20] Through the case law related to Article 6 of the ECHR, these principles have become understood as fundamental for the protection of human rights and freedoms. This is also why it is paramount to address current threats against judicial independence in some European countries since the protection of human rights is thereby also threatened.

The seven categories I have identified are, ordered from those most rigorously protected by judges to those less so, as follows:

1. The responsibility of a judge for the functioning of the judicial procedure,
2. The responsibility of a judge for access to judicial procedure,
3. The responsibility of a judge for legality,
4. The protection of fundamental rights and freedoms, and the balancing of those rights and freedoms,
5. The protection of economic rights, and the balancing of those rights,
6. The protection of other types of rights,
7. The supervision of the relations between the other two branches of government.

---

[14] Rt. 1976 p. 1. See Sunnqvist (2014a) pp. 702–707 for a more detailed discussion.

[15] Germer (1973).

[16] Rytter (2001).

[17] Smith (1990), Smith (1993) pp. 328–329.

[18] Proposition to the parliament 2009/10:80 pp. 147–148.

[19] See for a more detailed discussion Sunnqvist (2014a) p. 1059–1070, Sunnqvist (2015), Sunnqvist (2017).

[20] Cf. also Smith (1993) p. 239–242.

Numbers 4, 5 and 7 relate to the Norwegian cases, the discussions in the Danish and Norwegian literature and the *travaux préparatoires* to the latest Swedish constitutional amendments. Numbers 1 through 3 relate to the increasing importance of procedural rights: the right to a fair trial and the legitimacy in judging and in measures taken by the state against individuals. Number 6 relates to the many welfare rights included in the EU Charter of Fundamental Rights and, for example, the Convention on the Rights of the Child; it is still not fully clear exactly how these rights, that are sometimes rather vague, will be interpreted by the Nordic supreme courts.

4 Arrangements Securing the Independence of Courts

Procedural rights and the right to a fair trial relate closely to the institutional independence of courts and the judges. The judicial protection of constitutional rights requires an independent judiciary that can assess whether a statute is in contravention to the constitution or not. It is required for the courts to be independent, i.e. that the judges are irremovable. A further essential characteristic for an independent judiciary, highlighted especially in many eastern European countries after the fall of the Berlin Wall and the dissolution of the Soviet Union, is that the judiciary should be represented by a judicial council.

According to articles 2 and 3 of the Universal Charter of the Judge, adopted by the central council of the International Association of Judges in 1999 and updated in 2017, a judicial council is defined as follows:

> In order to safeguard judicial independence a Council for the Judiciary, or another equivalent body, must be set up, save in countries where this independence is traditionally ensured by other means.
>
> The Council for the Judiciary must be completely independent of other State powers.
>
> It must be composed of a majority of judges elected by their peers, according to procedures ensuring their largest representation.
>
> The Council for the Judiciary can have members who are not judges, in order to represent the variety of civil society. In order to avoid any suspicion, such members cannot be politicians. They must have the same qualifications in terms of integrity, independence, impartiality and skills of judges. No member of the Government or of the Parliament can be at the same time member of the Council for the Judiciary.
>
> The Council for the Judiciary must be endowed with the largest powers in the fields of recruitment, training, appointment, promotion and discipline of judges.
>
> It must be foreseen that the Council can be consulted by the other State powers on all possible questions concerning judicial status and ethics, as well as on all subjects regarding the annual budget of Justice and the allocation of resources to the courts, on the organisation, functioning and public image of judicial institutions.[21]

---

[21] Universal Charter of the Judge, adopted by the IAJ Central Council in Taiwan on November 17th, 1999, updated in Santiago de Chile on November 14th, 2017; https://www.iaj-uim.org/universal-charter-of-the-judge-2017/

Even though this document was adopted among judges themselves, the concept of a judicial council, and the demand that one should be organised in order to protect judicial independence, has been widely accepted outside of the judiciaries also, especially by different fora within the Council of Europe, such as its parliamentary assembly,[22] the council of ministers[23] and the Venice Commission.[24] The European Network of Councils for the Judiciary (ENCJ), co-funded by the EU, accepts as members only national institutions from EU member states which are independent of the executive and legislative branches, or are autonomous, and which ensure the final responsibility for supporting the judiciary in the independent delivery of justice.[25]

The Nordic country with the best safeguards for the independence of its judiciary is Denmark. The administrative office, *Domstolsstyrelsen*, is accepted as an independent judicial council by the ENCJ. It was organised in 1999 in its current form, for the precise purpose of safeguarding judicial independence.[26] The Danish administrative office was partly used as a model for its Norwegian counterpart, *Domstolsadministrasjonen*, established in 2002.[27] Finland has established its own such administrative office, *Domstolsverket*, in 2020, which has a board consisting of eight members, six of whom are judges.[28] The board appoints the director of the office.[29] In Iceland, similarly, the administration of the courts was transferred to an administrative office, *Dómstólasýslan*, in 2016.

The most problematic of the Nordic countries in this area is Sweden. Swedish courts were originally administered directly by the Ministry of Justice and partly by the courts of appeal, but a national courts administration was set up in the 1970s. At that time, the government believed that the courts were not so different from public administrative agencies and authorities.[30] This led to the present situation, where the administrative office, *Domstolsverket*, has a director general appointed by the government, through whom the government might well exert influence over the judiciary. Happily, the government has refrained from doing so. There were discussions over the years about reforming the office,[31] and in 2018, the parliament took an unanimous legislative initiative to rearrange the administrative office and—as an effect

---

[22] Resolutions no. 1685 (2009) and 2040 (2015), www.assembly.coe.int.

[23] Recommendations Rec. (1994) 12 and Rec. (2010) 12, www.coe.int.

[24] See e.g. the opinion 16 January 2020 no. 977/2019, Sect. 9, www.venice.coe.int.

[25] Article 6 (1), Statutes, Rules and Regulations of the International Not-For-Profit Association European Network of Councils for the Judiciary (i.n.p.a), https://www.encj.eu/statutes.

[26] Christensen (2003).

[27] NOU [Norges Offentlige Utredninger] 1999:19.

[28] https://valtioneuvosto.fi/sv/artikeln/-/asset_publisher/1410853/uudelle-tuomioistuinvirastolle-johtokunta.

[29] https://oikeus.fi/sv/index/ajankohtaista/tiedotteet/2019/06/tuomioistuinvirastonylijohtajaksirik ujaakkola.html.

[30] Proposition to parliament 1973:90 p. 233, see also SOU [Statens Offentliga Utredningar] 1972:15 pp. 190–191.

[31] Sunnqvist (2014a) pp. 856–857.

of events in Poland—to write into the constitution the number of, and retirement age for, supreme court justices.[32] This legislation is currently being prepared.[33]

The establishments of courts by law is an important safeguard. Recently, the new Icelandic court of appeal was scrutinised by the European Court of Human Rights.[34] Since a new court was erected, the judges were to be appointed by the parliament. However, the minister of justice suggested, in part, other judges than had been proposed by the judicial council, without giving the reasons for doing so. The parliament then approved the minister's proposal through one joint vote instead of one vote for each judge. This process failed to follow the established rules, and the European Court of Human Rights did not consider the court of appeal as a court established by law.

5 A 'Rule-Of-Law-Check' of Other Judiciaries

In many countries in eastern Europe, the independence of the judiciaries is currently under threat. Hungary and Poland, for example, are among EU countries where the development of an independent judiciary has gone in the wrong direction,[35] even though the judiciaries of both countries after the fall of the Berlin Wall and the dissolution of the Soviet Union were organised with, among other safeguards, judicial councils.[36] Most relevant to this chapter, however, is that the developments in Poland and Hungary are not simply the problems of our European neighbours to be denounced from afar. Quite the contrary, the national courts of the Nordic EU countries Denmark, Finland and Sweden might be called upon directly to assess the independence of their colleagues, judges in other EU member states.

Before discussing the protection of judicial independence through other national courts, we must examine *Aranyosi & Căldăraru* v. *Generalstaatsanwaltschaft Bremen*.[37] The *Aranyosi* case concerned whether the Hungarian prisons under review had such a low human-rights standard that handing people over to Hungary to serve

---

[32]Report of the parliamentary constitutional committee 2017/18:KU36, Decision in Parliament 18 April 2018.

[33]Directive 2020:4, *Förstärkt skydd för demokratin och domstolarnas oberoende*.

[34]ECtHR, Judgment [GC] 1 December 2020, Guðmundur Andri Ástráðsson v. Iceland, appl. no. 26374/18.

[35]See e.g. the CCJE 'Report on judicial independence and impartiality in the Council of Europe Member States 2017', CCJE-BU(2017)11 (published in February 2018); as regards Hungary 'Report on the fact-finding mission of the EAJ to Hungary', May 3rd, 2019; https://www.iaj-uim.org/iuw/wp-content/uploads/2019/05/Report-EAJ-Hungary.pdf, and as regards Poland See Marcin Matczak, 'Poland's Constitutional Crisis: Facts and interpretations', 2018;

https://www.iaj-uim.org/iuw/wp-content/uploads/2018/07/Polands-Constitutional-Crisis-Facts-and-interpretations.pdf.

[36]Hungary: Országos Bírói Tanács (National Judicial Council), Poland: Krajowa Rada Sądownictwa (National Council of the Judiciary).

[37]CJEU Judgment 5 April 2016, Case C-404/15 and C-659/15 Paul Aranyosi and Robert Câldâraru (ECLI:EU:C:2016:198).

prison sentences according to the European Arrest Warrant (EAW) procedure would violate Art. 4 of the EU Charter—'No one shall be subjected to torture or to inhuman or degrading treatment or punishment'. The Court of Justice of the European Union (CJEU) stressed the principles of mutual recognition and mutual confidence between member states but also ruled that these principles had limits that could 'in exceptional circumstances' provide protection for citizens, e.g., when there is a real risk that the individual concerned will be exposed to inhuman or degrading treatment. Later, the European Court of Human Rights found that the Hungarian prison conditions had improved,[38] meaning that the factual situation underlying the individual assessments made in the *Aranyosi* judgment had changed.

The present government in Poland has taken measures to weaken the independence of its judiciary and the judicial review of legislation. Poland's Judicial Council and Constitutional Court can no longer work independently, and disciplinary proceedings are instituted against judges who act independently. What was initially brought before the CJEU was a 'reform' aimed at lowering the retirement age for Supreme Court justices, thereby enabling the government to choose which judges could remain on the court and to appoint new ones. This would affect, among others, the first president of the court, Małgorzata Gersdorf.

This question also came before the CJEU in the context of the EAW. In the LM case, the CJEU ruled, just as in *Aranyosi*, that an individual assessment must be done. The executing judicial authority must examine whether, in the circumstances of the case, there are substantial grounds to believe that the individual will be dealt with by a court whose independence and impartiality are compromised.[39]

In this context, it should be noted that the CJEU earlier in 2018 decided a case in which the court stressed certain criteria for the assessment of the independence and impartiality of a court—criteria that were repeated in the LM case and that created an avenue for national courts to ask the CJEU about their own independence.[40] This might be a solution to the problem that Polish courts, for example, are, at the time of this writing, moving increasingly towards losing their independence, which, according to normal CJEU standards, would render inadmissible their questions for preliminary rulings. This consequence would effectively sever the lifeline between the CJEU and those national courts, like Poland's, whose independence is under attack.[41]

The Commission has also brought proceedings before the CJEU, and the court has declared that by lowering the retirement age of the judges appointed to the Polish Supreme Court, by applying that measure to the judges already appointed to that

---

[38]ECtHR Decision 23 November 2017, Domján v. Hungary, appl. no. 5433/17.

[39]CJEU Judgment 25 July 2018, Case C-216/18 PPU Minister for Justice and Equality [LM] (ECLI:EU:C:2018:586).

[40]CJEU Judgment 27 February 2018, Case C-64/16 Associação Sindical dos Juízes Portugueses (ECLI:EU:C:2018:117).

[41]In this context, have benefitted very much from discussions with Professor Xavier Groussot. Cf. his presentation at the annual meeting 2019 at the Swedish Association of Judges, https://domareforbundet.se/index.php?special=download&hash=e1d3c401a2bcc5a4ca024047da211f90&_benonce=0a794010ee.

court before 3 April 2018, and by granting the President of the Republic discretion to extend the period of judicial activity of judges of that court beyond the newly fixed retirement age, Poland has failed to fulfil its obligations under Article 19(1) TEU.[42] At the time of this writing, a case is pending in which the Commission seeks an order declaring that Poland has failed to fulfil its obligations under the second subparagraph of Article 19(1) in the Treaty of the European Union and the second and third paragraphs of Article 267 in the Treaty on the Functioning of the European Union. These violations include: allowing the content of judicial decisions to be treated as a disciplinary offence so far as concerns judges of the ordinary courts; having such alleged offences be tried by a court that is not independent; and limiting, by the possibility of the initiation of disciplinary proceedings, the courts' right to refer questions for a preliminary ruling to the CJEU.[43] The marshal of the Polish senate asked the Venice commission to assess Poland's proposed changes to the laws regarding the Supreme Court and the National Council for the Judiciary, and the commission concluded that Poland should re-establish the independence of the National Council for the Judiciary and transform the (non-independent) disciplinary chamber of the Supreme Court to an ordinary chamber of that court.[44]

The CJEU's judgment in the LM case means that EU-member state national courts, including those in the Nordic countries Denmark, Sweden and Finland, may have to assess whether the independence of the judiciary in another member state is endangered, and if so, whether this could affect an individual who is to be surrendered to that state's judicial authority. The national court performing the assessment can request from the issuing judicial authority any supplementary information that it considers necessary in determining whether there is a risk that the individual will be dealt with by a compromised court.

The Supreme Court of Ireland was the first European supreme court to handle these difficult issues. The court criticised the way the CJEU required from it to do the assessment whether surrendering the individual to the Polish courts would put him at risk of not having a fair trial. The court held as follows:

> It should be said that the test posited in the judgment of the C.J.E.U. is not one that is easy to apply. Normally, it might be said that where systemic deficiencies of any kind are identified, it becomes unnecessary to identify the possibility of those deficiencies taking effect in an individual case. This is particularly so where the value concerns one that is essential to the functioning of the system of mutual trust. . . . It is also inescapable in the logic of the judgment of the C.J.E.U. that it is possible that there should be systemic deficiencies apparent at the level of the court before whom the individual is to be tried and, yet, for it to be determined that surrender should not be refused because it has not been established that those deficiencies will operate at the level of the individual case, having regard to the person charged, the offence with which he is charged, and the factual context which forms the basis of the European arrest warrant (para. 75 of the L.M. judgment).[45]

---

[42] CJEU Judgment 24 June 2019, Case C-619/18 European Commission v. Republic of Poland (ECLI:EU:C:2019:531).

[43] Case C-791/19 Commission v. Poland. An interim decision was granted April 8, 2020.

[44] Opinion 16 January 2020 no. 977/2019, Sect. 9; https://www.venice.coe.int/webforms/documents/?pdf=CDL-PI(2020)002-e.

[45] Minister for Justice & Equality v. Celmer, S:AP:IE:2018:000,181, Sect. 81.

It is, of course, extremely difficult to assess whether general changes in a court system have reached the point that there is a great enough risk that precisely the person to be surrendered will not receive a fair trial. As the Irish Supreme Court mentioned elsewhere in its decision, this is rather an issue to be tried in such cases as *Commission* v. *Poland* however 'extremely serious' and 'troubling'[46] the situation in Poland is. Notwithstanding, a German court, Oberlandesgericht Karlsruhe, has indeed decided against the surrender of a suspect to Poland because of doubts whether a fair trial will be granted there. This decision entailed the German court asking the Polish authorities detailed questions about the independence of their courts.[47] The fact that these issues are being addressed directly in this way, will hopefully persuade the Polish government (and others with similar policies) to respect judicial independence. These examples tend to reinforce the value of judicial independence, and the support thereof, in the Nordic countries.

This brings me to the question about the persuasive power of these judgments. A decision entered by an Irish or a German court is not a binding authority to a Nordic court, but such a decision may provide, thus far, the only available guidance for Danish, Finnish and Swedish courts to themselves try the independence of other national courts, as the Irish and German courts did the courts in Poland. The nature and extent, therefore, of the persuasive authority[48] of the Irish Supreme Court's judgment will be of critical importance going forward.

6 Case Law and Interpretation of Precedents in the Nordic Countries

The growing case law on constitutional matters in the Nordic countries raises the question: how are these cases to be interpreted? The literature has generally been scarce on the interpretation of precedents in the Nordic courts, and the courts have no generally used theories about *ratio decidendi, obiter dicta* or distinguishing. Also entering into this issue is the difference in the length and degree of detail found in Supreme Court judgments; whereas the Danish courts still give very short reasons for their judgments, the Norwegian Supreme Court has a tradition of lengthy opinions in a style more similar to judges' opinions in common-law courts.[49] Meanwhile, the Swedish Supreme Court has over the last decades transitioned from brevity to lengthier discussions on law and facts. This lack of definite standards, and the stylistic dissimilarities among the Nordic courts, has provoked discussions about how judgments should be interpreted.

The importance of court judgments as a source of law, whether and to what extent they are binding or how to understand their persuasive authority, has come

[46]Minister for Justice & Equality v. Celmer, S:AP:IE:2018:000,181, Sect. 87.

[47]Oberlandesgericht Karlsruhe, Beschluss vom 17.2.2020 – 301 AR 156/19.

[48]See Glenn (1987).

[49]Cf. Blume (1989).

under recent discussion, especially in Sweden. The background is that there has been no generally accepted method for interpreting precedents. Professor of private law Christina Ramberg has recently authored discussions on the Swedish Supreme Court's approach to the interpretation of precedents, especially as regards private law. Ramberg prescribed a method to identify and to apply the legal rule that follows from a precedent. In the first step, identifying the rule, she has enumerated three models—the rule model, the result model and the purpose model. These three models can be used for different types of precedents. The rule model identifies rules or principles explicitly used by the Supreme Court, for example, *pacta sunt servanda*. The result model relates to the facts of the case and the practical outcome based on those facts. Finally, the purpose model focuses on the court's balancing the reasons for and against different solutions. The next step, after identifying the legal rule through the method outlined above, and after determining a precedent's relevance or irrelevance, and whether there are reasons to overrule it, is to apply the rule. This entails ascertaining whether the facts in the precedent and the present case are similar or dissimilar, that is, whether the precedent should be followed or can be distinguished.[50]

The model Christina Ramberg suggests has provoked discussions about the interpretation of precedents in both Swedish criminal law and constitutional law. In criminal law, the interest of unity in the application of law has enjoyed particular importance, especially when accounting for the principle of legality. The judgments of the Supreme Court, therefore, are not only considered to have persuasive authority but also to be binding to some degree.[51] In constitutional law, however, many expert observers find the role of precedents to be less clear.[52]

In my view,[53] there is, as regards most precedents, reason to combine Ramberg's rule model and result model. Nordic courts often identify a rule or a principle to be applied to the case, and such rule or principle can sometimes be construed very broadly. I think, therefore, that the power of a precedent often becomes clearer if one keeps in mind the facts present in the case and the outcome. Only then can one see how the Supreme Court actually applied the rule or principle, and one can then analyse whether the present case is similar to or different from the precedent.

I further think that Christina Ramberg does well to single out the precedents where supreme courts engage in balancing the reasons for and against different solutions—what she calls the purpose model. It is my overall impression that this method is much used in Nordic constitutional cases wherein, for example, restrictions to the freedom of expression must be deemed necessary to a democratic society, or restrictions to the right to property must be found to be based on a public interest. These decisions often depend on balancing the reasons for restricting a right against the right itself. The historical basis for this type of reasoning can be found in the configuration of many ECHR articles.

---

[50] Ramberg (2017).

[51] Borgeke and Månsson (2019) pp. 19–23.

[52] Nergelius (2017).

[53] Sunnqvist (2016).

Another principle that could be identified is that new obligations for citizens cannot be introduced through case law but instead require legislative support. This is a fundamental principle in Nordic law, embodied in the concept of *hjemmel* in Denmark and Norway and the 'principle of legality' in Sweden and Finland, and also extends beyond criminal law. It is an interesting question in its own right how far the courts' power to develop law through precedent might extend into areas of law which have not been covered by legislation.[54]

7 The Relationship Between the ECHR and National Constitutions in Nordic Case Law

Nordic supreme courts have acted differently regarding the relationship between similar constitutional rights preserved by international bodies like the ECHR and in their own national constitutions. The Norwegian Supreme Court seems not to hesitate to use distinct but nonetheless similar standards in parallel, including standards that are not legally binding.[55] By contrast, Danish lawyers are more keen to maintain a separation between the Danish constitution and the ECHR, apparently because the Danish constitution is extremely difficult to amend, which motivates the courts to avoid effectively amending it by interpreting it in light of the ECHR and the case law of the European Court of Human Rights.[56]

In two cases the Supreme Court of Sweden has tried to distinguish between the role of the ECHR as a treaty, on the one hand, and as incorporated into Swedish law as a statute, on the other.[57] Sweden is bound by the ECHR as a treaty, but that treaty-status does not make the ECHR directly applicable in Swedish courts. Therefore, the ECHR has been adopted verbatim into Swedish statutory law; there is also a section of the Swedish constitution forbidding the legislature to write laws that contravene the ECHR.[58]

The first of these two cases concerned an individual's right to compensation in the form of damages or leniency in punishments when court proceedings lasted too long and the right to a trial within reasonable time had been set aside.[59] The Supreme Court in its decision wrote that the ECHR has a 'double importance'.[60] As a treaty, the ECHR is relevant if the case concerns whether Swedish legislation or case law differs from the ECHR in such a manner that constitutes a breach of the treaty. This could be the case if an entire 'regime in Swedish law',[61] that is an established

[54] Lassahn (2017) pp. 18–32, 241–262.

[55] Skoghøy (2013), Kierulf (2018) pp. 255–257.

[56] Christensen (2011) pp. 254–257.

[57] NJA 2012 p. 1038 and NJA 2013 p. 502.

[58] Chap. 2 Sect. 19 Instrument of Government (*regeringsformen*).

[59] NJA 2012 p. 1038.

[60] NJA 2012 p. 1038 Sects. 13–16.

[61] NJA 2012 p. 1038 Sect. 14 ('*den svenska ordningen*').

set of rules or procedures, is contradictory to the ECHR and must be set aside or modified. If, however, a court is to decide a single case where a provision of the ECHR is relevant and a statute could be interpreted in conformity with the ECHR, it is not controversial that any court makes its own interpretation of the articles in the convention.

Professor of public law Hans-Gunnar Axberger has recently criticised this case law, arguing that it causes unclarity.[62] Indeed, as a judge, I believe that it is virtually impossible to differentiate between judging according to a rule in a treaty and to the same rule in a Swedish statute. But another point comes with the distinction: that the Supreme Court has itself distinguished between single cases wherein the articles in the convention can be brought with little controversy into discussion about the construction of a law and cases wherein an entire 'regime' in Swedish law called into question. Such a 'regime' could involve, for example, whether the Swedish system of tax surcharges is contravening the *ne bis in idem* principle in Article 4 of Protocol 7 to the convention.

The Supreme Court had to address exactly this problem in 2013. The Supreme Court clarified that its discussion about a 'regime', in contrast to a single case, did refer to precisely these more controversial issues of conformity between the ECHR and Swedish law.[63] The Supreme Court then outlined reasons for a certain degree of judicial restraint if a 'regime' of some dignity was to be found in contravention of the ECHR. The Supreme Court introduced four aspects for courts to consider:

1. The importance of the right in question,
2. The type of legislation affected,
3. Legal and practical consequences that will follow if the court sets aside the 'regime', and
4. Whether the legislature has had opportunities to adapt the Swedish law to the ECHR requirements.

The case must be viewed with an understanding that the Swedish 'regime' regarding tax surcharges had been controversial for a long time, and that the Supreme Court in an earlier case had taken a position of judicial restraint.[64] The earlier instance of judicial restraint can be explained by the lack of certainty at that time what the ECHR actually required,[65] though it is rather more difficult to explain the restraint that prevailed in another case in 2010 when the case law of the European Court of Human Rights was clearer.[66]

The Supreme Court found that the Swedish 'regime' of tax surcharges was to be set aside. Its main arguments did not relate in detail to the four aspects above since the CJEU had already set aside the Swedish 'regime' as regards the value-added

[62]Axberger (2018) pp. 771–777.

[63]NJA 2013 p. 502.

[64]NJA 2000 p. 622.

[65]Sunnqvist (2014b) pp. 390–393.

[66]NJA 2010 p. 168. Cf. the ECtHR judgments 10 February 2009 Zolotukhin v. Russia, appl. no. 14939/03, and 16 June 2009 Ruotsalainen v. Finland, appl. no. 13079/93.

tax, but as regards the third and fourth aspects, the court noted that the 'regime' was already partly set aside, which made the consequences of setting aside the rest of the 'regime' less interfering, and that the legislature had known since 2009 of the developing case law of the European Court of Human Rights concerning the *ne bis in idem* principle.[67] The court also noted that the *ne bis in idem* principle was protected both according to the ECHR and the EU Charter of Human Rights, and that the right ought to be equally treated in the two articles.[68] The Supreme Administrative Court reached the same conclusion as did the Supreme Court.[69]

We might better conceive this distinction drawn between a 'regime' and a single case by understanding the Supreme Court's need at the time of a vehicle to free itself from its own earlier restraint. In the 2012 case, the Supreme Court also held that when a court in a single case interprets the ECHR, it might do so in a way that gives wider rights to individuals than what follows from the Convention and the case law of the European Court of Human Rights.[70] Such construction permits courts to expand rights guaranteed under the ECHR, but not to restrict them.

Professor Axberger has criticised the view that influence of the European systems of human rights is always beneficial and instead champions the fundaments of the national legal systems.[71] I would counter that fundamental rules in national procedural law—which have their background in a common European legal culture from the Middle Ages onwards[72]—such as the right to a fair trial, have only gained importance through the case law concerning ECHR Art. 6. A dialogue within the judiciary and between judiciaries, and between courts and legislators, continues to develop these principles to the benefit of individual citizens.

A more nationally oriented body of case law built upon these common European principles can be seen in two recent cases decided by Sweden's Supreme Court. In the first, the Swedish Supreme Court invoked a new rule in the Swedish constitution about the right to a fair trial.[73] In the second, it interpreted the constitutional right to property in a new way.[74] In this latter case, the Supreme Court invoked a theory of proportionality brought into Swedish law through the Supreme Administrative Court[75] and with its origins on the continent, especially in German law. Without the influences from the European Court of Human Rights and the CJEU, this strengthening of our national constitutional rights would have been unlikely to occur.

---

[67]NJA 2013 p. 502 Sect. 58.

[68]NJA 2013 p. 502 Sect. 59.

[69]HFD 2013 ref. 71.

[70]NJA 2012 p. 1038 Sect. 15.

[71]Axberger (2018) pp. 782–786.

[72]Brundage (2008).

[73]NJA 2015 p. 374.

[74]NJA 2018 p. 753.

[75]RÅ [Regeringsrättens årsbok] 1999 ref. 76.

8 Concluding Remarks

The legal developments I have summarised here show that the Nordic courts have taken a step forward, no longer simply applying the statutes provided by the legislature, but acting as independent institutions empowered to balance rights and interests according to both their national constitutions and to international charters of rights; they have articulated reasons for their assessments, reasons that can afterwards elicit discussion and interpretation and enter into dialogues on legal matters both in the international sphere and in other countries. What remains—as always, it seems—is to find the way to safeguard the independence of the courts in the future. The recent lessons from Poland and Hungary show, unfortunately, that edifices that might quite recently have been firmly established can with shocking rapidity be torn down.

In the EU, at least, the interaction between national courts and both international courts and courts of other nations shows that the attacks on independence of courts in one country quickly sparks reactions from the other member states. This, comfortingly, shows that the EU system and mutual recognition mean that a country cannot hide behind its national sovereignty, but must continue to respect the principles of rule of law and the *Rechtsstaat,* the independence of the judiciary, and the protection of human rights. We have accumulated enough historical experiences already to show us why we need these principles. Still, it remains unclear whether other countries' reactions will in fact be able to stop the deterioration of the rule of law and the *Rechtsstaat.*

The notion of persuasive authority discussed here gives reason to examine the historical experiences that remind us why protecting human rights, the rule of law and *Rechtsstaat,* and the independence of the judiciary, is necessary. The necessity to discuss these experiences seems to be growing today, and our desire to avoid a repetition of any abuses of these agreed upon ideals means that we lawyers have ahead of us a task that is complex and difficult but vitally important.

References

Axberger HG (2018) Rättigheter. Sverige, EKMR och EU:s rättighetsstadga. Svensk Juristtidning 2018, pp 759–786, 849–875

Brundage JA (2008) The medieval origins of the legal profession. Canonists, civilians, and courts. University of Chicago Press, Chicago, London

Blume P (1989) Retsafgørelser Som Retskilde. Ugeskrift for Retsvæsen 1989B:201–214

Borgeke M, Månsson Ch (2019) Studier rörande allmän straffrättspraxis m.m. Jure, Uppsala

Bull T (2018) Institutions and divisions of power. In: Krunke H and Thorarensen B (eds), The Nordic Constitutions. A Comparative and Contextual Study. Hart Publishing, Chicago/London

Christensen JP (2003) Domstolene – den tredje statsmagt. Magtudredningen. Århus

Christensen JP (2011) Højesteret og statsmagten In: Højesteret – 350 år. Gyldendal, Copenhagen

Germer P (1973) Ytringsfrihedens væsen. Juristforbundet, Copenhagen

Glenn HP (1987) Persuasive authority. McGill Law J 32(2):261–298

Halpérin JL (2019) The triumph of judicial review: the evolution of post-revolutionary legal thought. In: Moréteau O, Masferrer A, Modéer KÅ (eds) Comparative legal history. Edward Elgar Publishing, London, pp 262–283
Helgadóttir R (2009) Status presens: judicial review in Iceland. Nordisk Tidsskrift for Menneskerettigheter 27:185–193
Husa J (2019) Constitutional mentality. In: Letto-Vanamo, P et al (eds), Nordic law in european context. Springer, Cham
Kierulf A (2018) Judicial review in Norway: A Bicentennial Debate. Cambridge University Press, Cambridge
Lassahn P (2017) Rechtsprechung und Parlamentsgesetz. Mohr Siebeck, Tübingen
Nergelius J (2017) Prejudikat(o)bundenhet inom den konstitutionella rätten: var ne bis in idem ett unikum? Svensk Juristtidning 2017:783–794
Nylund A, Sunde JØ (2019) Courts and Court Proceedings In: Letto-Vanamo P et al. (eds), Nordic Law in European Context. Springer, Cham
Ramberg C (2017) Prejudikat som rättskälla i förmögenhetsrätten. Wolters Kluwer, Stockholm
Rytter JE (2001) En differentieret strategi for domstolsprøvelse af love. Tidsskrift for Rettsvitenskap 2001:715–746
Skoghøy JEA (2013) De nordiske domstolene og Den europeiske menneskerettskonvensjon. Svensk Juristtidning 2013:397–424
Smith C (1990) Jus og politikk: samspill og konflikt. Lov og Rett 68(7):426–430
Smith E (1993) Høyesterett og folkestyret: Prøvingsretten overfor lover. Universitetsforlaget, Oslo
Smith E (2018) Judicial review of legislation. In: Krunke H, Thorarensen B (eds), The Nordic constitutions: A comparative and contextual study. Hart Publishing, Oxford
Suksi M (2018) Common roots of nordic constitutional law? Some observations on legal-historical development and relations between the constitutional systems of five Nordic Countries. In: Krunke H, Thorarensen B (eds), The Nordic constitutions: A comparative and contextual study. Hart Publishing, Oxford
Sundberg JWF (1983) Haegerstroem and Finland's struggle for law. Rothman & Co., Littleton CO
Sunnqvist M (2014a) Konstitutionellt kritiskt dömande: förändringen av nordiska domares attityder under två sekel. Institutet för rättshistorisk forskning, Stockholm
Sunnqvist M (2014b) 'Klart stöd'-doktrinens historia och dubbelförfarandeförbudets framtid. Europarättslig tidskrift 2014(2):389–399
Sunnqvist M (2015) Seven categories of constitutional critical judging: An interpretation of Nordic case-law. Giornale di Storia Costituzionale 30 / II 2015:141–153
Sunnqvist M (2016) Mord, prejudikattolkning och lagtolkning. Svensk Juristtidning 2016:541–553
Sunnqvist M (2017) Praktiskt konstitutionellt dömande. Lunds Domarakademi, Lund

Privatisation and Flexibilisation of Nordic Court Proceedings

Institutional Aspects of the Nordic Justice Systems: Striving for Consolidation and Settlements

Anna Nylund

Abstract This chapter maps the structure of the Nordic justice systems and explores whether and why one could argue that there is a 'Nordic' structure. The aim is also to examine recent changes and to investigate whether these entail a cultural shift in some or all Nordic countries. It examines shifts in the intended functions of the courts; changes in the court structure; and the use of alternative dispute resolution outside courts. It argues that the while the private functions of Nordic courts have been accentuated in recent decades in that courts are increasingly expected to facilitate amicable solutions, while alternative dispute resolution outside courts has also been important. It also discusses how the ideal of the generalist judge has been important in consolidating the Nordic court structure. While most of these changes are congruent across the Nordic countries, and have hence strengthened the Nordic court culture, differences among the countries regarding recourse against administrative decisions are growing. New differences among the Nordic countries have emerged and these do not follow the existing divide between the East-Nordic and the West-Nordic countries.

1 Introduction to the Nordic Justice Systems

The basic tenets of the court systems are the same across the Nordic countries: a simple three-tier, uniform court system with limited specialisation.[1] The deeply-rooted ideal is a system where almost all cases follow the same route through the court system and where specialist judges are almost non-existent.[2] Unified, stream-lined courts ensure the coherence of the legal system and congruity across different

[1]Finnish administrative courts consist of only two tiers. For an overview of the Nordic court systems, see Nylund and Sunde (2019).

[2]Letto-Vanamo (2021).

A. Nylund (✉)
Faculty of Law, UiT, The Arctic University of Norway, Hansine Hansens veg 18, 9037 Tromsø, Norway
e-mail: anna.nylund@uit.no

L. Ervo et al. (eds.), *Rethinking Nordic Courts*, Ius Gentium: Comparative Perspectives on Law and Justice 90, https://doi.org/10.1007/978-3-030-74851-7_11

legal fields in the absence of coherent, comprehensive codes. The system minimises jurisdictional conflicts and the risk of incompatible outcomes across court systems. The structure of the court system splits the Nordic countries into two groups: the West-Nordic countries—Denmark, Iceland and Norway—have only general courts, while the East-Nordic countries—Finland and Sweden—have both general and administrative courts.

Another characteristic of Nordic justice systems is the search for pragmatic solutions. The extensive use of out-of-court dispute resolution mechanisms, in both civil and criminal cases, is a manifestation of pragmatism. The Nordic justice systems thus extend far beyond formal courts, and courts are essentially a last resort for resolving disputes. In recent decades, ADR has migrated from the fringes of the justice system into the courts, which strengthens the legal-cultural elements related to finding amicable solutions. The shift towards ADR has also occurred in the domain of criminal justice, where restorative processes and victim-offender mediation have been promoted during the past few decades.

This chapter maps the structure of the Nordic justice systems and explores whether and why one could argue that there is a 'Nordic' structure. The aim is also to examine recent changes and to investigate whether these entail a cultural shift in some or all Nordic countries. It examines the functions of the courts, changes in the court structure, and the use of alternative dispute resolution outside courts by studying two very different processes—consumer dispute resolution (CDR) and victim-offender mediation (VOM). These two examples have been selected because they are present in all four countries studied and because they represent two different ideologies of alternative justice: CDR provides justice through a simplified process, and VOM offers an alternative process that generates different outcomes. This chapter also analyses whether and how these have changed during the past decades and whether the basic traits of Nordic court culture have been diluted or perhaps even strengthened.

2 A Transition of the Functions of Courts

2.1 The Intended Functions of Courts

The functions of courts and court proceedings has been vividly debated in Nordic legal scholarship. Civil procedure scholarship generally operates with five functions: private, public, norm-clarification/norm-creation, checks and balances, and enforcement of EU/EEA law and the European Convention on Human Rights (ECHR).[3]

The private function refers to courts serving the interests of citizens, businesses and associations in two distinct, yet partly intertwined ways: first, by enabling them to

[3]Eldjarn (2016), pp. 53 ff.; Lindblom (2007); Lindblom (2017); Komiteamietintö 2003:3 Tuomioistuinlaitoksen kehittämiskomitean mietintö, Oikeusministeriö, pp. 69 ff.; NOU 1999: 19 Domstolene i samfunnet. Administrativ styring av domstolene. Utnevnelser, sidegjøremål, disiplinærtiltak.

enforce their legal rights (i.e., to have efficient methods to counteract infringements of their rights and assaults by fellow citizens) and second, by providing dispute resolution processes resulting in final and enforceable outcomes.[4] In this second respect, dispute resolution does not imply outcomes that mirror the law; rather, it implies facilitating constructive dialogue between the parties to engender pragmatic solutions. In criminal and administrative cases, court proceedings protect citizens from 'arbitrary and inequitable use of state power'.[5] The public function encompasses the state having an interest in enforcing the law: the rule of law necessitates that the legal rules must be rendered effective by equal and efficient enforcement. Rule by law (i.e., using the law as the predominant tool of governing and moulding society) also requires that laws are effectively implemented and that private individuals are required to obey the law.[6] Effective enforcement of the law is also likely to result in voluntary compliance and even shape people's moral beliefs.[7] In criminal law, the public functions and aspects related to the rule of law are far more important than dispute resolution.[8]

The third function, that of norm clarification and norm creation, is primarily a task for supreme courts. The fourth function is to provide checks and balances to ensure that administrative authorities, and to some extent the legislature, obey the law. Finally, courts ensure effective and equivalent application of EU law and ensure that national law and practice complies with the requirements of the ECHR and other international human rights instruments. Since the three latter functions are discussed in more detailed in other parts of this volume,[9] this chapter focuses solely on the first two functions—the private and the public.

In addition to the above-mentioned functions that involve adjudication, or are at least connected with adjudication, courts in the Nordic countries (and elsewhere) also have administrative functions, in the form of non-litigious cases (*iurisdictio voluntaria, domstolsärende, hakemusasia*),[10] such as registrations of wills, guardianship cases, marriage, divorce, and land registers. Often, there is no disagreement between the persons concerned, and adjudication is only needed when a real dispute arises. To a large extent, these tasks have been transferred from courts to other authorities,

Midlertidige dommere. Justis -og politidepartementet. Oslo, pp. 117–119; Robberstad (2018), pp. 1–6; Robberstad (1998); Betænkning nr. 1401 (2001) Reform af den civile retspleje I: Instansordningen, byrettens sammensætning og almindelige regler om sagsbehandlingen i første instans. Retsplejerådet, København, pp. 83 ff.; Bang-Pedersen et al. (2017), pp. 29–30; and Bellander (2017), pp. 87 ff.

[4]Bedner (2010), p. 51.

[5]Bedner (2010), p. 50. For more detailed observations on the Nordic criminal justice systems, see Helenius (2021), Bedner (2010), p. 50. For more detailed observations on the Nordic criminal justice systems, see Helenius (2021).

[6]Møller and Skaaning (2014), pp. 13 ff., Tamanaha (2004), pp. 91 ff.

[7]Tyler (2006).

[8]Landström (2011), pp. 30 ff. See also, e.g., Øyen (2016), pp. 24–25.

[9]Nylund (2021), Sunnqvist (2021) and Thorsteinsdóttir (2021).

[10]The concept of non-litigious matters does not exist in Danish and Norwegian law.

since the cases seldom require a judge to be involved. Courts are specialists in adjudicating disputes (and resolving disputes through other processes), whereas other authorities are better equipped to operate registers, administer guardianships and grant divorces.[11] In Sweden, and to some extent in Norway, undisputed pecuniary claims and eviction cases are subject to direct enforcement (i.e., the parties do not have to go through courts to obtain a judgment). If the debtor (i.e., the defendant) contests the claim, the creditor must request that the case is transferred to regular civil proceedings, or else the debt collection proceedings come to an end. Uncontested claims have increasingly been transferred away from courts to administrative organs despite the fact that establishing the existence of the claim is de facto adjudication, and that administrative organs—enforcement officers—thus adjudicate claims.[12]

As a result of the ideal of courts as purely adjudicative organs, many of these cases have been transferred to administrative authorities.[13]The formal (independence) and procedural (impartiality, equality of arms, etc.) fair trial rights only apply to adjudication; courts should only have tasks directly related to these; and retaining non-litigious cases is primarily a manifestation of tradition, rather than the outcome of a deliberate selection of the most appropriate and efficient organisation. Administrative authorities can provide services of equal or even better quality than courts do, while letting courts specialise in rendering justice.[14]

2.2 *Accentuating the 'Private' Functions of Courts*

In parallel with emphasising courts as adjudicative organs, Nordic courts increasingly serve private functions by delivering non-adjudicative dispute resolution methods, particularly in civil cases, and by supporting out-of-court dispute resolution.[15] A broader spectrum of dispute resolution processes has been implemented in two distinct ways: by emphasising the role of judges in facilitating settlement while acting in their role as judges during the course of regular court proceedings, and by introducing court-connected mediation, which is a parallel track to litigation with a separate process.

Judges in the Nordic countries have long had a right to promote settlement. In his rule for judges, Olaus Petri stressed in the sixteenth century the virtues of settlement

[11]E.g., Työryhmämietintö 2007:6, pp. 23–24; NOU 1999: 22 (1999) Domstolene i første instans. Førsteinstansdomstolenes arbeidsoppgaver og struktur. Oslo, Justis- og politidepartementet, Sects. 3.4 and 4; and Ds 2019:31 Konkursförfarandet, Departementsserien, pp. 131 ff.

[12]For a more detailed discussion, see Nylund (2019a). For a discussion of the problematic aspects of this arrangement, see also Wallerman Ghavanini (2020).

[13]Komiteamietintö 2003:3, pp. 114 ff. and pp. 134 ff.; NOU 1999: 22, pp. 26–27 and 46 ff.; Betænkning nr. 1398 (2001) Domstolenes strukturkommission. København; Regeringens skrivelse 1999/2000:106 (2000) Reformeringen av domstolsväsendet – en handlingsplan. Stockholm, pp. 8–10 and 15–16.

[14]Komiteamietintö 2003:3, pp. 339–341, and Regeringens skrivelse 1999/2000:106, pp. 15 ff.

[15]Petersen (2021).

in *inter alia* rule ten: 'All law is to be wielded with wisdom because the greatest right is the greatest wrong; and there must be mercy in justice as well.'[16] Conciliation Boards (*forliksråd)* were introduced in Denmark and Norway in 1795 to establish a forum where a panel of lay judges would resolve disputes.[17] In recent decades, the right to promote settlement has been fortified and turned into a duty to assess whether promoting settlement is appropriate at every stage of civil proceedings. Danish, Finnish and Swedish law requires the court to facilitate settlement in all civil cases, unless the court finds that settlement is unlikely due to the character of the case, the position of the parties or other similar circumstances.[18] Norwegian law only imposes a duty to consider whether settlement is suitable and to act accordingly.[19] The differences in the wording of the duty to promote settlement do not necessarily translate into differences in practices. Hence, one can argue that pragmatic solutions are a quintessential element of Nordic court culture.

Civil procedure rules in the Nordic countries do not regulate how a judge should proceed when assessing whether promoting settlement is appropriate and how to assess the timing of these efforts, nor are the efforts themselves regulated in more detail.[20] However, judges must refrain from any action that could render them partial, or at least raise concerns with regard to their impartiality, such as meeting privately with one party. Finnish judges are explicitly allowed to suggest a specific outcome;[21] Danish judges can do so when appropriate, although the matter is not regulated in detail;[22] and Norwegian judges are explicitly prohibited from doing so.[23] In Sweden, judges are allowed to meet privately with each party (caucus), without the other party being present;[24] in the other Nordic countries, private meetings are considered inappropriate, as they jeopardise the impartiality of the judge.[25] According to a Danish study, judges lack a shared understanding of what promoting settlement entails and how judges should proceed when promoting settlement. Some judges believe encouraging the parties to negotiate suffices, others discuss the advantages of amicable solutions and the disadvantages of continuing litigation, and still others point out common ground.[26] Considering the limited regulation, the divergence among judges is not surprising.

---

[16]Tontti (2000).

[17]Vindeløv (2007), pp. 2–5.

[18]Danish Administration of Justice Act Sect. 268, Finnish Code of Judicial Procedure Chap. 5 Sect. 26 and Swedish Code of Judicial Procedure chapter 42 Sect. 17.

[19]Norwegian Dispute Act Sects. 8–1 and 8–2.

[20]Bengt Lindell (2019), pp. 248 ff., and Camilla Bernt (2011) discuss these in detail.

[21]Finnish Code of Judicial Procedure Chap. 5 Sect. 26.

[22]Bang-Pedersen et al. (2017), pp. 109–110.

[23]Norwegian Dispute Act Sect. 8–2.

[24]Lindell (2019), pp. 262–265, and SOU 2007:26 Alternativ tvistlösning. Betänkande av Utredningen om alternativa former för tvistlösning vid tingsrätt. p. 76.

[25]HE 114/2004 vp (2004) Hallituksen esitys Eduskunnalle riita-asioiden sovittelua ja sovinnon vahvistamista yleisissä tuomioistuimissa koskevaksi lainsäädännöksi. Helsinki, p. 6; Bernt (2011), pp. 286–288; Bernt (2015); and Adrian (2012), p. 96.

[26]Adrian et al. (2015).

The Nordic countries have relatively high settlement rates. In 2019, the proceedings in first courts in Denmark resulted in settlement in 18% of general civil cases.[27] In Finland, the ratio of settlements was 33% of rulings in civil cases in 2019.[28] In Norway, 24% of general civil cases were resolved by the means of an out-of-court settlement and 14% by an in-court settlement.[29] Sweden has no official statistics available, but a 2005 study found that a third of civil cases resulted in settlement.[30] Additionally, some cases end in withdrawal as a result of settlement.[31] At least in Finland, a cultural shift has taken place, as a result of which the preparatory stage of civil proceedings is essentially a dialogue in which the parties and the judge cooperate to identify the key disputed issues and to find a pragmatic solution, rather than each party attempting to persuade the judge using legal argumentation.[32] As a result, many judges perceive themselves as settlement judges.[33] This trend is also reflected in increasingly benign attitudes towards plea bargaining.[34]

Court-connected mediation, in which courts run, administer and monitor mediation programs and oversee mediators, has been introduced in Denmark, Finland and Norway. In Denmark and Norway, a judge or other suitable person can act as a mediator, and courts are obliged to maintain a list of approved mediators. In Finland, only judges can mediate. Court-connected mediation is regulated in some detail in law.[35] Sweden is different in this regard, as courts do not manage and run mediation programs themselves; the Swedish Courts Administration has a list of mediators.[36] Furthermore, the Swedish Code of Judicial Procedure Chap. 42 Sect. 17 subsection 2 only states that the court has the power to decide that the case be transferred to 'special mediation' (*särskild medling*) if the parties consent and that it must stay

[27] Afgørelsestyper inden for forældreansvarssager og ægteskabssager https://www.domstol.dk/om/talogfakta/statistik/Pages/civilesager.aspx (accessed 15 June 2020).

[28] Oikeusministeriö (2020), Tuomioistuinten työtilastoja 2019, Oikeusministeriön julkaisuita. Tominta ja hallinto 2020: 4, p. 34.

[29] NOU 2020: 11 Den tredje statsmakt. Domstolene i endring. Oslo, Justis- og beredskapsdepartementet, p. 52. Moreover, 5% were dismissed, 2% withdrawn and 1% through other types of rulings or no ruling was recorded, and 41% of all incoming cases were resolved by a judgment on the merits. Additionally, 13% were resolved by an in-court settlement in court-connected mediation. An in-court settlement is binding and enforceable in the same manner as a judgment on the merits, whereas an out-of-court settlement has the same status as any contractual agreement. The number of settlements is significantly higher in labour disputes.

[30] SOU 2007:26, p. 107.

[31] Riksrevisjonens undersøkelse av saksbehandlingstid og effektivitet i tingrettene og lagmannsrettene Dokument 3:3 (2019–2020), pp. 81 and 90.

[32] Haavisto (2002).

[33] Ervo (2016). Mark Galanter (1985) made a similar observation on American judges in the mid-1980s.

[34] See Ervo (2021).

[35] Danish Administration of Justice Act Sects. 271–279; Finnish Act on mediation in civil matters and confirmation of settlements in general courts 394/2011; and Norwegian Dispute Act Sects. 8–3–8–7.

[36] For a more detailed discussion on court-connected mediation, see Linnanmäki (2021) and, e.g., Adrian (2016). See also Adrian (2014).

the proceedings during mediation, but it does not regulate the mediation process in more detail.[37] One could argue that since court involvement and oversight of the mediation process is almost non-existent in Sweden, the scheme cannot be labelled court-connected mediation.[38]

The use of court-connected mediation varies significantly among the Nordic countries. In Denmark, only 1.7% of general civil cases were directed to court-connected mediation in 2017. Judges mediated 53% of the cases, and the parties settled the case in half of mediated cases.[39] In 2019, 23% of the incoming civil cases in Norwegian courts were directed to court-connected mediation, and the parties entered into settlement in 65% of the cases.[40] In Finland, 25% of civil cases were directed to court-connected mediation in 2018, with a settlement rate of 71%.[41] There appears to be no obvious explanation for the variation in the setup and use of mediation in Nordic courts.[42]

As increased focus on settlement demonstrates, Nordic courts have a bifocal approach to justice and dispute resolution: they facilitate amicable settlements, which enables the parties to design the outcome according to their wishes and needs (private justice), and they provide 'justice through the law' and promote the rule of law through formal, adjudicative processes.[43] This development is more pronounced in Finland and Norway, where court-connected mediation has become an integral part of civil procedure,[44] whereas Danish and Swedish courts are more hesitant to embrace mediation.

Perhaps part of the hesitance towards court-connected mediation arises from attractive alternatives. In Denmark, courts resolve many disputes by a judge's announcement—a process wherein the judge announces his or her view on the outcome of the case when the main hearing is concluded, unless a party requests that the court make a formal ruling.[45] The court can base the outcome either on legal rules or on what it considers to be a fair and equitable solution. In the latter case, it must inform the parties that a ruling based on legal arguments might differ from the outcome the court recommends. In Sweden, judges can meet privately with the parties when promoting settlement and, thus, do not need to resort to court-connected mediation to avail themselves of private meetings.

---

[37] Lindell (2019), pp. 266–270.

[38] Adrian (2016).

[39] Domstolsstyrelsen (2018) Statistik for civile sage – retsmægling 2017. https://www.domstol.dk/om/talogfakta/statistik/Pages/civilesager.aspx (accessed 26 June 2020).

[40] Riksrevisjonen (2019) Riksrevisjonens undersøkelse av saksbehandlingstid og effektivitet i tingrettene og lgamannsrettene. Dokument 3:3 (2019–2020) https://www.riksrevisjonen.no/global assets/rapporter/no-2019-2020/Domstolene.pdf (accessed 15 June 2020), p. 83.

[41] Data obtained from the Finnish Court Administration. On file with the author.

[42] Adrian (2014).

[43] For theoretical discussions on these concepts, see, e.g., Nolan-Haley (1996), Nolan-Haley (1998), Nolan-Haley (2011), Riskin and Welsh (2007), Welsh (2001), Welsh (2001), Welsh (2002) and Welsh (2004).

[44] See, e.g., Kjelland-Mørdre et al. (2020), pp. 142 ff; Bernt (2015); and Bernt et al. (2014).

[45] Bang-Pedersen et al. 2017, pp. 110–111.

3 Court Structure and the Role of Courts

3.1 Consolidation of Courts

Courts with general jurisdiction with generalist judges epitomise the institutional elements of Nordic procedural culture. While increased legal complexity with a 'denser' regulation, and an emphasis on productivity and minimising the cost of operating courts puts these basic tenets under pressure, they still remain a beacon for developing the structure of the court system.

Until the turn of the millennium, the Nordic countries had a large number of district courts—general courts of first instance. Many of the courts were very small, with only one or two professional judges aided by one or two deputy judges.[46] Courts heard many simple criminal cases, although a 'decriminalisation' had already taken place by changing the formal status of the sanction from criminal to administrative and thus alleviating the workload of (general) courts.[47]

Since the 1990s, general courts in Nordic countries have undergone reorganisation, with a dramatic reduction in the number of courts. The number of courts has been reduced from 82 to 24 in Denmark and from 70 to 20 in Finland.[48] In Sweden, the number has been reduced from 96 to 48,[49] and in Norway from 92 to 23.[50]

> Norwegian Conciliation Boards (*forliksråd*) are interesting in this respect. Although not formally courts, they have mandatory jurisdiction on most pecuniary, non-family civil cases unless the value of the claim is above NOK 200,000 (approximately € 20,000). The majority of cases are uncontested and the Board can pronounce a judgement only if the case is sufficiently simple.[51]

Small courts have several disadvantages; for example, the illness of a judge brings most proceedings to a halt, recruiting judges is challenging and judges hear fewer cases than in larger courts. Judges often have no experience hearing complex cases; hence, parties in commercial cases opt for larger courts or arbitration.[52] A study commissioned by the Norwegian Courts Commissions indicates that the criminal sanctions imposed by small courts more often deviate from the sanctions courts issue on average.[53] Larger courts offer higher quality proceedings and outcomes and are more efficient.

---

[46] E.g., Betænkning nr. 1401 (2001), Komiteamietintö 2003:3 and NOU 1999:22.

[47] Halila et al. (2018).

[48] Betænkning nr. 1401 (2001) and HE 270/2016 vp Hallituksen esitys eduskunnalle laeiksi tuomioistuinlain ja eräiden muiden lakien muuttamisesta.

[49] Regeringens skrivelse 1999/2000:106, pp. 13–14 and 44 ff.

[50] Prop. 11 L (2020–2021) Endringer i domstolloven (domstolstruktur)

[51] See Nylund (2020), p, 50–51 and Jensen (2021), part 2.3.

[52] NOU 2019: 17, pp. 40 and 46–48, SOU 2003:5 (2003) Förändringar i tingsrättsorganisationen – en utvärdering av sammanläggningar av tingsrätter 1999–2001. Justitiedepartementet, Betænkning nr. 1401 (2001), Chap. 9, and NOU 1999:22, pp. 22 ff and 89 ff.

[53] NOU 2019: 17, p. 45.

The increasing density and complexity of legal regulations as well as the increasing factual complexity of cases poses a challenge to the Nordic ideal of generalist judges. To address this problem, 'moderate specialisation' of judges has been implemented in mid-size and larger courts. Large courts are divided into sections specialising in criminal or civil cases, or even certain subgroups of these, such as white-collar crime, labour law or family law. Alternatively, some judges specialise in, for example, cases involving children or court-connected mediation. To maintain coherence, some types of cases are distributed among all judges in a section or even across sections, and judges rotate among the sections at regular intervals (e.g., 3–5 years).[54]

The disinclination toward special courts is persistent across the Nordic countries. Government reports from the Nordic countries articulate the same reasons for and against special courts.[55] The advantages of special courts are specialist knowledge, tailoring proceedings to the needs of the specific types of cases and potentially more efficient proceedings. The disadvantages are associated with difficulty to recruit judges, insufficient caseload to maintain efficient proceedings, inconsistent and incoherent case law emanating from different courts and weakening the coherence of law. The reports also list measures that enable general courts to gain the same advantages as special courts would: partial specialisation, using expert judges or experts, and flexible procedural rules. When necessary, the general procedural rules can be combined with a few special rules that are applicable only for selected types of cases.

As a result, functional consolidation has taken place by merging special courts with general and administrative courts.[56] This functional consolidation is a token of the strong inclination towards general courts and generalist judges. Finnish land courts (i.e., courts hearing land cadastral matters) have been merged with district

[54]NOU 2017: 8 Særdomstoler på nye områder? Vurdering av nye domstolsordninger for foreldretvister, barnevernsaker og utlendingssaker Justis- og beredskapsdepartmentet, Familie -og likestillingsdepartementet. Oslo, pp. 36–39; NOU 2019: 17, pp. 79–80. See e.g. description of how the work is organised at the Aarhus District Court https://www.domstol.dk/aarhus/om-retten-i-aarhus/organisation/ (accessed 15 June 2020); order for procedure at Helsinki District Court https://oikeus.fi/karajaoikeudet/helsinginkarajaoikeus/material/attachments/oikeus_karaja oikeudet_helsinginkarajaoikeus/liitteet_oikeus_karajaoikeudet_helsinginkarajaoikeus/plWhzY F0L/Helsingin_karajaoikeuden_tyojarjestys_2019.pdf (accessed 15 June 2020); the order of procedure at Helsinki Administrative Court https://oikeus.fi/hallintooikeudet/helsinginhallinto-oikeus/material/attachments/oikeus_hallintooikeudet_helsinginhallinto-oikeus/liitteet_oikeus_ hallintooikeudet_helsinginhallinto-oikeus/9RsdNS6VV/Helsingin_hallinto-oikeuden_tyojarjes tys.pdf (accessed 15 June 2020); information on moderate specialisation at the Oslo District Court https://www.domstol.no/Enkelt-domstol/oslotingrett/om-domstolen/virksomheten/mod erat-spesialisering/; information on how cases are distributed in Stockholm District Court domstol.se/stockholms-tingsratt/om-tingsratten/organisation/var-verksamhet/ (accessed 15 June 2020).

[55]Betænkning nr. 1401 (2001), pp. 252 and 305; Komiteamietintö 2003:3, pp. 334–339; NOU 2017: 8, p. 50; and Regeringens skrivelse 1999/2000:106, pp. 58–59.

[56]Komiteamietintö 2003:3, pp. 383–385.

courts, and Norwegian land appellate courts with general appellate courts.[57] The Swedish environmental (water) courts have been merged with selected district courts, whereas the administrative parts of Finnish water courts have been incorporated into administrative bodies and the adjudicative functions with the Vaasa administrative court.[58] Practically no special courts remain in Sweden as separate units, although some of them form a section of another court, such as the Market Court that has become a section of the Stockholm district court.[59] The Nordic Labour Courts and the Danish Maritime and Commercial High Court remains the exception to the rule of general courts.[60]

Functional consolidation has also been achieved by concentrating some cases to a single or a few selected courts (e.g., the district courts in Oslo and Stockholm have exclusive jurisdiction in patent matters).[61]

Geographic and functional consolidation combined with 'moderate specialisation' enable the Nordic countries to uphold the pragmatic, 'non-specialist' ('lay') elements in Nordic legal culture: even if lawyers and attorneys are increasingly specialised, the judges hearing the cases are not specialists. Hence, the legal counsels of the parties cannot resort to highly specialised, legal-technical arguments as easily as they could if the judges were specialists as well. Moderate specialisation also secures the position of courts as guardians of the coherence of the legal system.

Finally, the increased independence of courts is reflected in the establishment of separate administrative bodies for the administration of courts in all Nordic countries. Detaching courts from ministries of justice and other political organs is an important step in ensuring the independence of the judiciary.[62]

4 Persistent Differences in Attitudes Toward Administrative Courts

There are palpable differences among the Nordic countries in the adjudication of administrative cases. In 2019, the number of incoming administrative cases was

---

[57] HE 86/1999 vp (1999) Hallituksen esitys Eduskunnalle maaoikeuksien lakkauttamisesta erityistuomioistuimina ja siihen liittyväksi lainsäädännöksi. Helsinki; https://www.domstol.no/jordskifterettene/om-jordskifterettene/jordskiftevirksomheten-i-et-historisk-perspektiv/ (accessed 15 June 2020) and Regeringens proposition 2009/20:215.

[58] HE 114/1998 vp (1998) Hallituksen esitys Eduskunnalle hallinto-oikeuslaiksi ja siihen liittyväksi lainsäädännöksi. Helsinki and Regeringens proposition 2009/20:215 Mark- och miljödomstolar Miljödepartementet.

[59] A closer look at the courts of Denmark https://www.domstol.se/patent--och-marknadsdomstolen/om-patent--och-marknadsdomstolen/ (accessed 15 June 2020).

[60] https://domstol.dk/media/lacbg0w5/profilbrochure_uk.pdf (accessed 15 June 2020), p. 10.

[61] Norwegian Patent Act Sect. 3, and Swedish Patent Act Sects. 65 and 66.

[62] Sunnqvist (2021) and Nylund (2019c).

19,961 in Finland[63] and 176,760 in Sweden[64] but only approximately 800–1,000 in Denmark and Norway.[65] Considering that Denmark, Finland and Norway have almost the same number of inhabitants, around 5.4 million, one would expect these numbers to be much more similar. The Finnish Social Security Appeal Board (SSAB, *Sosiaaliturva-asioiden muutoksenhakulautakunta)* explains part of the gap between the Finnish and Swedish numbers. With 41,165 incoming cases in 2019,[66] the SSAB almost closes the gap between the two countries. The Norwegian Insurance Court (*trygderetten*) is a de facto appellate court in social security matters and contributes to closing part of the gap, but it can only account for a fraction of the difference.[67] The main explanatory factor seems to be that recourse against administrative decisions is organised within administrative bodies in Denmark and Norway, and that courts, therefore, seldom review administrative decisions, except in cases concerning a narrow range of issues, such as child protection.[68] For instance, Norwegian courts have only a handful of incoming cases related to environmental law, whereas Finnish and Swedish courts have several thousand environmental cases.[69]

Review of administrative decisions is recognised as part of the rule of law, since it enables citizens to react to abuses of power by challenging unlawful decisions and since review of decisions by courts is one of the main mechanisms constituting checks and balances. These principles are recognised in all Nordic countries. Hence, the following question arises: why are the differences in the incoming cases so pronounced?

The differences in the conception of the ideal method for reviewing administrative decisions are pronounced. The Finnish and Swedish systems value review by independent and impartial courts, while the Danish and Norwegian systems are based on a belief in the superiority of administrative review. Unlike administrative courts, where judges are generalists, administrative bodies have specialist knowledge and

---

[63]Oikeusministeriö (2020), Tuomioistuinten työtilastoja 2019, Oikeusministeriön julkaisuita. Tominta ja hallinto 2020: 4, p. 23.

[64]Domstolsverket 2020, Court Statistics 2019, https://www.domstol.se/globalassets/filer/gemensamt-innehall/styrning-och-riktlinjer/statistik/court_statistics_2019.pdf (accessed 15 June 2020), p. 27.

[65]No official statistics are available. Betænkning nr. 1401 (2001), p. 107 and Difi-rapport 2014:2 (2014) Viltvoksende nemnder? Om organisering og regulering av statlige nemnder. Oslo, Difi - Direktoratet for forvaltning og IKT, p. 48. The Danish Chamber Advocate represented Danish government bodies in 3,638 cases in district courts in 2019, https://oes.dk/media/36430/statens-forbrug-hos-kammeradvokaten-i-2019.pdf (accessed 15 June 2020). However, this includes both civil and administrative cases.

[66]https://www.samu.fi/wp-content/uploads/2020/03/SAMU-Vireasia-Tammi-Joulu-2019.pdf (accessed 15 June 2020).

[67]The Norwegian Insurance Court had 3 908 incoming cases in 2018, https://www.trygderetten.no/statistikk?p_lang=2 (accessed 15 June 2020). The Norwegian functional equivalent of the Finnish SSAB and Swedish administrative courts in social security matters is *NAV Klageinstans*, which is part of The Norwegian Labour and Welfare Administration, NAV. For more details see Nylund (2019a), p. 433 with further references.

[68]Difi-rapport 2014:2.

[69]Nylund (2019b), pp. 93–94.

easy access to information and documents, which allows them to perform a thorough review of each case, as well as a mandate to review issues related to both legality and expedience of the decision. The review process and the institutional organisation of the review body are tailored to the type of cases handled, since the rules regarding administrative review are general; this results in a timely and efficient process wherein the private party, at least ideally, does not need legal assistance. These advantages are pronounced when the administrative review board finds for the private party: the review board has the power to reverse the decision, and in these situations, the private party does not have to wait for the administrative body to make a new decision. Danish and Norwegian lawyers believe that review performed within the administration fulfils the foundational values of efficiency, the rule of law and the ability of administrative organs to control and rectify their own decisions. In these systems, court proceedings are, and should be, a last resort.[70]

The differences in court structure are undoubtedly of vital importance in this regard, since different procedural rules apply in general courts and administrative courts. Civil litigation is party-driven and adversarial; the parties produce the evidence, and the losing party pays the cost of litigation. Appointing a legal counsel is usually necessary; hence, the government uses specialised counsel in Denmark through an arrangement with a private law firm and in Norway through the Attorney-General's office.[71] Although administrative proceedings are also party-driven and adversarial, the court has a more pronounced role in the proceedings and can *inter alia* order other authorities to provide relevant information. Furthermore, the party constellation differs: unlike in civil litigation, in administrative court proceedings, the government organisation is not formally a party, and thus the government does not have a specialised legal counsel to assist during court proceedings. The parties are only liable for their own costs, and since the government does not use a fairly expensive, specialised legal counsel, and the court sometimes pays for (parts of) the cost of evidence, the total costs, are lower and differences in access to legal advice are not pronounced.[72] Therefore, the threshold for initiating court proceedings is lower for administrative courts. Nevertheless, administrative recourse can render equal, or even superior, justice to court proceedings, provided that the institutional and procedural rules regarding administrative recourse proceedings support quality outcomes.

The differences in recourse against administrative decisions have long historical roots. The Swedish system can be traced back to *Kammerkollegiet,* a government organ in charge of monetary, fiscal and customs policies, from which *Kammarrevisionen*—later *Kammarrätten* (Chamber Court)—was separated in 1695 to form a separate organ for adjudication and auditing. However, this organ was not fully

[70]NOU 2019: 5 Ny forvaltningsolv. Lov om saksbehandling i offentlig forvaltning. Oslo, Justis- og beredskapsdepartementet, p. 366–367.

[71]The Attorney-General is separately funded, and hence litigation entails no direct costs for the government body using the services of the Attorney-General, in spite of the fact that when the government prevails, the private party must reimburse the government.

[72]See, e.g., Bragdø-Ellenes (2014) and Aer (2003). For environmental cases, see Nylund (2019b).

independent. The Chamber Court gradually morphed into an administrative court. In 1909, the Supreme Administrative Court was founded, and the Chamber Court became a lower court.[73] Since Finland was a part of Sweden until 1809, it followed a similar path, except the former Chamber Court itself became the Supreme Administrative Court.[74]

Finnish and Swedish administrative courts have gradually cut their organisational, functional, economic and regulatory ties to the administration and formed a parallel track to general courts. Although their powers are limited to reviewing the legality of administrative decisions, they have been given increased powers to review aspects concerning expedience, both formally and by the increase in the role of general principles of public administration and administrative law.[75] The recourse system is two-pronged: it separates recourse based on legality from recourse based on expediency, where administrative courts hear the former and the government the latter. The increasing importance of EU law and the growing role of principles of administrative law have challenged the two-pronged approach and shifted the balance towards administrative courts.[76] The right to seek recourse against administrative decisions as an essential element of the rule of law has been emphasised in Finland since the Finnish civil war in 1918, whereas Swedish commentators have been sceptical towards 'elitist' courts and have seen recourse to the government as an equivalent path to review by administrative courts.[77]

Concomitantly with growing powers and organisational independence of administrative courts, administrative appeals boards have been merged with administrative courts, which has contributed further to administrative courts becoming relatively powerful state organs. For instance, migration cases are delegated to some administrative courts in Sweden,[78] and environmental cases to the Vaasa Administrative Court in Finland.[79] The main exception to the consolidation of administrative courts is that of cases related to social security benefits in Finnish law, for which a tribunal—the SSAB—hears the appeals. Its rulings are subject to appeal to the Insurance Court. The SSAB is interesting, as it has gradually been transformed from several bodies that were organisationally, institutionally and economically a part of the administration of the Social Insurance Institution of Finland (*Kela*) into an organisationally and financially independent tribunal, a de facto court. The predecessors of the board relied on staff employed by the administration to prepare the cases, most (or even all) of the judges had part-time, limited-term positions, and the regular rules of administration applied, whereas the proceedings in the SSAB are essentially governed by

[73]Wenander (2019), p. 438.

[74]https://www.kho.fi/fi/index/korkeinhallinto-oikeus/historia.html (accessed 15 June 2020).

[75]Mäenpää (2019), SOU 1994:117 Domstolsprövning av förvaltningsärenden. Slutbetänkande av Fri- och rättighetskomittén.

[76]Wenander (2019).

[77]Wenander (2019).

[78]Gothenburg, Luleå, Malmö and Stockholm (https://www.domstol.se/hitta-domstol/migrationsdomstolar/) (accessed 15 June 2020).

[79]See above Sect. 3.1.

the Administrative Judicial Process Act[80] and the Courts Act.[81] To make the SSAB more robust and to secure a sufficient caseload and number of judges and other staff, it was formed as a merger of two boards. As with general courts, very small units face difficulties in recruiting qualified judges compared with larger organisations. Having a broader variety of cases is also likely to attract potential judges, while simultaneously contributing to ensuring a coherent approach to social security benefits. The latter is not attainable, since many health-related benefits follow another track. The Finnish government estimated that the costs each case generates for the Board and the parties would remain roughly the same, while the quality of rulings is likely to increase (i.e., the rule of law will be improved).[82] The SSAB is in essence a special administrative court that—in combination with the Finnish Insurance Court, where appeal is sought against SSAB rulings—forms a branch of social courts.

The development of recourse against administrative decisions in Denmark and Norway has been very different. Since courts have reviewed administrative decisions in Denmark and Norway since the eighteenth century, there has been no perceived need for administrative courts. Due to the high costs and duration of civil litigation, a multitude of administrative appeals boards have been instituted to rule on appeals against administrative decision. Many of these have a limited caseload. A Danish report from 2001 identified 61 appeals boards: of these, about one third (21) had more than 100 cases per year, one third (24) had less than 50 cases and nine had no cases at all.[83] A Norwegian report found 53 appeals boards.[84]

In this regard, it is interesting to note the persistent resistance against administrative courts in Denmark and Norway. In fact, practically nobody advocates for establishing general administrative courts in these countries—at most, introducing administrative courts for a specific type of law, such as child protection and compulsory measures, is sometimes discussed.[85] The main arguments in support of specialised appeals boards or a superior administrative organs as the main bodies hearing recourse proceedings are that the proceedings can be tailored to each case, the judges are experts and the proceedings are less costly than in civil (and probably also administrative) litigation.[86] Recourse against decisions of local administrative bodies should stay within municipal or county organs to guarantee local self-governance.[87] By giving general courts competence to hear further appeals, the court system is streamlined, and a single branch of courts upholds the coherence of the legal system. Administrative courts, which in the Danish and Norwegian context refer to special

---

[80] Laki oikeudenkäynnistä hallintoasioissa 2019/808.

[81] Social Security Appeals Boards Act (Laki sosiaaliturva-asioiden muutoksenhakulautakunnasta) 2006/1299.

[82] Government Bill HE 167/2006, pp. 6–13 and Government Bill HE 74/2017, part 4.

[83] Betænkning nr. 1401 (2001), pp. 127–128.

[84] Difi-rapport 2014:2.

[85] NOU 2017: 8.

[86] NOU 2019: 5, pp. 371–374.

[87] NOU 2019: 5, p. 391 ff.

courts with jurisdiction limited to a specific area of law, arguably reduce the coherence of the legal system.[88] General courts are problematic, too: adversarial, party-driven proceedings are not appropriate, at least not in the first instance of recourse proceedings, and more 'inquisitorial' proceedings would require more specialisation of judges, which is unattainable.[89]

The disadvantage of the current Danish and Norwegian systems are that many appeals boards are organisationally dependent on the administration. Many boards are not detached from administrative organs, and sometimes it is the administrative organ that the appeals board is supposed to control that appoints the members of the board, that is the employer of the board members and administrative staff, and that even has the power to instruct the appeals board. Even independent bodies are relatively weak institutions with part-time, limited-term judges, who must rely on administrative staff (who do not have the independent position of a judge) to prepare the cases.[90] The irresolution regarding which powers should be assigned to the Norwegian Public Procurement Complaints Board (KOFA, *Klagenemnden for offentlige anskaffelser*) illustrates how the legislator is in doubt with regard to whether the Board is sufficiently competent: KOFA was assigned new powers, which later were withdrawn only to be returned again.[91]

The proceedings in complaint boards are often weakly regulated, which can result in the board not having a sound basis for its decision and in parties not having equal and appropriate opportunities to present their case (*audiatur et altera pars*).[92] Furthermore, highly specialised boards might reduce coherence of the legal system, since the scope of cases of each appeals board is limited. Additionally, recruitment of judges and administrative staff has often proved to be challenging.[93]

Some of the weaknesses with regard to administrative appeals boards can be easily remedied. The Norwegian Complaint Boards Secretariat (*Klagenemndssekretariatet*), established in 2017 to provide high-quality secretariat services to seven complaint boards, is an example of how the organisation of these bodies can be strengthened to enable them to render justice.[94] Consolidation of appeals organs is likely to advantageous because a larger case load is an incentive to establish an independent and specialised secretariat, and more detailed and tailored procedural rules, all of which improve the independence of the body. Thus, appeals boards do not necessarily render less justice than courts do, and when they are properly organised

---

[88] E.g., NOU 1999: 19, pp. 499–521; Betænkning nr. 1398 (2001); and Betænkning nr. 1401 (2001), pp. 135–142.

[89] Waage (2017), pp. 198 ff.

[90] Difi-rapport 2014:2, pp. 50 ff.; Difi-notat 2013:3 Forvaltningsdomstoler i Norge? Kort gjennomgang av begreper og synspunkter. Difi - Direktoratet for forvaltning og IKT, and Bragdø-Ellenes (2014, 2020), pp. 136–140.

[91] In 2012, the power to levy penalty charges was removed, only to be reintroduced in 2017. See Hagland and Bruserud (2016).

[92] Difi-rapport 2014:2, pp. 50 ff.; Difi-notat 2013:3; and Bragdø-Ellenes (2014).

[93] NOU 1999: 19, pp. 499–521; Betænkning nr. 1398 (2001); Betænkning nr. 1401 (2001), pp. 135–142; and Komitesamietintö 2003:3, pp. 392–394 and 415–416.

[94] www.klagenemndssekretariatet.no (accessed 15 June 2020).

and regulated, they can render better justice, since the procedure can be cheaper, faster and tailored to the specific type of cases instead of being based on general rules of procedure of administrative courts. The broader competence to review issues regarding expedience of complaint boards can also be an advantage for the rule of law,[95] as long as courts are able to exercise sufficient control.[96] The Finnish SSAB is a key example of how the difference between courts and appeals boards can be formal rather than substantive, and how relatively small organisational changes can result in a significant improvement of the independence of the body.

The practical implications of the absence of administrative courts is that administrative decisions are seldom subject to judicial review. Recourse against decisions that allow emission of environmentally harmful substances or other activities with adverse environmental effects serve as an example: Danish courts hear some and Norwegian courts hear only a handful of such cases each year, whereas Finnish and Swedish courts hear thousands of these cases.[97] Courts hearing few cases is likely to reduce the demand for in-depth knowledge in environmental law and other branches of administrative law. The de facto limited access to courts might also impact the interpretation and enforcement of *inter alia* rules protecting the environment: big companies who have been denied permission to make emissions can bear the costs associated with litigation and therefore challenge decisions to deny permission, whereas individual citizens and NGOs often cannot afford to challenge such permission. The Norwegian Government uses as a rule the Attorney General (*Regjeringsadvokaten*) as its legal counsel, which is funded over the state budget, not by billing each individual case.[98] In Denmark, since 2015 the Chamber Advocate (*Kammeradvokaten*) has been privately organised as a law firm, where government bodies pay for each individual case.[99] The power differences are thus often striking between the government and citizens. Additionally, the Danish Chamber Advocate and the Norwegian Attorney General are zealous advocates when representing government bodies in courts, and sometimes have an interest in resisting clarification, perhaps even obscuring, of the certain issues when the government has a weak case. This is in sharp contrast to the duty of the government to be objective and to provide for sufficient clarification on its own motion.[100] Consequently, to some extent, public authorities can *inter alia* bypass rules and proceedings concerning environmental law without facing sanctions.[101]

The so called NAV (Norwegian Labour and Welfare administration) scandal, which unfolded in November 2019, exemplifies the potential adverse consequences of the combination of the lack of independence of complaint boards and sufficient legal aid. NAV required the beneficiaries of certain welfare benefits to stay in Norway; even short-term trips abroad to visit family or have a short holiday were disallowed

[95] See also NOU 2019: 5, pp. 387–389.

[96] NOU 2020: 11, pp. 71–72.

[97] Nylund (2019b) and Anker et al. (2009).

[98] Bragdø-Ellenes (2010).

[99] Waage (2016).

[100] Waage (2017), pp. 272 ff., and Zimmer (2013).

[101] Fauchald (2018), see also Sunde (2017).

and sanctioned, although this was clearly against the requirements of EU/EEA law. Additionally, NAV persistently disregarded rulings from the Norwegian Insurance Court that found the practice unlawful. It could do so partly because first recourse takes place in a complaint board that is part of the NAV organisation and, hence, would follow internal guidelines despite the Insurance Court finding these unlawful. The very limited, practically non-existent access to general courts exacerbated the problem.[102]

From a legal cultural perspective, the enduring—and growing—difference in attitudes between Denmark and Norway on the one hand and Finland and Sweden on the other hand is very interesting. The latter systems seem to believe that a clear demarcation between executive and adjudicative powers is the best way of ensuring the rule of law and that administrative courts ensure that the tenets of administrative law are applied equally in different types of cases, whereas the former countries recognise the some of the advantages of administrative courts but still believe that a decentralised structure of first appeals against administrative decisions is superior.

The differences in the attitudes towards administrative courts in Denmark and Norway on the one hand and Finland and Sweden on the other hand are profound, and there are few, if any, signs of convergence between the two blocks. On the contrary, the consolidation of administrative courts in Finland and Sweden has widened the gap. Finnish and Swedish courts have in practice a far more prominent position in fulfilling the private and public functions of courts in administrative cases than Danish and Norwegian courts do.

5 Alternative Dispute Resolution Outside Courts

Alternative dispute resolution has a long history in the Nordic countries, and formalised dispute resolution processes outside courts have been present for centuries. Today, the use of dispute resolution boards outside the formal court system to resolve disputes and render justice could be regarded as a manifestation of Nordic pragmatism. Many of these bodies, such as organisations that offer VOM, labour courts and bodies offering CDR, are designed to find practicable solutions and common ground rather to provide a highly adversarial process. Consequently, courts are a final resort: a case should be filed only once other methods of dispute resolution have been exhausted.

Out-of-court dispute resolution is pivotal in many areas of law.[103] The availability of family mediation[104] free of charge is likely to contribute to the relatively low ratio of child custody cases in court compared with the number of separating families.

---

[102] Boe (2020), Nylund (2019a).

[103] See also Petersen (2021).

[104] See, e.g., Haavisto (2018), Nylund (2018), Ryrstedt (2012) and https://familieretshuset.dk/ (accessed 15 June 2020).

However, this section focuses on two areas in which the Nordic countries have been at the forefront, namely CDR and VOM (or restorative justice).

5.1 Consumer Dispute Resolution

The Nordic consumer dispute resolution systems were developed in the 1970s and 1980s, with each country opting for a slightly different design. The two-pronged design, consisting of dispute resolution boards as the 'private' prong that resolves individual disputes and the consumer ombudsman as the public prong, forms the tenets of the systems. The 'private' prong consists of two sub-divisions: a publicly funded consumer dispute resolution body with broad subject-matter competence and privately funded bodies competent to hear disputes related to specific types of goods or services, such as banking and insurance, or laundry and dry cleaning. Despite the fact that the fragmented structure of CDR makes establishing the exact number of cases processed arduous, the considerable number of cases resolved annually by these boards is one factor explaining the comparably low number of civil cases in Nordic courts.[105] The public prong—consumer ombudsmen and authorities—have an important role in monitoring trading and marketing practices and in enforcing consumer law.[106] The Nordic consumer dispute resolution (CDR) systems have served as an inspiration for EU law.[107]

Sweden has a National Board for Consumer Disputes (*Allmänna reklamationsnämnden*), which is competent to hear practically all consumer disputes regardless of the type of purchase object or service concerned. In contrast, the Danish and Norwegian systems consist of a number of consumer dispute resolution (CDR) boards, most of which are highly specialised.[108] The Finnish system is located somewhere between the two, being neither highly centralised nor decentralised.[109]

In Finland and Sweden, the decisions of consumer dispute resolution boards are not binding and enforceable as a judgement.[110] In Denmark and Norway, decisions of public CDR bodies are binding. In Denmark, the decision is only binding on the trader, and the trader can avoid being bound by the decision by declaring that he or she does not wish to be bound by the decision within 30 days of the date

---

[105]See, e.g., Hodges (2014). For a discussion on the advantages and disadvantages of dispute resolution boards, see Betænkning nr. 1398 (2001) and Betænkning nr. 1401 (2001), pp. 148–153.

[106]E.g., Viitanen (2007).

[107]E.g., Hodges (2014) and Hodges et al. (2012).

[108]See Kristoffersen (2019) for details about the Danish system and NOU 2010:11 Nemndsbehandling av forbrukertvister, Barne-, likestillings- og inkluderingsdepartementet, Chapters 3.2 and 8.

[109]Viitanen (2007).

[110]Laki kuluttajariitalautakunnasta (Consumer Disputes Board Act) 2007/8 p. 20 and Förordning (2015:739) med instruktion för Allmänna reklamationsnämnden (Decree containing instructions for the National Board for Consumer Disputes).

the decision.[111] In Norway, the decision is binding on both parties, unless one party initiates court proceedings.[112] The Norwegian CDR system is different from those of the other Nordic countries, in that traders can initiate CDR processes in the Norwegian Consumer Authority (*Forbrukertilsynet*), whereas normally this is a privilege of consumers. The Norwegian Consumer Authority also hears disputes arising from sales of goods between two individuals, neither of whom is a trader.[113]

Despite these formal differences, the systems function similarly. The EU Consumer ADR Directive[114] introduced mediation as the first step of CDR processes in all Nordic countries. While mediation has some advantages, the parties to consumer disputes often have disparate power both economically and in terms of knowledge of their legal rights and obligations, making mediation problematic. The consumer risks entering into disadvantageous agreements if they do not know their rights. The availability of bodies offering consumers information and advice mitigates this problem.[115] If the consumer and trader do not settle their case in mediation, the consumer can initiate 'adjudicative' proceedings at a CDR board. Proceedings are written, free of charge or low-cost, and designed for self-represented parties and are thus very popular. The decisions of CDR bodies have evolved into a set of 'case law', which is important for ensuring equal application of the law and predictability and for preventing disputes from arising. The majority of traders voluntarily comply with the decisions. Consumer organisations often 'blacklist' traders who do not comply, thus creating an incentive to comply regardless of whether or not the outcome is formally binding.[116]

5.2 *Victim-Offender Mediation*

The famous article 'Conflicts as Property'[117] by the Norwegian criminologist Nils Christie marked the genesis of restorative justice processes in Norway, which later spread to the other Nordic countries. Christie reprehended lawyers for being professional thieves, who by solving the conflict in lieu of the parties efficiently bar the

[111] Lov om alternativ tvistløsning i forbindelse med forbrugerklager (Act on alternative dispute resolution regarding consumer complaints) 30 April 2015, Sect. 32.

[112] Lov om Forbrukerklageutvalget of 17 February 2017 nr. 7 (Act relating to the Consumer Disputes Commission), Sects. 7 and 12.

[113] Act relating to the Consumer Disputes Commission Sect. 1 subsection 2 and Lov om godkjenning av klageorganer for forbrukersaker of 17 June 2016, nr. 29 (Act relating to authorisation of alternative dispute resolution entitites in consumer matters), Sect. 23.

[114] Directive 2013/11/EU of the European Parliament and of the Council of 21 May 2013 on alternative dispute resolution for consumer disputes and amending Regulation (EC) No 2006/2004 and Directive 2009/22/EC (Directive on consumer ADR), O.J. L165/63 (2013).

[115] Hodges (2014) and Komiteamietintö 2003:3, pp. 280–284.

[116] Hodges (2014).

[117] Christie (1977).

parties from renegotiating their relations and social rules and from gaining an understanding of each other's views and experiences related to the incident. Hence, the lay element is pronounced in the Norwegian context, with trained volunteers serving as mediators. The involvement of the employees at the local Mediation Service Offices (*konfliktrådet*) is limited to coordinating and administrative support.[118]

Mediation can be either linked to criminal proceedings (i.e., considered 'criminal' mediation) or independent of them (i.e., considered 'civil' mediation). In 'criminal' mediation, the process is either an alternative to the criminal investigation and court proceedings or an alternative to or part of the sanction. The accused person must plead guilty to or at least admit the factual basis for the criminal investigation to qualify for victim-offender mediation. Many 'civil' mediations are, in fact, related to a criminal offence: the police encourage the victim of the crime to attempt mediation rather than to file a report, or the police or prosecution has decided to dismiss the case. Since 2016, mediation has been an integral part of youth punishment and youth follow-up, two sanctions aimed at youth offenders ages 15–18. These sanctions replace imprisonment and fines, respectively. In 2019, the total number of cases was 7,386, including 554 youth sanctions and youth follow-ups and 2,207 'civil' mediations.[119]

Denmark and Finland have enacted similar processes. The Danish process, called *konfliktråd*, entered into force in 2010 and is administered by the police. In 2019, the number of mediations was 564, approximately the same as in 2011.[120] In Finland, the Finnish institute for health and welfare has overseen local mediation offices since 2006.[121] The process has a criminal and a civil prong, as in Norway. In 2018, the number of 'criminal' mediations was 14,789 and the number of 'civil' mediations was 737.[122] The Swedish system is decentralised and less regulated compared to mediation in the other Nordic countries. No statistics are available for Sweden.[123]

Studies on VOM processes show that both victims and offenders are satisfied with the processes.[124] However, the impact on recidivism is limited or non-existent and that the restorative elements are often limited in practice.[125]

---

[118] https://www.konfliktraadet.no (accessed 15 June 2020) and Holmboe (2019).

[119] Konfliktrådet, Årsrapport 2019. https://www.konfliktraadet.no/getfile.php/4683565.2268.lwlitpzbuttjbt/%C3%85rsrapport+for+2019+fra+Sekretariatet+for+konfliktr%C3%A5dene++-+korrigert+27.4.2020.pdf (accessed 15 June 2020), p. 6.

[120] https://konfliktraad.dk/ (accessed 15 June 2020).

[121] Ervasti (2018) and https://thl.fi/en/web/thlfi-en/statistics/information-on-statistics/quality-descriptions/mediation-in-criminal-and-civil-cases (accessed 15 June 2020).

[122] https://thl.fi/fi/tilastot-ja-data/tilastot-aiheittain/sosiaalipalvelut/rikos-ja-riita-asioiden-sovittelu (accessed 15 June 2020).

[123] For a critical account of the organisation and regulation of victim-offender mediation, see Jacobsson et al. (2018).

[124] Gade et al. (2020) and Eide and Gjertsen (2009).

[125] Andrews and Eide (2019), Kyvsgaard (2016), p. 26 and Medling i går, i dag och i morgon. En kort skrift om melding vid brott. Brottsförebyggande rådet 2008. https://www.bra.se/download/18.cba82f7130f475a2f180007582/1371914724337/2008_medling_igar_idag_imorgon.pdf (accessed 15 June 2020), p. 15.

Victim-offender mediation and restorative justice processes follow roughly the same pattern as court-connected mediation: it has become an integral part of the justice system in Finland and Norway, is used to a lesser extent in Denmark and exists only at the fringes of the Swedish justice system.

6 Concluding Remarks

Nordic courts and justice systems have undergone structural, organisational and functional changes, which have amplified many of the legal cultural hallmarks. A strong preference for general courts over special courts is the most central and discernible of these, despite the fact that the adjudication of administrative cases takes place in a myriad of complaints boards in Denmark and Norway. Another key element is the continued unequivocal support for generalist judges. The increased support and use of 'moderate specialisation' dilute the ideal to some extent, while keeping the core of the principle intact.

Nordic courts occupy a less central role in the justice systems than in many other countries, since many other organs provide dispute resolution services, particularly in small cases. The role of courts in the Norwegian justice system is less central than in the other Nordic countries due to the small number of administrative cases, the role of the Conciliation Boards and enforcement agency in resolving undisputed pecuniary claims and the wide powers of CDR bodies and restorative processes. In comparison, the Swedish justice system is by design much more court-centred. Interestingly, some of the Nordic traits are primarily present in the formal court system, such as the idea of judges and courts as generalists, whereas boards at the fringes of the justice system are specialised.

In civil cases, the function of courts is disjointed. On the one hand, the adjudicative role of courts has been accentuated by transferring non-litigious, undisputed cases from courts to other organs. On the other hand, facilitating settlement and conciliation are increasingly a task of courts, whether it is part of the ordinary court proceedings or a separate mediation process or whether victim-offender mediation and restorative justice processes are used as a criminal sanction. The private function of courts has broadened beyond the formal, legal definition of a final judgment, to encompass dispute resolution through dialogue and active search for mutually agreeable solutions. Thus, Nordic courts have taken steps in the direction of the multi-door courthouses, where the disputants can utilise the dispute resolution process of their choice.[126] This has strengthened the pragmatic element in Nordic court culture.

While many of the developments are common to the Nordic countries, such as consolidation of the court structure, judicial settlement efforts or CDR, other developments uphold pre-existing divides or even create new ones. The differences in the view of the role of courts in administrative law cases and the attitudes towards administrative courts are tangible and unaltered. Court-connected mediation and

[126]Sander (1976).

victim-offender mediation have become intrinsic elements of the Finnish and Norwegian justice systems and court cultures. The reception of mediation has, in comparison, been tepid in Sweden, and partly also in Denmark. Perhaps a new division is emerging in Nordic court culture between the north (Finland and Norway) and the south (Denmark and Sweden)—that is, between countries where mediation is absorbed into court culture becoming an intrinsic part of it and countries that are more sceptical toward to mediation.

References

Adrian L (2012) Mellem retssag og rundsbordssamtale: retsmægling i teori og praksis. Jurist- og økonomforbundets forlag, Copenhagen

Adrian L (2014) Court-connected mediation in Danish civil justice: a happy marriage or a strained relationship? In: Ervo L, Nylund A (eds) The future of civil litigation: access to courts and court-annexed mediation in the Nordic countries. Springer, Cham, pp 157–186

Adrian L (2016) The role of court-connected mediation and judicial settlement efforts in the preparatory stage. In: Ervo L, Nylund A (eds) Current trends in preparatory proceedings: a comparative study of Nordic and former communist countries. Springer, Cham, pp 209–231

Adrian L, Bager S, Petersen CS (2015) Perspektiver på forligsmægling. Juristen 3:98–106

Aer J (2003) Oikeusturva ja oikeudenmukainen oikeudenkäynti hallintolainkäytössä. Oikeustiede-Jurisprudentia XXXVI Jyväskylä

Andrews T, Eide AK (2019) Mellom hjelp og straff: fungerer nye straffereaksjoner for ungdommer etter intensjonen? NF rapport nr. 2/2019, Nordlandsforskning, Bodø

Anker HT, Fauchald OK, Nilsson A, Suvantola L (2009) The role of courts in environmental law: a Nordic comparative study. Nord Environ Law J 1:9–33

Bang-Pedersen UR, Christensen LH, Petersen CS (2017) Den civile retspleje. Pejus, Hellerup

Bedner A (2010) An elementary approach to the rule of law. Hague J Rule Law 1:48–74

Bellander H (2017) Rättegångskostnader:om kostnadsbördan i dispositiva tvistemål. Iustus förlag, Stockholm

Bernt C (2011) Meklerrollen ved mekling i domstolene. Fagbokforlaget, Bergen

Bernt C (2015) Mediation of legal disputes in Norway. Institutionalized, pragmatic and increasingly popular. In: Esplugues C, Marquis L (eds) New developments in civil and commercial mediation. Springer, Cham, pp 511–545

Bernt C, Mykland S, Sky PK (2014) Evaluering av rettsmekling i jordskifterettene 2012: Sentrale funn, problemstillinger og implikasjoner. Lov og Rett 6:334–359

Boe EM (2020) Forsvarlig systeminnretning i forvaltningen. Lov og Rett 3:129–140

Bragdø-Ellenes SC (2010) Regjeringsadvokatens betydning for rettssikkerheten i forvaltningen, for menneskerettighetenes gjennomslag og for prøvingen av lovers grunnlovsmessighet. Lov og Rett 8:490–504

Bragdø-Ellenes SC (2020) Alminnelig og spesialisert tvisteløsning: i og utenfor domstolene. In: Duy IN et al (eds) Uten sammenligning: Festskrift til Eivind Smith 70 år. Fagbokforlaget, Bergen, pp. 127–150

Bragdø-Ellenes SC (2014) Overprøving av forvaltningsvedtak i Norge, Sverige og Frankrike. Universitetsforlaget, Oslo

Christie N (1977) Conflicts as property. Br J Criminol 1:1–15

Eide A K and Gjertsen H (2009) Med ! eller ? Virkninger av, og utfordringer ved, gjenopprettende rett som alternativ eller supplement til straff. NF-rapport nr. 14/2009, Nordlandsforskning, Bodø

Eldjarn E (2016) Materiell prosessledelse. Cappellen Damm Akademisk, Oslo

Ervasti K (2018) Problem-Solving Justice in Criminal and Civl Justice in Finland. Utrecht Law Review 3:19–30
Ervo L (2016) Swedish-Finnish Preparatory Proceedings: Filtering and Process Techniques. In: Ervo L, Nylund A (eds) Current Trends in Preparatory Proceedings: A Comparative Study of Nordic and Former Communist Countries. Springer, Cham, pp 19–56
Ervo L (2021) Plea Bargaining Changing Nordic Criminal Procedure: Sweden and Finland as examples. In: Ervo L, Letto-Vanamo P, Nylund A (eds) Rethinking Nordic courts. Springer, Cham
Fauchald OK (2018) Klimarettssaken og amerikanisering av norske domstoler. Lov og Rett 03:158–169
Gade CBN, van Mastrigt S, Christensen SRB, Andersen LK, Strang H, Sherman LW (2020) Forurettedes og gerningspersoners oplevelse af at mødes i konfliktråd. Foreløpige spørgeshemaresultater fra Konfliktråd Impact Project (KIP), Aarhus Universitet, Aarhus
Galanter M (1985) A settlement judge, not a trial judge: Judicial mediation in the United States. JL & Soc'y 1:1–18
Haavisto V (2002) Court work in transition: an activity-theoretical study of changing work practices in a Finnish district court. University of Helsinki
Haavisto V (2018) Developing family mediation in Finland: the change process and practical outcomes. Nordic Mediation Research, Cham, Springer, pp 41–66
Hagland B, Bruserud H (2016) Er regel "uten virkning" en regel uten virkning? In: E Hjelmeng (ed) Ugyldighet i privatretten: minnebok for Viggo Hagstrøm. Fagbokforlaget, Bergen, pp 223–244
Helenius D (2021) Nordic and European Judicial Cooperation in Criminal Matters. In: Ervo L et al (eds) Rethinking Nordic Courts. Springer International Publishing, Cham
Hodges C, Benöhr I, Creutzfledt N (2012) Consumer ADR in Europe. Bloomsbury Publishing
Hodges CJS (2014) Consumer ombudsmen: better regulation and dispute resolution. ERA Forum 4:593–608
Holmboe M (2019) Konfliktrådsloven: en kommentar. Juridika, Oslo
Jacobsson M, Wallin L, Fromholz E (2018) Victim offender mediation in Sweden: An activity falling apart? In: Nylund A et al (eds) Nordic mediation research. Springer International Publishing, Cham, pp 67–79
Jensen C (2021) Small Claims Procedures in the Scandinavian Countries. In: Ervo L, Letto-Vanamo P, Nylund A (eds) Rethinking Nordic courts. Springer, Cham
Kjelland-Mørdre K, Rolland AL, Steen KS, Gammelgård P, Anker C (2020) Konflikt, mekling og rettsmekling. Universitetsforlaget, Oslo
Kristoffersen S (2019) Det offentlie forbrugerklagesystem i et retssikkerhedsmæssigt perspektiv. Samfundslitteratur, Copenhagen
Kyvsgaard B (2016) Evaluering av konfliktråd. Justitsministeriets forskningskontor, København
Landström L (2011) Åklagaren som grindvakt: en rättsvetenskaplig studie av åklagarens befogenheter vid utredning och åtal av brott, Iustus Förlag AB.
Letto-Vanamo P (2021) Courts and proceedings: some Nordic characteristics. In: Ervo L, Letto-Vanamo P, Nylund A (eds) Rethinking Nordic courts. Springer, Cham
Lindblom PH (2007) The growing role of the courts and the new functions of judicial process: fact or flummery? Scand Stud Law 1:281–310
Lindblom PH (2017) Access to justice and the courts' role. In: Lindblom PH (ed) Progressive procedure. Iustus, Stockholm, pp 155–169
Lindell B (2019) Alternativ till rättskipning. Förhandling, medling, processförlikning, tvistlösningsnämnder och skiljeförfarande. Iustus, Stockholm
Linnanmäki K (2021) Mediation: a change in Finnish court culture? In: Ervo L, Letto-Vanamo P, Nylund A (eds) Rethinking Nordic courts. Springer, Cham
Mäenpää O (2019) Deference to the administration in judicial review in Finland: Deference to the administration in judicial review, Springer, Cham, pp 181–201
Møller J, Skaaning S (2014) The rule of law: definitions, measures, patterns and causes. Springer, Cham

Nolan-Haley JM (1996) Court mediation and the search for justice through law. Wash. ULQ 1:47
Nolan-Haley JM (1998) Informed consent in mediation: a guiding principle for truly educated decisionmaking. Notre Dame L. Rev. 3:775
Nolan-Haley JM (2011) Is Europe headed down the primrose path with mandatory mediation. NCJ Int'l L. & Com. 4:982
Nylund A (2018) A dispute systems design perspective on Norwegian child custody mediation. In: Nylund A, Ervasti K, Adrian L (eds) Nordic Mediation Research. Springer, Cham, pp 9–26
Nylund A (2019a) Comparing the efficiency and quality of civil justice in Scandinavia: the role of structural differences and definitions of quality. Civ Justice Q 4:427–439
Nylund A (2019b) Klima, miljø og domstoler i et komparativt perspektiv. In: Fauchald OK Smith E (eds) Mellom jus og politikk. Grunnloven § 112. Fagbokforlaget, Bergen, pp 101–117
Nylund A (2019c) Accountability and transparency in the course of civil justice in the Nordic countries. In: D Mitidiero (ed) Accountability e Transparência da justica civil. Uma perspectiva comparada. Revista dos Tribunais, São Paulo, pp 251–267
Nylund A (2020) Civil procedure in Norway. Wolters Kluwer, Alphen aan den Rijn
Nylund A (2021) Europeanisation of Nordic civil procedure: does the map match the terrain? In: Ervo L, Letto-Vanamo P, Nylund A (eds) Rethinking Nordic Courts. Springer, Cham
Nylund A, Sunde JØ (2019) Courts and court proceedings. In: Letto-Vanamo P et al (eds) Nordic Law in European Context. Springer, pp 201–213
Petersen CS (2021) The public policy-implementing role of Nordic courts in civil dispute resolution. In: Ervo L, Letto-Vanamo P, Nylund A (eds) Rethinking Nordic courts. Springer, Cham
Riskin LL, Welsh NA (2007) Is that all there is: the problem in court-oriented mediation. Geo. Mason L. Rev. 15:863
Robberstad A (1998) Mellom tvekamp og inkvisisjon: straffeprosessens grunnstruktur belyst ved fornærmedes stilling, Universitet i Oslo
Robberstad A (2018) Sivilprosess. Fagbokforlaget, Bergen
Ryrstedt E (2012) Mediation regarding children: is the result always in the best interests of the child? A view from Sweden. Int J Law Policy Fam 2:220–241
Sander FE (1976) The multi-door courthouse. Barrister 3:18
Sunde JØ (2017) Klimasøksmål og demokrati. Nytt Norsk Tidsskrift 4:354–365
Sunnqvist M (2021) The Changing Role of Nordic Courts. In: Ervo L, Letto-Vanamo P, Nylund A (eds) Rethinking Nordic Courts. Springer, Cham
Tamanaha BZ (2004) On the rule of law: history, politics, theory. Cambridge University Press, Cambridge
Thorsteinsdóttir H (2021) Globalisation and court practice in Iceland: new case law of the Supreme Court in relation to the EEA Agreement and European Convention on Human Rights. In: Ervo L, Letto-Vanamo P, Nylund A (eds) Rethinking Nordic courts. Springer, Cham
Tontti J (2000) Olaus Petri and the rules for judges. Assoc J Soc Leg Theory 1:113
Tyler TR (2006) Why people obey the law. Princeton University Press, Princeton, New Jersey

The Public Policy-Implementing Role of Nordic Courts in Civil Dispute Resolution

Clement Salung Petersen

Abstract This chapter explores the role of Nordic courts in safeguarding certain public values and interests, whether substantial or procedural, in the three types of civil dispute resolution that can potentially lead to state enforcement, namely civil litigation, arbitration and mediation. First, it shows how Nordic courts in civil litigation may take on an'active role' vis-à-vis the parties but that the legal contours of this role remain unclear and controversial. Secondly, it shows how current and proposed statutory frameworks governing arbitration and mediation give national courts an important role in safeguarding public values and interests which raises important questions in law concerning the role of courts as gatekeepers of access to court and state enforcement for private actors. The chapter concludes with a discussion of the need for developing a clearer and more coherent approach to defining this public policy-implementing role of courts across all three types of civil dispute resolution. It is argued that such a coherent approach is needed and that it will be valuable to analyse the public policy-implementing role of courts in a Nordic context, since the Nordic countries generally share many of these relevant public values and interests.

1 Introduction

During the twentieth century, the Nordic welfare states established a clear social dimension in their laws. This significantly changed the view on the state into what we today usually refer to as the 'Nordic model', in which the state actively protects and promotes social values through economic and social policies.[1] Today, both the Nordic countries and the European Union continue to use law as an important instrument to safeguard certain economic, social and political values and interests in society. Examples of such 'public values and interests' include protection of weaker parties (e.g., consumers and employees); safeguarding the functioning of markets (e.g.,

[1] See, e.g., J. H. Petersen (2019).

C. S. Petersen (✉)
Faculty of Law, University of Copenhagen, Karen Blixens Plads 16, 2300 København, Denmark
e-mail: clement.petersen@jur.ku.dk

L. Ervo et al. (eds.), *Rethinking Nordic Courts*, Ius Gentium: Comparative Perspectives on Law and Justice 90, https://doi.org/10.1007/978-3-030-74851-7_12

competition law, financial regulation, and free movement law); safeguarding third-party interests (e.g., company law and insolvency law); and broader public interests (e.g., combatting corruption, fraud, money laundering, etc.).[2] Meanwhile, private actors have come to play a significant societal role in the Nordic countries with regard to providing goods and services of essential importance to markets and welfare. In this regard, private actors often establish and enforce private legal orders to help them operate on multi-jurisdictional markets, and such private governance of their activities may affect the public values and principles promoted by state governance.[3] Because of these societal developments, disputes about civil rights and obligations may increasingly concern public values and interests such as consumer protection, workers' rights, equal treatment, fair market practices, environmental protection, social policy, and health.[4]

With regard to civil dispute resolution, we have seen increasing support for the use of consensual arbitration (hereinafter 'arbitration') and mediation as private and usually confidential alternatives to civil litigation in public courts.[5] Recent research even suggests that arbitration (instead of civil litigation) should become the default mode of dispute resolution in transnational commercial disputes.[6] Under the New York Convention on Arbitration of 1958 and the newly enacted Singapore Convention on Mediation of 2019, states and their national courts must generally recognise and enforce arbitral awards and mediated settlement agreements, even though national courts may also exercise some (limited) judicial control over the arbitration/mediation procedure and its outcome. As a result, three distinct forms of civil dispute resolution can now provide private actors with access to state-enforced civil justice—namely, civil litigation, arbitration and mediation. At the same time, state legislation requires public courts to enforce arbitration agreements and mediation agreements, respectively, by (to some extent) limiting access to civil litigation.[7]

These developments raise important questions concerning the role of courts as gatekeepers of access to the court and access to state enforcement in disputes about civil rights and obligations. A question of particular importance in this regard is the public policy-implementing function of courts with regard to safeguarding the fundamental procedural guarantees enshrined in ECHR Article 6 and preventing (the enforcement of) substantive outcomes that violate certain public values and interests like those mentioned above. How and to what extent shall courts in the three forms of civil dispute resolution safeguard such specific rights and obligations from state legal

---

[2] Cordero-Moss (1999) and Cordero-Moss (2018).

[3] On this development and its legal implications in private law and civil dispute resolution, see Hansen et al. (2020) with references.

[4] Hansen et al. (2020).

[5] On the privatisation of civil justice, see, e.g., Genn (2012) and Hess (2019).

[6] Cuniberti (2015).

[7] See, in particular, Article 8 of the UNCITRAL Model Law on International Commercial Arbitration, 1985, with amendments as adopted in 2006, and Article 14 of the UNCITRAL Model Law on International Commercial Mediation and International Settlement Agreements Resulting from Mediation, 2018, amending the Model Law on International Commercial Conciliation, 2002. See also Sect. 3.2 below.

orders, whether substantive or procedural, irrespective of the will of the parties, before providing them with access to state enforcement? With the developments mentioned above, this question has become fundamentally important for understanding the role of courts and the interplay between state legal orders and private ordering in the age of globalisation. Nonetheless, legal scholarship traditionally analyses the public policy-implementing role of courts in arbitration separately from the similar role of courts in civil litigation. With the newly enacted Singapore Convention on Mediation, similar questions will potentially arise in the Nordic countries (if they adopt the convention) with regard to mediation.

Against this background, the aim of this chapter is to explore how the above-mentioned developments affect the role of Danish, Norwegian and Swedish courts in safeguarding public values and interests, whether substantial or procedural, in the three types of civil dispute resolution that can potentially lead to state enforcement—namely, civil litigation, arbitration and mediation. First, it will show how courts in civil litigation in Denmark, Norway and Sweden increasingly may take on an 'active role' *vis-à-vis* the parties but that the legal contours of this role remain unclear and controversial. Secondly, it will show how current and proposed statutory frameworks governing arbitration and mediation (as distinct alternatives to civil litigation) give national courts an important role in safeguarding public values and interests, and that this role raises important questions in law concerning the role of courts as gatekeepers of access to court and state enforcement for private actors. Thirdly, it will discuss the need for developing a clearer and more coherent approach to defining the public policy-implementing role of courts across all three types of civil dispute resolution, including the potential benefits of doing so in a Nordic context. Because of language barriers, the analysis will not include Finnish and Icelandic law but focus on Danish, Norwegian and Swedish law. All references to 'Nordic' in the analyses will thus refer to these three Nordic jurisdictions, unless otherwise explicitly stated.

2 Civil Litigation

2.1 Role of Courts

Party autonomy is a fundamental value in the modern Nordic laws on civil procedure.[8] The courts shall only adjudicate a dispute if requested by a party, and it is generally for the parties to define their legal dispute and adduce relevant evidence. In dispositive civil disputes, courts shall traditionally be passive and not seek to influence the choices of the parties with regard to their claims, allegations and evidence. This passive role of courts in civil procedure reflects a mid-19th-century liberalist view on the state and, in this sense, represents a 'liberal procedural ideology'.[9]

[8] Petersen (2014) with references.

[9] See, e.g., Westberg (1988), p. 33, and van Rhee (2005), p. 11.

As mentioned, civil disputes increasingly concern matters governed by statutory law in which the welfare state seeks to promote certain public values or interests.[10] This active role of the Nordic welfare states as regulators has challenged the liberal procedural ideology governing the state as adjudicator (through its state courts). State courts in civil litigation can thus (potentially) play an important, active role in safeguarding public values and interests promoted by the state (as strongly emphasised by Franz Klein in his seminal work Pro Futuro (1891)).[11] With the development of the Nordic welfare states, it is therefore not surprising that exceptions to the traditionally passive role of courts have also gradually emerged in the Nordic countries.[12] Significant examples of such court activity include investigating issues of fact or law *ex officio*, providing judicial guidance or giving hints and feedback to the parties, *ex officio* ordering a self-represented party to take on legal representation, and promotion of settlement.

The aim of the following analysis is to explore the public policy-implementing role of courts—that is, how courts take an active role in civil litigation to safeguard public values and interests. The analysis will comprise the adjudicatory role of courts (Sect. 2.2), the settlement-promoting role of courts (Sect. 2.3) and the role of courts in court-connected mediation (Sect. 2.4, which also defines the concept of court-connected mediation).

2.2 *Court Adjudication*

2.2.1 Jura Novit Curia

When analysing the public policy-implementing role of court adjudication in the Nordic countries, the starting point is the principle usually referred to as *iura novit curia*, which means that courts have an *ex officio* obligation to identify and apply the relevant law correctly regardless of the legal arguments of the parties. This principle will often allow Nordic courts to apply relevant statutory law that seeks to promote public values and interests. However, under the principle of party presentation courts generally cannot go beyond the ambit of the dispute as defined by the parties in their claims and allegations. This can create tension if the parties rely on statements of fact that do not allow the court to address aspects of the dispute that concern public values or interests. Parties may have an interest in disregarding such aspects of the dispute, so the ability of a court to give hints and feedback to the parties concerning such an issue might not be sufficient to convince the parties to establish a factual basis for doing so. In this context, the pertinent question is whether courts can or must raise and consider issues of fact *ex officio*, if none of the parties has explicitly relied upon them, when the facts are necessary to consider aspects of the dispute that

[10] See examples mentioned in Sect. 1 above.

[11] See van Rhee (2005), pp. 11–13.

[12] See, in particular, Taksøe-Jensen (1979), Westberg (1988) and Eldjarn (2016).

concern public values or interests. Furthermore, Nordic courts might be unable to apply statutory law because of conflict-of-law rules.

To understand the public policy-implementing role of Nordic court adjudication in further detail, it becomes relevant to distinguish between different types of legal rules. More specifically, the analysis will distinguish between the fundamental legal principles and values in the state legal order typically referred to as public policy (ordre public) in private international law and international procedural law[13] (2.2.2), mandatory protection rules (2.2.3) and other rules (2.2.4).

2.2.2 Safeguarding Public Policy (Ordre Public)

If relevant for safeguarding rules of public policy (ordre public) in civil litigation, Nordic courts may set aside the principle of party presentation. Danish and Norwegian civil procedure law provides statutory support for this.[14] In Swedish civil procedure law, courts may also rely on certain facts *ex officio* in dispositive civil disputes (so-called *officialfakta*) despite the lack of clear statutory support for this in the Swedish Judicial Code.[15] Illustrative examples from Danish case law concern claims for specific performance of contractual obligations which involve a criminal offense, as well as the collection of debt originating from undeclared work (moonlighting) or bribes.[16] An illustrative example from Swedish case law concerns *ex officio* enforcement of public law requirements concerning acquisition of certain types of property.[17]

In recent decades, Danish courts seem to have increasingly used this *ex officio* power to safeguard public policy in civil litigation. This has raised the difficult question to what extent public policy concerns should bring courts to take action *ex officio*. As an example, courts must decide whether the fact that a service provider has offered his services as undeclared work affects only a claim for payment for the services or any claim based on such contract, including remedies for the service provider's breach of contract. In the latter case, public policy concerns might leave people in private law relationships without legal protection under the rule of law. Some commentators have criticised the Danish courts for going too far in this regard.[18] The aim here is not to go into a thorough analysis of these questions but merely to show that an active public policy-implementing role of courts raises legal questions that are unclear and also quite controversial.

---

[13] See, e.g., Hess and Pfeiffer (2011).

[14] See Sect. 338 in the Danish Administration of Justice Act (which allows Danish courts to also rely on 'allegations that the parties cannot waive') and Sect. 11–4 in the Norwegian Civil Dispute Act.

[15] See Westberg (1988), p. 83, and Ekelöf and Edelstam (2002), pp. 64–65.

[16] Petersen (2019), p. 495.

[17] See Ekelöf and Edelstam (2002), pp. 64–65.

[18] See Tromborg (2015), Faldborg and Troelsen (2016).

Where domestic law allows *ex officio* application of rules of public policy, it is for the national court to apply any applicable fundamental rules of EU law, such as the antitrust provisions in the Treaty on the Functioning of the European Union.[19] In general, EU law does not require national courts 'to abandon the passive role assigned to them by going beyond the ambit of the dispute defined by the parties themselves and relying on facts and circumstances other than those on which the party with an interest in application of those provisions bases his claim'.[20] However, when Nordic courts (as discussed above) may rely on other facts *ex officio* to safeguard domestic public policy, a similar obligation will apply with regard to EU public policy under the principle of equivalence.[21]

2.2.3 Safeguarding Mandatory Statutory Protection

Both the Nordic welfare states and the EU have enacted mandatory statutory laws that aim to protect so-called 'weaker parties' such as consumers and employees. Some of these mandatory rules are 'absolute' and thus have the same character as the fundamental rules of public order discussed above. Other statutory protection rules allow the weaker party to waive the protection *ex ante* (after the rise of a dispute). These rules can also raise difficult questions about the role of courts in civil litigation, which I will illustrate below by focusing on two distinct procedural situations in which such questions may arise.

The first situation arises when a weaker party appearing before a court in a civil litigation omits arguments concerning the relevant mandatory statutory protection laws. This omission may be due to a deliberate choice made by the weaker party to waive the statutory protection, but it may also be due to a lack of awareness of his/her rights under the applicable statutory law. As mentioned, courts generally have an obligation to identify and apply the relevant law correctly regardless of the legal arguments of the parties (*iura novit curia*), but courts must respect the principle of party presentation and thus cannot go beyond the factual ambit of the dispute as defined by the parties (see *supra* 2.2.1). Unlike the rules of public order discussed in Sect. 2.2.2, Danish, Nordic and Swedish courts have no general power to *ex officio* include facts not relied upon by the parties in order to make mandatory statutory protection rules applicable.[22] Instead, the court may provide judicial guidance or give hints and feedback to the weaker party about the potential relevance of the mandatory rules. If the weaker party is self-represented, in some situations the court can also order the weaker party to take legal representation. Danish, Norwegian and Swedish courts only have a duty to take on such an active role in dispositive disputes in

[19]This follows from the so-called principle of equivalence developed in the CJEU case law; see, e.g., Lenaerts et al. (2014), p. 118.

[20]See *Van Schijndel*, ECLI:EU:C:1995:441.

[21]See e.g. Lenaerts et al. (2014), p. 118.

[22]This follows from Sect. 338 of the Danish Administration of Justice Act, Sect. 11 of the Norwegian Dispute Act and Sect. 17:3 of the Swedish Judicial Code.

a few specific circumstances. In particular, Nordic courts often have a duty to provide judicial guidance to self-represented parties. In Danish law, this follows explicitly from Sect. 339(4) of the Danish Administration of Justice Act. A similar duty exists without explicit statutory support under Norwegian law and Swedish law.[23] In other cases, Danish, Norwegian and Swedish courts have no duty but generally a wide discretion to provide judicial hints and feedback to the parties. There seems to be no clear guidelines in these countries concerning when courts should exercise this discretion to safeguard mandatory statutory protection laws.

Danish courts have a wide discretion to take on the active role described above under Sect. 339(1)-(3) and Sect. 259(2) of the Danish Administration of Justice Act. In 2001, the Danish Administration of Justice Committee discussed the need for clearer rules about the role of Danish courts with regard to providing judicial hints and feedback to safeguard mandatory statutory protection laws. The committee concluded that it would return to this pertinent question in the future.[24] As of 2019, the committee still has not addressed this question, and it remains unclear whether Danish courts should generally exercise their discretion to give hints and feedback to safeguard mandatory statutory protection laws.

Norwegian courts also have a wide discretion to provide judicial hints and feedback to the parties in dispositive civil disputes under Sect. 11–5 of the Norwegian Dispute Act. According to the preparatory works to the Norwegian Dispute Act, courts should follow some of the principles that are applicable in non-dispositive civil disputes in dispositive civil disputes as well (e.g., to provide hints and feedback in cases involving a weaker party vis-a-vis a strong party).[25] The scope of any such duty, including a duty to provide judicial hints and feedback to ensure that a weaker party is aware of his/her rights under mandatory statutory laws, generally remains unclear.[26]

Swedish courts also have discretion to provide judicial hints and feedback under Sects. 42:8 and 43:4 of the Swedish Judicial Code. In connection with a significant reform of these rules, an expert committee addressed the implications of potentially relevant mandatory statutory protection laws in dispositive civil disputes.[27] According to the majority view in the committee, mandatory statutory protection laws should not lead to a more active role of courts in dispositive civil disputes, whereas three members of the committee argued that if such laws could be potentially relevant courts should take on a more active role in their safeguarding.[28] The subsequent bill that implemented the law reform left this question quite open.[29] Today, the scope of any duty of courts to provide hints and feedback remains unclear.[30]

---

[23] See Skoghøy (2017), p. 966, and Lindell (2012), p. 295.

[24] Retsplejerådet (2001) Betænkning 1401 om Reform af den civile retspleje I, p. 315.

[25] Ot.prp. no. 51 (2004–2005) p. 177.

[26] See Eldjarn (2017), pp. 210–212 with references.

[27] SOU 1982:26.

[28] SOU 1982:26, pp. 114, 609, 610 and 616.

[29] Prop 1986/87:89, p. 106, and Westberg (1988), p. 619.

[30] Ekelöf and Edelstam (2002), p. 45; Westberg (2012), p. 330; and Lindell (2012), p. 293.

A second situation arises when courts render a default judgment. Do courts have a duty to enforce (potentially) applicable mandatory statutory protection laws, or is it justifiable to assume that the lack of response from the defendant (as the protected weaker party) constitutes an *ex post* waiver of the statutory protection? Courts may enforce such rules by applying them *ex officio*. However, in some cases it might not be entirely clear that such laws apply, or their application might require the court to rely on facts or circumstances not put forward by the plaintiff. Should courts in such situations have an obligation to start an *ex officio* investigation of the relevant facts (to clarify whether the mandatory rule applies)? Alternatively, the court could provide judicial guidance to the defendant about (the possible relevance of) the mandatory statutory protection rule.

Courts in Denmark, Norway and Sweden can render a default judgment without making a full inquiry on the factual and legal basis for the claims put forward by the plaintiff. A Danish court must ascertain that the plaintiff's claim is justified based on the statement of claim and any other information available to the court.[31] A Norwegian court must ascertain that the plaintiff's claim does not appear to be obviously incorrect ('åpenbart uriktig').[32] These rules on default judgments explicitly address whether the court should seek to safeguard mandatory statutory protection laws.

In Denmark, the development of consumer protection laws in the 1970's led to a call for more active courts in safeguarding consumer rights, and in the early 1980's, Danish courts appeared to be open for undertaking a more active role.[33] However, recent research shows that it is difficult to find a consistent approach in Danish case law to such a more active role and that the Danish high courts have actually limited the district courts from undertaking such a role when rendering default judgments.[34] Currently, it remains unclear to what extent Danish courts actively seek to safeguard statutory mandatory protection laws in connection with default judgments.[35]

The CJEU has taken a more extensive approach to ensuring the effectiveness of EU law on protection of consumers against unfair contractual terms, which 'are not binding on the consumer'. Thus, the CJEU has developed a number of *exofficio* obligations of national courts to safeguard the mandatory statutory protections against unfair contractual terms.[36] Under this case law, a national court is required to assess of its own motion whether a contractual term falling within the scope of EU consumer protection law is unfair. A national court has an obligation to examine this issue of its own motion, when it has available to it the legal and factual elements necessary for the task. Generally, these *ex officio* obligations in EU consumer law also apply in connection with default judgments. However, the scope of these *ex officio* obligations

---

[31] See Sects. 352 and 360 of the Danish Administration of Justice Act.

[32] See Sect. 16–10(2) of the Norwegian Civil Dispute Act.

[33] Zahle (1983), Rosenmeier (1984).

[34] Christensen (2008).

[35] C. S. Petersen (2019).

[36] For an overview, see, e.g., Trstenjak (2013); Lenaerts et al. (2011), pp. 131–136; and Hess and Law (2019), pp. 111–129.

of national courts is also quite unclear, and it is doubtful whether national courts live up to their obligations under EU law in this regard.[37]

2.2.4 Safeguarding Other Rules of Law

The 'liberal procedural ideology' with (generally) passive courts empowers the parties to take care of their own interests. Parties may not always be able to do this in a way that will ensure their legal rights under the rule of law. This makes it pertinent to consider whether courts should have certain duties to safeguard legal rights under the rule of law beyond the scope of rules of public policy and mandatory statutory protection laws (discussed above). As an example, German judges have quite extensive responsibilities to undertake a certain amount of positive activity during civil proceedings in the interest of ensuring a fair and just outcome.[38]

As mentioned in Sect. 2.2.3 above, Danish, Norwegian and Swedish courts generally have a duty to provide judicial guidance to self-represented parties in dispositive civil disputes. When a party has legal representation, these Nordic courts have a quite wide discretion to provide hints and feedback. Even though legal scholarship has developed some general guidelines for whether or not to exercise this discretion, it generally remains a controversial question whether and to what extent Nordic courts should provide judicial hints and feedback with an aim to safeguard civil justice under the rule of law.[39]

2.3 *Court Promotion of Settlement*

Promoting settlement is an important role of Nordic courts in civil litigation, particularly before or during first instance proceedings. Generally, Nordic courts have significant discretion with regard to whether, when and how they will promote settlement in civil litigation.[40]

Promoting settlement clearly supports the dispute resolution function of courts. In contrast, its relationship with the other functions of courts in civil litigation, particularly the need of society to have its laws respected and clarified, is less clear.[41] It seems clear that a Nordic court should not promote a settlement which will clearly

[37] See the comprehensive analysis in Hess and Law (2019).

[38] See Murray and Stürner (2004), p. 155 and pp. 166–177.

[39] On Danish law, see C. S. Petersen (2019) with references. On Norwegian law, see Skoghøy (2017) and Eldjarn (2016), both with references. On Swedish law, see Westberg (1988) and Lindell (2012), both with references.

[40] See, e.g., Bang-Pedersen et al. (2017), pp. 108–111; Skoghøy (2017); and Lindell (2012), pp. 303–310.

[41] For a comparative overview of the functions of Nordic courts in civil litigation, see Petersen (2014) with references.

violate the public order (ordre public), including mandatory provisions from which the parties cannot derogate by agreement.[42]

In other situations, courts appear to have wide discretion to promote settlement without having regard to the rules of law. Swedish law traditionally subscribed to the view that the estimated outcome of the dispute under the rule of law (which can be subject to significant uncertainty at an early stage of the proceedings) should guide the promotion of settlement by courts. In recent decades, this view on the role of courts in civil litigation has changed, such that courts should generally promote settlement if doing so meets the interests and needs of the parties.[43] This change clearly favours the dispute resolution function of courts. With regard to Norwegian law, Skoghøy argues that a legally correct decision should be the guiding star ('ledetråd') for the promotion of settlement by courts.[44] However, it is not a role of Norwegian courts to control whether a party, by entering into a settlement, waives mandatory statutory protection laws, which a party is entitled to waive in a civil litigation.[45] With regard to Danish law, empirical research shows that there is no clear view on this matter amongst Danish judges.[46] In recent years, the Danish Ministry of Justice and the Danish Court Administration have asked consultancy firms to analyse Danish civil litigation. The consultancy reports suggest using the number of settled civil cases as an important benchmark, and they refer to the courts with the statistically highest number of settled cases as 'best practice'.[47] These consultancy reports reflect a view that the primary (or perhaps only) function of the Danish civil justice system is (or should be) dispute resolution.

2.4 Court-Connected Mediation

Court-connected mediation[48] is now part of the civil justice systems in Denmark, Norway and Sweden. Based on a facilitative mediation model, court-connected mediation focuses, in particular, on the needs and interests of the parties, not on rights

[42] On Norwegian law in this regard, see NOU 2001:32, pp. 725–726, and Skoghøy (2017), p. 33.

[43] Lindell (2012), pp. 307–309.

[44] Skoghøy (2017), p. 33.

[45] Schei et al. (2009), p. 829, and NOU 2001:32, pp. 725–726.

[46] Adrian et al. (2015).

[47] Deloitte (2013), Implement Consulting Group (2015).

[48] Adrian (2016), p. 213, provides the following general description of court-connected mediation in a Nordic context: 'Court-connected mediation is a voluntary settlement activity conducted by one or more neutral third parties who assist the parties in reaching their own solution in a pending court case. The court is engaged in the mediation—an engagement that can range from minimally providing a controlled list of mediators to which the parties can be referred to a full in-house service. The service is to some extend regulated by law, decrees, ethical guidelines, court rules or similar instruments. Mediation can take place at any point in time after the case is filed and before the final ruling.'

and obligations under the rule of law.[49] However, in this context, courts can also play an important public policy-implementing role by controlling that a settlement agreement does not violate rules of public policy (ordre public). Norwegian law generally does not require courts to safeguard mandatory statutory protection, which a party can waive by agreement.[50] In court-connected mediation under Danish law, the mediator must terminate the mediation if it is necessary to do so to prevent the parties from entering during the mediation into an agreement that involves a criminal activity or in any other way contravenes mandatory law.[51]

Against this background, the public policy-implementing role of courts in court-connected mediation appears to be limited to ensuring that courts do not support agreements that will violate public policy (ordre public), including mandatory provisions from which the parties cannot derogate by agreement.

2.5 Reflections

The analyses above show how the public policy-implementing role of Nordic courts in civil litigation is in several respects unclear and in some respects also controversial. As a general observation, Nordic courts appear to have a quite wide discretion, but only few duties, to take on a public policy-implementing role. In particular, it remains unclear to what extent courts should exercise their discretion to safeguard mandatory statutory protection laws or even legal rights in general. Views differ, presumably reflecting different political views on the role of the state *vis-a-vis* private autonomy, and the law generally leaves it to the discretion of judges in the individual case to decide the extent of their public policy-implementing role.

The analyses also show how EU law has created more explicit and potentially more far-reaching *exofficio* obligations, particularly in EU consumer law. Even though these obligations are also subject to significant uncertainty, they lead to a fragmented civil justice system in the Nordic countries, since the public policy-implementing role of courts will differ depending on whether or not the disputes concern matters regulated by EU law.

[49] For an overview, see,e.g., Nylund et al. (2018).

[50] See Sect. 19–11(3) of the Norwegian Dispute Act and Schei (2009), p. 829, with references.

[51] See Sect. 276(2) of the Danish Administration of Justice Act.

3 Arbitration and Mediation

3.1 Role of Courts

The Nordic countries generally support consensual arbitration as an alternative to civil litigation in commercial disputes. The UNCITRAL Model Law on Commercial Arbitration (Model Law) constitutes the basis for the Danish Arbitration Act (DAA) and the Norwegian Arbitration Act (NAA), whereas the Swedish Arbitration Act (SAA) has a different form but still generally follows the Model Law in substance.[52] All three Nordic countries have adopted the New York Convention on Arbitration of 1958.

Mediation, as a separate form of dispute resolution unconnected to court litigation, has only more recently attracted the interest of legislators. The EU has adopted Directive 2008/52/EC on certain aspects of mediation in civil and commercial matters, which is binding neither on Denmark (Article 1(3) and Recital 30 of the Directive) nor on Norway (no EEA relevance). The Swedish Act No 2011:860 transposes this Directive into Swedish law. The Norwegian Dispute Act includes some rules on extra-judicial mediation (see Chapter 7 of the Act). Denmark has not adopted any similar legislation.

Important legal frameworks for mediation are now emerging at the international level, including the UNCITRAL Model Law on International Commercial Mediation 2018 and the newly enacted Singapore Convention 2019. Against this background, a recent report from an expert committee established by the Danish Arbitration Institute has drafted a proposal for a new Danish Mediation Act.[53]

The aim of the following analysis is to explore the potential public policy-implementing role of courts in disputes, which the parties submit to consensual arbitration or mediation as an alternative to civil litigation. Specifically, the aim is to explore to what extent national courts can safeguard public values and interests in such arbitration or mediation. The analysis will comprise the legal implications of arbitration and mediation agreements as waivers of the right of access to a court (Sect. 3.2), the role of courts during a pending arbitration or mediation (Sect. 3.3), court control of arbitral awards (Sect. 3.4) and court control of mediated settlements (Sect. 3.5).

---

[52] See, e.g., Juul and Thommesen (2017) on Danish law, Woxholth (2013) on Norwegian law, and Lindskog (2012) on Swedish law.

[53] See Voldgiftsinstituttet (2018).

3.2 Waiver of the Right of Access to a Court

3.2.1 Arbitration

It is a fundamental feature of modern arbitration laws based on the Model Law that when an action is brought before a national court in a matter that is the subject of an arbitration agreement, the court shall refer the parties to arbitration, unless the court finds that the arbitration agreement is null and void, inoperative or incapable of being performed. Thus, an arbitration agreement generally constitutes a waiver of the right of access to a court under the rule of law. Under the case law from the European Court of Human Rights (ECtHR), persons may waive their right to a court under Article 6 of the ECHR in favour of arbitration. The waiver must be permissible, must be established freely and unequivocally and must be attended by minimum safeguards commensurate to its importance.[54]

The above-mentioned principle that courts should normally refer parties to arbitration applies in the Nordic countries.[55] It is, however, subject to certain restrictions. Only disputes concerning legal relationships with respect to which the parties have an unrestricted right of disposition may be submitted to arbitration (sometimes referred to as the requirement of 'arbitrability'. If a dispute involves issues that concern public policy, it may not be 'arbitrable'.[56] Further restrictions can apply in specific types of disputes, most notably consumer law disputes.[57]

A judgment from the Danish Supreme Court provides an illustrative example of how the public interest may affect 'arbitrability'.[58] The dispute arose between the Association of Danish Pharmacies, which is the employer and professional organisation of the pharmacies in Denmark, and one of its members. The dispute was formally about an alleged violation by the member of a rule in the bylaws of the association, but this rule mirrored a Danish statutory rule, which concerned the pricing of drugs for sale on the Danish market. This statutory rule was part of the general public law regulation of pharmacies in Denmark. In accordance with the bylaws of the association, the association submitted the dispute to arbitration and the arbitral tribunal rendered an arbitral award stating that the member had violated the bylaws and therefore should pay a 'fine' to the association. The member started a court action for setting aside this arbitral award, which was eventually heard by the Danish Supreme Court. The Supreme Court stated that the parties could not submit this kind of dispute to arbitration, because it concerned an alleged violation of a

[54] For an overview of this case law, see Council of Europe/European Court of Human Rights (2019) Guide on Article 6 of the European Convention on Human Rights. Right to a fair trial (civil limb). Updated to 31 August 2019. Council of Europe, p. 31.

[55] See DAA Sect. 8, NAA Sect. 6, and SAA Sect. 4.

[56] For a general discussion of this matter, see, e.g., Werlauff (2008); Werlauff (2009); SOU 1994:81, pp. 172–174; and Cordero-Moss (2018).

[57] See DAA Sect. 7(2), NAA Sect. 11, SAA Sect. 6.

[58] See judgment from the Danish Supreme Court of 17 February 1999, reported in the Danish Weekly Law Reports as U 1999.829 H.

public law rule, which in essence was aiming to safeguard general public interests. The Supreme Court therefore set aside the arbitral award.

When national courts deny access to a court and instead refer a party to arbitration, they support arbitration as an alternative to court litigation. However, as the analysis above shows, courts can still control whether the dispute is capable of settlement by arbitration and, if not, provide full access to the court despite the arbitration agreement. Since the restrictions on access to arbitration reflect important public values and interests, this control constitutes an important public policy-implementing role of courts *vis-à-vis* arbitration as an alternative to court litigation.

3.2.2 Mediation

In the same vein, courts may have to consider whether they shall deny access to the court upon request from a party who wants to mediate the dispute under the terms of an agreement to mediate. This is a challenging question, since mediation is a consensual process that supports the autonomy of the disputing parties to make their own decisions about the dispute. If after a dispute arises, a party is determined not to mediate, one could argue that a general mediation agreement is unenforceable (as an 'agreement to agree' or an 'agreement to negotiate in good faith').[59] However, more detailed mediation agreements, requiring parties not to initiate judicial or arbitral proceedings during a specified period or until a specified event has occurred, might provide courts with a basis for at least suspending a civil litigation.[60] Article 14 of the UNCITRAL Model Law on Commercial Mediation takes steps in this direction, as do the new Danish General Conditions for the provision of works and supplies within building and engineering (the 'AB System').[61]

Eventually, however, courts cannot deny access to the court because of a mediation agreement, since mediation against the will of a party is a *contradictio in adjecto.* In this respect, courts therefore cannot support mediation as a means of dispute resolution to the same extent as arbitration.

---

[59] Case law from common law jurisdictions has previously followed this line of argumentation. For an overview of relevant case law, see Brooker (2013), pp 42–82.

[60] See Hansen et al. (2020) with references.

[61] This new 'AB System' introduces a multi-tiered dispute resolution system, which can include different types of mediation. For details, see https://www.byggerietsregler.dk/.

3.3 *Role of Courts during Arbitration and Mediation*

3.3.1 Arbitration

Nordic courts can support a pending arbitration in several ways. They can assist in the appointment of arbitrators.[62] They can also assist in the collection of evidence, which can be a prerequisite for summoning a witness against his/her will and for the effective production of documents under applicable disclosure rules.[63] Moreover, arbitral tribunals with a seat in Denmark can request that a Danish court make a preliminary reference to the CJEU.[64] In the same vein, an arbitral tribunal with a seat in Norway can request that a Norwegian court make a preliminary reference to the EFTA Court.[65]

Even though an arbitration agreement generally constitutes a waiver of the right of access to a court for resolving the specific dispute, Nordic courts can still play a role in controlling certain aspects of a pending arbitration upon request of a party. Most importantly, national courts can control the competence of the arbitral tribunal, including whether the dispute is capable of settlement by arbitration.[66] Courts can also control the impartiality and independence of arbitrators[67] and the costs of the arbitral tribunal.[68]

The above-mentioned rules enable national courts to safeguard certain fundamental aspects of due process in arbitration, including those institutional and procedural requirements of Article 6 ECHR that the parties have not waived by entering into an arbitration agreement.[69]

3.3.2 Mediation

The focus here is on mediation used as an alternative to civil litigation. Since mediation is a consensual dispute resolution process, court control of a pending mediation process does not play the same role as in arbitration (as discussed above). However, the legislative frameworks on mediation (such as those discussed above) can empower the courts to control the costs of the mediator(s).[70]

---

[62] See DAA Sect. 11, NAA Sect. 13, and SAA Sects. 12 and 14–17.

[63] See DAA Sect. 27(1), NAA Sect. 30(1) and SAA Sect. 26.

[64] See DAA Sect. 27(2).

[65] See NAA Sect. 30(2).

[66] See DAA Sect. 16, NAA Sect. 18, SAA Sect. 2.

[67] See DAA Sect. 13, NAA Sect. 15, SAA Sect. 10.

[68] See DAA Sect. 34, NAA Sect. 39, SAA Sect. 41.

[69] On the applicability of ECHR Article 6 to arbitration, see, e.g., Jaksic (2002), Jaksic (2007) and Krumins (2019).

[70] Section 7–4 of the Norwegian Dispute Act and Sect. 18 of the proposal for a Danish Mediation Act.

Courts may support mediation in ways comparable to the way courts can support arbitration. Courts may assist in the appointment of mediators.[71] They may also support mediation by enforcing confidentiality obligations (e.g., in connection with restrictions on admissibility of evidence in subsequent civil litigation).[72]

3.4 Court Control of ADR Outcomes

3.4.1 Arbitral Awards

When an arbitral tribunal has rendered an arbitral award, the courts shall generally recognise that award as binding and enforceable. However, a court may subsequently control certain aspects of the arbitral award in setting aside proceedings, provided the arbitration took place within the jurisdiction of the court or in proceedings concerning recognition and enforcement of the award.[73] These provisions in the three Nordic arbitration acts include an exhaustive list of grounds for setting aside or refusing recognition and enforcement of arbitral awards, which are identical to or largely correspond to those in the UNCITRAL Model Law, which again largely reflect those in the New York Convention. These grounds include certain serious violations of due process or other procedural irregularities and an excess of power by the arbitral tribunal (*ne ultra petita*).[74]

Furthermore, the legislative frameworks allow some limited control by national courts of the substantive outcome in arbitral awards, which courts can use to safeguard certain public values and interests. First, courts can control (*ex officio*, if necessary) whether the arbitral award is contrary to public policy (ordre public). Public policy also comprises fundamental principles of EU law such as the previously mentioned antitrust rules in the Treaty on the Functioning of the European Union.[75] Second, courts can control (*ex officio*, if necessary) that the dispute was capable of settlement by arbitration. This includes the fundamental requirement that disputes must concern legal relationships with respect to which the parties have an unrestricted right of disposition. In the Nordic countries, this notably includes the explicit consumer protection restrictions mentioned in Sect. 3.2.1 above. These grounds enable national courts to safeguard the 'strongest' public values and interests such as those discussed in Sect. 2.2.2 above.

---

[71] See e.g. Section 7–2 of the Norwegian Civil Dispute Act and Sect. 7 of the proposal for a Danish Mediation Act.

[72] See, e.g., Sect. 7–3(6) of the Norwegian Civil Dispute Act, Sect. 5 of the Swedish Mediation Act, Sect. 15 of the proposal for a Danish Mediation Act, and Article 7 of the Mediation Directive.

[73] For details, see DAA Sect. 37–39, NAA Sects. 42–47 and SAA Sects. 33–36.

[74] *Ibid.*

[75] *Eco Swiss*, ECLI:EU:C:1999:269.

With regard to mandatory statutory protection laws and other rules of law (as discussed in Sects. 2.2.2, 2.2.3 above), national courts generally have no competence to control whether the arbitral tribunal has applied such law correctly. Nordic arbitration laws do not impose any duty on arbitrators to provide guidance or to give hints and feedback to the parties in an arbitration.

In conclusion, Nordic courts can generally safeguard public values and interests only if they are inherent in fundamental rules of public policy (ordre public) or in matters excluded as 'not capable of settlement by arbitration under the Nordic arbitration laws.

3.4.2 Mediated Settlements

Even when the parties have chosen to mediate and have reached a settlement, courts can generally control the binding effect and validity of such a mediated settlement. However, under the newly enacted Singapore Convention, certain mediated settlement agreements (agreements resulting from mediation and concluded in writing by parties to resolve a commercial dispute) shall generally become directly enforceable under the conditions laid down in the Convention. The Convention includes an exhaustive list of grounds for refusing to grant relief to enforce a settlement agreement (see Article 5 of the Convention), which largely resembles the regulation known from the New York Convention on Arbitration (mentioned in Sect. 3.1 above). The Convention will thus generally enable national courts to safeguard public values and interests to the same (limited) extent as in arbitration (as described in Sect. 3.4.1 above). The grounds in the Convention for refusing to grant relief also address some special issues arising in mediation, including the potential implications of a mediator having unduly influenced the parties' decision to enter into the settlement agreement. These grounds will enable national courts to safeguard certain fundamental due process principles in mediation.

3.5 Reflections

The analyses show that national courts can play an important role in safeguarding public values and interests in both arbitration and mediation. Courts shall perform this role within the applicable statutory frameworks, which currently provide courts with some instruments to control arbitration and mediation, both with regard to preventing enforcement of arbitral awards or settlements that are contrary to certain public values and interests and with regard to safeguarding certain (minimum) procedural guarantees in arbitration and mediation.

Under the current statutory frameworks, the scope of this role of national courts will depend, in particular, on the scope of the grounds for setting aside, or for refusing recognition and enforcement of, arbitral awards and the ground for refusing to grant relief based on a mediated settlement agreement. Apart from the specific procedural guarantees offered by these frameworks, the public policy-implementing role of courts will depend on national laws regarding when the 'subject matter of the dispute is not capable of settlement by' arbitration or mediation and the legal concept of public order (ordre public). Both of these legal concepts are today subject to significant legal uncertainty, but they both enable courts to limit access to state enforcement if necessary to avoid a violation of certain (strong) public values and interests.

4 The Public Policy-Implementing Role of Nordic Courts

This chapter has explored the public policy-implementing role of Nordic courts in civil litigation, arbitration and mediation. It generally shows that courts can play an important role in safeguarding public values and interests in a broad sense, whether procedural or substantial, in all three types of civil dispute resolution, but to varying degrees.

The analyses show that Nordic courts have an important role in safeguarding due process. In civil litigation, this role of courts is subject to detailed regulation, including the requirement of ECHR Article 6. In arbitration, national courts can play a role in safeguarding the mandatory due process guarantees in the statutory frameworks governing arbitration, which generally reflect those guarantees of ECHR Article 6 which the parties do not waive by entering into the arbitration agreement. In mediation, national courts can also play a role in safeguarding certain due process requirements, including ensuring that the mediator has not unduly influenced the mediated settlement.

The analyses also show that courts play an important role in safeguarding rules of public policy (ordre public) in all three types of civil dispute resolution. The concept of 'public policy' traditionally comprises the most fundamental public values and interests in a society; at the same time, however, it remains a flexible legal concept that can take into consideration important developments in society as well as in the law. Arguably, courts should take a consistent approach to defining the concept of 'public policy' (ordre public) across all three types of civil dispute resolution, which should take into consideration the significant developments mentioned in Sect. 1 above. The scope of the concept of 'public policy' can be crucial in defining the reach of state legal orders *vis-a-vis* private legal orders in our currently globalised world.[76]

With regard to mandatory statutory protection laws, which do not fall within the concept of public policy (ordre public), the analyses show significant differences across the three types of civil dispute resolution. In civil litigation, courts can play an active role in safeguarding such mandatory statutory protection, particularly through judicial guidance of self-represented parties. In many cases, however, Nordic courts have no duty, but a wide discretion, to take on such an active role. In some cases raising issues of EU law, courts must use this discretion to safeguard, for example,

[76] See Hansen et al (2020).

consumer protection. In these regards, the de facto public policy-implementing role of courts in civil litigation is generally fragmented and unclear. In arbitration, the Nordic arbitration acts provide significant protection of certain public values and interests (in particular, consumer protection laws) through the restrictions mentioned in Sect. 3.2.1 above. Outside the scope of these restrictions, national courts generally cannot safeguard mandatory statutory protection laws in arbitration, unless they fall within the concept of public policy (ordre public). The same is true in the case of mediation. The analyses thus show that the choice of civil dispute resolution can significantly affect the legal effects of such mandatory statutory protection laws. The increasing focus on arbitration and mediation as alternatives to civil litigation makes it pertinent to consider the potential for developing a more consistent approach to the public policy-implementing role of courts in all three types of civil dispute resolution.

With regard to other rules of law, the role of courts in safeguarding any public values and interests associated with such laws is generally limited. In civil litigation, courts may have a duty to provide judicial guidance, particularly to self-represented parties. Apart from such explicit duties, courts generally have a wide discretion, but no duty, to give hints and feedback to the parties, and such rules of law generally do not limit their competence to promote settlement. In arbitration and mediation, courts generally cannot play a public policy-implementing role with regard to such other rules of law.

The societal developments mentioned in Sect. 1 above make it relevant to consider developing a clearer and more consistent approach to defining the public policy-implementing role of courts across all three types of civil dispute resolution. This will require further analyses of the legal frameworks and concepts mentioned above in light of the relevant public values and interests. Since the Nordic countries generally share many of these relevant public values and interests, it will arguably be valuable to analyse this public policy-implementing role of courts in a Nordic context. This represents an important task for future Nordic legal research in this area.

References

Adrian L (2016) The role of the court-connected mediation and judicial settlement efforts in the preparatory stage. In: Ervo L, Nylund A (eds) Current trends in preparatory proceedings. A comparative study of Nordic and former communist countries. Springer, Cham

Adrian L, Bager S, Petersen CS (2015) Perspektiver på forligsmægling. Juristen 3:98–106

Bang-Pedersen UR, Christiansen LH, Petersen CS (2017) Den civile retspleje. Pejus, Copenhagen

Brooker P (2013) Mediation Law: Journey through Institutionalism to juridification. Routledge, Oxfordshire

Christensen LH (2008) Rettens prøvelse i udeblivelsessager – særligt i forbrugerforhold. Erhvervsjuridisk Tidsskrift 2:129–144

Cordero-Moss G (1999) International Commercial Arbitration: Party Autonomy and Mandatory Rules. Tano Aschehoug, Oslo

Cordero-Moss G (2018) Norsk ordre public som skranke for partsautonomi i internasjonale kontrakter og internasjonal tvisteløsning. Universitetsforlaget, Oslo

Cuniberti G (2015) Rethinking international commercial arbitration: towards default arbitration. Edward Elgar Publishing, Cheltenham
Deloitte (2013) Analyse af civile sager. Deloitte
Ekelöf PO, Edelstam H (2002) Rättegång. Första häftet. Norstedts Juridik, Stockholm
Eldjarn E (2016) Materiell prosessledelse. Cappelen Damm Akademisk, Oslo
Faldborg A, Troelsen K (2016) Sort arbejde – kan det betale sig? Erhvervsjuridisk Tidsskrift 3:200
Genn DH (2012) Why the privatization of civil justice is a rule of law issue, 36th F A Mann Lecture, Lincoln's Inn. https://www.ucl.ac.uk/laws/sites/laws/files/36th-f-a-mann-lecture-19.11.12-professor-hazel-genn.pdf
Hansen et al (2020) Private governance and the potential of private law. Eur Rev Private Law 2–2020:333–374
Hess B, Pfeiffer T (2011) Interpretation of the public policy exception as referred to in EU instruments of private international and procedural law. PE 453.189. European Parliament, Brussels
Hess B (2019) Privatizing dispute resolution and its limits. In: Loïc Cadiet et al (eds) Privatizing dispute resolution: trends and limits. Nomos, Baden-Baden, pp 17–46
Hess B, Law S (2019) Implementing EU consumer rights by national procedural law. Luxembourg Report on European Procedural Law Volume II. Beck/Hart/Nomos
Implement Consulting Group (2015) Analyse af rets- og forligsmægling. Implement Consulting Group
Jaksic A (2002) Arbitration and human rights. Peter Lang, Bern
Jaksic A (2007) Procedural guarantees of human rights in arbitration proceedings: a still unsettled problem? J Int Arbitr 24:159–171
Juul J, Thommesen PF (2017) Voldgiftsret. Karnov Group, Copenhagen
Krumins T (2019) Arbitration and human rights—lack of setting-aside proceedings as a violation of the ECHR (PhD Thesis, University of Copenhagen 2019). University of Copenhagen, Copenhagen
Lenaerts K, Maselis I, Gutman K (2014) EU procedural law. Oxford University Press, Oxford
Lindell B (2012) Civilprocessen. Iustus Förlag, Uppsala
Lindskog S (2012) Skiljeförfarande: en kommentar. Norstedts Juridik, Stockholm
Murray PL, Stürner R (2004) German civil justice. Caroline Academic Press, Durham, North Carolina
Petersen CS (2014) A Comparative perspective on recent Nordic reforms of civil justice. In: Ervo L, Nylund A (eds) The Future of Civil Litigation. Springer, Cham, pp 9–29
Petersen CS (2019) Den civile retspleje under forandring. In: Ulrik Rammeskow Bang-Pedersen et al. (eds) Retsplejeloven 100 år. DJØF Forlag, Copenhagen
Petersen JH (2019) Nordic models of welfare states. In: Letto-Vanamo P et al (eds) Nordic Law in European Context. Springer, Cham, pp 21–39
Rosenmeier HP (1984) Nogle aktuelle spørgsmål ved retternes behandling af borgerlige sager, hvor sagsøgte udebliver. Advokaten 7:117–120
Schei T et al (2009) Tvisteloven: Kommentarutgave Bind I. Universitetsforlaget, Oslo
Skoghøy JEA (2017) Tvisteløsning. Universitetsforlaget, Oslo
Taksøe-Jensen F (1979) Materiel procesledelse i borgerlige sager. Juristforbundets forlag, København
Tromborg NW (2015) Aftaler i strid med loven – en analyse af de senere års praksis. Erhvervsjuridisk Tidsskrift 4:261–268
Trstenjak V (2013) Procedural Aspects of European Consumer Protection Law and the Case Law of the CJEU. European Review of Private Law 2:451–478
Van Rhee CH (2005) Introduction. In: van Rhee CH (ed) European Traditions in Civil Procedure. Intersentia, Cambridge, pp 3–22
Voldgiftsinstituttet (2018) Behovet for en lov om mediation. Voldgiftsinstituttet
Werlauff E (2008) Privat voldgift med offentligretlige delspørgsmål. Ugeskrift for Retsvæsen 19:152–159

Werlauff E (2009) Private Arbitration of Incidental Public Law Issues. European Business Law Review 4:565–577
Westberg P (1988) Domstols officialprövning. En civilprocessuell studie i anslutning till RB 17:3 p 1. Juristförlaget i Lund, Lund
Woxholth G (2013) Voldgift. Gyldendal juridisk, Oslo
Zahle H (1983) Udeblivelsesdomme. Om parternes udeblivelse i civile dispositive retssager. Juristforbundets Forlag, København

Mediation: A Change in Finnish Court Culture?

Kirsikka Linnanmäki

Abstract The topic of this chapter is court-connected mediation and how mediation has affected the court culture in civil cases in Finland. The focus is on the three following dimensions of the mediation system: on legislative, theoretical, and practical changes. The main normative change was the act that came into force in 2006. The new legislation led gradually to changes in practice as well. A significant amount of cases in the District Courts go to mediation today. The law defines judges also as mediators, and in practice many judges are trained and experienced mediators. Also, the theoretical framework for courts has expanded, since mediation theories constitute a relevant basis for the mediation process. The change in culture is also multidirectional. Not only has mediation moved into the legalistic court culture, but also the legal context affects mediation. Mediation has changed court culture by providing an alternative to court trial and it has brought new dimensions to the definition, role and function of courts of law.

1 Introduction

Culture can be defined in various ways and can refer to a variety of things. It can be defined as a way of life of a particular group of people at a particular time.[1] Culture is also a compass that provides the direction or glue that holds groups together.[2] It can be said that people make culture.[3] The concept of culture is a rather abstract social construction that is affected and cross-affected by many things. Likewise, the changes in court culture can be defined in various ways depending on context and perspective.

[1] Cambridge Dictionary https://dictionary.cambridge.org/dictionary/english/culture (last visited 17th of June 2020).

[2] Tharp (2009), p. 2.

[3] Menkel-Meadow (1993), p. 6.

K. Linnanmäki (✉)
University of Helsinki, Yliopistonkatu 3, 00014 Helsinki, Finland
e-mail: kirsikka.linnanmaki@helsinki.fi

L. Ervo et al. (eds.), *Rethinking Nordic Courts*, Ius Gentium: Comparative Perspectives on Law and Justice 90, https://doi.org/10.1007/978-3-030-74851-7_13

Court culture is also part of the larger legal culture.[4] In addition, it reflects the general atmosphere in the society. Traditionally, courts have represented broad stability and predictability. Court culture can be attached to court cases, to the norms that guide procedures and resolutions, to court personnel and their education and to court customers. Also, the views of court culture depend on the various functions that are related to the courts. This chapter, which can be defined as sociolegal, describes and analyses whether and how mediation has changed court culture in Finland and will focus on the norms that regulate court proceedings, behaviour patterns or practices and traditions in courts.[5]

Court culture can be divided into different spaces of time. Kaijus Ervasti has outlined the Finnish court and justice culture over five periods: (1) early law of local community (until the sixteenth century), (2) pre-modern law (from the sixteenth century to the nineteenth century), (3) modern law (from the nineteenth century to 1950s), (4) the law of the welfare state (from the 1950s to 1990) and (5) post-modern law (from 1990 onwards). According to him, the distinctive features of the development of the Finnish law system at the beginning of the twenty-first century are: (1) the growth of regulation and the globalisation of sources of law, (2) the disintegration of jurisprudence to several disciplines, (3) the decrease in civil proceedings and the increase in alternative dispute resolution, and (4) the privatisation of justice.[6] Here, the focus will be on the post-modern law, the increase of alternative dispute resolution (especially mediation)[7] and the privatisation of justice.

Mediation has definitions in various sources such as legislation, research, handbooks and brochures, as well as in practice. Mediation can be understood in many ways, and different goals and details can be highlighted. Practices are also diverse. Mediation can, for example, be defined narrowly, referring to the modern, professional mediation process, or broadly, referring to various processes aiming at amicable resolution. Mediation as a system can also be divided into three different elements: theoretical models, applications in context, and mediation in action.[8] In this chapter, mediation refers only to court-connected mediation in civil cases, and thus out-of-court mediation and mediation in criminal and administrative cases are not included.

---

[4]Ervasti (2005), p. 352.

[5]Various elements of defining culture, see Schein (2010), pp. 14–18.

[6]Ervasti (2005), pp. 352–371.

[7]Regarding the history of mediation in Nordic countries, see Ervasti (2018), pp. 226–227.

[8]Ervasti and Nylund (2014), pp. 139, 148. Regarding the mediation system with various definitions and perspectives in Nordic countries, see also Ervasti (2018).

2 Normative Change

2.1 *Legislative Changes*

Before 2006, modern, professional mediation was not an option in the Finnish courts in civil cases. A court trial was the only available option. The procedure of court trial is regulated in detail in the Code of Judicial Procedure (4/1734). Just to mention some of the main characteristics, the judge presides over the procedure, the advocates present the case, and evidence is presented. The process and the conversations are meant to be formal, and the resolutions are to be motivated. The process and the outcome are open for complaint. The legal evaluation of the case (i.e., the judgement) is based on what is considered to be the legal truth according to legislation and requires due motivation.

During the trial, the parties can also come to an agreement. The courts have a general duty to support amicable resolutions (i.e., settlement) in dispositive cases. The actual proceeding for or method of promoting agreements is not regulated in detail, and there seems to be no clear theoretical background for the process itself. The promotion of settlement takes place in the framework of court trial and the norms of fair trial.[9] The court can also confirm the agreement between the parties instead of giving a judgement in the case (the Code of Judicial Procedure, Chap. 5, Sect. 26 and Chap. 20).

Following the examples from Denmark and Norway, in 2006 the Finnish general courts (administrative courts are thus excluded) were by law given the option to provide court-connected mediation as an alternative process to a court trial in dispositive cases, however including child custody and contact cases[10] (which also include indispositive elements).[11] Court-connected mediation is regulated in the Act on Mediation in Civil Matters and Confirmation of Settlements in General Courts (394/2011, the Mediation Act, the law was reformed in 2011 due to the implementation of the EU-directive 2008/52/EY, but the original sections about mediation remained mainly untouched). Mediation is thus regulated in a separate law, apart from the Code of Judicial Procedure, to underline its alternative nature to court trial. In addition to mediation in the district courts, mediation is by law also available in the appellate court instances.

The Mediation Act regulates the mediation process on a very general level. It is left for the mediators and the parties to decide the process in more detail on a case by case basis. Some main principles, such as the aim of amicable resolution, free will and consent of the parties, as well as the neutrality and objectivity of the mediator, are regulated. The Act also requires that the mediator be a judge; thus, no one outside the court can act as the mediator in court-connected mediation. However,

---

[9] See, Ervasti (2004).

[10] Regarding the background and aims of the regulation, see Government bill HE 114/2004 vp.

[11] See, e.g., Aaltonen (2009), p. 132 and the referenced literature, Tolonen and Linnanmäki 2020, p. 310–313.

the mediator can have assistance in the process, either procedural or substantial, from an expert (Sect. 5). The Act does not define the experts as mediators, since the role of the mediator in court includes among other things the power to confirm the reached agreement.[12]

The phases or techniques of mediation are not regulated in detail. The preparatory works, however, propose four phases and highlight the mediator's communication skills.[13] In principle, no evidence or legal evaluation is required. Child custody and contact cases, however, constitute an exception in the legislation. Specifically, the Mediation Act requires that the child's best interests shall be taken into consideration in mediation (Sect. 10). The specific methods for this, however, are not regulated, and the evaluation of the child's best interests is left up to the individual mediator. The preparatory works, however, require that the legislation regarding child custody and contact shall be taken into consideration in mediation as well.[14] During the past decade, more interest has been paid to how mediation can support the best interests of the child. This interest has been inspired by the Norwegian child-friendly models (using, e.g., psychologist expertise (*sakkyndige*) in various roles and combining mediation with court trial) on one hand and the English and Australian models (systemic and child-focused) on the other hand.[15]

Court-connected mediation involves many changes for court personnel, advocates as well as court customers. First, according to the law, judges are also mediators, when they are addressed to and serving on a mediation case (Act on Mediation Act, Sect. 5). Today, judges are not only experts of law and legal questions but also are responsible for the mediation process. Second, according to law, mediation aims to achieve amicable resolution and promote mutual understanding between the parties (Sects. 3 and 7). Court customers, the parties of the cases, are given different kind of responsibility and self-determination in mediation compared to in the court trial. They need to discuss their own case together with the other party. Thus, the parties, instead of their advocates, act the main roles in their process and create their own private justice. For the parties, mediation is also less risky, since they are the ones deciding the outcome and as the parties are, according to law, responsible for their own costs only (Sect. 27).[16] Third, advocates are also expected to understand and adopt different roles, even though the law does not separately regulate their special role in mediation. They however need to know the differing legislation and other norms and practices between mediation and court trial, as well as to advise their clients to choose the best alternative for their case.[17]

The confirmation of an agreement can follow either court trial or mediation. The confirmation requires request and consent from both parties. According to law, the settlement may not be confirmed if it is contrary to law or clearly unreasonable or if

[12]Government bill HE 114/2004, various pages.

[13]Government bill HE 114/2004.

[14]Government bill HE 114/2004, pp. 48–49.

[15]See, Ministry of Justice (2013), pp. 47, 53, 70.

[16]See also Government bill HE 114/2004, various pages.

[17]Ministry of Justice (2016), p. 84–104.

it violates the right of a third party. It is further regulated that the decision of the court on the confirmation of the settlement in the case is subject to appeal in accordance with the provisions on appeal of a judgment (the Code of Judicial Procedure, Sect. 3 and 5, Chap. 20, Mediation Act, Sect. 8). However it can be noted that mediation and court trial can give very different premises to evaluate the possible obstacles to the confirmation.

Mediation has meant normative changes and additions in the court culture. At the same time, some questions regarding mediation remain unregulated or simply linked to the legalistic framework and to the Code of Judicial Procedure. One explanation for this is that mediation was retrospectively added to the already existing court system, and the whole of the system with its new element was not opened for comprehensive re-evaluation or re-design.[18] As a result, there remains some incoherence and even confusion between the various proceedings. In legislation, the general procedural framework for court-connected mediation is a combination of the Mediation Act and the Code for Judicial Procedure. The framework can be seen as a combination of (a) the legalistic court context, which highlights the objective criteria for justice, and (b) mediation as a flexible alternative highlighting the parties' subjective experiences in creating justice.[19]

2.2 *Theoretical Changes*

Before 2006, mediation theories were not given much attention in courts or in procedural law. However, the 1993 change with regard to settlement promotion and the oral preparatory stage gave some attention to the conflict resolution theories.[20] Mediation took this development even further, since it is an alternative to court trial and in many ways a different process. The two alternatives are based on different theoretical backgrounds and are also differently regulated.[21] Court trial is regulated by several hundred paragraphs in the Code of Judicial Procedure accompanied by a large amount of case law, whereas only very few general provisions regulate mediation and the amount of case law is very limited. Regarding mediation, the process is guided mostly by cross-scientific mediation theories and ethics.[22] The mediation process has its typical phases, but it is also flexible for case-by-case adaptation. Mediation has

---

[18]Regarding system design, see Ury et al. (1993), Menkel-Meadow (2006), Ervasti and Nylund 2014, pp. 552–553.

[19]Regarding the different discourses, see Ervasti (2005), p. 369.

[20]Regarding the change of court trial, see Haavisto (2002), pp. 165–251, 260–262, 287, Ervasti (2004), p. 433, Ervo (2014), Ervo (2017), p. 679.

[21]Ervasti (2011), pp. 8–11, 25.

[22]Ervasti (2011), pp. 16–19, 79, Ervasti and Nylund (2014), pp. 41–42, 558.

thus also changed (or expanded) the theoretical framework for court proceedings, which can also be seen as part of the normative change.[23]

The Finnish legislator has taken into account the existence of mediation theories. Court-connected mediation is, in its preparatory works, linked to facilitative and evaluativemediation models.[24] This applies to child custody and contact cases as well. However, the child's best interests shall also be taken into account. From the wide selection of mediation theories that exist today, the theoretical background for the Finnish mediation legislation is of course selective.[25] However, during the below-mentioned pilot project, the English model of systemic mediation[26] seemed to be also one source of inspiration.[27] On one hand, the Finnish co-mediation creates its own special application and practices. On the other hand, many links and similarities to international discussions can be noted.[28]

The mediation theories, as understood here, are based on cross-scientific research and other literature focusing especially on the mediation process, phases and techniques, as well as mediation principles and ethics. They constitute an important framework for mediation training, practices and research.[29] The role of mediation theories in mediation practices can be compared to the role of legal theories in legal practises. Legal theories play an important role in defining the perspectives from which legal sources are viewed and individual cases are handled and resolved. Legal theories support lawyers into reflecting and justifying their practices.[30] It is evident that mediation has gained ground in today's courts. This is due to legislation and the high case numbers, as described below. Thus, the importance of mediation theories has also become part of court culture. Mediation theories are part of mediation training provided to judges, as described below. Today, knowledge of mediation is also included in legal studies.[31] Since 2006, court-connected mediation has also interested researchers of procedural law.[32] Mediation has thus expanded the norms, values, behavioural patterns and traditions of the Finnish courts.

According to the general theoretical perspective adopted in Finland (in legislation, in the preparatory works, in research and in mediation training),[33] the mediator is

[23]Regarding division of norms into rules and principles, see, e.g., Aarnio (1989), p. 78, Pajulammi (2014), p. 271.

[24]Government bill HE114/2004, pp. 4, 22. The concepts of facilitative and evaluative mediation were introduced by Riskin (1996).

[25]See also Nylund (2014), pp. 325–326.

[26]Parkinson 2011.

[27]See Ministry of Justice (2013) and (2016).

[28]Government bill HE 186/2013, Aaltonen (2015).

[29]For a description of conflict and mediation theories, see Ervasti and Nylund (2014), pp. 41–42.

[30]Syrjänen (2012), p. 339.

[31]According to University of Helsinki's website, the course of general procedural law includes alternative conflict resolution and inter alia knowledge of the Mediation Act (https://courses.helsinki.fi/fi/200250/125443008).

[32]E.g., Knuts (2006), Ervasti (2011).

[33]See, e.g., Government bill HE 114/2004, Knuts (2006), various pages, Ervasti (2011), pp. 8–19, 47–52, Ministry of Justice (2013), pp. 22–24 and (2016), pp. 104–115, Ervasti (2018), p. 231.

a facilitator of discussions between the parties and does not provide resolutions or even opinions to the parties.This lack of ruling authority is very different from the traditional role of a judge. The mediator is an expert in the mediation process and in promoting communication, but not necessarily in the content of the case (as in arbitration or court trial). The parties' self-determination to define their own interests and to negotiate their own agreements is the cornerstone of mediation. Mediation provides an opportunity for creative, tailor-made resolutions that can meet the parties' needs and are not only limited to the provisions of law. This differs from the judge's traditional role as well. The mediation process is informal and flexible and is based on trust and the neutrality and objectivity of the mediator. As a process, mediation is based on special techniques (e.g., questioning and active listening) and different phases that diverge from the ones in court trial and are not regulated by law.

In today's society, mediation, especially in the court context, however occurs in the shadow of the law.[34] The legal and social frames cannot be ignored for the process and the resolution to be generally recognised and accepted. The mediation process and the reached agreement should therefore not infringe upon the parties' or a third party's legal rights. In addition, a case is suitable for court-connected mediation only if a legally defined dispute exists; other conflicts are thus excluded.[35]

Child custody and contact disputes in particular illuminate the collision between the legalistic and alternative perspectives. One example is the child's role in the process. In Finland, children are not legal parties to these disputes (Act on Child Custody and Contact Right, Sect. 14).[36] The role of children in mediation is likewise deduced from the law that regulates child custody and contact issues and that is procedurally focused on court trials.[37] It can be noted that the legalistic approach is dominant in this respect. An alternative approach could emphasise the perspectives of family systems and conflict resolution. It could recognise the importance of children's voices in family systems and communications when resolving family conflicts. The alternative perspective could give reason to view the child's role differently from the legalistic perspective. Mediation can be more informal, constructive and even healing compared to a court trial. Thus, it can meet the child's legal rights differently as well. For example, the need to protect children from the process could be different in the different processes.[38]

[34]The term is originally from Mnookin and Kornhauser (1979).

[35]Government bill HE 114/2004, p. 29.

[36]Government bill HE 224/1982, p. 6.

[37]This is confirmed by the Finnish Legal Affairs Committee Statement 4/2005.

[38]Linnanmäki (2019), pp. 185–186.

3 Changes in Practice

3.1 Mediation Has Become a Popular Alternative in District Courts

Before 2006, mediation was not an available alternative in the Finnish courts, and disputed cases were handled only in court trials. However, the court practices changed after the 1993 reform, becoming more informal and actively controlled and highlighting the parties' contributions to establishing their case and their expanding initiatives in particular, as well as attempts to reach a settlement instead of giving a verdict.[39] Nonetheless, the practices by which settlements are promoted within the trial context are various, changing between facilitating communication, evaluating the case and using pressure.[40]

Court-connected mediation started to emerge in practice quite slowly during the first years. Initially, mediation was not very popular, despite many investments in mediation training inspired by Nordic and English and North American models and trainers.[41] A new phase started in 2011, when a specific specialist-assisted application of court-connected mediation was piloted in child custody and contact disputes in selected courts, accompanied by a large-scale training and promotions for professionals and in general media. In the pilot project, four district courts offered co-mediation in child custody and contact disputes, where an expert—a social worker or psychologist—assisted the judge mediator.[42] In 2014, this model was made nationwide and permanent in legislation.[43] During the pilot project in 2011–2014, a significant rise in mediation case numbers in courts occurred. Simultaneously, there was a development and research project underway regarding facilitative mediation in family social services.[44] There was thus a strong interest in developing family mediation services in Finland in the 2010s.

---

[39] Haavisto (2002), pp. 289–290.

[40] Ervasti (2004), various pages.

[41] See Ervasti (2011), p. 50 and Fig. 1 below.

[42] Ministry of Justice (2013 and 2016).

[43] Government bill HE 186/2013.

[44] Haavisto et al. (2014).

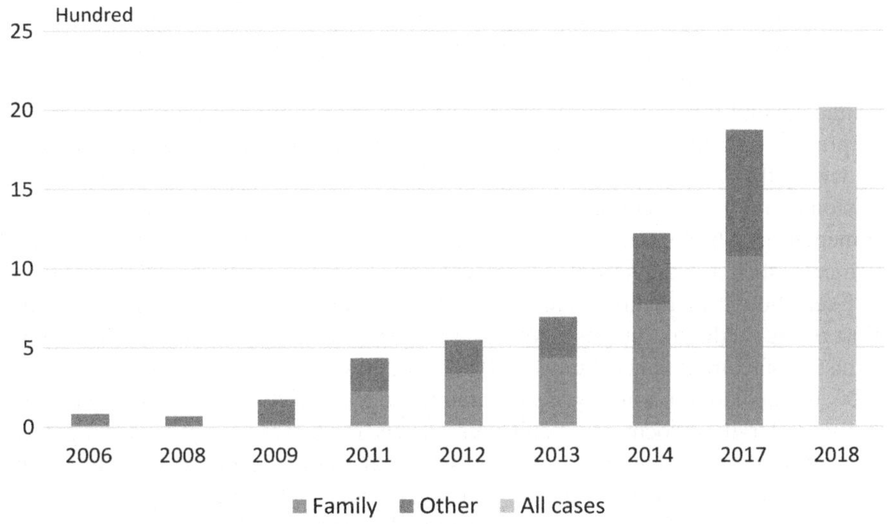

Fig. 1 Mediation in Finnish district courts in civil cases (family and other) 2006–2018 (Salminen and Ervasti (2014), p. 603, Linnanmäki (2019), p. 2.)

The mediation statistics regarding the district courts show that the mediation case numbers have risen significantly in the past ten years.[45] More than half of the mediation cases are now family conflicts, and the rest are other civil conflicts such as neighbour- or work-related matters. Thus, court-connected mediation has now become an established practice in the district courts in Finland. However, there is some local variation among district courts,[46] with some being more active than others in promoting mediation, investing in mediation training for mediators and other lawyers and even promoting mediation in the media.[47] In 2011, there was a great rise in mediation case numbers, mainly because of the above-mentioned pilot project. In 2018, more than 2000 cases in district courts went to mediation. This number represents a significant share of the approximately 8000 disputed civil cases (in the court case system, they are called 'broad claims') in the district courts. Mediation is especially popular in child custody and contact disputes. In general, the number of cases in the courts has not changed much but the popularity of mediation has clearly increased.[48]

Mediation is experienced to be different from a court trial in practice as well. Mediation has changed and expanded the behaviour and practices in many of the Finnish district courts. The roles of the parties, the mediators and the legal advisers of the parties in mediation are, in practice, different from the roles in court trial.

---

[45] Salminen and Ervasti (2014), p. 603, Linnanmäki (2019), p. 2.

[46] Salminen and Ervasti (2014), pp. 604–606.

[47] Savela (2017).

[48] See Ministry of Justice (2018), Ervasti (2018), p. 236.

In mediation, the parties are acting in the main roles, and the legal advisers are not presenting or pleading the case on behalf of the parties. The mediator has no decision-making power but, rather, serves to promote the parties' communication and mutual ground for fruitful discussion. The mediation conversation is informal, and the process is flexible; however, it typically follows a certain structure and techniques to identify the parties' deeper interests and needs. The opening phase of the mediation session is important in order to give the parties a clear picture of the characteristics of mediation. The agreements can be tailor-made and include elements beyond legal elements, such as behavioural elements.[49]

Even though mediation training is not a prerequisite in legislation, in practice most of the mediating judges have taken a special training provided by the Finnish Ministry of Justice (since January 2020, National Courts Administration). Before 2006, no mediation training was provided for judges. Now, basic mediation training and special training focusing on child custody and contact cases is provided regularly. The training is complementary and consists of mediation theory and practical exercises. In practice, mediation training has been found to be important for amending the various professional roles of judges and advocates.[50]

Settlements as such, however, are not new in the district courts in Finland. As Kaijus Ervasti points out, 'Nordic conflict resolution culture and court culture has been very pragmatic in promoting settlement and avoiding full-scale trial.'[51] Even before the court-connected mediation was launched, approximately one third of the broad, disputed claims were resolved by settlement in courts. The promotion of settlements is not regulated in detail and, as mentioned above, is practised in various ways.[52] In practice, the 1993 change in legislation was followed by a clear change towards more amicable, communication-based and future-oriented processes.[53] The number of settlements has thus not changed much over the years, since even today about one third of these cases are resolved by settlement in either court trial or mediation.[54] What has partly changed is the process by which the settlement is achieved.[55]

[49]Regarding the changes in practice, see Ministry of Justice (2016), various pages, Linnanmäki (2019), pp. 240–294.

[50]Regarding mediation training for judges in practice, see Ervasti (2011), pp. 47–52, Ministry of Justice (2013), pp. 22–24 and (2016), pp. 104–115, Linnanmäki (2019), p. 238. According to my own experience, some district courts have also developed their own training and support for mediators.

[51]Ervasti (2018), p. 227.

[52]Ervasti (2004), various pages.

[53]Haavisto (2002), pp. 289–290, Salminen and Ervasti (2015), pp. 606–612. See also Ervo (2017), p. 679.

[54]Ministry of Justice (2018), p. 35.

[55]An interesting detail regarding court culture change is that in the court statistics provided by the Ministry of Justice in 2018, the absence of the word *mediation* (*sovittelu*), even though court-connected mediation is an established practice in the district courts.

3.2 Interrelation Between the Elements of the Mediation System

Mediation has entered district courts in significant numbers and brought a new alternative to court legislation and practices. However, a more detailed examination of mediation cases reveals that the mediation practises are diverse. Especially in child-related cases, the practices have partly developed apart from the legislation and the original theoretical background for court-connected mediation. Moreover, the differences between theoretical background, legislation and mediation practices are not unique to Finland; research in other Nordic countries has had similar findings.[56] The combination of legal and alternative perspectives is a challenge for courts and mediating judges and can lead to imbalance of the various elements of the mediation system, including theoretical models (developed in mediation research and other literature), applications in context (e.g., in court and regulated by legislation) and mediation practices in action.[57]

According to law and the preparatory works, mediation should follow the general, mainly facilitative and interest-based approach[58] on which the basic mediation training in Finland is based.[59] However, in practice, the child custody and contact cases are balancing between the facilitative and evaluative mediation model.[60] This is due to the promotion of the best interests of the child within the mediation framework. The legislator has painted the mainly facilitative framework for mediation and left it for the mediators and experts to define how to promote the best interests of the child in practice. Thus, the roles of the mediator and the expert are mostly defined in practice. The practices and the training programme have developed different emphases regarding these roles.

The role of the expert has some evaluative elements. One element of her/his role is to provide, for example, general information regarding children's development. The mediator, on the other hand, leads and facilitates the conversations and, if necessary in order to settle the case, can also take a directive role. The mediator can also be a legal expert in the case, who can provide neutral, general legal information to the parties.[61] It can be noted that the mediator and the expert both have significant power to guide the interpretation of the best interests of the child.[62] The mediation practices have also had rather evaluative and directive as well as settlement-oriented

[56] See, e.g., Mykland (2011), pp. 160–186, Adrian (2012) various pages, Ervasti (2018), pp. 240–241 and the referenced research.

[57] Ervasti and Nylund (2014), p. 139, Ervasti (2018), p. 229.

[58] Government bill HE 114/2004, p. 22. See also Ervasti (2018).

[59] Ministry of Justice (2016), p. 105, Ervasti (2011), pp. 47–52, 79.

[60] Aaltonen (2015), p. 44, Linnanmäki (2019), p. 297.

[61] Aaltonen (2015), p. 110–118, Ministry of Justice (2013), pp. 45–60.

[62] Linnanmäki (2019), pp. 263, 279.

elements.[63] According to mediators, the pure facilitative techniques are not always sufficient when promoting the best interests of the child in mediation.[64]

Thus, in practice, mediation is a combination of facilitative and evaluative approaches. The practices have developed partly apart from the legal and theoretical framework behind the process. One reason for this could be the lack of special provisions regarding the mediation framework for the child-related cases. Another reason may be that the facilitative techniques and the broad perspective on conflict resolution are not always fully implemented in order to reach a settlement effectively under the institutional pressure. The gaps between theory, legislation and practices, however, can raise some questions regarding the procedural safeguards.[65]

One example regards the parties' self-determination—one of the cornerstones in mediation. As mentioned above, according to the law, the confirmation of agreement requires the request and consent of both parties, which can be seen as an expression of self-determination. In a previous study,[66] however, absence of an explicit request or consent to confirm the agreement appeared. When reflecting on the mediation theories, however, one can ask whether it should be the parties who have the final word and will in how the mediation ends and what is the content of the agreement.

The legislation regulates case screening only on a very general level. According to Sect. 3 in the Mediation Act, the case shall be suitable for mediation, which means mainly that the parties can dispose the case. Mediation shall also be meaningful regarding the parties' claims. In child-related cases, the best interests of the child shall also be taken into account (Sect. 10). However, as already noted, the best interests of the child is open to various interpretations. In practice, the standards and timing for case screening vary. For example, family violence or substance abuse as such are not, by law, absolute hindrances for mediation in Finland; rather, they impose special requirements to adjust the mediation process and the evaluation of the best interests of the child.[67]

As mentioned above, the Norwegian model inspired the Finnish co-mediation model. However, the Norwegian model has faced criticism, since various proceedings and roles (mediator, evaluator, psychologist and judge) are mixed, which causes confusion and risk with regard to the procedural safeguards.[68] For example, some

---

[63]Linnanmäki (2019), regarding the difference between amicability and contractuality and their roles in the legal system, see Koulu (2014), pp. 171–172.

[64]Aaltonen (2015), pp. 44–45.

[65]About the process safeguards in mediation, see Ervasti and Nylund (2014).

[66]Linnanmäki (2019), especially pp. 289–290. The research included observations of six mediation sessions in various Finnish District Courts and 26 interviews with mediators and experts, advocates and parties during 2015–2016. The data were rather low in representativeness but gave a broad picture of each of the cases. No children were interviewed. This is because they did not participate in the mediation sessions and were not heard, which has been a common practice in Finland (regarding this practice, see Ministry of Justice (2013), pp. 74–75 and (2016), pp. 72–73).

[67]Ministry of Justice (2013), pp. 95–191, Ministry of Justice (2016), pp. 34–35, 90, Aaltonen (2015), pp. 181–202.

[68]Nylund (2018), p. 19, Bernt (2018), p. 130. See also Mykland (2011), p. 176.

parties have experienced pressure to settle their case and directions for the settlement.[69] In this respect, the Finnish solution, where the mediation is a separate proceeding from court trial, has some benefits, since the mediator has no authority to decide the case. However, in Finland, too, the roles of the judge and the mediator as well as the expert can also be mixed. The mediator has the final say in whether the agreement can be confirmed[70]; the role is in this respect judicial and evaluative. In practice, it has been noted, that the mediators may have been more directive and evaluative than the law suggests, in an effort to reach the best interests of the child. Mediation in child custody and contact disputes especially balances between facilitative and evaluative mediation models and between alternative and legal discourses.[71]

3.3 Mediation and the Appellate Courts

As mentioned above, court-connected mediation is, by law, also available in the appellate court instances (Mediation Act, Sect. 1), meaning the Courts of Appeal (hovioikeus) and the Supreme Court (Korkein oikeus).[72] However, there has thus far not been exact information available regarding how much mediation is or not used in these instances in practice. As illustrated in the descriptions below, the Courts of Appeal have had at least some individual mediations. Concerning the Supreme Court, its role is to use the highest jurisdiction to supervise legal practices by its own resolutions, as well as to give preliminary rulings (Supreme Court Act, 665/2005). The (alternative) conflict resolution role has not been highlighted as one of the Supreme Court's functions.[73] However, some individual cases in the higher courts have *concerned the appropriateness of the mediation process and the confirmed settlement* in district courts or in the courts of appeal. In these cases, the interaction between the legal and alternative perspectives is very interesting. Some examples will be described and analysed in more detail below.

In one case in the Helsinki Court of Appeal,[74] one of the parties in the case claimed that there had been no prerequisites for mediation in the district court, that there was a failure in the mediation process and that the confirmed agreement was invalid since the other party had manipulated her during the mediation. She claimed that the agreement about child maintenance did not meet her wishes or the best interests of the child in question. The Court of Appeal found that there were prerequisites

[69] Koch (2008), Bernt (2018), various pages.

[70] This role of the mediator is not explicitly regulated in the Mediation Act, but it is stated in the Government bill HE 114/2004, p. 33.

[71] See Linnanmäki (2019), p. 318, Aaltonen (2015), p. 44.

[72] Expert assistance (co-mediation) in child-related disputes is, according to legislation, provided to district courts only (Act on Child Custody and Contact Right, Chap. 3a).

[73] See even the Supreme Court's website (www.korkeinoikeus.fi/en).

[74] HelHO 717/2019.

for mediation, that no failure in the process existed and that there was no reason to change the agreement or return the case to the district court, since the claimant had failed to prove her perspective and claims. Her claims and views, however, during or after the mediation session, played no significant role in this decision. The District Court judge—who served as the mediator—was asked to give a statement about the mediation session, and her views were taken into account in the decision.

Regarding the court culture changes, it can be noted that the evaluation of the case in the Court of Appeal was strongly based on a legalistic perspective, legal issues and evidence, even though it was about mediation, an alternative to legal decision-making based on parties' self-determination and free will and a non-decisive role of the mediator. It is also interesting that, even though mediation should never diminish the parties' right to legal proceedings, and even though the claimant wanted the case to be handled in a court trial, the confirmed agreement was not nullified or returned to the district court for new proceedings. In addition, the mediator was heard even though there is a prohibition in the law against the mediator witnessing in the court about the mediation session without the consent of the parties. This issue was not problematised in the court decision. It also seems, that the mediation process itself and its theoretical background did not get attention in the decision.

Mediation should promote the free will and mutual understanding of the parties. This is the core of mediation as an alternative. If one or both of the parties feel the processes and agreements have been pushed, directed or manipulated, the process and the agreement cannot meet this goal of mediation. However, it is understandable that court decisions, such as confirmation of an agreement, cannot be nullified or returned to new proceedings merely because one party starts to regret the outcome if no signs of resistance were apparent in the mediation session. Nullification or returning of a case to a new proceeding on this basis would obviously be contrary to the legal certainty of the court decision. It is also of importance that the other party of the case can count of the certainty of the decision. Agreements as such are also highly legal by nature.[75] However, the balance between the legalistic and alternative perspectives is challenging. There are neither specific requirements nor guidelines in legislation to evaluate mediation as an alternative process.

In 2018, the first case about court-connected mediation was handled in the Supreme Court of Finland.[76] The court considered whether the Court of Appeal should have confirmed the agreement in the case after a mediation session. The question also concerned the duration of the mediation session. The mediator had confirmed the agreement only after (not at the end of) the mediation session, based on an e-mail conversation between the parties and the mediator. One of the parties declared in her e-mail that she did not want the agreement to be confirmed. Despite this, the Court of Appeal confirmed the agreement anyway. The Supreme Court found that the Court of Appeal had acted wrongly in confirming the agreement, repealed the resolution and returned the case to the Court of Appeal.

---

[75] See Hietanen-Kunwald (2018), various pages.

[76] KKO 2018:55.

It can be noted that in this case the Supreme Court paid attention to the special characteristics of mediation. It stated that the process is an alternative to court trial and thus regulated separately but that the confirmation of the agreement is a legal decision made by the court. According to the Supreme Court, the agreement is confirmed by the same rules that regulate the confirmation of an agreement during the court trial. Moreover, a complaint about the agreement is to be made by the same rules; in other words, there are no exceptions concerning mediation. While the Supreme Court did not expressly point this out, it seems that the mediation process itself is thus not open for complaint by the parties. This is the case despite the fact that there is a fine line between the process and the agreement with regard to infringements of access to justice. However, what is highlighted in the judgment is that mediation is based on the free will and consent of the parties. If the parties wish to end the mediation, they can do so at any time and are not required to justify this choice. The confirmation of the agreement requires consent and request from both parties.

In this Supreme Court case as well, the mediator (i.e., the judge who confirmed the agreement) was asked to give a statement about the mediation session and the steps prior to confirming the agreement. The prohibition to witness about mediation was not seen as an obstacle. Thus, the interpretation of the legal norms seems to be that the prohibition to witness applies only to the resolution of the substantive parts of the case or other cases handled in court.

In 2020 the Supreme Court gave another decision regarding mediation (KKO 2020:75). In this case the Supreme Court reversed a final decision of a district court. It stated that the settlement confirmed in a court-connected mediation manifestly based on misapplication of the law, since a public purchase witness (kaupanvahvistaja) did not witness the purchase of a real property, which is an absolute requirement in the law for a valid purchase and for the buyer to be granted title to the property. This Supreme Court decision clearly shows that, even though creative outcomes as such are possible and one asset in mediation as an alternative process, certain absolute formal requirements need to be followed in mediation too when confirming agreements, in order for the parties to implement their legal rights. It can however be noted, that the Supreme Court did not state much about mediation itself and how the requirements regarding the confirmation of the agreement reflect the mediation process.

4 The Many Faces of Change

Mediation has opened the paradigm of courts and procedural law towards more alternatives in legislation, in practice, and in theory. The districts courts in Finland today are multidoor courthouses[77] providing both court trial and mediation.[78] Judges not only interpret legislation and case facts but also promote settlements and creative

[77] Regarding this concept, see Sander (1964).

[78] This is aligned also in Government bill HE 114/2004, p. 4.

conflict resolution in mediation. Also, the law recognises judges as mediators. In practice, many district court judges in Finland today are also specialised and trained mediators.

The basis for Finnish court-connected mediation is in parties' self-determination and freedom of agreement.[79] The law does not separate various types of conflicts; thus, in principle, all cases are considered equally. The only particular exception stated in the Mediation Act concerning the substance of the case is that of cases involving children (Sect. 10). This is understandable, since child custody and contact disputes constitute a significant share of the disputed cases in courts. Another reason for this may be that children's matters have been important in the Finnish welfare state. According to law, the child's best interests need to be taken into account when mediating child-related cases. The child's best interest is not defined in detail. However, in confirming the agreement, the legislation regarding child custody and contact is expected to be taken into account.[80] The mediation process in child custody and contact cases is not regulated in any more detail. The child's best interest is thus open to various interpretations.[81]

Mediation in the court context is affected by the legal context. Mediation in court is a hybrid[82] balancing between the legalistic and the alternative traditions, occurring in the shadow of the law. However the law and its shadows[83] have changed as well. The law is more pluralistic and fragmented, than before and it is no longer always clear what is the law and what is the shadow.[84] This is due to both internationalisation and privatisation. The emphasis of human rights affects the interpretations of law and makes law in some respect more flexible and reflexive. Thus, the previously criticised legalisation of mediation[85] is today inevitable. The legalisation also differs from the traditional perspective due to the fragmentation and reflexivity of the legal context.[86]

Law could regulate certain questions regarding mediation in more detail. For example, at the moment there is no regulation on mediation training. The guarantee for due mediation process is however dependent on the individual mediators. Also some special characteristcs regarding mediation could be regulated separately rather than by referring to the regulation designed for court trials. In this way mediation theories would not need to compete for attention with the legal interpretations. The traditional role of the courts is to apply law, and law in their activities binds the judges.

[79]Government bill HE 114/2004, pp. 5, 52.

[80]Since December 2019, however, there has been an amendment to the law that the child's views shall be taken into account if possible in mediation too.

[81]Linnanmäki (2019), various pages. See also Salminen (2018).

[82]The term 'hybrid' has been used in various ways, in referring to processes mixing alternative and legal elements (such as evaluation and mediation or arbitration and mediation), as well as mixing different mediation models (such as facilitative and evaluative). See Lindell (2000), p. 26, Knuts (2006), p. 55, Kovach and Love (1998), Bernt (2011), p. 67, Lowry (2004), p. 115, Ervasti and Nylund (2014), pp. 73, 167.

[83]The expression is originally presented by Mnookin and Kornhauser (1979).

[84]Linnanmäki (2019), p. 306.

[85]See Ervasti and Nylund (2014), pp. 188, 555.

[86]See Linnanmäki (2019), various pages.

But what about mediation and the mediator? One can thus ask, whether there is need to regulate the roles of mediator and judge more separately in order to promote the alternative nature of the mediation process in courts.

By adding regulation—legislation or soft law—the mediation paradigm is of course moving away from its unregulated origins and total freedom of the parties.[87] It can also stiffen the flexible nature of mediation. New directions in the life span of mediation are however taken in accordance with today's society. This can lead towards more appropriate alternatives, more training, evolution of processes, new skills and standards, and to new system designs.

5 Conclusion

Court-connected mediation has affected the court culture in Finland with regard to civil cases. This change has occurred on normative, practical, and theoretical levels. Mediation has changed the culture by bringing an alternative that is more informal, client-centred and conflict resolution-oriented. However, it has also made the court culture and the courts' role more diverse. Court-connected mediation is not just mediation, since the legalistic perspective dominates the courts' functions as well as the interrelation between court trial and mediation. The judges are balancing between different roles of legal resolution providers as well as facilitators and evaluators.

In 2006, the law introduced court-connected mediation in Finland. The purpose of doing so was to add alternatives in courts and to promote agreements between the parties. Simultaneously legislation defined judges in mediation as mediators. In practice, many judges today are also trained and experienced mediators. The mediation alternative has also expanded the theoretical dimension of court culture, since mediation theories play a significant role as the framework for mediation.

Since 2006, the amount of mediation cases has risen significantly in the district courts. In 2018, more than 2000 cases in court went to mediation. Mediation is especially popular in child custody and contact disputes. The number of cases in mediation represents a large share of the disputed civil claims (about 8,000 per year) in the district courts. Measured in case numbers, mediation thus has an established role as an alternative process to court trial in Finnish District Courts and has changed the court culture significantly. Before the mediation alternative was introduced, about one third of all broad claims in the district courts were settled, and the number has not changed radically over the years. However, the process by which settlement is reached has partly changed. Mediation can promote more durable and tailor-made settlements, even though the realisation of this objective in mediation practices in Finland has not yet been comprehensively researched.[88] The material differences and similarities between mediated agreements and court decisions is an interesting topic for future research as well.

---

[87] Regarding the history of mediation, see, e.g., Ervasti and Nylund (2014), pp. 51–61, 138.

[88] In Denmark and Norway, see Adrian and Mykland (2014).

In legislation, and according to experiences from practice, mediation has many differences compared to a court trial. The court context, however, creates a special framework for mediation. In the court context as it is regulated today, it is a challenge to fit together the three elements of mediation—theoretical models, applications in legislation, and mediation in action.[89] The requirements placed by legislation and the institutional framework are natural characteristic for courts. However, a multidoor courthouse also needs multiple theoretical and legislative frames. Also, the cases in the appellate courts emphasise that there can exist complications of bringing together the legalistic and alternative discourses.

The change in court culture and court paradigm due to mediation is also multidirectional. Not only has mediation affected the courts, but the legal context has also shed its light on mediation. Mediation has become partly regulated and drawn into a legal context.[90] Mediation is a private and alternative process on the one hand but is also part of the social and legal context on the other hand. This balancing between various functions and roles is evident in the Finnish courts of law today, and it also shapes the court culture.

References

Aaltonen AK (2009) Lapsioikeus ja lapsen oikeus tuomioistuimissa. Edita, Helsinki
Aaltonen AK (2015) Huoltoriitojen sovittelu tuomioistuimessa. Kauppakamari, Helsinki
Aarnio A (1989) Laintulkinnan teoria: yleisen oikeustieteen oppikirja. WSOY, Juva
Adrian L (2012) Mellem retssag og rundbordssamtale: retsmægling i teori og praksis. Jurist- og Økonomforbundets Forlag, København
Adrian L, Mykland S (2014) Creativity in court-connected mediation: myth or reality? Negot J 4:421–439
Bernt C (2011) Meklerrollen ved mekling i domstolene. Fagbokforlaget, Bergen
Bernt C (2018) Custody mediation in Norwegian courts: a conglomeration of roles and processes. In: Nylund A et al (eds) Nordic Mediation Research. Springer, Cham, pp 105–132
Ervasti K (2004) Käräjäoikeuksien sovintomenettely: empiirinen tutkimus sovinnon edistämisestä riitaprosessissa. Oikeuspoliittinen tutkimuslaitos, Helsinki
Ervasti K (2005) Tuomioistuinkulttuurin kehityslinjoja. Oikeus 4:352–375
Ervasti K (2011) Tuomioistuinsovittelu Suomessa. Oikeuspoliittinen tutkimuslaitos, Helsinki
Ervasti K (2018) Past, present and future of mediation in Nordic countries. In: Nylund A et al (eds) Nordic Mediation Research. Springer, Cham, pp 225–245
Ervasti K, Nylund A (2014) Konfliktinratkaisu ja sovittelu. Edita, Helsinki
Ervo L (2014) Nordic court culture in progress: historical and futuristic perspectives. In: Ervo L, Nylund A (eds) The future of civil litigation. Access to courts and court-annexed mediation in the Nordic countries. Springer, London, pp 383–407
Ervo L (2017) Välimiesmenettely vaihtoehtoisena riidanratkaisumenettelynä Suomessa ja Ruotsissa. Defensor Legis 4:661–679

---

[89] See Ervasti and Nylund (2014), p. 139, Ervasti (2018), p. 229.

[90] Regarding the convergence between court trial and mediation especially regarding mandatory mediation, see Macfarlane 2002, p. 308.

Finnish Legal Affairs Committee Statement 4/2005 vp. Lakivaliokunnan mietintö. Hallituksen esitys riita-asioiden sovittelua ja sovinnon vahvistamista yleisissä tuomioistuimissa koskevaksi lainsäädännöksi

Government bill HE 224/1982 vp, Hallituksen esitys eduskunnalle laeiksi lapsen huollosta ja tapaamisoikeudesta ja holhouslain muuttamisesta sekä niihin liittyvien lakien muuttamisesta

Government Bill HE 114/2004 vp, Hallituksen esitys Eduskunnalle riita-asioiden sovittelua ja sovinnon vahvistamista yleisissä tuomioistuimissa koskevaksi lainsäädännöksi

Government Bill HE 186/2013 vp, Hallituksen esitys eduskunnalle laeiksi lapsen huollosta ja tapaamisoikeudesta annetun lain, riita-asioiden sovittelusta ja sovinnon vahvistamisesta yleisissä tuomioistuimissa annetun lain 5 ja 10 §:n sekä sosiaalihuoltolain 17 §:n muuttamisesta

Haavisto V (2002) Court work in transition: an activity-theoretical study of changing work practices in a Finnish district court. University of Helsinki, Helsinki

Haavisto V et al (2014) Perheasioiden sovittelun uudet tuulet: havaintoja, mallinnuksia ja arvioita FASPER-hankkeen pohjalta. Unigrafia, Helsinki

Hietanen-Kunwald P (2018) Mediation and the legal system. Extracting the legal principles of civil and commercial mediation. Unigrafia, Helsinki

Knuts G (2006) Förfarandegarantier vid domstolsanknuten medling. Suomalainen Lakimiesyhdistys, Helsinki

Koch K (2008) Evaluering av saksbehandlingsreglene for domstolene i barneloven: saker om foreldreansvar, fast bosted og samvær. Barne- og likestillingsdepartementet, Oslo

Koulu S (2014) Lapsen huolto- ja tapaamissopimukset: oikeuden rakenteet ja sopivat perheet. Lakimiesliiton kustannus, Helsinki

Kovach KK, Love LP (1998) Mapping mediation: the risks of Riskin's grid. Harvard Negot. L Rev. 3:71–110

Lindell B (2000) Alternativ tvistlösning. Iustus förlag, Uppsala

Linnanmäki K (2019) Lapsen etu huoltoriidan tuomioistuinsovittelussa: lapsioikeutta, sovitteluteoriaa ja empiriaa yhdistävä tutkimus. Alma Talent, Helsinki

Lowry RL (2004) Evaluative mediation. In: Folberg J et al (eds) Divorce and family mediation: models, techniques and applications. The Guilford Press, New York, pp 72–91

Macfarlane J (2002) Culture change: a tale of two cities and mandatory court-connected mediation. J Dispute Resolut 2:241–325

Menkel-Meadow C (2006) Exporting and Importing ADR: 'I've Looked at Life from Both Sides Now'. Dispute Resolut Mag 5–8

Ministry of Justice (2013) Report 25. Asiantuntija-avusteista huoltoriitojen sovittelua koskeva kokeilu käräjäoikeuksissa 1.1.2011–31.12.2013. Loppuraportti

Ministry of Justice (2016) Report 12. Ei niin suurta riitaa, ettei sopu sitä sovita

Ministry of Justice (2018) Court statistics

Mnookin RH, Kornhauser L (1979) In the shadow of the law: the case of divorce. The Yale L J 88:950–997

Mykland S (2011) En studie av mekleratferd i norske rettsmeklinger. NHH. Institutt for strategi og ledelse. PhD. thesis No 2011/02

Nylund A (2014) Access to justice: Is ADR a Help or Hindrance? In: Ervo L, Nylund A (eds) The future of civil litigation: access to courts and court-annexed mediation in the Nordic countries. Springer, London, pp 325–344

Nylund A (2018) A dispute systems design perspective on Norwegian child custody mediation. In: Nylund A et al (eds) Nordic Mediation Research. Springer, Cham, pp 9–26

Pajulammi H (2014) Lapsi, oikeus ja osallisuus. Talentum, Helsinki

Parkinson L (2011) Family mediation. Appropriate dispute resolution in a new family justice system. 2nd edn. Jordan Publishing Limited, Bristol

Riskin L (1996) Understanding mediators' orientations, strategies, and techniques: a grid for the perplexed. Harvard Negotiation Law Rev 1:7–51

Salminen K (2018) Mediation and the best interests of the child from the child law perspective. In: Nylund A et al (eds) Nordic Mediation Research. Springer, Cham, pp 209–222

Salminen K, Ervasti K (2015) Tuomioistuinsovittelun yleistyminen ja tuomioistuimen tehtävät. Lakimies 5:591–612

Savela A (2017) Kohti sovinnollisempaa riidan ratkaisua: kokemuksia tuomioistuinsovittelun kehittämisestä Oulun käräjäoikeudessa. In: Riekkinen J (eds) Oikeutta oikeudenkäynnistä täytäntöönpanoon: Juhlajulkaisu Tuula Linna. Alma Talent, Helsinki, pp. 330–345

Schein EH (2010) Organizational culture and leadership, 4th edn. Jossey Bass, San Francisco

Syrjänen J (2012) Tuomarin harkinnan rajat: irti legalismin taakasta. Oikeustiede – Jurisprudentia XLV:335–391

Tharp BM (2009) Defining ‘culture’ and ‘organisational culture’: from anthropology to the office. Haworth, Philadelphia PA

Tolonen H, Linnanmäki K (2020) Uudistunut lapsenhuoltolaki. Alma Talent, Helsinki

Ury WL et al (1993) Getting disputes resolved: designing systems to cut the costs of conflict. Jossey-Bass, San Francisco

Plea Bargaining Changing Nordic Criminal Procedure: Sweden and Finland as Examples

Laura Ervo

Abstract A plea bargaining system is a novelty and originally a legal transplant in Northern European countries. It exists—in some form—for instance in Finland, Norway and Denmark, whereas in Sweden only the system of crown witnesses is likely to be introduced. In this chapter plea bargaining is put into the East-Nordic—Finnish and Swedish—contexts. How does plea bargaining fit into the East-Nordic court culture? Which ingredients does the contemporary legal culture consist of? In which way is court culture changing due to the new values in the society? Or are the amendments made primarily to reduce the costs of the state? Fairness, procedural justice, conflict resolution, negotiated law, pragmatically acceptable compromise, procedural truth, court service, communication and interaction are examples of the topics that are currently discussed in Finland and Sweden. At the same time, the use of written proceedings and proceedings in the absence of an accused are increasing. Is the plea bargaining system a step towards a more effective and economic criminal procedural system or is it mirroring new type of thinking concerning criminal proceedings? In this chapter, these elements are discussed. Finland is used as a main example. The Finnish situation is also compared with Sweden.

1 Starting Points

Many Nordic and Baltic countries have recently adopted a plea-bargaining[1] system. It exists—in some form—in Finland, Estonia, Norway, Denmark, and Latvia.[2] In Sweden, plea bargaining is not possible, but recently a discussion on crown witnesses,

[1]According to the Oxford English dictionary, plea bargaining refers to an arrangement between prosecutor and defendant whereby the defendant pleads guilty to a lesser charge in exchange for a more lenient sentence or an agreement to drop other charges.

[2]Ervo (2014a), pp. 97–98 and Oikarainen (2012), p. 752–753.

L. Ervo (✉)
School of Law, Psychology and Social Work, Örebro University, 70182 Örebro, Sweden
e-mail: Laura.ervo@oru.se

L. Ervo et al. (eds.), *Rethinking Nordic Courts*, Ius Gentium: Comparative Perspectives on Law and Justice 90, https://doi.org/10.1007/978-3-030-74851-7_14

as one variant of plea bargaining,[3] has arisen.[4] As a procedural instrument, plea bargaining is quite new in Northern Europe. How does it fit into our traditional court culture, or is the court culture no longer the same?

There are controversial trends in criminal proceedings. On the one hand, fairness, procedural justice, conflict resolution, negotiated law, pragmatically acceptable compromise, procedural truth, court service, communication, interaction, plea bargaining, and anonymous witnesses are good examples of the currently discussed topics.[5]

Based on those new trends, the values in the criminal jurisdiction seem to be softening. The individual's rights are stressed. The parties are more subjects than objects in the investigation made at courts. The decision power is going to be taken from the judge to the court's clients. The service culture has landed in the public sector, including even the courts, which traditionally have been formal and power-packed institutions. From that perspective, criminal proceedings have recently become closer to civil proceedings.[6]

Still, there are at the same time trends in the opposite direction, which means efficiency in the name of economy. The written proceedings in simple and clear criminal cases as well as proceedings in the absence of an accused are good examples. The possibility of solving a criminal case in the absence of the accused is quite widespread both in Sweden[7] and in Finland.[8] The plea-bargaining system is also one step towards a more effective and economic criminal procedural system.

The development described above is rather confusing. What is going on in the Nordic criminal procedural law and why? Are these changes mirroring the current values in the society, and is the culture therefore changing?[9] Or are all these steps taken only to favour the treasury ministry and to intensify the state economy? Are there other practical needs, like the fight against organised crime, behind this change? Is it the development about privatisation, intensifying criminal proceedings, or is this change linked with the cultural change in mentalities? Does not the society share the same values any longer? Is also the way of thinking is changing?

Finland and Sweden are chosen as examples because the current situations of those neighboring countries vary quite dramatically in terms of the acceptance of plea bargaining. Finland has accepted and adopted plea bargaining into its criminal procedural system, while the discussion in Sweden has been rather unwelcoming. Still, the discussion on crown witnesses continues in Sweden. Because of this controversial situation between two East-Nordic countries which otherwise share quite

---

[3]Lauri (2010), p. 12.

[4]https://www.regeringen.se/pressmeddelanden/2019/11/en-starkt-rattsprocess-och-en-okad-lagforing/, accessed 28 June 2020.

[5]See, e.g., Ervo (2014a), p. 99 and Määttä (2013), p. 647.

[6]Määttä (2013), p. 647.

[7]The Swedish Code for Juridical Procedure, Chap. 46, Sect. 15 a.

[8]Chap. 8, Sects. 11 and 12 in the Finnish Criminal Procedure Act.

[9]See also Pesonen (2011), p. 72.

similar legal cultures[10] and even a common history, they offer a fruitful context to discuss the opportunities and obstacles when adopting legal transplants and, in this case, considering whether plea bargaining can fit well into the Nordic legal culture or is likely to change it.

2 Plea Bargaining in the East-Nordic Countries

2.1 Plea Bargaining in Finland

In Finland, the plea bargaining system has existed since 2015.[11] It is based on the confession and the consent of the victim. The aim is to save resources by having easier proceedings in these negotiated cases. Plea bargaining covers even the police investigation level. Investigation can be focused on the confessed crime only, whereas the other suspected but more unclear crimes are not investigated at all in the plea-bargaining context. This can mean, for instance, bargaining even on an investigation and not only by way of proceedings and then sanction.[12]

The Finnish Criminal Investigation Act (805/2011), Chap. 3, Sect. 10a (672/2014) covers restriction of a criminal investigation on the basis of a confession.[13]

The decision of a prosecutor to waive of discontinue the criminal investigation and the commitment of the prosecutor to request a mitigated sentence are biding. They may be withdrawn only if the confession is withdrawn or in the view of new evidence in the case the decision or the commitment had been based on essentially incomplete or erroneous information.[14] Plea bargaining may not be used for serious crimes. If the suspected offence is punishable by a sentence of imprisonment for more than six years or an important public or private interest requires that the criminal investigation be conducted. Additionally, there is a list of crimes which are not suitable for plea bargaining.[15] Therefore, plea bargaining can be used only for minor crimes without a significant interest to prosecute.

The Finnish Criminal Procedure Act (689/1997),[16] Chap. 5(b) covers proceedings on the basis of a plea of guilty (670/2014). There are some specific guarantees for legal relief in the plea-bargaining procedure. Namely, proceedings on the basis of a plea of guilty shall normally be held within 30 days of when the case becomes

[10]See Ervo (2021).

[11]On the legislative history and background, see Kananen-Ahjoharju (2012), pp. 28–45 and Linna (2012), pp. 126–131.

[12]Ervo (2014a), p. 105.

[13]The Act can be found as an English translation on the web: https://www.finlex.fi/fi/laki/kaannokset/2011/en20110805_20150736.pdf, accessed 28 June 2020.

[14]The Finnish Criminal Investigation Act, Chap. 3, Sect. 10a, Paragraph 4.

[15]The Finnish Criminal Investigation Act, Chap. 3, Sect. 10a, Paragraph 5.

[16]In its entirety, the Act can be found as an English translation on the web: https://www.finlex.fi/fi/laki/kaannokset/1997/en19970689_20150733.pdf, accessed 28 June 2020.

pending. In addition, the prosecutor and the defendant shall be present in person in the proceedings on the basis of a plea of guilty. Also, the injured party shall be reserved an opportunity to be present if, his or her claim is not being presented by the prosecutor.[17] In the beginning of the proceedings on the basis of a plea of guilty, the prosecutor shall clarify the content of the proposal for judgment and the other circumstances connected with it, and present to the necessary extent the criminal investigation material dealing with the case. After that, the court shall inquire of the defendant, whether or not he or she continues to admit the offence and consents to the consideration of the case in this kind of simplified procedure. The court also checks whether or not he or she understands also in other respects the content and significance of the proposal for judgment. It is a duty of the court to seek to ensure that the proposal corresponds to the intent of the defendant. Then the court will reserve the defendant an opportunity to otherwise comment on the proposal for judgment and the criminal investigation material. After that, the court reserves the injured party an opportunity to comment on the proposal for judgment. Then other claims are heard and the parties are provided with an opportunity to present their closing statement. The court shall ensure that the case is dealt with appropriately and that irrelevant matters are not mixed into the case. The court shall use questions to eliminate ambiguities and deficiencies in the statements of the parties.[18]

Finally, the court shall issue a judgment according with the proposal for judgment if the defendant has made the admission and given the consent and no reasonable doubt remains regarding the voluntary and valid nature of the admission, taking into consideration also the criminal investigation material concerning the case. The court convicts in accordance with the proposal for judgment if there is otherwise no bar to acceptance of the proposal. If the court does not issue the judgment referred above, the case is withdrawn. If the case is dismissed without considering the merits, statements by the defendant that have been given in connection with the plea bargaining, may not be used as evidence in a criminal case.[19]

Because in Finland plea bargaining covers even the police investigation level as described above, investigation can then be focused on the confessed crime only, whereas the other suspected but more unclear crimes are not investigated at all in the plea bargaining context. By that mean, it is allowed to bargain also on an investigation and not only by way of proceedings and then sanction. However, fact bargaining is not allowed. By following the plea bargaining rules, the suspect may by bargaining 'choose' the crimes which will be investigated. Later on, there will be simplified proceedings. Also the sanctions which are used are milder than in normal cases. In the Finnish model, the state get benefits in the form of resource savings, and the accused get benefits in the form of limited police investigations, simplified procedures and milder sanctions.[20]

[17] The Finnish Criminal Procedure Act, Chap. 5(b), Sect. 2.

[18] The Finnish Criminal Procedure Act, Chap. 5(b), Sect. 3.

[19] The Finnish Criminal Procedure Act, Chap. 5(b), Sects. 4 and 5.

[20] Ervo (2014a), p. 105. On more detailed presentation of the plea bargaining in Finland, see Illman (2015), pp. 142–162.

2.2 The Crown Witnesses in Sweden

When plea bargaining was suggested for Finland, legislators pointed out as benefits the efficiency and the appropriate allocation of resources to simplify the criminal proceedings. What was extremely interesting was that, at the same time, the Swedish legislature rejected the plea bargaining without any deeper discussion. It was simply stated that it did not fit into the Swedish system.[21] It is very seldom that the East-Nordic legislators have such different perspectives. As I have explained elsewhere,[22] the Nordic legislators collaborate very much, and Swedish and Finnish legal reforms in particular often follow each other. Normally, Sweden is a role model that Finland follows, especially if the Swedish experience has been positive. In particular, the reforms in procedural law have traditionally followed the Swedish example. Therefore, this novelty, which is a legal transplant and quite a big step from civil law towards common law,[23] is an exception in the East-Nordic legislative culture, which otherwise is very collaborative.[24]

Even if normal plea bargaining was rejected in Sweden, the use of crown witnesses,[25] which is can be seen as one variant of plea bargaining, is currently debated in Sweden, and investigations are being made to determine whether this system should be adopted in Sweden. A crown witness is a defendant who receives mitigation of his or her sentence because he or she has participated or assisted in the investigation of someone else's crime. Mitigation is currently not included in the Swedish equitable grounds. The question of crown witnesses has already arisen several times in the Swedish political debate. In January 2019, the Prime Minister of Sweden announced that further inquiry regarding crown witnesses should be made.[26] The next step was taken in December 2020, when the government introduced its so-called 34-point program, which includes efforts to combat gang crime. The possibility of using crown witnesses is mentioned in the program. It should be investigated whether crown witnesses could be a solution in this fight and whether the system could be adopted to Sweden. The deadline for that report is in May 2021.[27] It is thus currently unknown whether the Swedish development in this question will follow the Finnish model. In Finland, plea-bargaining was also previously considered to be something negative that did not fit into the Finnish court culture.[28] Changes in the

[21] Ervo (2014a), p. 109 and Government Bill (Finland) 58/2013.

[22] Ervo (2021).

[23] See Oikarinen (2008), pp. 11–53 and (2012), pp. 754–759, Pesonen (2011), p. 72 and Vilkko (2011), p. 40.

[24] See Ervo (2021).

[25] For more about crown witnesses as one version of plea bargaining, see Lauri (2010), pp. 30–35.

[26] Bentelius (2019), p. 1.

[27] https://www.regeringen.se/regeringens-politik/ett-tryggare-sverige/34-punktsprogrammet-regeringens-atgarder-mot-gangkriminaliteten/#bryt_tystnadskulturen, accessed 12 February 2021.

[28] Linna (2010), pp. 227–235, Kananen-Ahjoharju (2012), pp. 46–81, Loiva (2008), pp. 73–81, 90, Oikarinen (2012), pp. 754–759 and Pesonen (2011), p. 43–57. Also, the relation between the right

paradigm caused the way of thinking to change, and plea bargaining became more acceptable over time.[29]

According to the Swedish inquires, the attitude toward crown witnesses has been predominantly negative. Additionally, the adoption of crown witnesses in the Swedish legal tradition has resulted in criticism in literature. Based on the named empirical studies, even if the crown witness system is economically efficient, there is no place in the Swedish legal system for it. Even this aspect of economic efficiency is challenged in the inquiries by saying that there is no scientifically proven rise in efficiency due to such a system.[30] Based on this background in attitudes, it will be exciting to see, if the system finally is adopted into the Swedish legislation or not.

However, in the Supreme Court case NJA 2009 p. 599, the court admitted mitigation for persons who, as a consequence of the fact that they named accomplices, would have to live their lives under serious threat. By doing so, the court indirectly opened up to the possibility of applying the system of crown witnesses in Swedish law through the case law.[31] Still, this possibility to open new chances to act in the case law has not been found to be widely applicable, and, according to the Swedish legal tradition, it is the parliament as a legislator that should react and legislate on the possibility to make such a change. As I have explained elsewhere,[32] these type of very creative solutions in the form of precedents to create new rules to meet new demands do not traditionally fit into the Swedish court culture.

3 From Fairness Towards Feelings

3.1 From Sollen to Sein

The traditional German concepts of ‘sein’ and ‘sollen’ have become closer to one another in terms of procedural fairness. Even if normative fairness and procedural justice from that point of view are based, for instance, on article 6 of the ECHR and other norms (sollen), the factual situation and the real feelings (sein) of the parties nowadays have much significance in the quality control of fairness. In this shift, the role of parties has changed from being subservient towards clients.[33]

Traditionally, it has been stressed that these concepts must be separated, and it has not been permissible to draw legally valid conclusions from sein, as only sollen has been decisive. In the contemporary paradigm, this distinction has been softened,

not to incriminate oneself and the plea bargaining system have been found to be problematic and is discussed in detail. Linna (2010), pp. 236–254 and Ridha (2014), p. 34.

[29] Oikarainen (2012), pp. 744–747 and Vilkko (2011), pp. 40–46.

[30] Bentelius (2019), p. 1.

[31] See Bentelius (2019), where the case has been widely commented upon.

[32] Ervo (2021).

[33] Ervo (2014a), p. 101.

and the concepts are—by many scholars—nowadays regarded as more parallel than opposing.[34]

As described above, the aim of truth finding is disappearing. Instead, the way to the result should be fair, and the parties should be satisfied, indicating sein. The ingredients for this satisfaction need to be scooped from sein. The highly-valued sollen has lost its significance, whereas the instrumental way of thinking, as well as reality-based fairness, strongly affecting the court culture in addition to strengthening the use of 'sein' as a source, partly in decision making but especially in designing the way to it.[35]

This change is a strong piece of evidence on the change of the paradigm in the contemporary criminal proceedings.[36]

3.2 *Perceived Procedural Justice*

There has also been a change from the normative procedural justice towards a perceived procedural justice, which means that it is not sufficient that proceedings fulfill the requirements of normative procedural justice but that parties and other actors, like witnesses and experts as well as all actors involved in proceedings, should subjectively feel that the procedure was fair. This aspect of justice has been stressed by many scholars in the contemporary literature since 1990's.[37]

According to that paradigm, the most important function in the adjudication is that the contextual decisions, with which the parties are satisfied, are produced through fair proceedings. In achieving these aims, the communication and interaction of judges and parties are the most important tools.[38]

4 From Truth Finding Towards Negotiations

Truth finding is no longer trendy. It is old-fashioned. Traditionally, the aim of procedure has been to find out the material truth.[39] According to the earlier Chap. 17, Sect. 2 (571/1948) in the Finnish Code of Judicial Procedure, it was stated that 'after having carefully evaluated all the facts that have been presented, the court shall decide

---

[34]Ervasti (1998), p. 377, Ervo (2016), p. 280, Ervo (2005), p. 83, Lappi-Seppälä (1997), p. 201; Niemi (1996), p. 128, Searle (1988), p. 175, 1988 and Ukkonen (2013), p. 28.

[35]See Ervo (2005), p. 83 and Ervo (2016), p. 280.

[36]See also Ervo (2013b), pp. 51–71 and Ervo (2016), pp. 290–291.

[37]Ervasti (2004), p. 168; Haavisto (2002), p. 20, Laukkanen (1995), p. 214, Takala (1998), pp. 3–5, Tala (2002), Tyler (1990), p. 94 and Virolainen and Martikainen (2003), p. 5.

[38]Ervasti (2004), p. 168, Ervo (2014a), p. 101, Haavisto (2002), p. 20, Laukkanen (1995), p. 214, Jukka-Pekka Takala (1998), pp. 3–5, Tala (2002), pp. 21–23, Tyler (1990), p. 94, Virolainen and Martikainen (2003), p. 5.

[39]See, e.g., Tolvanen (2003), p. 1016 and (2006), p. 1329.

what is to be regarded as the truth in the case.' This had been interpreted to refer to the material truth as an aim. In 2015, this Chap. 17 was reformed and now Sect. 3, which covers criminal cases, is as follows (12.6.2015/732):

> In a criminal case, the plaintiff shall prove the circumstances on which his or her request for punishment is based. A judgment of guilty may be made only on the condition that there is no reasonable doubt regarding the guilt of the defendant.

This amendment came into force on 1 Jan 2016. After the reform, Chap. 17, Sect. 2, which covers civil cases, is as follows:

In a civil case, the party shall prove the circumstances on which his or her claim or objection is based, The wording used here is 'shall prove'. This can refer to a preponderance of evidence when a 51% probability is enough to win the case.[40] Therefore, there is quite a lot of space for uncertainty. The advantage in the preponderance of evidence is a better chance to decide the case on its material bases—in other words, according to the substantive law. Namely, if the decision is 'not proven', the decision is based on the procedural law and the case is left as open what the material basis is concerned.[41]

The above-cited wording of Sect. 2 in Chap. 17 covered both civil and criminal cases. As already stated, it was interpreted to refer to the material truth as an aim despite the fact that concrete decisions have always been based on the procedural truth and there have been many restrictions in the law of evidence in truth finding. Still, the material truth as an idealistic aim was seen to be important and to correspond with the contemporary values earlier before the reform, whereas this idealism has today lost its position, and the majority of scholars seem to think that it is not worth mentioning; often, it even causes clear resistance when discussed.[42] Truth finding has lost its fascinating value as an idealistic goal, and daily life realism has replaced it.

Often, truth finding is even found to be something illegal or totalitarian. In the modern society, it has been linked with overly strong police power, lack of human rights, torture and so on—with something, which is anything else but idealistic,[43] whereas in olden times the truth was something positive, the opposite of the false or lies. It was found to be fair as such, whereas today it is seen as a risk to a fair trial. This change described above, verifies the change in the way of thinking. The concept of the truth is interpreted in a different way, which indicates the changed values in the court culture.[44]

In Sweden, this has been the case before, and both the aim and the result in the proceedings have been based on the procedural truth only. According to the Swedish Code for Judicial Procedure, Chap. 35, Sect. 1:

> The court shall determine what has been proved in the case after conscientious evaluating everything that has occurred in accordance with the dictates of its conscience.

[40] HE 46/2014 p. 46 and Saranpää (2010), p. 177.

[41] Saranpää (2010), pp. 260–264.

[42] See, e.g., Ervo 2012, pp. 1–16.

[43] Lehtimaja (1981), pp. 170–174 was already making such observations in the 1980s, and a similar way of thinking seems to have increased since them among scholars. Tolvanen (2003), and (2006).

[44] See, e.g., Tolvanen (2003), p. 1016 and Tolvanen (2006), p. 1329.

If we look at history, the circle—described above—seems to be closed. In the past, the power to sanction belonged to the village communities. In addition, the family and relatives played a significant role in 'criminal procedure', which was based on the aim to find the public peace again and to avoid the spiral of revenge. The significance of the truth became more important only later, when the central power started to develop and the power to punish was moved to the state. In Sweden (of which Finland was a part at that time), the private settling of crimes was finally forbidden in 1540. By that royal act, the criminal proceedings were moved to the state monopoly.[45] Today, it looks as if we are returning to these earlier times and 'ancient venues' by increasing the private decision-making power not only in civil proceedings but also in criminal procedure.[46] The state is giving back its power to decide. By doing so, the meaning of truth finding is losing significance. The reason for this change seems to be related to the state economy. The lack of interest in having a monopoly in adjudication results in decreasing possibilities to fund all public sectors. However, at the same time, values in the society are changing. It seems no longer to be important to have a strong, powerful and power monopolizing state; instead, individualism and the ability to gain more space to disposee one's own business is more important than being an obedient servant.[47]

Conflict resolution has been a current trend in civil proceedings for decades. Now, it even affects criminal proceedings. Even in the context of criminal proceedings, the parties should be satisfied, and the conflict between them should be solved by legitimate means and in a comprehensive way.[48] For instance, Tolvanen describes the contemporary criminal proceedings be noting that the first step is to qualify the current conflict, and then the parties try to prove their views to be correct. After this procedure, the result will be legitimate despite the facts of what really happened in the case.[49]

Courts are no longer state organs that use the sovereign's power to punish; instead, they are more of an independent body, to which the most important tasks belong to protect the fundamental rights of citizens.[50] Even the realisation of criminal responsibility can mean that the conflict is just solved. The conflict can be solved by the parties' friendly settlement. By doing so, the material truth in the case will be disregarded.[51] Still, in criminal cases, there is always also the public interest to consider. However, the common factors in both civil and criminal procedures today are communication, interaction, cooperation and fair trial as the most important aims.[52]

---

[45]Ervo (2014b), pp. 386–390, Letto-Vanamo (1995), pp. 85–101 and Nousiainen (1993), pp. 319–320.

[46]Vilkko (2011), pp. 43–46.

[47]See Ervo (2014a), pp. 386–391 and pp. 392–394.

[48]Tolvanen (2003), p. 1016 and Tolvanen (2006), p. 1329.

[49]Tolvanen (2003), p. 1016 and Tolvanen (2006), p. 1329.

[50]Tolvanen (2003), p. 1027.

[51]Tolvanen (2003), p. 1027.

[52]Tolvanen (2006), p. 1343.

According to this conflict resolution function, the most important values in criminal procedure are that the parties are satisfied with the result and that the procedure is effective, cost-effective and functional. The material truth has lost its status, and even the procedural truth is developing in such a way that the parties may be permitted to dispose on it. By doing so, it is possible to start to talk about the negotiated law as a result, not only in the civil cases but also partly in the criminal proceedings. This is a fundamental change in the criminal procedural paradigm.[53]

The restorative justice and mediation in criminal cases are affecting in a similar way to the change of the paradigm. According to the restorative justice, conflicts can be seen as our property and resources.[54] Based on restorative justice, the accused should face both the conflict and the victim. They should participate in the conflict resolution by themselves. It is not healthy to externalise the conflict to a too much serving court who does all for us. It should be totally the opposite; the criminal procedure should be based on the actor's personal participation, wherein they work for the solution of the case. Plea bargaining fits very well into this current picture of criminal proceedings and mirrors the contemporary values.[55]

5 From the Right to be Heard to the Right to Decide

The post-modern court culture in civil litigation is based on communication and interaction between the parties and the judge. Similar trends can be found even in criminal proceedings.[56] There has been a big change from the adjudication, material truth and a substantively correct judgment towards the ideal of negotiated law and pragmatically acceptable compromise. The development has gone from the judicial power towards court service.[57] The role of parties has been changed from the role as a subservient towards the role of clients. Additionally, party autonomy has been one of the key words especially in the Swedish procedural law discussion since 1990's.[58]

Plea bargaining can be seen as a procedural instrument where party autonomy covers procedural issues, or it can be seen as a substantive tool where the parties

---

[53]See, e.g., Ervo (2013a), pp. 47–55.

[54]Christie (1998), pp. 113–132.

[55]See Ervo (2012), pp. 13–15 and Linna (2010). Illman took up the possibility that confessions based on plea bargaining do not necessarily correspond with the material truth. It is interesting that he still used the concept of the material truth in 2015. He seemed to appreciate the material truth as an aim, while the possibility that confessions do not correspond was something negative. Illman (2015), p. 162. Also, Sahavirta has paid attention to the problem wherein false confessions do not correspond with the material truth. This can lead to problems in finding these types of false confessions binding. Therefore, plea bargaining can cause problems in res judicata. Sahavirta (2018), pp. 73–75.

[56]Ervo (2012), p. 15.

[57]Ervasti (2004), p. 433, Haavisto (2001), pp. 98–102 and Haavisto (2002), pp. 165–251, 260–262 and 287.

[58]Ervo (2009), pp. 21–41.

agree on issues which belong to criminal law. In this distinction, the nature and scope of confession play the main role. The other important issue is the role of the parties, especially if the consent of the victim is needed, as well as how much the parties will attend to negotiations and decision making versus the prosecutor as a state representative primarily addressing the issue ex officio.

Especially in Sweden, the ultimate functions of proceedings have been discussed for decades. Conflict resolution has often been seen as a very important function, especially of civil proceedings, and with this development the perspective has been changed from external to internal and from a retrospective to a prospective point of view.[59]

When discussing civil cases and the party autonomy concerning substantive matters in Sweden, Lindell has placed an emphasis on judicial relief in this context. According to him, the content of judicial relief is not only the idea to achieve a judgment, which has been achieved strictly according to substantive law. Rather, it also covers access to a certain procedure where consensus on the substantive legal matters exists. To reach this consensus, the agreed-upon result must not correspond with the substantive law only; rather, there is also space to find a suitable solution that to some extent opposes the law. The reason for this is public peace. Lindell thinks that the idea of confirming a settlement that covers the substantive law is not as radical or as impossible as it appears at first glance, and that it is possible to extend the party autonomy to cover fully even the substantial matters in the legislation.[60]

Concerning the criminal law, a similar context is plea bargaining, where the parties partly gain the power to decide the substantive—that is, criminal—law in the way which binds courts. Therefore, the role of courts is radically changing. It is seen clearly to be that of a client's conflict solver and not that of a state adjudicator that decides the case in the name of society and follow the law. Still, plea bargaining has often been seen as a technical instrument only, and its links to party autonomy as well as an understanding of substantive criminal law have not been addressed. The direct reason for this development may be the current governmental lack of resources, but the change cannot be made without accepting fundamental changes in the understanding of the criminal law and the criminal procedural law. These changes in the fundamental basis necessitate corresponding societal values to be valid and followed. If this adoption of very new instruments like plea bargaining works well in practice, it is at the same time a proof of the existence of new societal values.

6 Conclusions

Plea bargaining, written proceedings and procedure in absentia are contemporary, if not new, at least East-Nordic trends, which have been adopted or widened recently.

---

[59]Ervasti (2002), pp. 56–62, Leppänen (1998), pp. 32–41, Lindell (2003), pp. 82–101, Lindblom (2000), pp.46–58 and Virolainen (1995), pp. 80–89.

[60]Lindell (1988), p. 68.

Theoretically, they are based on an agreement between the state authorities (a prosecutor or a judge and a suspected/accused).

Not only in civil procedure but also in criminal proceedings, the law can be seen as a negotiable compromise, not only between the victim and the accused but also between the state authorities and the parties. This is true especially in plea bargaining or when choosing the written procedure or the procedure in absentia.

Plea bargaining, written proceedings and procedure in absentia are concrete tools to realise the new paradigm and its elements, which includes conflict resolution, restorative justice, party autonomy and procedural truth. The use of these tools entails a new way of thinking and a substantial change in values.

However, the change is probably not totally controlled but at least partly accidental. The goal and need to put the state economy into balance affects the paradigm in a similar way. Still, due to the almost total lack of protests or wide scientific discussions, not to mention revolutions, the change seems to correspond with the current societal values. Therefore, it is not only about saving money and a budget-based way of thinking but also a change in a paradigm based on the surrounding new societal values.

The above described phenomena are more apparent in countries that have had a greater need to balance their budgets like Finland, compared with Sweden, which normally has a quite stable economy.

When plea bargaining was suggested for Finland, legislator pointed out the efficiency and the appropriate allocation of resources to simplify the criminal proceedings. At the same time, Swedish legislators rejected the plea bargaining without any deeper discussion beyond mentioning that it did not fit into the Swedish system.

However, Sweden has now started a similar discussion on crown witnesses to tackle organised crime. The system of planned crown witnesses is similar to plea bargaining, but the goal with this amendment is not the same. In Sweden, the purpose is to better address the war on organised crime, not to benefit the state economy or simplify proceedings.

In this sense, the societies and needs in the East-Nordic neighboring countries vary. In Finland, organised crime has not (yet) been as large a problem as it is in contemporary Sweden. However, the state economy has been in deep crisis in Finland, whereas Sweden's economy is more stable. The changes are leading to similar results, but the reasons seem to be different. Still, in both countries the general audience as well as scholars seem mainly to accept the changes and do not protest very much. Therefore, the prevalent values in those societies seem to correspond with each other. They also differ from the earlier criminal procedural values. The change in the criminal procedural paradigm seems to be reality in both contemporary East-Nordic societies.

Based on the discussion above, it is the author's opinion that the criminal process has moved towards party autonomy. Several examples that indicate this change has been identified in this chapter. The role of parties, their decision power and the significance of the 'atonement' are increasing in value, whereas the state's monopolistic penal authority is losing its significance. The big shift is in moving away from the material truth and the penal authority towards a societal solution to the conflict where the parties are in focus. The state is blessing this change because it corresponds with its economic aims. The paradigm change seems to be motivated not only by the changing societal values, which legislation always needs to mirror to be acceptable in a democracy, but also from the economic crisis and resulting unstable state economy in many European countries. This is an effective combination to put new theories and values into practice.

References

Bentelius H (2019) Passar ett kronvittnessystem i svensk rättsordning? En kritisk diskussion kring kronvittnen i svensk rätt. University of Lund, Lund

Christie N (1998) Konflikt Som Eiendom. Tidskrift for Rettvitenskap 90:113–132

Ervasti K (1998) Eräitä näkökohtia empiirisen tiedon hyväksikäyttämisestä oikeustieteessä. Lakimies 3:364–388

Ervasti K (2002) Lainkäytön funktiot. Lakimies 1:47–72

Ervasti K (2004) Käräjäoikeuksien sovintomenettely: empiirinen tutkimus sovinnon edistämisestä riitaprosessissa. Oikeuspoliittinen tutkimuslaitos, Helsinki

Ervo L (2005) Oikeudenmukainen oikeudenkäynti. Werner Söderström Osakeyhtiö, Helsinki

Ervo L (2009) Party autonomy and access to justice. In: Jokela A et al (eds) Europeanization of procedural law and the new challenges to fair trial. Europa Law Publishing, Groningen, pp 21–41

Ervo L (2012) Tie totuuteen. In: Hyttinen T (ed) Rikoksesta rangaistukseen: Juhlajulkaisu Pekka Viljanen 1952-26/8–2012. Turun yliopisto, Turku, pp 1–16

Ervo L (2013a) Changing civil proceedings: court service or state economy? In: Nekrošius V (ed) Recent trends in economy and efficiency of civil procedure. Vilnius University Press, Vilnius, pp 51–71

Ervo L (2013b) Öiglase kohtupidamise väljavaated kriminaalasjades: tulevikuvisiooniid ja praegune olukord Skandinaavias ja Europas. Juridica 1:47–55

Ervo L (2014a) Nordic court culture in progress: historical and futuristic perspectives. In: Ervo L, Nylund A (eds) The Future of civil litigation: access to courts and court-annexed mediation in the Nordic countries. Springer, Cham, pp 383–407

Ervo L (2014b) Plea bargaining as an example of the recent changes in the Finnish criminal procedural paradigm. Baltic J Law Politics 1:97–112

Ervo L (2016) Facing people through language use: linguistic tools to make proceedings fair. Int J Legal Discourse 2:277–293

Ervo L (2021) Culture and mentality in East-Nordic courts. In: Ervo L et al (eds) Rethinking Nordic courts. Springer, Cham

Haavisto V (2001) Sovinnot: ikkuna tuomioistuintyön muutokseen. In: Pohjonen S (ed) Sovittelu ja muut vaihtoehtoiset konfliktinratkaisujärjestelmät. Werner Söderström Osakeyhtiö, Helsinki, pp 89–119

Haavisto V (2002) Court work in transition: an activity-theoretical study of changing work practices in a Finnish district court. University of Helsinki, Helsinki

Illman M (2015) Plea bargaining enligt finskt rätt. Tidskrift utgiven av Juridiska Föreningen i Finland 2:142–162

Kananen-Ahtoharju M (2012) Syytteistä sopiminen osaksi Suomen rikosrprosessia? Lainvalmisteluprosessin analysointi & oikeusturvaongelmien jäsentäminen vastaajan näkökulmasta. Pro gradu –thesis May 2012 University of Helsinki, Faculty of Law. Published in Edilex 22.8.2012 www.edilex.fi/lakikirjasto/9011

Lappi-Seppälä T (1997) Rikosoikeustutkimus, kriminaalipoliittinen orientaatio – ja metodi. In: Häyhä J (ed) Minun metodini. Werner Söderström Osakeyhtiö, Helsinki, pp 189–218
Laukkanen S (1995) Tuomarin rooli. Suomalainen Lakimiesyhdistys, Helsinki
Lehtimaja L (1981) Aineellinen totuus ja järkevä epäilys. Lakimies 170–174
Lauri A (2010) Kruununtodistajajärjestelmän ja sitä muistuttavien piirteiden soveltuminen suomalaiseen rikosprosessiin. Turun yliopisto, Turku
Leppänen T (1998) Riita-asiain valmistelu todistusaineiston osalta. Suomalainen Lakimiesyhdistys, Helsinki
Letto-Vanamo P (1995) Käräjäyhteisön oikeus. Oikeudenkäyttö Ruotsi-Suomessa ennen valtiollisen riidanratkaisun vakiintumista. Helsingin yliopisto, rikos-ja prosessioikeuden sekä oikeuden yleistieteiden laitos, Helsinki
Lindblom PH (2000) Processens funktioner: en resa i gränslandet. In: Lindblom PH (ed) Progressiv process: spridda uppsatser om domstolsprocessen och samhällsutvecklingen. Iustus, Uppsala, pp 593–632
Lindell B (1988) Partsautonomins gränser. Iustus, Uppsala
Lindell B (2003) Civilprocessen. Iustus, Uppsala
Linna T (2010) Puntarissa plea bargaining: vastassa oikeusturva ja itsekriminointisuoja. Oikeustiede - Jurisprudentia XLIII 43:189–262
Linna T (2012) Rikosvastuun huojennus: suomalainen plea bargaining hakee muotoaan. In: Hyttinen T (ed) Rikoksesta rangaistukseen. Juhlajulkaisu Pekka Viljanen 1952 – 26/8–2012. Turun yliopisto, Turku, pp 117–134
Määttä P (2013) Rikosasian joutuisa käsittely: perusoikeus ja tuomarin velvollisuus. Lakimiesliiton kustannus, Helsinki
Niemi M (1996) Päämäärien valtakunta. Konventionaalinen analyysi lainopillisen tiedon edellytyksistä ja oikeusjärjestelmän perusteista. Suomalainen Lakimiesyhdistys, Helsinki
Nousiainen K (1993) Prosessin herruus. Suomalainen Lakimiesyhdistys, Vammala
Oikarainen J (2012) Syyteneuvottelu ja tunnustamisoikeudenkäynti oikeuspoliittisena kysymyksenä – uhka vai mahdollisuus? Lakimies 5:742–763
Pesonen AE (2011) Tunnustaminen ja syytteestä sopiminen osaksi suomalaista rikosprosessia: käyttökelpoinen lisä keinovalikoimaan vai kyseenalaista kaupankäyntiä? Oikeuspoliittista keskustelua tunnustamisen muuttuvasta merkityksestä. Pro gradu – thesis February 2011 Eximia cum laude approbatur, University of Turku, Faculty of Law. Published in Edilex 5.9.2011 https://www.edilex.fi/lakikirjasto/8044
Ridha S (2014) Plea bargaining suhteessa rikoksesta syytetyn itsekriminointisuojaan. Published in Edilex 23.12.2014 www.edilex.fi/acta_legis_turkuensia/14602. Published earlier in: Acta Legis Turkuensia 2014 Turun yliopiston Oikeustieteen Ylioppilaiden Yhdistys Lex ry
Sahavirta A (2018) Luottamuksella lopullisuuteen? Oikeusvoiman vaikutukset syyteneuvottelumenettelyssä. Itä-Suomen yliopisto, Kuopio
Saranpää T (2010) Näyttöenemmyysperiaate riita-asiassa. Suomalainen Lakimiesyhdistys, Vammala
Searle JR (1988) Speech acts. An essay in the philosophy of language. Cambridge University Press, Cambridge
Takala JP (1998) Moraalitunteet rikosten sovittelussa. Oikeuspoliittinen tutkimuslaitos, Helsinki
Tala J (2002) Luottamus tuomioistuimiin: mitä se on ja tarvitaanko sitä lisää? Lakimies 1:3–33
Tolvanen M (2003) Asianosaisten määräämistoimista rikosprosessissa. Defensor Legis 6:1009–1027
Tolvanen M (2006) Asianosaisten ja tuomioistuimen roolit todistelussa. Lakimies 7–8:1325–1343
Tyler TR (1990) Why people obey the law? Yale University Press, New Haven
Ukkonen IT (2013) Hyveen ja yhteisön mahdollisuus modernissa oikeudessa. University of Helsinki, Helsinki
Vilkko N (2011) Plea bargain–menettely Suomessa. Bookwell Oy, Vaajakoski

Virolainen J (1995) Lainkäyttö: oikeudenkäynnin perusteet ja lainkäyttöelimet siviili-ja rikosprosessissa. Lakimiesliiton kustannus, Helsinki
Virolainen J, Martikainen P (2003) Pro et contra: tuomion perustelemisen keskeisiä kysymyksiä. Talentum, Helsinki

Small Claims Procedures in the Scandinavian Countries

Christina Jensen

Abstract All the Scandinavian countries have some form of special proceedings for small claims. Still, there has not been formal cooperation between the countries. This means that Sweden, Denmark and Norway have quite different approaches to some procedural questions concerning small claims. The goal of this article is to analyse whether the implementation of small claims procedures has had any effect on the Scandinavian civil procedure. There is no doubt that the introduction of small claims procedures has a direct effect purely by being an addition to the ordinary proceedings. The question of more interest here is whether the implementation has some indirect effects on the Scandinavian way of approaching procedural questions. Mainly, the article will focus on the effect of the rules limiting the possibility of obtaining cost reimbursement from the losing party in small claims cases. For example, there is an assumption that the mentioned cost limitations will increase the number of self-represented parties. More self-represented parties demand more of the judge, for example when it comes to giving guidance.

1 Introduction

Special procedures for claims of lower value have become a staple in most European countries.[1] This is also the case in Norway, Sweden and Denmark, which all have small claims regulations, although there are clear differences in the structure. This text aims to identify some aspects of the small claims procedure that have influenced how Scandinavian countries approach procedural questions.

Two of the other Nordic countries will not be further discussed in this article. Iceland does have small claims procedures, but the source material is neither available in any Scandinavian language nor English, which excludes the procedures from this article. Finland does not have a small claims procedure, at least not of the kind

[1] CEPEJ (2014), p. 260.

C. Jensen (✉)
Faculty of Law, UiT, The Arctic University of Norway, Hansine Hansens veg 18, 9037 Tromsø, Norway

L. Ervo et al. (eds.), *Rethinking Nordic Courts*, Ius Gentium: Comparative Perspectives on Law and Justice 90, https://doi.org/10.1007/978-3-030-74851-7_15

this article discusses.[2] Through its membership in the European Union, Finland is required to implement the European Small Claims Procedure, which is not the topic of the article. Finland does have procedural rules that aim to limit costs and time spent on smaller cases, but these are more like order-for-payment procedures than small claims procedures, since the claims must be uncontested.[3] In this article, the focus is on procedures concerning contested claims, and how these are handled by the courts. Therefore, Finnish procedural aspects that have common features with small claims procedures will not be discussed further here.

Since the focus of the article is Scandinavia, it might be natural to assume that there has been some form of cooperation between the countries. However, this is not the case, at least not formally. In fact, there are examples of significant differences among the three countries, especially with regard to the degree of EU impact on procedural rules.

Still, there are clear signs of common inspiration in the reasoning behind implementing small claims regulations. First, the main goals of having special procedures for small claims are the same. The procedure should be more effective than the ordinary procedures, and it should limit the parties' financial risks associated with going to court. Secondly, all three countries have obligations to secure a fair trial, in accordance with the ECHR article 6 number 1.

There have also been communications between lawyers in the different countries concerning the procedure for small claims, in a more informal way compared to official law making. For example, one of the topics during the 35th Nordic Law Meeting '*Nordisk juristmøte*' in 1999 was small claims.[4] Therefore, even though there has not been any formal cooperation, it is a legitimate hypothesis that it should be possible to identify some similar developments for the Scandinavian courts.

The problems with small claims and court proceedings have also been similar in the countries. Mainly, the procedures in the Scandinavian courts have been too expensive and too time consuming, and often the parties have different procedural experience.[5] These factors may reduce the expectation of fairness in the court proceedings, which again can make people with small claims choose to give up the claim instead of taking it to court. This is generally seen as a restriction of 'access to justice'. The introduction of small claims procedures in the Scandinavian countries has a common goal: to make the courts accessible to people with small claims by reducing the costs and the time spent on the case and to reduce differences between experienced parties and parties that have never been to court before. The procedural rules should secure a proportional treatment of the cases.[6]

---

[2]Nylund (2016), p. 77.

[3]See, e.g., The Finnish Code of Judicial Procedure chapter 5 Sect. 3, concerning the procedure for uncontested claims.

[4]This is a meeting held regularly since 1872, where participants from all the Nordic countries discuss different legal challenges, with the goal to learn from each other.

[5]Jensen (2021), pp. 33–40.

[6]For Norway, see Lov 17.6.2005 no. 90 Tvisteloven (hereafter The Dispute Act) Sect. 10–1 (1); for Sweden, see Law committee report 2004/05: 131, p. 78; and for Denmark, see The Danish Standing Committee on Procedural Law (Retsplejerådet) report no. 1436/2004, p. 41.

In the following, I will firstly discuss what constitutes a small claim in the different countries. Secondly, I will present the main structure of the different procedures. Thirdly, I will discuss differences in the cost rules. Finally, I will analyse the different effects these rules have had, or may have, on the procedure.

2 The Application of the Small Claims Procedures

A necessary condition for discussing small claims is to understand what constitutes a small claim in each of the countries. There are three questions of particular interest for this subject. The first is which monetary amount the countries have set as the limit between ordinary proceedings and small claims proceedings. The second is what kinds of cases are not suitable for judgment after a simplified procedure and therefore fall out of the small claims scope. The third is what the definition of a small claim entails for the number of cases dealt with under the small claims procedures.

2.1 The Monetary Limit

As a main rule, the usage of the special procedural rules for small claims depends on the monetary value of the contested claim. This is the case, for example, in England and Germany, as well as in the Scandinavian countries.[7] Among the Scandinavian countries, there is quite a large difference in what constitutes a 'small' claim.

Norway has the highest threshold for small claims. All claims that are valued less than approximately 13,000 EUR are considered small claims, with some exceptions.[8] The typical Danish small claims are of lower value than approximately 6700 EUR, which is less than half the Norwegian limit.[9] Sweden has a noticeably lower limit than the two other countries, at only approximately 2200 EUR.[10]

However, the Swedish limit does change somewhat from year to year, as it depends on the price base amount, which the Swedish government adjusts every year.[11] This differs from the Norwegian and Danish thresholds, as these are set as a fixed amount. Consequently, there needs to be a change in the law if the limits are to change in the latter countries. Such changes are under discussion in Norway, where there is a suggestion to increase the limit to approximately 25,500 EUR, which is double

[7] See The Civil Procedure Rules 1998 no. 3132 Sect. 26.6 and *Gerichtsverfassungsgesetz*, 27 January 1877 Sect. 23 no. 1.

[8] The Dispute Act Sect. 10–1 (2) a.

[9] *Lovbekendtgørelse* 14.11.2018 no. 1284 *Retsplejeloven* (hereinafter Administration of Justice Act) Sect. 400 (1).

[10] Lov 1942:740 *Rättegångsbalken* (Hereafter Swedish Code of Judicial Procedure) Sect. 1–3d (1).

[11] Swedish Code of Judicial Procedure Sect. 1–3d (1).

the amount that divides small claims from ordinary claims today.[12] If this change is made, it will increase the differences in what constitutes a small claim among the Scandinavian countries.

There is no consensus across the borders concerning non-monetary claims and the usage of small claims procedures. In Norway, the small claims procedure excludes non-monetary claims, unless the parties agree on using it and the court finds it reasonable.[13] In Sweden, the simplified procedure is only applicable to monetary claims, with no exceptions.[14] Both the Swedish and the Norwegian solutions therefore differ from the Danish one. The main rule in the latter is that the small claims procedure is applicable in both small monetary claims cases and cases concerning claims of no monetary value.[15]

2.2 *Excluded Cases*

The principle of proportionality does not set aside the principle of procedural fairness in small claims cases, as stated, for example, by the European Court of Human Rights in Pönka versus Estonia.[16] Some cases have high societal importance or are so complicated, either legally or factually, that they are not suited for simplified procedures. This means that the ordinary procedural rules must regulate some cases, even though they may concern lower value claims.

In all three countries, the small claims procedures are not applicable to cases concerning public interests.[17] For example, child custody cases and cases about coercive matters are excluded. This rule stems from a belief that some cases are so important to the society that efficiency and costs should have less impact on the procedure. Therefore, simplified procedures are not suitable for these kinds of cases.

In addition, the courts must use the ordinary procedural rules in cases of high importance outside the specific case or cases that demand a more thorough hearing. In the evaluation of importance, the perspective is that of the party. This rule is the same in all three countries.[18] It is therefore not of relevance in this respect if the case has, for example, high importance for interest groups. However, high importance for an interest group can be a factor in the consideration of the need for a more thorough

[12] Hearing proposal from the Norwegian Ministry of Justice and Public Security, dated July 2018, no. 18/3837, p. 39 and Proposal 133L (2018–2019), p. 36.

[13] The Dispute Act Sect. 10–1 (2) c.

[14] Swedish Code of Judicial Procedure Sect. 1–3d (1). In addition, see Westberg (2013), p. 96.

[15] Administration of Justice Act Sect. 400 (1) no. 1.

[16] Judgement of 8 November 2016, paragraph 30.

[17] For Norway, see The Dispute Act 10–1 (3) c; for Sweden, see Swedish Code of Judicial Procedure Sect. 1–3d (2); and for Denmark, see Administration of Justice Act Sect. 400 (1) no. 2.

[18] For Norway, see The Dispute Act 10–1 (3) d; for Sweden, see Swedish Code of Judicial Procedure Sect. 1–3d (1) and (2); and for Denmark, see Administration of Justice Act Sect. 402 (1) no. 1 and 2.

hearing of the case, at least from the Norwegian perspective.[19] In Swedish and Danish law, the question concerning the relevance of interest groups as an argument for a more thorough hearing seems unanswered.

2.3 *The Usage of the Small Claims Procedures*

The small claims procedures will only make the court procedures more effective if it is used. It is therefore necessary to discuss the actual usage of the procedures in the Scandinavian countries.

Danish courts have the highest percentage of small claims cases of the Scandinavian countries. Over half of the civil cases brought before the Danish courts are small claims cases.[20] In Sweden, the number is lower. Only a fourth of civil cases brought before the Swedish courts are small claims cases, which is natural because of the low monetary limit.[21] The lowest share of small claims among the Scandinavian countries is in the Norwegian court system, where only about one tenth of civil claims are small claims.[22] As we can see, even though Norway has the highest monetary limit, the percentage of cases judged after the small claims regulations is the lowest, being less than half the percentage of small claims in Sweden and less than a fifth of the small claims in Denmark.

The reason for the discrepancy is most likely the extensive use of Conciliation Boards in Norway.[23] The Conciliation Board in Norway is a formalised form of mediation with the possibility of obtaining a judgment. The judges are always laymen. Before the district court can hear a small claims case, it must go before the Conciliation Board, with some exceptions.[24] The most important exception is when an official complaints board has heard the case on its merits.[25] Still, small claims cases in general need to undergo a hearing by some kind of board before the district court can hear them.

Neither Sweden nor Denmark has Conciliation Board hearings as a requisite for a district court hearing. Small claims cases will therefore generally have their first

[19] See judgment from the Norwegian Supreme Court, HR-2018–1369-U paragraph 12.

[20] Statistics from Denmark: https://www.domstol.dk/om/organisation/domstolsstyrelsen/organisationsdiagram/Documents/Civile%20sager%20-%20byretter%20-%20modtagne-afsluttede%20sager.pdf (last visited 1 May 2019). In 2018, 45,657 civil cases came to the district courts. Of these, 23,268 were small claims cases.

[21] Statistics from Sweden: https://www.domstol.se/upload/Lokala_webbplatser/Domstolsverket/Statistik/Domstolsstatistik%202018.pdf (last visited 1 May 2019). In 2018, 85,617 civil cases came to the district courts. Of these, 20,480 were small claims cases.

[22] Statistics from Norway: https://www.domstol.no/no/domstoladministrasjonen/publikasjoner/arsrapport/tema-13/domstolene-i-2017/ (last visited 1 May 2019). There are no statistics concerning small claims cases in Norway from 2018.

[23] Jensen (2021) pp. 112 and 125.

[24] The Dispute Act Sect. 6–2 (2) a.

[25] The Dispute Act Sect. 6–2 (2) c.

hearing at the courts. In Norway, if the parties get a judgment from the Conciliation Board, there is not necessarily a need for a second judgement from the district court. For example, the judgment from the Conciliation Board is enforceable.[26] As long as the losing party does not appeal the judgment from the Conciliation Board, the winning party can enforce the ruling in the same way as a district court decision. This is probably the main reason for the low number of Norwegian small claims cases in the first instance courts, compared to Sweden and Denmark.

A second reason for the large difference in the number of small claims cases may be the fact that Denmark also includes non-monetary cases, which neither of the other two countries do. Without detailed statistics that show how many small claims cases concerns non-monetary claims in Denmark, this remains merely a speculation.

3 Procedural Steps in the Small Claims Procedures

3.1 Norway

The Norwegian small claims procedure came to force on 1 January 2008. Chapter ten of the Dispute Act (*tvisteloven*) regulates the procedure. In addition, the Dispute Act has several chapters that are common for both the ordinary procedure and the small claims procedure. Still, the interpretation of these rules may also be affected by the fact that the case concerns a small claim.[27]

The first stage of the case starts with a writ of summons and a written reply.[28] After this, the preparatory stage starts. Based on the written summons and the written reply, the court sets up a plan for the case and gives the parties necessary guidance. Still, the parties are responsible for the preparatory stage. The communication between the parties and the court shall be in writing at this stage, and there is no room for preparatory meetings. In legal theory this restriction has been deemed illogical, as an active use of the preparatory stage generally is seen as an effective addition to civil procedures.[29]

In small claims cases, the main rule is that the case is heard by a single judge. There is a possibility of adding two expert lay judges within a week of the hearing, but it is rarely used.[30] Small claims cases therefore have limited possibility for lay participation. The judge that prepares the case is generally the same judge that hears the case.

When the preparatory stage is finished, the main hearing commences. Ideally, the case should be fully prepared at this stage. Small claims hearings should ideally be

[26] Lov 26.06.1992 no. 86 om tvangsfullbyrdelse (The Enforcement Act) Sect. 4–1 (1) a.

[27] NOU 2001:32 A, p. 341 and Jensen (2021) p. 90.

[28] The Dispute Act section 10-2 (1) together with Sects. 9-2 and 9-3.

[29] See Nylund (2016) p. 73 and Jensen (2021), pp. 93–95.

[30] The Dispute Act Sect. 10–3 (3).

finished within 2–3 h.[31] The hearing should be less formal and simpler compared to the ordinary procedure. For example, the judge and the lawyers do not wear capes, and the court can adjust the proceedings to a greater extent with fewer obligatory stages.

If one or both of the parties are displeased with the result, it is possible to appeal the judgment. However, there are limitations. If the case concerns a claim valued below 13,000 EUR, the second instance court must agree to hear the case.[32] Approval by the second instance court is rarely given, so in reality small claims cases in general only get one hearing.[33]

3.2 Denmark

The road towards special procedures for small claims in Denmark started in 1979.[34] Several propositions came and were turned down. The process towards the small claims procedure of today started in 2002.[35] The revision of the Administration of Justice Act that implemented the small claims procedure came to force 1 January 2008.[36]

The Danish small claims procedure is designed much like the Norwegian procedure. The Administration of Justice Act has a separate chapter including the main rules for the hearing of small claims, chapter 39. As in The Dispute Act, the small claims chapter is supplemented by general chapters in the law.

A writ of summons and a written reply commence the court case. Based on these, the court takes responsibility for the preparation of the case, which is the opposite of the Norwegian solution.[37] Identifying and presenting relevant procedural acts is still the responsibility of the parties. However, the court may reject some acts, mainly evidence, if they are not deemed necessary or proportionate. Since the court has been given an extra responsibility for the case during the preparatory stage, this is where the main adjustments of the case should happen. The preparation is mainly written, but since 2012 it has been possible to have preparatory meetings.[38]

---

[31]The Norwegian Justice Department report Ot.prp. no. 51 (2004–2005) p. 359 and Vangsnes (2018), p. 156.

[32]The Dispute Act Sect. 10–6 and Sect. 29–13 (1).

[33]The Norwegian Justice Department report Innst. O. no. 110 (2004–2005), p. 65.

[34]Law committee report 1979/886 *om behandling af sager af mindre værdi ved domstolene.*

[35]The Danish Standing Committee on Procedural Law (Retsplejerådet) report no. 1436/2004, p. 440.

[36]Act no. 538, 8 June 2006 § 1 no. 102.

[37]Administration of Justice Act Sect. 406 no. 2. See also Dahlager (2010) p. 56.

[38]Administration of Justice Act Sect. 406 no. 4 and law proposition 14. December 2011 no. 58 *om ændring af retsplejeloven m.m.*, no. 6.2.2.2.

The main hearing of the case should be finished within a few hours.[39] This requires a well-prepared case, as time-consuming discussions about questions in the hearing generally are not possible. Time restrictions on the main hearing constitute one of the reasons why the judge is given proportionally more responsibilities during the preparatory stage compared to the ordinary procedures. The hearing itself is quite like an ordinary case, where the parties present evidence and closing arguments. However, the parties should not present their perspectives on the facts separately.[40] The court oversees the preparation of the case and therefore does not require the facts in the case to be repeated.

In Denmark, there are no general restrictions on the possibility to appeal the judgment in a small claims case.[41] There are only restrictions for monetary claims valued lower than approximately 2680 EURO.[42] If this limit is exceeded, the second instance court must accept the case before the case can be heard again.

3.3 Sweden

Sweden was the first of the Scandinavian countries to have a separate procedure for small claims, at least in a form that can compare to small claims procedures today.[43] The small claims law (*småmålslagen*) regulated the procedure in full. The law must have been a success, as it inspired a revision of the ordinary procedure, where special rules for small claims were implemented in the Swedish Code of Judicial Procedure. The small claims law was therefore removed. After 1988, the Swedish procedural rules have in general been meant to be more flexible, and therefore it has been possible to make the procedure in the single case proportionate to the interests at stake, based on for example the value of the claim.[44]

The general focus on efficiency has had a direct impact on the regulation of the small claims rules. Whereas the ordinary procedure is highly flexible, the need for special regulations of small claims cases is more limited. In the Swedish Code of Judicial Procedure, there are therefore only a few special rules concerning small claims. These relate firstly to the number of judges preceding the case. There is only one judge presiding over small claims cases, whereas under the normal rule three judges preside in civil cases.[45] As a consequence, it is not possible to have lay judges.

---

[39]The Danish Standing Committee on Procedural Law (Retsplejerådet) report no. 1436/2004, p. 45 and Kirk (2011) p. 137.

[40]Administration of Justice Act Sect. 407 (1).

[41]Administration of Justice Act Sect. 410.

[42]Administration of Justice Act Sect. 368 no. 1.

[43]For example, Norway has had some special procedures for claims of lower value in earlier days, but the rules have been very limited, with the consequence that they were rarely used; see Official Norwegian Report NOU 2001:32 p. 318.

[44]Law committee report 1986/87:89 p. 68.

[45]Swedish Code of Judicial Procedure chapter 1 Sect. 3d (1).

Secondly, there are separate limitations for cost reimbursement in small claims cases. All other procedural questions depend mainly on the discretion of the judge. In the decisions, the goal of an efficient but fair procedure is of high importance.[46]

In the preparatory stage, the judge decides if it is necessary to have preparatory hearings, if the preparation of the case shall be in writing or if a combination of the two will be used.[47] In small claims cases, where the focus on efficiency is of high importance, the preparation is mainly written. Only in exceptional circumstances will the court allow oral preparation.[48]

The final hearing is as, a main rule, oral. The parties present their perspectives on the case, evidence is presented, and the parties present their closing arguments. Based on the oral hearing, the court gives judgment.

In theory, if one or both of the parties disagree with the judgment, they can appeal. In Sweden, however, there are quite strict limitations on the possibility of appeal. All cases must be approved by the second instance court before being allowed a second hearing.[49] The threshold is very high, which means that in practice small claims generally will not be allowed a second hearing. It has also been claimed that the Swedish civil procedure is mainly a one-instance procedure.[50]

In Sweden, the courts may also be inclined to use the European Small Claims Procedure.[51] This is not the case in Norway or Denmark. Norway is not a part of the EU, and Denmark is exempt from the regulation.[52] The regulation does not have rules concerning the topics discussed in this article and will therefore not be included in the discussions.

4 Limitation of Costs

There seems to be a worldwide consensus about the need for cost limitations as a tool to reduce the risk of taking small claims to court.[53] The costs related to taking a small claim to court should be predictable for the parties. Still, the extent of the limitations differs. Here I will outline the most central aspects of the Norwegian, Danish and Swedish procedural rules which aim to reduce the parties' costs in small claims cases. Cost-reducing rules are directly linked to securing the 'access to justice' of people with small claims, as the high court costs have constituted one of the main restrictions to access to the courts for this group of claimants.

---

[46]Swedish Code of Judicial Procedure chapter 42 Sect. 6 s paragraph.

[47]Swedish Code of Judicial Procedure chapter 42 Sect. 9 first paragraph.

[48]Lindell (2017) p. 354.

[49]Swedish Code of Judicial Procedure chapter 49 Sect. 12.

[50]Westberg (2013), p. 250.

[51]Regulation (EC) 861/2007, O.J. L199/1 (2007) and Regulation (EU) 2015/2421, O.J. L341/1 (2015).

[52]See Regulation (EC) 861/2007, O.J. L199/1 (2007), The preamble paragraph 37.

[53]Kramer and Kakiuchi (2015), p. 27.

I will focus on costs that arise from representation by a lawyer. The countries may also have lower court fees in small claims cases, but these are generally quite low in the Scandinavian countries. All the countries also accept reimbursement of necessary travel expenses and expenses for witnesses.[54] The biggest differences in cost limitations are therefore mostly visible with regard to lawyer representation.

4.1 Norway

The Dispute Act Sect. 10–5 limits the reimbursement the parties can get in a small claims case. In ordinary cases, the main rule is that the winner of the case gets full reimbursement from the losing party.[55] This is also the main rule in small claims cases; however, the definition of 'full reimbursement'is quite limited when it comes to legal representation.

Firstly, the limits depend on the value of the claim. Cost reimbursement is only possible for up to 20 percent of the value of the claim. If the claim is valued at 3000 EUR, the reimbursement is limited to 600 EUR. Secondly, there are limits for minimum and maximum reimbursements. The party should always get approximately 260 EUR reimbursed, but never more than approximately 2600 EUR. The limit for maximum reimbursement is usually not necessary, as 20 percent of 13,000 EUR, the small claims threshold, is 2600 EUR. The only time the maximum will be reached is in cases in which the parties have agreed to use the small claims procedure in a case concerning a claim valued above 13,000 EUR.

There is a narrow exception to these restrictions. If a party 'has brought or resisted an action clearly without grounds for doing so' the restrictions may be lifted.[56] The same is the case when a party has increased the opposing party's costs through negligent behaviour.

The party that seeks reimbursement of costs must also show that the costs are necessary.[57] This is another example of the principle of proportionality and its practical meaning in small claims cases. The parties should always aim to reduce their costs within the maximum cost limit.

[54]For Sweden, see Swedish Code of Judicial Procedure chapter 18 Sect. 8a (2) no. 3 and 4. For Denmark, see Administration of Justice Act Sect. 408 no. 1 together with Sect. 316 no. 1. For Norway, see The Dispute Act Sect. 10–5 (1).

[55]The Dispute Act Sect. 20–2 (1).

[56]The Dispute Act Sect. 10–5 (2).

[57]The Dispute Act Sect. 20–5 (1).

4.2 Denmark

In Denmark, there is no direct link between small claims and limitation of costs. Instead, there are limitations only for the small claims of lowest value.[58] The first threshold is approximately 1340 EUR. If the claim is of lower value then this, the winning party can only get reimbursement for approximately 335 EUR. If the case concerns a claim of even lower value, such as approximately 670 EUR, there are even more limitations, and the possibility for reimbursement reduces to a maximum of approximately 200 EUR.

For claims valued higher than 1340 EUR, there are no special restrictions. Since small claims can be valued up to approximately 6700 EUR, there are several cases in which the parties can get full reimbursement for costs. This way of differentiating the limits accounts for the different needs of cases concerning extremely low values compared to cases concerning values close to the small claims limit.

Finally, as in Norway, the expenses that can be reimbursed must be necessary.[59] It is therefore possible that the parties must endure further restricted cost reimbursement.

4.3 Sweden

The most restrictive cost limitations are in the Swedish small claims procedure. In the ordinary procedure, as in the other two countries, the main rule is that the winning party gets full compensation from the other party for the costs of going to trial. In small claims cases, this is not the case; instead, the winning party can only get reimbursement for one hour of legal advice.[60] If the case gets appealed to the second instance court the party can be reimbursed for another hour. In addition, the amount cannot exceed the hourly rate set by the government.[61] This amount is usually lower than the ordinary hourly rate set by lawyers.

As in the other two countries, the party must also show that the expenses have been necessary.[62] However, this is a restriction with little effect concerning lawyers' expenses in Sweden. Since the amount of legal advice are already limited to an hour, it is not likely that the judge will find this expense unnecessary. As noted previously, it is not a goal of the small claims procedure to hinder the parties from seeking any advice from a lawyer.

---

[58] Administration of Justice Act Sect. 408 (1).

[59] Administration of Justice Act Sect. 316.

[60] Swedish Code of Judicial Procedure chapter 18 Sect. 8a (2) no. 1.

[61] Swedish Code of Judicial Procedure chapter 18 Sect. 8a and code no. 1996:1619 Sect. 4 (2). See also Almkvist and Elofsson (2013), p. 156.

[62] Swedish Code of Judicial Procedure chapter 18 Sect. 8.

5 The Effects of Cost Limitations

The goal of limiting the possibility of compensation for cost is to reduce the risk of going to court. However, this is not the only way the limitations affect the court proceedings. When the parties must pay their own costs, they may choose not to be represented in the case or to have only limited representation. Less representation can affect the expectations the parties may have of the presiding judge. What the cost limitations entail for the procedure and the courts is the subject here.

5.1 Self-Represented Parties

When the possibility for the parties to get a reimbursement of the lawyers' fees is limited, there is a risk that the parties might choose to represent themselves to save money. In this way, the cost risks are limited. Therefore, it is natural to assume that small claims procedures may increase the number of self-represented parties, since these are closely related to cost limitations. However, it is unclear whether this is actually the case in Scandinavia. As of 2019, statistics related to the number of self-represented parties in small claims cases in the Scandinavian countries are lacking. Even though there is no factual basis to conclude on this question for Scandinavia, there are indications that this prediction has come true in other countries.[63] There is no reason to believe that the Scandinavian countries should be affected differently, at least over time.

Despite the lack of statistics, all three countries have assumed that the small claims procedures will increase the number of self-represented parties. This has had an impact on how the small claims rules are to be interpreted, which to some extent follows from the law in Norway and Denmark, but not in Sweden.[64] In Sweden, the same idea is presented in the preparatory works.[65]

5.2 Case Management

In all three countries, the court is generally given more responsibility for securing more efficient progress in small claims cases compared to the ordinary procedures. Since the claims are of low value, the resources put into the case can quickly become disproportionate. This kind of case must therefore be handled with a greater focus on efficiency compared to the procedure in ordinary cases. If the parties are self-representing, the judges' responsibility generally increases, as mentioned above.

---

[63] Andrews (2003), pp. 534–535, Voet (2015), p. 157 and Sorabji (2015), p. 172.

[64] For Norway, see The Dispute Act Sect. 11–5 (6); for Denmark, see Administration of Justice Act Sect. 339.

[65] Law committee report no. 1986/87:89, p. 107.

This is a consequence of the parties' lack of judicial experience combined with the fact that the main hearing still should be finished within few hours.

One of the most visible ways in which case management is introduced in the law is in the possibility for the judge to set deadlines.[66] If the parties do not finish the requested procedural act by the deadline, the act as a rule ends up being the subject of preclusion. This is intended to have both a disciplinary effect and a cost-reducing effect.[67] The disciplinary aspect arises when the parties present procedural acts in a timely manner because they do not want it to be precluded. It is also assumed that the earlier the parties present procedural acts, the more efficient the procedure will be.[68]

Denmark can be said to have the most extensive case management in small claims, as the responsibility for the preparation is given to the judge. Since the judge is the one who asks for necessary procedural acts, the parties have less possibility to unnecessarily extend the preparatory stage. In Sweden and Norway, where the main responsibility is with the parties, a passive judge may cause delays. Still, all three countries have tools to make sure that the case progresses effectively.

5.3 *Judicial Guidance*

Lastly, it must be assumed that the judge, to achieve a fair and efficient trial, must give the parties more judicial guidance in small claims cases then in ordinary cases. This presumed increase in guidance comes as a consequence of the above-mentioned assumption of an increase of self-representing parties in these cases. This assumption is common for all three countries, as shown above. One of the general problems with small claims, from a procedural perspective, has been to reduce the differences between 'one-shot litigants' and 'repeat players'.[69] The most common way to approach this is to allow for more guidance for the party without procedural experience. Some commonality is therefore to be expected between the countries. However, the extent of the guidance does differ.

In Norway, the judge is permitted to give quite extensive guidance about procedural questions.[70] This applies in both ordinary cases and small claims cases. However, it is assumed that the judge can go even further in giving guidance in small claims cases. This must be seen in relation to the cost limitations. When the law limits the possibility for representation, even if only implicitly, the judge must have an increased responsibility to ensure that the parties understand the procedural

[66]For Sweden, see Swedish Code of Judicial Procedure Sect. 42–15 and Sect. 42-15a; for Norway, see the Dispute Act Sect. 11–6; and for Denmark, see Administration of Justice Act Sect. 406 no. 3.

[67]Jensen (2021) pp. 203–205.

[68]Nylund (2016) p. 7.

[69]Cappelletti (1976) p. 679 and Lindblom (2000) p. 311.

[70]See the Dispute Act Sect. 11–5 first paragraph.

steps. A party should not lose the case merely because of misunderstandings about procedural rules. In addition, it is assumed that there are few arguments against procedural guidance.[71] This is especially the case in small claims cases, where the parties are in more dire need of procedural guidance compared to ordinary cases (where the parties most likely get procedural guidance from a lawyer).

With regard to guidance about substantial questions, it is assumed that the judge must be more restricted compered to procedural guidance. This is a consequence of the rules concerning impartiality in general legislation, as well as the Constitution Sect. 95 and ECHR art. 6 no. 1.[72] The latter two state that the judge must be impartial at all stages of the case. Extensive guidance about the substantial questions in the case, at least when one of the parties needs guidance more than the other, may give an impression of partiality. The principle of impartial judges is also relevant in Danish and Swedish procedural law, as the ECHR is binding for all the Scandinavian countries.

Still, it assumed that the judge can give quite a lot of guidance about substantive questions in small claims cases. Again, this increase in guidance must be seen in relation to the expectation of more self-representing parties.[73] However, the lack of preparatory meetings may reduce the judges' possibility to give guidance in small claims cases. It is more difficult to give guidance by writing, and it is often a bit too late to give guidance during the final hearing. Guidance is therefore possible to a wide extent in small claims cases in theory, but perhaps not in practice. However, the judge can never give the parties advice about the case, even in small claims cases.[74]

The Swedish approach is quite similar to the Norwegian one. There are no special rules concerning judicial guidance in small claims cases. Still, it can be argued that parties in small claims cases are obliged to receive more guidance than parties in ordinary cases. This is stated, for example, in the preparatory works.[75]

It is generally assumed that the judge has an obligation to give guidance about procedural questions.[76] This is based on similar ideas as in Norway. Since the parties only get reimbursed for one hour of legal counsel in small claims cases, the necessity of procedural guidance may be assumed to be even larger in Sweden than in the neighbouring countries.

The Danish judge has similar options to give the parties guidance as in Norway and Sweden. The primary aim of guidance is to clarify what the procedural acts the parties present should add to the case. Furthermore, the possibility of giving guidance is wider for procedural questions and smaller for substantial questions.

The Danish rules, however, seen to go a bit further than the other two countries' with regard to substantive questions. For example, the judge may give the parties

---

[71]See NOU 2001:32 A, p. 140.

[72]See the Norwegian Constitution, 17 May 1814 § 95 and the European Convention on Human Rights article 6 no. 1.

[73]Nylund (2016), p. 73.

[74]The Dispute Act Sect. 11–5 (7).

[75]Law committee report 1999/2000:26 *Effektivisering av förfarandet i allmän domstol*, no. 12.

[76]Westberg (2013), p. 157.

advice.[77] This is unheard of in Norwegian and Swedish law, where the judge is banned from giving the parties advice.[78] Guidance may be given, but not to the extent of advising the parties about what to do. A reason for this difference may be the fact that in Denmark, the same judge does not both give guidance and deliver the judgement. In Norway and Sweden, the same judge usually does both, which increases the possibility of doubt as to impartiality.

Moreover, even though it may seem that Swedish and Norwegian law clearly forbids the judge from giving advice, it must be noted that the line between guidance and advice is, to some extent, blurred in all three countries. Thus, it is possible that that the practical application of the rules is more similar than it seems from the outset.

When one compares the three countries' restrictions concerning judicial guidance in small claims cases, they may at first seem a bit different. Still, the main guidelines are similar. The extent of guidance to be given in small claims cases is larger compared to ordinary cases. The increased responsibility of the courts to give guidance is perhaps one of the most visible procedural changes that has a direct connection to the introduction of small claims procedures in the Scandinavian countries. Even in Sweden, where all cases should be handled with flexibility, parties in small claims cases should get more guidance then in ordinary cases. This similarity must be seen in connection with the problems with small claims and 'access to justice'. One of the issues with small claims cases has been that the parties have had different experiences with the courts, which can make the procedure uneven and therefore unfair, especially for self-representing parties. Introducing more guidance may reduce the impact of this kind of unevenness in small claims cases.

6 Conclusions

This chapter began by asking whether the small claims procedures have affected the Scandinavian courts and proceedings. Based upon the analyses above, it seems clear that they indeed have done so. The Danish and Norwegian civil procedure has gotten a new track, which is an entirely new procedural element, while Sweden removed the small claims law but used it as an inspiration for the ordinary law. Even without a separate track, the Swedish procedure has therefore been affected by the earlier small claims regulations. The more interesting question is how and to what extent the small claims procedure has had an impact on the Scandinavian procedures. As mentioned in the introduction, within the scope of this article it is not possible to draw full conclusions. Based on the analysis above, some aspects that have affected the approach to procedural questions have been identified.

---

[77] The Danish Standing Committee on Procedural Law (*Retsplejerådet*) report no. 1436/2004, p. 457.

[78] For Norway, see The Dispute Act Sect. 11–5 (7). For Sweden, see Law Committee report 1986/87:89, p. 107.

The most obvious impact of the small claims procedures is the visibility of the principle of proportionality. This principle is of importance in the ordinary proceedings in Scandinavia. Still, the introduction of small claims proceedings shows how the principle may outweigh other important procedural principles. For example, the preparation stage is, at least to some extent, downplayed compared to ordinary cases, and the possibility to appeal small claims cases is reduced.

Another way in which the small claims procedures may impact civil procedures is by affecting the way the judges approach the question of judicial guidance. In small claims cases, the Scandinavian judge should give the parties more extensive guidance, as shown above. However, it is possible that the judges will give more similar guidance over time, without it necessarily depending on the classification of the case. Since judges in general will preside in both ordinary and small claims cases, the entrance of small claims procedure may increase the amount of guidance given in ordinary cases as well. This is at least a possibility if the increased guidance is seen as an effective tool in the procedure. For the time being, this is only speculation, as this hypothesis requires further research to reach a conclusion.

Also, the introduction of small claims procedures increases the impact of judicial discretion. This is seen, for example, in the different rules based on the idea of flexibility, discussed above under Chap. 18.3 and 18.5. Common among the Scandinavian countries is the fact that the small claims regulations to a great extent depend on the discretion of the judge. Judicial discretion is typical for the Nordics, but with the introduction of the small claims procedures, it has especially intensified in the Scandinavian countries. The combination of the bigger impact of the principle of proportionality and increased judicial discretion does give the Scandinavian judge more responsibility when it comes to managing the case compared to how it was before the entrance of small claims procedures. This is the case, for example, for the main hearing in small claims cases. In all three countries, the judge is given almost full discretion in deciding which steps are necessary to take, and which can be skipped, to make sure the hearing is efficient and proportional.

The small claims procedure, and the special importance of the principle of proportionality, may seem partly to constitute a reduction of the quality of civil procedure in Scandinavia. Still, the introduction of small claims proceedings is a clear sign that the principle of access to justice is of high importance in the Scandinavian countries. Even though some procedural aspects are reduced in small claims cases, the special proceedings also reduce the risk of costs, which can open the courts for people with small—but, to them, important—claims. This is an important addition to the Scandinavian Civil Procedure which arguably outweighs some of the procedural reductions. Without these associated restrictions, the costs related to the cases could skyrocket, potentially making it impossible for the parties to take their cases to court at all.

References

Almkvist G, Elofsson N (2013) Rättegångskostnader i förenklade tvistemål. Svensk Juristtidning 2:150–168
Andrews N (2003) English civil procedure: fundamentals of the new civil justice system. Oxford University Press, Oxford
Cappelletti M (1976) Access to justice. Rabel J Comp Int Private Law 40:669–717
CEPEJ (2014) European judicial systems (2012 data): efficiency and quality of justice, Council of Europe
Dahlager C (2010) Få ret. Nyt Juridisk Forlag, København
Jensen C (2021) Småkravsprosessen. Gyldendal, Oslo
Kirk H (2011) Sagsomkostninger i civile sager. Thomson Reuters, København
Kramer XE, Kakiuchi S (2015) Relief in small and simple matters in an age of Austerity. Working paper XV congress of procedural law. http://ssrn.com/abstract=2610773 Accessed 27 May 2020
Lindblom PH (2000) Progressiv process: spridda uppsatser om domstolsprocessen och samhällsutvecklingen, Iustus, Uppsala
Lindell B (2017) Civilprocessen: rättegång samt skiljeförfarande och medling. Iustus, Uppsala
Nylund A (2016) Introduction to the preparatory stage of civil proceedings. In: Ervo L and Nylund A (eds) Current trends in preparatory proceedings: a comparative study of Nordic and former communist countries. Springer, Cham
Nylund A (2016) Preparatory proceedings in Norway: efficiency by flexibility and case management. In: Ervo L and Nylund A (eds) Current trends in preparatory proceedings: a comparative study of Nordic and former communist countries. Springer, Cham
Sorabji J (2015) Austerity's effect on english civil justice. Erasmus Law Rev 4:159–173
Vangsnes J (2018) Sivilprosess i et nøtteskall. Gyldendal, Oslo
Voet S (2015) Relief in Small and Simple Matters in Belgium. Erasmus Law Rev 4:147–158
Westberg P (2013) Civilrättskipning. Norstedts juridik, Stockholm

Conclusions on Nordic Courts and Court Proceedings

The Past, Present and Future of Nordic Courts

Anna Nylund

Abstract Based on the insights from the previous chapters in this volume, this concluding chapter discusses key traits of Nordic courts: colloquial legal language, generalist judges, 'unrefined' and fragmentary laws, high trust in the state and judges, and corporatism. The development of these traits over time is explored as well as the emergence of new traits that could be labelled 'Nordic'. It also discusses how two current trends—Europeanisation and privatisation of dispute resolution processes—influence Nordic courts. The question whether a unified Nordic procedural culture still exists is raised. Finally, the future of Nordic courts is discussed.

1 Introduction

This study of the Nordic legal mind and its historical, societal and linguistic contingencies, as well as its current manifestations in the structure, processes and practises of the justice system demonstrates a vibrant, regional procedural culture. The 'Nordic' traits identified in the contributions in this book demonstrate pragmatism expressed in, among other things, a belief in the benefits of amicable solutions; keeping the law and justice system 'accessible' (which translates into a colloquial legal language and lay participation); a belief in the 'good' state that manifests in high trust in judges and discretionary rules; corporatism;[1] and a legislative tradition consisting of single acts rather than codes, in which preparatory works, case law and legal scholarship are important supplements. The Nordic Supreme Courts have taken up the challenge of being guardians of human rights and EU law and they have transformed into courts of precedent that contribute actively and openly to the development of the law. Additionally, we have seen how courts are used to actively

[1] See Nylund (2021a), Sect. 4.2.

A. Nylund (✉)
Faculty of Law, UiT, The Arctic University of Norway, Hansine Hansens veg 18, 9037 Tromsø, Norway
e-mail: anna.nylund@uit.no

L. Ervo et al. (eds.), *Rethinking Nordic Courts*, Ius Gentium: Comparative Perspectives on Law and Justice 90, https://doi.org/10.1007/978-3-030-74851-7_16

enforcing government policies, particularly those regarding protection of weaker parties (e.g., consumers and employees).

Based on the insights from the previous chapters in this volume, this concluding chapter discusses key traits of Nordic courts and how these traits have developed over time, and how new hallmarks of Nordic courts and court proceedings have emerged. It also discusses how two current trends—Europeanisation and privatisation of dispute resolution processes—influence Nordic courts. The question whether a unified Nordic procedural culture still exists is raised. Finally, the future of Nordic courts is discussed.

2 Nordic Legal Language as a 'Colloquial' Language

Pragmatism and lay culture characterise Nordic courts and court proceedings, as opposed to a 'learned', highly professionalised procedural culture and 'rigid', formalistic court proceedings. According to Pia Letto-Vanamo,[2] a strong peasant culture and late urbanisation and industrialisation characterise the Nordic countries. Until the 1800s and even later, disputes were resolved by panels consisting either entirely of lay persons or of a mixture of judges with at least some formal legal training and lay judges. The judge was not a stranger from a completely different social stratum who imposed almost incomprehensible rules; rather, one was judged (at least in the case of peasants, craftsmen and traders) by one's equals, who would attempt to find an equitable, practicable solution. In this setting, developing advanced legal concepts and coherent codes easily amenable to deductive reasoning is futile, if not plainly impossible. As Ditlev Tamm explains, the first written laws were vernacular and were only to a very limited degree and indirectly influenced by Roman law and Canon law.[3] Although the persons who redacted the laws might have studied law at a university or encountered learned law in other ways, the laws were written with the reality of very low professionalisation of judges in mind. The codes enacted in the seventeenth and eighteenth centuries were also compilations of earlier law rather than products of direct transplantation of 'learned' law or manifestations of legal innovations. Continental European 'learned' legal thinking had a very modest impact on them, which is hardly surprising considering that the academic community was almost non-existent and could not have undertaken the tremendous work to craft codes that adhered to the ideals of the Enlightenment. As mentioned, low professionalisation would have made the effort futile, since the use of general concepts and deductive reasoning necessitates formal legal training.[4]

The language and terminology used in contemporary Nordic procedural law still reflect the 'lay' elements. For instance, the committee that drafted the Norwegian Dispute Act discussed whether and how the language used should and could be

[2] Letto-Vanamo (2021).

[3] Tamm (2021).

[4] Sunde (2021).

accessible for citizens.[5] The committee found that the language should be accessible for everyone. As a result, it abolished *inter alia* the term *kjæremål* to refer to interlocutory appeals; instead, appeal (*anke*) now refers to both appeals of judgments (i.e., rulings on the merits) and interlocutory appeals, despite the fact that the procedural rules governing the two are different.[6] Of course, one can question whether the terminological changes have increased the accessibility of the Dispute Act, considering that understanding the concept of interlocutory appeals requires prior knowledge of procedural law. Nevertheless, the example illustrates how simple language is still a foundational value of Nordic legal culture.

The language used in court rulings also reflects the pragmatic, 'lay' approach: the language is, relatively speaking, fairly accessible and not very technical. It does not reflect the ideal of a distant judge who mechanically applies technical rules.[7] Likewise, the language is sober and the style of matter-of-fact argumentation lacks the persuasiveness and eloquence that is associated with rulings in common law jurisdictions.[8] Ideally, the average citizens who are willing to make an effort to comprehend the ruling should be able to understand the reasoning of the court.[9] Despite the ideal of accessible language, the use of complex sentence structures, such as the passive voice, and of difficult words is common in legal language, and even in mediated agreements, although these are supposed to reflect the wishes of the parties.[10]

Linguistic unity has been pivotal for Nordic law: lawyers can understand texts written in Danish, Norwegian and Swedish without having to resort to a dictionary, and the legal terminology is mostly shared, despite some differences. Nevertheless, Finnish and Icelandic law are, as a rule, not available to speakers of the other languages. Instead, communication between Finland and Iceland and the other Nordic countries is mainly one-way: Finnish and Icelandic lawyers generally read at least one of the other languages, but the same is not true in reverse. Since Swedish is an official language of Finland, some legal texts, such as statutes and government bills, are available in Swedish.[11]

[5]NOU 2001: 32 Rett på sak, p. 150.

[6]The terminological choice can be ascribed at least partly to the fact that the rules concerning appeals of rulings on the merit and appeals of procedural rulings were formally merged. Still, different rules and principles apply for the two categories of appeals; the rules are simply interwoven.

[7]Mattila (2016), pp. 111–112, 218–222, 241 and 258–260.

[8]Mattila (2016), pp. 11–112, 318–331 and 339.

[9]Bogason and Örlygsson (2019).

[10]E.g., Dahlberg-Larsen (2015), Kjær (2015), Adrian and Mykland (2018).

[11]Tamm (2021).

3 'Generalist' Judges and 'Unrefined', Broad Laws

Nordic procedural law remained archaic well into the twentieth century. The repeated failure of attempts at modernising court proceedings in the Nordic countries during the nineteenth century and early twentieth century could be attributed partly to the lay character of Nordic law at that time. The reforms were direly needed to expedite court proceedings and to improve the factual and legal basis of the ruling by moving from piecemeal, written proceedings to oral proceedings with witness testimony and legal arguments presented orally, as well as to modernise concepts, ideas, beliefs and practices. Still, the laborious and costly process of turning a system founded on medieval law into a state-of-the-art process of the time caused significant delays, except in Denmark.[12] In Finland, the rules were modernised as late as the 1990s, partly due to the fact that profound legislative reforms regarding courts were impossible during the Russian period, and the turbulent period before, during and after the Second World War brought reforms to a halt.[13] Since German and Austrian procedural law and legal thinking formed the backbone of the Nordic reforms, despite the fact that they were adapted to Nordic legal culture, contemporary procedural law still has a strong kinship with these systems.[14]

Contemporary Nordic societies are far from peasant, rural or under-developed societies. Nevertheless, the historical characteristics are still palpable in Nordic legal culture. One example of this can be found in the Nordic court structure and aversion towards judicial specialisation, which in turn has resulted in the same procedural rules being applied in practically all civil cases and a second set of rules governing criminal cases.[15] The Nordic countries, except Norway, still have only a single act governing both civil and criminal proceedings.[16] In Finland, supplementary rules for criminal proceedings are provided in a separate act, although the Code of Judicial Procedure forms the backbone of both civil and criminal court proceedings.[17] Regulating court proceedings in a single act contributes to maintaining coherence across civil and criminal procedure and having general rules that fit a wide range of different cases and that do not require specialist knowledge. Family law cases are, in contrast, regulated in a fragmented manner, with procedural rules amending or supplementing the general procedural rules scattered across different acts or even left partially unregulated.

Since the Nordic countries have a 'piecemeal' legislative technique (i.e., a multitude of legal sources, including statutory law, case law, preparatory works, legal scholarship, etc.), courts have a pivotal role in amalgamating the sources to create a

---

[12] Hjort (2021), Sect. 2.

[13] Ervo (2021a).

[14] Hjort (2021).

[15] Hjort (2021), Letto-Vanamo (2021) and Tamm (2021).

[16] Retsplejeloven in Denmark and Rättegångsbalken in Sweden.

[17] Oikedenkäymiskaari and Laki oikeudenkäynnistä rikosasioissa. The government considered including the rules in the Code of Judicial Procedure but found that the result would be complicated and confusing (HE 82/1995, p. 19). This argument is not very convincing, however, considering that Denmark and Sweden have all the relevant rules in the same act.

coherent system. This requires high trust in courts to loyally enforce the policies that the legislature and executive branch have adopted, while also promoting equal access to justice by searching for a pragmatic and equitable solution.[18] Courts are expected to pursue the same policy goals as the legislator, the goals that the Parliament has identified as pivotal. The design of the small claims programs in Nordic courts is a manifestation of the idea of enforcement of policies, in that the judge has an active role in managing the case to reduce costs and enabling self-represented parties to argue their cases to render their legal rights effective.[19] Laura Ervo explains that, in Finland, the fact that legislation has often been outdated has resulted in the courts having to step in to modernise the law through interpretation.[20]

Anna Nylund posits that a streamlined court system consisting of general (and 'general' administrative) courts with broad jurisdiction and judges that adjudicate all types of cases is pivotal for attaining legal coherence.[21] However, the ideal of general courts does not preclude the use of special courts and dispute resolution boards, since all cases have the capacity of eventually reaching general (or 'general' administrative) courts, either a lower court or the Supreme Court or Supreme Administrative Court. These specialised dispute resolution bodies also enable corporate decision-making.

4 High Trust in the Good State Underpins Nordic Procedural Culture

Trust among citizens and trust in the government permeate Nordic culture and legal culture. Flexible, general procedural rules represent an embodiment of trust. Judges can adapt the proceedings according to the needs of the case at hand and their individual preferences, since the public and the government trust that judges obey the law and that they will use their discretion wisely and to the benefit of the parties and the legal system, as Christina Jensen demonstrates.[22] The proliferation of mediation could be interpreted as an expression of high trust in courts and the good state, as well as in pragmatism and thus the rejection of excessive formalism and legalism. The potential tension between protecting and enforcing legal rights and private ordering through settlement has been overlooked, at least so far.[23] Facilitating settlement is considered a duty of judges and a natural function of courts. In the Nordic legal mind, dispute resolution outside courts does not jeopardise the access to justice or undermine the law as a tool of governance; rather, it is believed to enhance justice

[18] Sunde (2021).
[19] Jensen (2021).
[20] Ervo (2021a).
[21] Nylund (2021b).
[22] Jensen (2021).
[23] Ervo (2021b) and Petersen (2020).

by amplifying access to high-quality processes.[24] The use of lay judges is crucial in building and maintaining trust.[25]

Martin Sunnqvist identifies 'Nordic-ness' in the role of supreme courts in performing judicial review.[26] The Nordic countries do not have constitutional courts like many countries in continental Europe. Nordic supreme courts have been hesitant to exercise judicial review overtly, apart from the Norwegian Supreme Court. However, even the Norwegian Supreme Court exercised self-restraint in the post-war years until it re-embraced judicial review in the late 1970s and 1980s. The decrease in self-restraint coincided with a discussion of the protection of human rights in Danish and Norwegian law. The shift in Finnish and Swedish courts occurred more gradually, with the first cases where the court set aside were passed only at the turn of the millennium and, moreover, partly as the result of Europeanisation.

The turn towards human rights and the Europeanisation of law has resulted in Nordic supreme courts no longer being willing to blindly obey the Parliament: they have become the guardians of human rights, with procedural rights and equal access to justice forming the epitome of the new role of courts. However, they still defer to the Parliament. Often, they resolve the discrepancy between national legislation and the constitution, ECHR or EU law by defining the problem as one that arises in a specific context, rather than a possibly profound mismatch between the underlying legal 'regimes'. In this process, assessing the decision-making processes and procedures as well as the quality and transparency of the underlying reasoning (i.e., whether the decision-maker has taken into account and balanced different viewpoints and arguments in an appropriate manner) enables courts to circumvent some of the problems regarding the relationship between national and supranational law, notes Sunnqvist.[27] Focusing on processes and transparency is congruent with the requirements of ECHR and largely also EU law: Court must assess whether proceedings abide by the criteria of due process, and not necessarily the outcome as such.[28]

A power shift has also ensued from supreme courts becoming primarily courts of precedent; that is, the supreme court had the right to select a limited number of cases based on whether the case raises issues of interest for other cases or matters of principle. The Swedish Supreme Court was the first to evolve into a court of precedent in the 1970s.[29] The other Nordic courts have followed suit, and the final step was taken when Iceland introduced a court of second instance, *Landsrettur*, placed between the Supreme Court and the district courts. Except on Iceland, this development thus preceded Europeanisation, despite the fact that the influx of EU law and international human rights from the 1990s onwards has further propelled the transition in the role of Nordic supreme courts. As a result of the increased weight of case law as a source of law, court rulings must be longer, more detailed and the

[24] Linnanmäki (2021) and Nylund (2021b).

[25] Letto-Vanamo (2021) Sect. 4.

[26] Sunnqvist (2021) Sects. 2 and 3.

[27] Sunnqvist (2021).

[28] Pedersen (2016)

[29] Sunnqvist (2021).

legal profession must advance of techniques for determination of the *ratio decidendi* and for distinguishing cases.[30]

5 Europeanisation and Nordic Courts

The European law, primarily the ECHR and EU law, have had a tangible impact on Nordic courts and court proceedings, as many of the contributions in this volume demonstrate. Despite the variation in the formal relations to EU, in particular the Area of Freedom, Justice and Security,[31] differences in the underlying mechanisms of influence and the extent of the influence among the countries are relatively minor. The EEA and Schengen Agreements have been instrumental in this respect since they necessitate close cooperation in the justice sector as well.[32]

The Nordic conventions on judicial cooperation have served as a model for the foundational concept of mutual trust in EU judicial cooperation, as Dan Helenius explains.[33] The difference is that 'blind' mutual trust exists among the Nordic countries (i.e., they consider the systems of the other Nordic countries to be of an equal standard as the domestic system), and consequently they do not question the background of a request for cooperation. For instance, Helenius notes that since the rules governing criminal liability, the criminalised acts and the criminal sanctions are sufficiently similar, requiring double criminality is redundant. Thus, Nordic countries comply with requests without hesitation. The European rules do not preclude intra-Nordic conventions on judicial cooperation, and thus Europeanisation adds a layer on the pre-existing Nordic cooperation scheme.[34]

The influx of EU law and ECtHR case law has manifestly shifted the balance of power among the three state powers in favour of courts: courts are required—not just allowed—to interpret and apply statutory law in a manner that renders them compatible with the ECHR (and EU law) and, when necessary, to give primacy to the ECHR and EU law. The increasing role of the ECHR through the growing weight and density of ECtHR case law coincided with a national turn toward human rights and courts as the guardians of those rights. In their combined effect, the bourgeoning of human rights has driven courts to perform judicial review actively and openly, which has challenged and altered the idea of courts serving the people by yielding to the will of the Parliament. Even when the ECHR does not formally take precedence over acts of Parliament, it has in practice become intertwined with interpretation of

---

[30] Sunnqvist (2021).

[31] For a more detailed discussion on how international agreements can be—and are—used to tie the Nordic countries closer to the EU, see Nylund (2019a).

[32] For a more detailed discussion on the impact of EU law on the civil procedure law of EEA countries, see Nylund (2020a) and Nylund and Strandberg (2019).

[33] Helenius (2021).

[34] Helenius (2021).

the national constitution, except in Denmark.[35] As Sunnqvist notes, courts are even required to monitor whether courts and court proceedings of other EU Member States fulfil fundamental fair trial rights.[36] However, as Thorsteinsdóttir illustrates, Nordic courts have taken on their new role gradually and reluctantly.[37] As explained above, courts still tend to frame discrepancies as related to the specific case or specific issues and are hesitant to discuss the underlying, general differences.

Courts are, in essence, required to monitor the rule of law by protecting human rights derived from the ECHR, national law and other human rights instruments, such as the United Nations Covenant on the Rights of the Child,[38] the EU Fundamental Rights Charter[39] and the United Nations Convention on the Rights of Persons with Disabilities.[40] In contrast with the earlier approach, where courts were expected to respect the will of the majority, courts are now expected to protect the rule of law—the fundamental values of a liberal, democratic society and the rights of minorities—from infringements by the government.

In interpreting case law from European courts, Nordic courts must assess whether and which aspects of the case are applicable in the national context. Navigating the complex multi-layered European system is not an easy task: sometimes Nordic courts are accused of being overly cautious and minimising the room to manoeuvre nationally, while at other times they have been criticised for being overly confident and reluctant to engage in dialogue. The former applies especially to the ECHR and the latter to the issue of requesting preliminary rulings from the CJEU (or advisory opinions from the EFTA Court).[41] The ECHR and the EU system rely on national courts explaining how they have interpreted relevant laws and how they have balanced different arguments and values. Procedural aspects, access to court and open argumentation are paramount, and courts scrutinising above all procedural aspects of constitutionality is a logical consequence of this approach. The implementation of EU law has thus propelled congruous shifts in all Nordic countries.

The impact of EU and ECHR law on Nordic law is partly contingent on judges and lawyers having sufficient knowledge and understanding of EU and ECHR law—substantive law, legal principles and methods. Unless lawyers and judges recognise the relevance of EU law and have the skills to detect and analyse complex problems pertaining to EU law, they are likely to overlook it or refrain from invoking it. Anna Nylund argues that Nordic lawyers and judges tend to have insufficient skills in EU law and that weaknesses in the implementation of EU law generate additional hurdles for effective application of EU law.[42] Moreover, since requests for preliminary rulings (and advisory opinions in the EEA context) drive the development and refinement of

[35] Sunnqvist (2021) and Thorsteinsdóttir (2021).

[36] Sunnqvist (2021).

[37] Thorsteinsdóttir (2021).

[38] For a comparison of the Nordic countries in this regard, see Haugli and Nylund (2019).

[39] See, e.g., Nylund (2020a) for a discussion of its impact on civil procedure in EEA countries.

[40] Brennan et al. (2018) and Helgadóttir (2009).

[41] Nylund (2021c), Sunnqvist (2021) and Thorsteinsdóttir (2021).

[42] Nylund (2021c).

EU law, the relative passivity of Nordic courts in this respect reduces the footprint of Nordic law, legal principles, values and patterns of argumentation on EU law.

Furthermore, policymakers, and to some extent academics, in Nordic countries influence whether the response to Europeanisation is proactive or reactive. A proactive approach entails participation in the processes by which European procedural rules are forged and in making deliberate choices when implementing European procedural law in national law, not just treating European procedural rules as 'technical' rules that can be implemented mechanically.

6 Changing Role of Courts: Privatisation and Enforcement of Policies

The expectations courts face are increasingly bifurcated: on the one hand, settlement in all its forms is promoted, resulting in individualised, privatised dispute resolution; on the other hand, courts are required to enforce selected government policies (i.e., provide for the public good).

Court-connected mediation, in which either a judge or a registered mediator serves as the mediator, was introduced as a parallel process to litigation in Norway in 1997 and has since spread to Denmark, Finland and Iceland.[43] Sweden differs in this regard, since courts do not have mediation programs themselves; they only encourage the parties to attempt mediation. Court-connected mediation fits Nordic courts and court culture in several ways, not least due to the innate pragmatism of these cultures and the ubiquity of dispute resolution processes available outside courts. In addition to court-connected mediation, judges have had the right to promote settlement as part of regular civil proceedings, and in recent reforms this right has transformed into a duty to promote settlement when appropriate. Cross-fertilisation seems to take place between court-connected mediation and litigation practices, particularly in the techniques that judges apply to promote settlement.[44] Court-connected mediation could also influence whether and how parties negotiate before they file a court case and thus also whether they decide to litigate. However, the findings related to the reciprocal impact between litigation and mediation are preliminary and indicate a need for more research on the underlying mechanisms and outcomes.

Despite court-connected mediation being relatively prevalent in the Nordic countries, which suggests that it could be characterised as a success, the quality of the mediation process has been questioned. Mediation theory promises a facilitative process and interest-based outcomes, where the parties jointly decide whether they wish to enter the process, the design of the process and the outcome.[45] Litigation, in contrast, offers an adversarial process resulting in an outcome defined by the rules of law, where one party can force the other to participate in the process and the

[43] Nylund (2021b) and Lög um meðferð einkamála (Civil Procedure Act Sect. 106 ff.).

[44] Nylund (2021b) and Ervo (2016).

[45] Linnanmäki (2021).

rules of civil procedure determine the procedure. As Kirsikka Linnanmäki observes, the legislation and case law on mediation does not fully support the vision of party self-determination by protecting the parties from direct or indirect coercion and by sustaining informed, deliberate decision-making.[46] She identifies several problematic aspects. The process of mediation, its structure and the intended outcomes are unclear; the mediator and the parties do not have a joint understanding of mediation, the role of the mediator and what defines a quality settlement. The role of the mediator is unclear in that the mediator should formally be an expert on the mediation process and not direct the outcome or provide any opinion of the outcome, yet the mediator often acts in a way that is contrary to these ideas. Hence, the self-determination of the parties and the confidential nature of the mediation process are not sufficiently protected, as Linnanmäki observes.

Plea bargaining is related to mediation in that it represents a form of 'negotiated', informal justice where the parties to a dispute are given more control of the process and the outcome than in regular court proceedings. The process is often cheaper and faster than regular proceedings, since the police does not have to investigate the crime in detail if the accused person confesses the crime. As Laura Ervo notes, plea bargaining constitutes a shift from the power of the state to the power of the individuals involved in the dispute and their communities.[47] Perhaps one could also argue that plea bargaining represents a 'postmodern' turn: truth is no longer considered to be absolute, rather it is relative and contextual. However, one could also argue that various forms of plea bargaining and related phenomena are introduced for pragmatic reasons. Spending less time on criminal offences that the defendant has agreed to plead guilty enables the police and courts to focus on cases in which the defendant has not done so.

Clement Salung Petersen discusses the intricate relationship between party autonomy and private ordering on the one hand and using law as a tool to promote and enforce policy goals on the other hand. He notes that while parties still determine the ambit of the dispute and are responsible for providing evidence, recent reforms have stressed case management[48] and the duty of the judge to provide guidance, primarily to self-represented parties.[49] The CJEU demands that national courts enforce parts of EU consumer and competition law on their own motion. As a result, courts must be more active during the court proceedings, and the duties of the judge vary depending on the subject matter of the case. Although active judges contribute to more equal access to justice and efficient enforcement of rules protecting public policy and weaker parties, relying on active judges as the primary mechanism for enforcing public policies is also controversial and even potentially counter-productive.[50] Furthermore, the variation in the degree to which judges are

---

[46]Linnanmäki (2021).

[47]Ervo (2021b).

[48]Nylund (2019b).

[49]Petersen (2021).

[50]Petersen (2021), Wallerman Ghavanini (2020), Andersson (2019), Fredriksen and Strandberg (2019) and Eldjarn (2016).

active could result in significant fragmentation of procedural rules, which is contrary to the Nordic tradition of operating with a single set of procedural rules.

Settlement and processes facilitating (early) settlement have long been a part of Nordic dispute resolution culture and are an essential part of the Nordic justice systems. Recent decades have witnessed a proliferation of processes facilitating settlement within the domain of court proceedings by mandating judges to actively promote settlement whenever appropriate, by introducing court-connected mediation, by directing cases to restorative justice processes and through various forms of plea bargaining and simplified proceedings when the accused person pleads guilty. The question arises whether it is possible to pursue two diametrically different aims simultaneously. The question of whether or not judges should review settlement agreements, and, if so, when and to what extent they should interfere, remains unanswered, as does the question of what exactly lies in the duty to promote settlement, what type of process court-connected mediation is and should be and which cases are appropriate for each process.[51] Furthermore, one could question whether current procedural rules regarding settlement in fact undermine the rule of law and 'neutralise' the constitutional dimensions of the growing role of courts.

Requiring courts to enforce certain rules on their own motion or catering to the needs of self-represented or weaker parties is as such not problematic; on the contrary, one could argue that it is part of the Nordic legal-cultural DNA. Instead, the problem is the variation in how courts and judges perceive the obligation to act, and the way considered most appropriate to exercise the obligation or power to interfere also differs. Moreover, the extent to and intensity with which the court reviews an arbitral award or a settlement agreement, and to which courts enforce selected rules on their own motion through guidance and other measures, also varies, as Petersen notes.[52] The consequences of a very strict approach or a too-lenient approach could be draconian. For instance, employers could circumvent obligations arising from employment contracts by characterising the contract as purchase of services and thus avoid both procedural and substantive rules protecting employees. The question is whether the court should intervene and declare the contract void or interpret it as if it were an employment contract. Significant variation in the approach courts and individual judges use will result in different outcomes and will contradict the epitome of the rule of law—that is, equal and predictable application of law. Fragmentation of procedural rules could also amount to a breach of intrinsic principles of the rule of law: Why does a consumer deserve far better protection than a tenant or employee who is in an equally weak position, and where the case at hand is likely to be crucial for the tenant or employee in question? Is a split justice system desirable, where some parts are permeated by a laissez-faire attitude toward justice and enforcement of legal rules in the name of privatisation, while other parts of the system depart from traditional 'adversarial' maxims of the parties defining the ambit of the dispute in favour of forceful promotion of selected policies? Petersen argues that a new path for

[51] Linnanmäki (2021), Nylund (2021b), Petersen (2021) and Adrian et al. (2015).

[52] Petersen (2021). See also Wallerman Ghavanini (2020), Andersson (2019), Fredriksen and Strandberg (2019) and Eldjarn (2016).

civil procedure law is needed to find a proper balance between the two approaches and to regulate when and how courts should intervene in private agreements and settlements and in implementing mandatory rules.[53]

Digitisation is an omnipresent trend, yet only Maria Astrup Hjort discusses it in detail.[54] One reason for this is that digitisation is not specific to courts and has so far not been disruptive. Whether a document is filed on paper or electronically has few implications, except that a party (in practice, legal counsel) or judge preparing for a court hearing does not have to carry binders full of documents in order to have access to all relevant documents.[55] Similarly, judges are likely to perceive examining an expert or a witness remotely via video as an improvement vis-à-vis conducting examination via telephone, because they can both see and hear the person who is examined. Until know, digitisation has been an incremental process. One can question whether the potential of new technology has been so far largely overlooked among Nordic courts.

The novel coronavirus pandemic illustrates the pragmatic Nordic approach: Problems are related to courts lacking the hardware and software to allow judges to conduct hearings remotely, even from their home office. Makeshift solutions were put in place during the first weeks of the pandemic, and these are gradually being replaced by more permanent and functional solutions. In civil cases, the main problem seems to be the transformation of work processes, not a resistance to technology as such.[56] In criminal cases, the problems are more profound, since the right to appear in person in front of the judge is a quintessential element of the rights of the accused. Additionally, the use of lay judges and multiple accused persons in the same case entail problems regarding sufficient social distancing.[57] Some courts have established a video link between two courtrooms to enlarge the rooms virtually, and many utilise only the larger courtrooms. Despite these measures, practically all courts have a significant backlog of cases that will take a few years to dispose of.[58] Although

---

[53]Petersen (2021) .

[54]Hjort (2021).

[55]See Ervo (2020), Krans and Nylund (2020), Nylund (2020b) and Petersen (2020).

[56]Ervo (2021b), Nylund (2020b) and Petersen (2020).

[57]E.g., Ervo (2020) and Justis- og beredeksapsdepartementetet, Utkast til høringsnotat om forslag til midlertidig lov om endringer i rettens sammensetning mv. for å avhjelpe konsekvenser av utbrudd av Covid-19, https://www.regjeringen.no/contentassets/9189a551f3cc4cdcb30dce395e114478/horingsnotat---forslag-til-midlertidige-endringer-i-prosessregelverket.pdf (accessed 24 June 2020).

[58]As of 24 May 2020, 6068 criminal cases, 1,485 civil cases and 311 administrative cases had been postponed in Finnish courts (https://tuomioistuinvirasto.fi/fi/index/loader.html.stx?path=/channels/public/www/tuomioistuinvirasto/fi/structured_nav/ajankohtaista/QwlQgYmkm accessed 2 June 2020) (accessed 24 June 2020). Dealing with the backlog is expected to take at least two years, https://tuomioistuinvirasto.fi/fi/index/loader.html.stx?path=/channels/public/www/tuomioistuinvirasto/fi/structured_nav/ajankohtaista/2020/OSXN0egSy (accessed 2 June 2020). In Norway, more than 1,200 cases were postponed. https://www.dn.no/jus/bergen-tingrett/rettssak/domstolene/over-1100-rettssaker-utsatt-pa-grunn-av-virusutbruddet/2-1-803400 (accessed 2 June 2020), and dealing with these is expected to take two years https://www.domstol.no/nyheter/domstolene-far-penger-fra-krisepakke/ (accessed 2 June 2020). In Sweden, the ratio of cancelled or postponed hearings has increased from 20.3% to 27.9% during the pandemic compared to the three

one can hardly expect courts to seize the opportunity to rethink the justice system by implementing new technologies amidst an unprecedented crisis, one can hope that policymakers, judges, lawyers and academics will do so in due time.

7 Nordic Procedural Culture: Unity and Division

At the onset of the early modern period, there were only two Nordic countries, Denmark-Norway, which included Iceland, and Sweden, which included modern Finland. The laws, legal terminology and court structure of these countries were dissimilar, yet founded on congruous roots, and law in both blocks was influenced by the same sources.[59] Norway and Iceland retained their ties to Denmark, and Finland preserved its strong connection to Sweden even after the political detachment from the 'mother' country.[60] The divide between East-Nordic and West-Nordic is still visible in the structure of the court system, where the East-Nordic countries have administrative courts and in legal terminology.[61] However, if we zoom in on each individual country, differences in judges' self-perception become perceptible.[62]

The size and significance of the East–West divide should not be exaggerated, however. Several factors offset the divergences between the East and the West. One of these factors can be seen in the purposeful and persistent—though not always entirely successful—efforts to nurture and sustain Nordic legal cooperation in all areas of law, including procedural law among legislators, policymakers, scholars and (Supreme Court) judges. In relatively small countries like the Nordic countries, strong bonds to neighbouring countries ensure the continuous input of ideas and an opportunity for discussing ideas.[63] Ervo analyses the persistently strong ties between Finland and Sweden by showing how Finnish lawyers still turn to Swedish law for innovations and inspiration.[64] In drafting new laws, the Nordic countries serve as a benchmark for identifying the need for reforms and societal trends, as Hjort notes.[65] Thus, the need for and content of reforms is put in a broader context, and arguments for the specific approach chosen for the reform can be extracted. Often, the resume of Nordic law is nevertheless simply an ornament, a ritual in both drafting of legislation and in academic treaties.

---

previous years https://www.domstol.se/globalassets/filer/gemensamt-innehall/styrning-och-riktlinjer/statistik/2020/installda-forhandlingar-tom-v.22-2020.pdf (accessed 2 June 2020). The number of remote hearings has doubled, https://www.domstol.se/globalassets/filer/gemensamt-innehall/styrning-och-riktlinjer/statistik/2020/diagram-veckovis-videokonferenssamtal-salar-vecka-1-22.pdf (accessed 2 June 2020).

[59] Letto-Vanamo (2021), Sunde (2021) and Tamm (2021).

[60] Hjort (2021) and Sunde (2021).

[61] Nylund (2021b).

[62] Ervo (2021a).

[63] Ervo (2021a), Letto-Vanamo (2021), Sunde (2021) and Tamm (2021).

[64] Ervo (2021a).

[65] Hjort (2021).

In seeking inspiration from the same countries and in being influenced by the same ideas, the Nordic countries maintain alignment. Often, the process of transplanting legal concepts and institutions entails adaptation to the Nordic legal and societal context. Sometimes coordination among the Nordic countries is organic: during the 1800s and the early decades of the 1900s, German (and Austrian) law was the main source of influence, whereas today, ideas originating from common law jurisdictions are in vogue.[66] The potential transplants are often discussed in informal settings and among scholars, but efforts to propel formal cooperation in procedural law have remained futile. Class action (collective redress) serves as an example. Instead of each country drafting its own set of rules, albeit using enacted or draft legislation from other Nordic countries as a blueprint, Nordic model rules could have been drafted in a joint effort when the Nordic countries decided to enact rules on class action. Nordic model rules could then be adapted to the needs and wishes of each country. Alternatively, the countries could have enacted temporary rules on class actions to test how the modalities chosen influence the number of class actions and the court proceedings. A joint trial period would have enabled the Nordic countries to function as a natural laboratory. One reason why Nordic model rules were not drafted is that each of the Nordic countries decided to introduce class actions at different times. Small claims proceedings illustrate how the Danish, Norwegian and Swedish rules are slightly different yet based on the same tenets, such as flexible rules leaving ample room for the judge to exercise discretion and active involvement of the judge in giving judicial guidance.[67]

There are also some notable, even foundational, differences among the Nordic countries in some respects. Traditionally, the demarcation has been located between the East and West Nordic countries, such as the differences in the attitude towards administrative courts. In this regard, the gap has widened due to the increased independence of administrative courts in the East Nordic countries concurring with the persistent legal-cultural resistance towards administrative courts. In the domains of court-connected mediation and victim-offender mediation, a new divide has emerged, as Finland and Norway have embraced mediation, while Swedish legal culture has been more reluctant to mediation.[68] A similar divide seems to apply to plea bargaining as well.[69] Perhaps some of the differences can be attributed to the ideal of 'legalism' among Swedish judges, in contrast to the more pragmatic attitude of Finnish (and Norwegian) judges.[70] Differences in the attitudes towards mediation has devitalised the East–West divide and created new divides.

---

66 Hjort (2021).

67 Jensen (2021).

68 Nylund (2021b).

69 Ervo (2021b).

70 Ervo (2021a).

8 The Future of Nordic Courts

What are the prospects of a distinct Nordic procedural culture amid Europeanisation, globalisation and privatisation of dispute resolution?

Being Nordic has never entailed a uniform court structure or uniform procedural legislation: instead, the similarity of the underlying ideas, values and concepts, as well as shared cultural, economic, and societal structures, have constituted the basis of the Nordic legal culture. Consequently, upholding 'Nordic-ness' does not require identical legislative changes in the Nordic countries; it is sufficient that processes such as privatisation and Europeanisation prompt similar changes in the underlying ideas and concepts. The increasing tendency of Supreme Courts to perform judicial review, courts' hesitation to engaging in dialogue with the Court of Justice of the European Union and the EFTA Court and the increased focus on courts facilitating settlement have resulted in the metamorphosis of the role of Nordic courts; however, since the changes are largely congruous, it is primarily the content of 'Nordic-ness' that has changed, while the degree to which courts and court proceedings can be labelled as 'Nordic' has remained largely unaltered. The EEA and Schengen Agreements have been pivotal in this respect, since they enable Iceland and Norway to participate in many of the processes, either formally or de facto.[71] Nevertheless, differences in the views on the functions and form of administrative courts maintain a divide among the Nordic countries, and the manner in which and degree to which mediation processes are integrated in the civil and criminal justice systems could also be a source of increasing differences.

The ideological mainstays of Nordic court proceedings appear to be almost immutable: the generalist judge is still the ideal; pragmatism and high trust in judges have resulted in general, flexible procedural rules; language is fairly simple and judges strive to write comprehensible rulings; and judges must seek to balance and forge information derived from various sources and sometimes unite various interests.

The networks, shared culture and (with the exception of Finland and partly Iceland) shared language preserve legal unity and a shared legal culture. Seeking assistance is easy when communication is less formal, or even informal, such as when sending an email or telephoning a colleague one knows by name, instead of having to proceed formally through a long chain of intermediaries such as the Prosecutor General or the Central Authority.[72] Often, both parties involved can use their first language. Nonetheless, Nordic lawyers have not fully tapped into the potential of cooperation, particularly regarding pre-emptive attempts to shape EU hard law

[71] The Maintenance Regulation, Council Regulation (EC) No 4/2009 of 18 December 2008 on jurisdiction, applicable law, recognition and enforcement of decisions and cooperation in matters relating to maintenance obligations, O.J. L7/1 (2009), is intertwined with the Convention of 23 November 2007 on the International Recovery of Child Support and Other Forms of Family Maintenance, in a manner that enables third countries, such as Iceland and Norway, to align their system with the internal EU system, see Lipp (2019) and Nylund (2019a).

[72] Helenius (2021).

with procedural implications and in ensuring quality implementation.[73] The future of Nordic procedural law thus depends to a large extent on whether Nordic lawyers attempt to maintain strong ties and find new methods of fruitful cooperation.

References

Adrian L, Bager S, Petersen CS (2015) Perspektiver på forligsmægling. Juristen 3:98–106

Adrian L, Mykland S (2018) Unwrapping court-connected mediation agreements. In: Nylund A et al (eds) Nordic Mediation Research. Springer, Cham, pp 83–103

Andersson T (2019) *Ex Officio* Application of the unfair terms directive cases against consumers: a Swedish perspective. In: Nylund A, Strandberg M (eds) Civil Procedure and Harmonisation of Law. Intersentia, Cambridge, pp 153–170

Bogason B, Örlygsson Th (2019) For Whom Are Judgments Written? In: Selvik, M-J Clifton, T Haas, L Lourenço and K Schwiesow (eds) The art of judicial reasoning: Festschrift in honour of Carl Baudenbacher. Springer, Cham, pp 223–231

Brennan C, Traustadóttir R, Rice J, Anderberg P (2018) 'Being Number One Is the Biggest Obstacle': Implementing the UN Convention on the Rights of Persons with Disabilities within Nordic welfare services. Nordisk Välfärdsforskning Nordic Welfare Research 1:18–32

Dahlberg-Larsen J (2015) Retssproget, juridisk magtutøvelse og demokrati. In: AL Kjær, L Adrian, CB Cederstrøm et al (eds) Retten i sproget. Samspillet mellem ret og sprog i juridisk praksis. Jurist- og Økonomforbundets Forlag, København, pp 61–72

Eldjarn E (2016) Materiell prosessledelse. Cappellen Damm Akademisk, Oslo

Ervo L (2016) Swedish-Finnish preparatory proceedings: Filtering and process techniques. In: Ervo L and A Nylund (eds) Current trends in preparatory proceedings: a comparative study of Nordic and former communist countries. Springer, Cham, pp 19–56

Ervo L (2020) Corona-jurisdiction in Finland. Septentrio Reports 5:20–22

Ervo L (2021a) Culture and mentality in East-Nordic courts. In: Ervo L et al (eds) Rethinking Nordic courts. Springer, Cham

Ervo L (2021b) Plea bargaining changing Nordic criminal procedure: Sweden and Finland as examples. In: Ervo L et al (eds) Rethinking Nordic courts. Springer, Cham

Fredriksen HH, Strandberg M (2019) *Ex Officio* Application of Eu Consumer Protection Law in Norwegian Courts. In: Nylund A, Strandberg M (eds) Civil Procedure and Harmonisation of Law. Intersentia, Cambridge, pp 171–191

Helenius D (2021) Nordic and European judicial cooperation in criminal matters. In: Ervo L et al (eds) Rethinking Nordic courts. Springer, Cham

Helgadóttir R (2009) The UN convention in Nordic domestic law-lessons learned from other treaties. In: Arnardóttir OM, Quinn G (eds) The UN convention on the rights of persons with disabilities, Brill Nijhoff, Leiden, pp 279–301

Hjort MA (2021) Sources of inspiration of Nordic procedural law: Choices and objectives of the legal reforms. In: Ervo L et al (eds) Rethinking Nordic Courts. Springer, Cham

Jensen C (2021) Small claims procedures in the Scandinavian countries. In: Ervo L et al (eds) Rethinking Nordic courts. Springer, Cham

Kjær AL (2015) Forandring, læring og 'sprogpolitikresistens' i Danmarks Domstole. In: AL Kjær, L Adrian, CB Cederstrøm et al. (eds) Retten i sproget. Samspillet mellem ret og sprog i juridisk praksis. Jurist- og Økonomforbundets Forlag, København, pp 45–60

Krans B, Nylund A (2020) Concluding remarks on Covid-19 and civil justice. Septentrio Reports 5:54–57

[73] Nylund (2021c).

Letto-Vanamo P (2021) Courts and proceedings: some Nordic characteristics. In: Ervo L et al (eds) Rethinking Nordic courts. Springer, Cham

Linnanmäki K (2021) Mediation: a change in Finnish court culture? In: Ervo L et al (eds) Rethinking Nordic courts. Springer, Cham

Mattila HES (2016) Comparative legal linguistics: Language of law, Latin and modern lingua francas, Routledge, Abingdon

Nylund A (2019a) Family maintenance and multi-speed integration: A Norwegian perspective. In: Nylund A, Strandberg M (eds) Civil procedure and harmonisation of law: the dynamics of EU and international treaties. Intersentia, Cambridge, pp 209–230

Nylund A (2019b) Case management in a comparative perspective: regulation, principles and practice. Repro - Revista Do Processo 292:377–398

Nylund A (2020a) Procedural autonomy, the EEA agreement and Norwegian law: the art of bridging a gap and maintaining it too. In: Krans B, Nylund A (eds) Procedural autonomy across Europe. Intersentia, Cambridge, pp 119–138

Nylund A (2020b) Civil procedure in Norway and Covid-19: some observations. Septentrio Reports 5:39–42

Nylund A (2021a) Rethinking Nordic courts: an introduction. In: Ervo L et al (eds) Rethinking Nordic courts. Springer, Cham

Nylund A (2021b) Europeanisation of Nordic civil procedure: does the map natch the terrain? In: Ervo L et al (eds) Rethinking Nordic courts. Springer, Cham

Nylund A (2021c) Institutional aspects of the Nordic justice systems: striving for consolidation and settlements. In: Ervo L et al (eds) Rethinking Nordic courts. Springer, Cham

Nylund A, Strandberg M (2019) Conclusions on civil procedure and harmonisation of law. In: Nylund A, Strandberg M (eds) Civil procedure and harmonisation of law: the dynamics of Eu and international treaties. Intersentia, Cambridge, pp 231–242

Pedersen JE (2016) Begrunnelse av rettsavgjørelser. Universitetsforlaget, Oslo

Petersen CS (2020) Denmark. Septentrio reports 5:15

Petersen CS (2021) The public policy-implementing role of Nordic courts in civil dispute resolution. In: Ervo L et al (eds) Rethinking Nordic courts. Springer, Cham

Sunde JØ (2021) The history of Nordic legal culture and court culture: the story of what should not have been, but still came to be. In: Ervo L et al (eds) Rethinking Nordic courts. Springer, Cham

Sunnqvist M (2021) The changing role of Nordic courts. In: Ervo L et al (eds) Rethinking Nordic courts. Springer, Cham

Tamm D (2021) Courts, law, language and culture. In: Ervo L et al (eds) Rethinking Nordic courts. Springer, Cham

Thorsteinsdóttir H (2021) Globalisation and court practice in Iceland: new case law of the Supreme Court in relation to the EEA Agreement and European Convention on Human Rights. In: Ervo L et al (eds) Rethinking Nordic courts. Springer, Cham

Wallerman Ghavanini A (2020) Manouvering procedural autonomy in Sweden. In: Krans B, Nylund A (eds) Procedural autonomy across Europe. Intersentia, Cambridge, pp 203–226

Index

L. Ervo et al. (eds.), *Rethinking Nordic Courts*, Ius Gentium: Comparative Perspectives on Law and Justice 90, https://doi.org/10.1007/978-3-030-74851-7

The manufacturer's authorised representative in the EU is Springer
Nature Customer Service Centre GmbH, Europaplatz 3, 69115 Heidelberg,
Germany. If you have any concerns regarding our products, please
contact ProductSafety@springernature.com

Printed and bound by CPI Group (UK) Ltd, Croydon, CR0 4YY
30/09/2026
02225453-0018